BECAUSE OF EVE

BECAUSE OF EVE
HISTORICAL AND THEOLOGICAL SURVEY OF THE SUBJUGATION OF WOMEN IN THE CHRISTIAN TRADITION

JOE E. EARLY, JR., PH.D.

Universal-Publishers
Irvine • Boca Raton

Because of Eve: Historical and Theological Survey of the Subjugation of Women in the Christian Tradition

Copyright © 2022 Joe E. Early, Jr. All rights reserved. No part of this publication may be reproduced, distributed, or transmitted in any form or by any means, including photocopying, recording, or other electronic or mechanical methods, without the prior written permission of the publisher, except in the case of brief quotations embodied in critical reviews and certain other noncommercial uses permitted by copyright law.

Universal Publishers, Inc.
Irvine & Boca Raton
USA • 2022
www.Universal-Publishers.com

ISBN: 978-1-62734-409-8 (pbk.)
ISBN: 978-1-62734-410-4 (ebk.)

For permission to photocopy or use material electronically from this work, please access www.copyright.com or contact the Copyright Clearance Center, Inc. (CCC) at 978-750-8400. CCC is a not-for-profit organization that provides licenses and registration for a variety of users. For organizations that have been granted a photocopy license by the CCC, a separate system of payments has been arranged.

Typeset by Medlar Publishing Solutions Pvt Ltd, India
Cover design by Ivan Popov

Library of Congress Cataloging-in-Publication Data

Names: Early, Joseph E. (Joseph Everett), 1970- author.
Title: Because of Eve : historical and theological survey of the subjugation of women in the Christian tradition / Joseph E. Early, Jr., PH.D.
Description: Irvine : Universal Publishers, 2022. | Includes bibliographical references and index.
Identifiers: LCCN 2022037852 (print) | LCCN 2022037853 (ebook) | ISBN 9781627344098 (pbk.) | ISBN 9781627344104 (ebk.)
Subjects: LCSH: Women--Religious aspects--Christianity. | Sex role--Religious aspects--Christianity.
Classification: LCC BT704 .E25 2022 (print) | LCC BT704 (ebook) | DDC 248.8/43--dc23/eng/20220826
LC record available at https://lccn.loc.gov/2022037852
LC ebook record available at https://lccn.loc.gov/2022037853

To my wonderful wife Tiffany, who would've been burned as a witch in the Middle Ages

TABLE OF CONTENTS

Foreword Dr. Stephanie Peek .... *ix*

Preface .... *xiii*

Acknowledgments .... *xix*

Chapter One: The Old Testament Depiction of Women 1

Chapter Two: The Greek Concept of Women 37

Chapter Three: Women in the New Testament 53

Chapter Four: The Perception of Women in the Patristic Era 73

Chapter Five: Women in the Middle Ages 127

Chapter Six: Women in the Reformation 173

Chapter Seven: Women in Seventeenth and Eighteenth-Century England and America 209

Chapter Eight: Women in Nineteenth-Century America 231

Chapter Nine: Women in the Twentieth and Twenty-First Centuries 251

Final Thoughts *307*

Bibliography *311*

Index *343*

FOREWORD

When I first arrived at college, I found myself sitting in a class on Jesus and the Gospels with a man that would become my favorite professor and a mentor to me throughout my undergraduate years. He taught the Gospels in ways that made them come alive. By the time I finished that first class, I knew I was going to study this text for the rest of my life. Furthermore, I knew that God was calling me to share what I had learned through the ministry of the church. With great confidence, I told everyone who would hear of it how God had called *me* to the ministry. While I was still unsure of the nature of my calling at age 18, I was surprised to find that many in my church, my community, and even some at my school were less than thrilled about my revelation. For some reason, I was allowed to learn at the feet of Jesus, but I was not permitted to speak of what I had learned in mixed company. I was told that women were not qualified to serve in many of the ways to which I felt called. I was told that Scripture "makes it clear" that women have a responsibility to get married and raise the next generation. I was even told by some that Scripture said I was a daughter of Eve and thus too easily deceived to be a proper minister.

Undeterred, and perhaps seeking some answers for myself, I became a biblical scholar. I thought that if I studied enough and was a thoughtful teacher and scholar, previous objections to my suitability would be found unjustified and naysayers rendered speechless. Sadly, I was incorrect. The more I learned, the more deeply I felt the push away from the evangelical circles I called home and the people who had taken great pains to cultivate my deep and abiding love of Jesus. I have since been called "Jezebel," "Delilah," and the more vague but equally stinging "heretic" for my views on women in the church and my willingness to preach the message of Jesus. It was made clear: there was no room for me at the men's table.

When I became a professor of religion, I started my teaching career at a small women's college in Alabama. I was determined to ensure that the young women in my intellectual and spiritual care were aware that women belonged wherever God called them. I wanted them to know that there was a place for them at the table—even if it meant building a new table. Responding to their inquiries, I set out to offer a class on women in the Christian tradition. I sought a book that could offer my students a thoughtful history of women in the Christian tradition as well as insight into the ways that history affected the modern church. In addition, I wanted a straightforward evaluation of the tradition, one that was unafraid to point out the more sordid and disappointing moments, both theologically and socially, that were part of our tradition. The Bible does not speak of women univocally; not all aspects of the text provide a positive perspective on women and we must decide what we do with those voices. Indeed, the history of the church has not looked kindly upon us. I wanted my students to know their history. At the time, I was left dissatisfied with what was available, either because of length, accessibility of the writing, or the lack of comprehensive coverage from a perspective that invited dialogue and critique. I wanted my students to see the big picture, to hear the whole story, and to be intrigued enough to ask questions and do their own research.

I wish that in my first class on women in the Christian tradition, I had had a book like this one. *Because of Eve* offers an unflinching evaluation of beliefs about women in the history of the tradition. It offers a thought-provoking and consistent narrative of women from the earliest books of our canon, through the New Testament, and into the modern era. This book provides an accessible resource for the history of belief with reference to women in the Christian tradition. It is comprehensive in its scope; it provides a thorough outline of the biblical witnesses on the topic and a thoughtful overview of the evolution of the Christian tradition through the past 2000 years, an undertaking of no small difficulty. Early demonstrates that while women were always heralded by Jesus as full participants in the kingdom and considered by Paul to be equal to men in the kingdom in his earliest writings, the later Pauline social context prompted a reconsideration of egalitarianism. By the Patristic period, the egalitarian focus was all but lost, sacrificing female participation on the altar of the patriarchy. Women would not again find solid footing in the church until the twentieth and twenty-first centuries.

More importantly, and refreshingly, this book calls readers to examine the current state of women in the church. While many women—I think here specifically of my students—have been given access to seminary and great theological educations, the opportunities for these women, especially those of an evangelical tradition, to live into their callings are limited. I so greatly appreciate Dr. Early's work of tracing the subjugation of women in the Christian tradition and his willingness to serve as an ally to a generation of women who desire to live into their God-issued callings. Perhaps this book will prompt discussions in classrooms and churches about the ways in which women have been neglected and subjugated in the Christian tradition and perhaps even prompt further reflection on the dangers of theological systems that demonize, belittle, or denigrate the fullness of the image of God in women.

I hope there will come a day when everyone in every church—but especially a young woman in the evangelical tradition—will be able to speak freely of what God has done for her and that to which God has called her and will be told, "Welcome to the table; we saved you a seat." I think this book is a useful step in that direction, as it calls us all to reckon with our history. For now, however, we read texts such as this one and remember that many of us sit in good company. Mary Magdalene never was a whore; she was the first woman called to preach on Easter morning. Many witches were just women with theological opinions, and far more educated and successful women than myself have been told to "go home" where we belong. I pray this book sparks a fresh conversation about the role of women in your Christian community and gives you hope that progress, though slow, is being made.

Stephanie Peek, Ph.D.

PREFACE

How I Became Interested

I am a Christian, Protestant, American man. I understand the irony that I chose to write this book. Moreover, I grew up an evangelical Southern Baptist and have three degrees from conservative Southern Baptist institutions of higher learning. This places me at the top of the American Christianity caste in many denominations. I often asked myself why am I in this fortunate position while females with equal training and often superior ability are less valued? The answer comes from a lifetime of study and observation.

I grew up in a wonderful Southern Baptist church. It is where I became a Christian and underwent the ordinance of baptism. Even though I've never considered myself a minister, this church also licensed and ordained me. The church did this for everyone who had attended seminary, even those who were planning careers in academia. It's a great church. It was and remains, however, very conservative. It is not a King James only fundamentalist church or anything like that, but it was very rigid concerning women's roles. To this day, women cannot serve as deacons or pastors. As a youth, I knew this was the rule and never questioned it. I cannot remember a woman praying aloud in the worship service, but women were expected to cook before and clean up after church dinners and fellowships. It is a happy church, and no one questions this arrangement. I just figured that it was in the Bible somewhere. Though I disagree with this aspect of my home church, I love it and attend services whenever possible.

I decided to attend seminary after college. I had initially planned to go to law school, but I decided I wanted to be a professor of religion instead. While working on my Master of Divinity degree, the Southern Baptist Convention began to push complementarianism. Accepting it seemed to be a litmus test for orthodoxy that would get me my Southern Baptist guild card at graduation. My professors would talk about how wives must "graciously submit." Many called their wives "good wives," as if they were seventeenth-century New England Puritans. I can remember only two women in my master's program, but I'm sure there were others. Both had sharp minds but looked very uncomfortable in class. The wives of the male students were encouraged to attend "seminary wives" classes. These wives received some biblical and theological training, but mostly the classes were concerned with how to take care of the home and be a proper, submissive pastor's wife. I remember thinking all this focus on women's submission was odd and that it seemed to clash with Galatians 3:28, but I was trying to get into a doctoral program and didn't want to ruin my chances, so I kept quiet.

By 2016, I was a tenured college professor who had just published a book, and I was looking for a new topic. One evening I went with one of my closest friends, a female professor of missions, to hear a lecture by the President of the Center for Biblical Equality, Dr. Mimi Haddad. She discussed how bad hermeneutics and Greek philosophy have more to do with the subordination of women than anything written in the Old Testament or by the Apostle Paul. The lecture mesmerized me. When I told my wife what I had heard, she said, "I guess you have your next book topic." As always, Tiffany was right.

The Purpose of the Book

In this work, I endeavor to provide a thorough examination of how the Church and Christian men sought to define women and the roles women must play within the church, home, and society for more than two thousand years. The book examines the works of theologians, decrees of councils, canon law, statements of faith, and a myriad of other pronouncements that affected their generation—and the following generation's—beliefs concerning women.

Each chapter considers the era in which these beliefs were voiced, as much of what was accepted as orthodoxy was reflected in or based on cultural beliefs.

The chapters are in chronological order, beginning with the Old Testament and Greek philosophy, and ending with the United States in 2021. Eve dominates much of the first chapter as many theologians perceive her as the one who seduced Adam and brought sin into the world. It also examines women and Jewish law, their relation to the cult, and their roles as wives and daughters. I discuss the importance of the two creation accounts as well as how men used women as a commodity. I also examine how women, such as Ruth, Delilah, and Tamar, were depicted as either nags, tricksters, or seducers. I examine the Apocrypha and its effect on the Christian interpretation of women.

Chapter two depicts how Greek philosophy played a major role in how New Testament writers and early and medieval Christian theologians defined women. It examines the place of women in classical Greek (Athenian) life (480 BCE—323 BCE) and in the philosophies of Plato, Aristotle, and the Jewish Hellenistic philosopher, Philo.

Like the Old Testament, New Testament traditions depict the authors as men. The New Testament, however, portrays women differently. It does not depict women as heroines, harlots, or seducers. Women were rarely the key actors in a narrative. Rather, the New Testament authors discussed women as figures in men's narratives. Along with customary Jewish teachings, some New Testament authors drew upon Greek concepts in their depictions of women. Chapter three also examines Roman and Jewish women's lives in the century prior to and during Jesus' life and how Jesus and Paul depicted the station of women.

Chapter four concerns theologians (Clement of Alexandria, Tertullian of Carthage, John Chrysostom, Jerome, and Augustine) of the Patristic era whose writings addressed women. Prominent themes include how these theologians perceived women in relation to the creation stories, original sin, wives' submission in marriage, women's effect on men, female chastity, and ministry and teaching. The chapter also concerns the importance of local synods, ecumenical councils, and writings that shaped the hierarchy of the growing church.

Chapter five discusses Thomas Aquinas' thoughts concerning women and their importance to future Catholicism, canon law, and the continuation of the men's fear that women were temptresses, weak-minded, and dangerous to men—especially the clergy. Attention is paid to the development of female monastic orders, the fear of nuns, and why they must be cloistered. The chapter concludes with an examination of the roots of misogynistic female stereotypes and how women became identified with witchcraft.

Chapter six concerns the Reformation and what it meant for women. The chapter closely investigates Desiderius Erasmus, Martin Luther, and John Calvin's writings concerning women. It also concerns women's place in the English Reformation and John Knox's writings.

Chapter seven moves the discussion to the New World in the seventeenth and eighteenth-centuries. It examines the Puritans, Separatists, Baptists, Quakers, Roman Catholics, and later Methodists' perception of the nature, role, and purpose of women in the seventeenth and eighteenth centuries. Special attention is given to the importance of Cotton Mather, John Milton, John Wesley, and Jonathan Edwards.

Chapter eight explores nineteenth-century events that had a direct effect on Christian women in the United States. Among these are the Second Great Awakening, the growth of the Baptist and Methodist denominations, and Charles Finney's revivals. There is also an examination of Catholic encyclicals, Female-led Mission societies, Dwight Laymen Moody's revivals, and the Holiness Movement's impact on Christian women.

Chapter nine examines how the Catholic Church, Fundamentalists, Evangelicals, mainline Protestant denominations, Pentecostals, and Black Protestants depicted the nature, role, and purpose of women in the twentieth and twenty-first centuries. Papal decrees, Southern Baptist confessions of faith, and the significance of Christians for Biblical Manhood and Womanhood are closely analyzed. The chapter also discusses how Christian men have responded to Christian women who demand equality in the church, home, and society.

The book concludes with my final thoughts on what the past tells us about the male Christian perception of women and what these perceptions also say about men. I also discuss what I believe history tells us about the future of Christian women. I have provided a comprehensive bibliography to offer additional material. When citing primary sources, whenever possible, I have included an online link to the source and the physical text. I hope the content of this book challenges you as much as it did me and that we will all learn lessons from the past to make a fairer and more equitable Christianity for everyone.

ACKNOWLEDGMENTS

There are many people to whom I owe a debt of gratitude for their help in writing this book. First and foremost is my wife, Tiffany, who allowed me to take over the entire dining room for six years so I could spread out all my research. She has been very patient with me, read and edited the entire book several times, and encouraged me when I wanted to quit. Dr. Twyla Hernandez also deserves special recognition. She read every word of my book several times, provided valuable insight, and kept me on track. As always, my dad was with me every step of the way and helped keep me on target. I would also like to thank all those who read and edited chapters for me within their expertise. Few books have been as reviewed and scrutinized by so many distinguished scholars. These professors include Dr. Melody Maxwell, Dr. Terry Wilder, Dr. Laura Anne Rodgers Levens, Dr. Bob Dunston, Dr. Brian Austin, Dr. Paul Gritz, Dr. Twyla Hernandez, Dr. Dwayne Howell, Dr. Susan Shaw, Dr. Mimi Haddad, Dr. Rex Butler, and Dr. Adam Harwood. I am indebted to Dr. Stephanie Peek for her wonderful foreword and Dr. Susan Shaw, Dr. Bill Leonard, Dr. Carey Ruiz, and Dr. Twyla Hernandez who provided endorsements. They were an immense help. I am also grateful to the group of friends known as the "Porch" who were always supportive, fun, and willing to offer constructive criticism. Finally, I would like to extend my gratitude to Campbellsville University and the administration who believed in my book enough to grant me a year's sabbatical to finish it. I am indebted to my friends, colleagues, and University.

CHAPTER ONE

The Old Testament Depiction of Women

The Israelites of the Old Testament lived in a patriarchal society. Its authors were also male; therefore, the male perspective dominates the Old Testament. The Old Testament God is depicted as male; the proper names for God, Yahweh, and Elohim are masculine. Most adjectives and metaphors used to describe God are also masculine.[1] When God acts, he performs tasks associated with men, such as fighting and ruling. Many passages (e.g., Isaiah 64:8, 1 Chronicles 29:10, and Malachi 2:10 and many more) depict God as a father. There are several, but fewer, passages (e.g., Hosea 13:8, Job, 38:29, Isaiah 42:14, 49:15, and 66:13) that depict God acting in a feminine or maternal way. Only males could be mediators between God and humans, as seen in the exclusively male Israelite priesthood. According to Ludwig Köhler:

> Yahweh's covenant with Israel is a covenant with those competent to enter into such a thing; that is to say, with the men; they represent the people. Woman has no place in this revelation; therefore, she is a constant danger to the work of God. The Decalogue addresses the man only […] The male is man, and the people of Israel consists of men.[2]

---

[1] Kristen E. Kvam, Linda S. Schearing, and Valerie H. Ziegler, eds. *Eve and Adam: Jewish, Christian, and Muslim Readings on Genesis and Gender* (Bloomington, IN: University of Indiana Press, 1999), 25.
[2] Ludwig Köhler, *Old Testament Theology* (Philadelphia, PA: Westminster Press, 1957), 69.

Unlike the gods of other pre-Christian Middle Eastern religions, the Israelite God does not need a female consort or mate. He has no family. This God is not dependent on or answerable to any other.

No single female image prevails in the Old Testament.[3] Sarah, Ruth, and Deborah are heroines but are imperfect. Esther is an exception, as she may be considered the greatest hero, male or female, of the Old Testament. Her actions save the Jewish people in Persia from the genocidal machinations of Haman. The majority of the depictions of women, however, are not so exalted and run the gamut from strong mothers and chaste wives to temptresses. The writer of Proverbs 31 imagines the qualities of an ideal wife. In contrast, Proverbs 1–9 describe the "Strange Woman"—the embodiment of the woman that men fear.

The history of how men in the Bible define women begins with Eve. Because she was the first woman, and because of her role in the Fall, men have presented her as the archetype of all women.

Eve

Even though she is the primary character of the first four chapters of Genesis, Eve does not play a major role in Israelite tradition. After the birth of Seth in Genesis 5:3, she disappears from the Old Testament. Eve does play an important role in the Pauline corpus and in Christian tradition. Only the Virgin Mary outpaces her in the Christian theological writings of the Patristic and Middle Ages. Because of this Christian emphasis, Eve merits special attention, especially in the two creation accounts.[4]

The First Creation Account—Genesis 1:26–29

In the first account, the world and all things in it already existed before the creation of humans. Over time God created man or

---

[3] Phyllis Bird, "Images of Women in the Old Testament," in *Religion and Sexism: Images of Woman in the Jewish and Christian Traditions*, Rosemary Radford Ruether, ed. (Eugene, OR: Wipf and Stock Publishers, 1998), 47.

[4] There has been a great deal of scholarly debate throughout the previous century as to whether Moses wrote the book of Genesis and the other books in the Pentateuch. Theologians who are discussed in this book, however, almost exclusively accept Mosaic authorship.

"them" together (26). The Hebrew word *Adam* is translated as "humanity." God, therefore, did not give his first human a name. Adam did not become a personal name until Genesis 5:1. By stressing the simultaneous creation, the creation story is told as one of equality. The relationship between man and woman was perfect, and neither gender held sway over the other.[5] God instructed them to "be fruitful and multiply" (28). Prior to this directive, God must have separated Adam into two different sexes.

Israelite tradition does not condemn act of sex. The negative connotations of sex originated with early Christianity. The couple was then told their purpose: to procreate and to assert dominion over other creatures.[6] The division of labor and the establishment of dominion were left to them. Perhaps because of its brevity, its egalitarian approach, its lack of detail, or the endearing story of Adam's rib, the first creation story has never been as popular in Christian tradition and theology as the second account.

The first creation account leaves the reader with several questions. Did the first human constitute one being, two, or something else? Does verse 26 teach that the first human was androgynous only to be separated into two distinct **sexes** in verse 27 when told to go forth and multiply? If understood in this manner, humanity's creation consisted of two steps: the creation of Adam, and God's division of Adam into male and female. This division allowed humanity to procreate and care for the rest of creation.[7] The androgynous creation found its way into Israelite legend and scholarship but found little traction in Christian theology and tradition. God presumably created male and female animals that were capable of reproduction.[8] Phyliss Bird argues that "male and female" do not refer to the image of God but rather to the sexual differentiations in the fertility

---

[5] John H. Otwel, *And Sarah Laughed: The Status of Women in the Old Testament.* (Philadelphia, PA: Westminster Press, 1977), 16.
[6] Gordon J. Wenham, *Genesis 1–15.* Word Biblical Commentary Series (Grand Rapids, MI: Zondervan, 1987), 33.
[7] Anne Lapidus Lerner, *Eternally Eve: Images of Eve in the Hebrew Bible, Midrash, and Modern Jewish Poetry* (Waltham, MA: Brandeis University Press, 2007), 37.
[8] David Clines, "What Does Eve Do to Help? And Other Readerly Questions in the Old Testament," *Journal for the Study of the Old Testament*, Supplement Series 94 (Sheffield: JSOT Press, 1990), 38.

blessing that follows.[9] The "male and female" statement could also refer to the way in which the command to "go forth and multiply" was given to both the man and woman.[10] This interpretation fits well with the egalitarian emphasis of the first creation account. Throughout literature, theories abound.[11]

Another pertinent question is why the writer added a second creation account. Perhaps Adam had two wives. One Mesopotamian legend (ca. 300 BCE) tells of a female night demon named Lilith who brought disease and death. In the Middle Ages, the *Alphabet of Ben Sira* integrated this story into Jewish mythology.[12] This text claims that Lilith was Adam's wife in the first creation account. According to the story, Lilith constantly refused to defer to or submit to Adam. While having sex with Adam, Lilith demanded to be on top. He refused and she fled the garden. Adam complained to God that she had deserted him. God sent three angels to return her to Adam. They found her at the Red Sea and told her that if she did not return to Adam one hundred of her offspring would die every day. Lilith refused, was punished, and became a demon who sought revenge by killing newborn babies. Lilith legends abound in Mesopotamian mythology, and the Israelites who returned from captivity in Babylon may have brought the legends with them. The Amplified Bible's translation of Isaiah 34:14 states, "The creatures of the desert will encounter jackals. And the hairy goat will call to its kind; Indeed, Lilith will settle there. And find herself a place of rest."[13] In many translations, she is also known as the "night demon."

Why is the Lilith legend important in Israelite tradition? One answer is that it explains the reason for two creation accounts. The other is that the author of the *Alphabet* may have been trying to teach men a lesson about women. Lilith was a defiant woman who did not know her place. She refused to be subservient to Adam.

---

[9] Phyllis Bird, "'Male and Female': Gen. 1:27b in the Context of the Priestly Account of Creation," *Harvard Theological Review* (1981), 147–150.
[10] Kvam, Schearing, and Ziegler, 25.
[11] Ibid.
[12] Ibid., 204.
[13] References to Lilith in this passage can be also be found in the New Revised Standard Version, the Common English Bible, the International Standard Version, and many others.

This story warned men to avoid women like Lilith and taught women God would punish them if they challenged male authority.[14] Although the Lilith legend is rarely mentioned in the Christian tradition, Lilith has not been forgotten. In the late twentieth century, she became an icon for feminism and the 1997–1999 concert series Lilith Fair was named after her.

The Second Creation Account—Genesis 2:4b–24

Genesis 2 reintroduces the story of the creation of the first couple. This is the more popular creation account in both Judaism and Christianity. It is also more patriarchal. Throughout the story, the female is called woman, not Eve. In this story, God created man (Adam) from the dust of the earth and breathed life into him (7). Then God determined that man should not be alone and needed a helper (18). Therefore, God created for him a woman fashioned from his rib (21). There is no mention of breathing life into the woman, or that the woman was created in the image of God. Having been created in the image of man who was created in the image of God, the woman was but an image of an image of God. The woman as depicted in the second account is an inferior creation to Adam.

In the second account, the order of creation is also important. God created Adam before creating the woman. Birth order had an important role in the Israelite and Christian tradition. With woman being drawn from Adam's side rather than having life breathed into her by God, she was the second creation and owed part of her very existence to Adam. The account, however, does not state that Eve is subordinate to Adam. The Apostle Paul (1 Corinthians 11:8–9 and 1 Timothy 2:13) is the first to claim that the order of creation placed Eve under Adam's authority.[15] Phyllis Trible, however, views the creation account differently. She believes that God made Eve the culmination of his creation by creating her last just as humanity was created after the animals but was yet superior to them.[16]

---

[14] Barbara Crandall, *Gender and Religion: The Dark Side of Scripture*, 2nd ed. (New York, NY: Continuum International Publishing Group, 2012), 90.
[15] John L. Collins, *A Short Introduction to the Hebrew Bible*, 3rd ed. (Minneapolis, MN: Fortress Press, 2018), 46.
[16] Phyllis Trible, "Depatriarchalizing in Biblical Interpretation," 36–37.

The second account also offers an unintended rationale for woman's creation. Woman was not created until after Adam had failed to find a satisfactory mate elsewhere.[17] God determined that Adam needed not only to reproduce, but he also needed companionship. God decided to create woman without having Adam ask. The creation of woman thrilled Adam, and in Genesis 2:23 he spoke for the first time. Just as Adam has named the animals, he named her, and "because she was taken out of man," he named her "woman." Genesis 2:24 states that "For this reason a man shall leave his father and his mother and be joined to his wife; and they shall become one flesh."

God also stated that the woman is to be Adam's *ezer* or helper. How should *ezer* be interpreted? Was she his equal helpmate or was she to be his servant? Were male superiority and female submission part of the original creation? Was Adam to lead, make decisions, and rule alone? Was Eve to submit to him? The interpretation of helper, therefore, determines whether or not this new relationship was one of submission.[18] Nowhere in the Hebrew scriptures is *ezer* used to mean "servant." Moreover, the scriptures often depicted God as an *ezer* to his people (e.g., Psalms 33:20; Psalms 115:9–11).[19] Reading submission into this account, therefore, is difficult.

In Israelite tradition, naming someone or something was a significant event.[20] Before the creation of woman, Adam named the animals; in doing so, he was given dominion over them. Adam named his mate twice. The first naming occurred in the second creation account (Genesis 2:23) when he provided her with the appellation "woman." The second naming happened after the Fall (Genesis 3:20) when she was subordinated to Adam. "Now the man called his wife's name Eve, because she was the mother of all the living." By giving her this significant name, Eve and her descendants were given the task of bringing all human life into the world. Despite this honor, Adam still named Eve just as he did all the other creatures.[21]

---

[17] The Babylonian Talmud, *Yebamot*, 63a says that only after Adam copulated with all the animals did Yahweh determine that none were appropriate for him and that something else was needed.
[18] Anne Lapidus Lerner, 74–75.
[19] William E. Phipps, "Adam's Bone of Contention," *Theology Today* 45, no. 1 (1988): 271.
[20] Anne Lapidus Lerner, 130.
[21] Phillips, 32.

No Old Testament naming of a human, however, connoted the idea of a superior naming an inferior. This incident, therefore, should be understood neither as an act of a greater naming a lesser nor the male's superiority to the female.[22]

Eve's Role in the Fall—Genesis 3:1–24

The story of Eve continued into what Christianity labels the Fall. Whereas God and Adam had been center stage in the creation accounts, Eve took the starring role in the Fall. She spoke to the serpent, broke God's prohibition concerning the tree, and provided her husband with the fruit.[23] The story of the Fall consists of four sections: the serpent and the first couple, awareness, their conversation with God, and punishments.

The Serpent and the First Couple—Genesis 3:1–6

The second creation account did not refer to the origins of the serpent. The account depicted the serpent only as wilier than the other animals. The serpent enticed the woman to break God's only rule. In Genesis 2:16–17, "The Lord God commanded the man, saying, "From any tree of the garden you may eat freely; but from the tree of the knowledge of good and evil you shall not eat, for in the day that you eat from it you will surely die." If this was a morality test, then the serpent could be seen as God's accomplice. Adam and Eve had the free will to obey or disobey. They could defy God.

God and Adam made this covenant before Eve was created. Under the covenant, Adam could live in the garden, tend it, and eat anything he desired—with one exception: he could not eat from the tree of knowledge of good and evil. As long as Adam kept his part of the covenant, God would allow him to stay in the garden.

Despite God's mandate and Adam's apparent relaying of it to her, the woman gave in to the serpent (Genesis 3:6). Adam, who was with her, said nothing. The text does not explain why he stood mute while the woman was violating God's order. Some translations of

---
[22] John H. Ortwell, *And Sarah Laughed: The Status of Women in the Old Testament* (Philadelphia, PA: Westminster Press, 1977), 17–18.
[23] Phillips, 55.

Genesis 3:6 state or imply that Adam was not there.[24] How this verse is translated is very important. If she were alone, she alone was culpable for breaking the covenant. If Adam were with her, Adam was as guilty as Eve, if not more so, because God had given the mandate directly to him and he did nothing to keep it from being broken. Whatever the case may be, he then joined in the sin by taking the fruit Eve offered him and eating it.

Awareness—Genesis 3:7

The man and woman knew immediately they made a grave mistake. As they were created in the image of God, their awareness came in the form of moral knowledge. They understood good and evil. After the fall, the couple lost their ability to follow God without moral considerations.[25] The first couple also realized that they were naked and covered themselves. When compared with Genesis 2:25, in which they recognized their nakedness and were not ashamed, the Fall account is implying something about their bodies.[26] Their new awareness included sexual knowledge.

The Conversation with God—Genesis 3:8–14

At that moment, God appeared in the garden and called for the man, who finally responded (8–9). Adam told God that he had hidden because he was naked (10). God then asked who told him he was naked (11). Since the man and the woman had already covered themselves with fig leaves (7), Adam's answer made little sense. His nakedness could not be covered up with clothes.[27] His shame had led him to feel naked before God. God knew what happened. He gave them a chance to repent (11), but neither did. Adam blamed the woman for leading him astray (12) and God for creating her.

---

[24] Revised Standard Version (1952), New English Bible (1970), Living Bible (1971), Good News Bible (1976), Revised English Bible (1989).
[25] Gerda Lerner, *The Creation of Patriarchy* (Oxford: Oxford University Press, 1986), 196.
[26] Alice Bach, ed. *Women in the Hebrew Bible: A Reader* (New York, NY: Routledge, 1999), 245.
[27] Ibid., 246.

This was the last time Adam speaks. The woman then blamed the serpent for deceiving her (Genesis 13). Neither took responsibility for their actions.

God's Punishments—Genesis 3:15–24

After Adam and Eve failed to repent, God cursed the serpent to be below all the other animals, to crawl on its belly, and to have constant enmity with the woman (14–15). The second account provided no reason as to why man was spared. The simplest explanation is that the serpent had tempted Eve and not Adam.[28]

God punished the woman by giving her pain in childbirth and placing her under his authority (16). This was the first statement of female subordination and is often quoted to support patriarchy. The woman of the first creation account lost her equality with man and the subjugation of the woman in the second account was now explicit. Adam then gave the woman her proper name, Eve, "because she will be the mother of all the living." Women, therefore, would find some redemption in motherhood.

God then reprimanded Adam for listening to his wife rather than obeying him (17). As stated in John Milton's *Paradise Lost*, Adam had chosen her over God and Adam had ignored what God ordained. For this reason, he, like the Israelites after him, would have to work much harder if they wanted to eat.

God then gave Adam and Eve new animal skins to cover themselves (21) and banished them from the Garden of Eden (23). God provided two reasons for their expulsion. First, after Adam and Eve ate from the forbidden tree, they, like God, knew right from wrong (22). Second, if they did not lose access to the tree, Adam and Eve would continue to eat from it and live forever (22). This section points out two of God's intentions for his human creation: to be obedient and to die. The only immortality God intended for humans was the kind that comes through procreation.[29] If this is the case, we are left with only speculations as to why God placed this dangerous tree in the garden.

---

[28] Anne Lapidus Lerner, 109.
[29] Gerda Lerner, 188.

Eve After the Garden

Genesis 4:1–2

After their expulsion from the garden, Adam and Eve had sex. She became pregnant and gave birth to Cain. Eve thanked God for his help in the creation of Cain, but also boldly took some of the credit for herself (1). Eve became pregnant again and gave birth to Abel (2). These births, however, led to the first murder.[30]

Genesis 5:3

As the story of Cain and Abel comes to the fore, Adam and Eve fade into the background. According to Genesis 5:3, one hundred and thirty years pass before we next hear from Eve, who has become pregnant with her third son. Eve thanked God for Seth, whom she considered a replacement for the murdered Abel. Seth's importance cannot be overstated. Genesis 5:3 states, "When Adam had lived one hundred and thirty years, he became the father of *a son* in his own likeness, according to his image, and named him Seth." Seth was in Adam's likeness and image, as Adam had been in God's. The only difference is in the order of "image" and "likeness." God created Adam in his image and likeness.[31] The text said nothing comparable about Cain or Abel. From Seth's lineage, God chose Noah to repopulate the earth after the flood, and Abraham who will be the patriarch of the Hebrews. Eve neither appeared nor was mentioned again in the Old Testament. Even though the deaths of other Israelite matriarchs were noted throughout the Old Testament, Eve's was not.

Other Influential Works Concerning Eve

Pseudepigraphal and Deuterocanonical Books

The Old Testament accounts of Eve were brief, vague, and left many questions unanswered. Several non-Old Testament writings elaborate on Eve and other biblical accounts and stories. The Pseudepigrapha ("false writings") are one such collection of writings.

---

[30] Anne Lapidus Lerner, 165.
[31] Ibid., 156–7.

They are considered false because the authors falsely claim to be patriarchs or prophets from the Old Testament era. Written between approximately 300 BCE and 200 CE, some of these books, such as Jubilees, 2 Baruch, 1 Enoch, and the Apocalypse of Moses, contain accounts of Eve.

Written between 300 BCE and 70 CE, the *Apocrypha* is composed of twenty books not found in the Old Testament but are included in *Septuagint* of the *Codex Alexandrinus* or the Latin Vulgate. Christian codices such as *Codex Vaticanus* and *Codex Sinaiticus* include the bulk of these books. Several of these books are considered canonical (deuterocanonical) by the Eastern Orthodox and Roman Catholic churches but not by Protestant churches. The books that mention Eve are Sirach, Tobit, 2 Esdras, and 4 Maccabees.

Written in Hebrew between 200 BCE and 175 CE and translated into Greek in 132 BCE, Sirach has many similarities to the Old Testament book of Proverbs. Sirach is wisdom literature. Its purpose is to address the deleterious effects of Hellenism on Judaism.[32] Arguably, it is also the most misogynistic book in the canon.[33] Though Sirach did not mention Eve, the story in 25:16–26, particularly verse 24, left little room for doubt that the author had her in mind. "From a woman sin had its beginning, and because of her we all die."

If Sirach is alluding to Eve in verse 24, it is probably the oldest attribution of the origin of sin to Eve. Earlier Israelite tradition attributed the origin of sin to women's copulation with angels (Genesis 6:1–4). This interpretation represented a more Hellenized interpretation of Eve as Greek mythological gods often had sex with women.[34] This Eve is similar to the Greek Pandora.

Sirach also alluded to Eve in 40:1. "Hard work was created for everyone, and a heavy yoke is laid on the children of Adam, from the day they come forth from their mother's womb until the day they return to the mother of all the living." Here, Sirach cites Adam's curse and Genesis 3:20 when Eve was called "mother

---

[32] Gale A. Yee, Hugh R. Page, Jr., and J.M. Coomber, eds. *The Apocrypha: Fortress Commentary on the Bible Study Edition* (Minneapolis, MN: Fortress Press, 2016), 999–1000.
[33] Pamela Eisenbaum, "Sirach," in *Women's Bible Commentary*, eds. Carol A. Newsom, Sharon H. Ringe, and Jacqueline E. Lapsley (Louisville, KY: Westminster John Knox Press, 2014), 509.
[34] Goodman, 92.

of all the living." The mother of the living, however, may be the earth, not Eve.³⁵

Written between 250 BCE and 175 BCE, the book of Tobit tells the story of two families devastated by tragedies who came together in marriage and were then blessed.³⁶ In the only account that mentioned Eve by name, the husband, Tobias, prays for his wife, Sarah, and their marriage. Tobias reiterated that a man needed a helper to live a full and content life. "You it was who created Adam, you who created Eve his wife to be his help and support; and from these two the human race was born. You it was who said, 'It is not right that the man should be alone; let us make him a helper like him'" (Tobit 8:6).

Written in the first century of the common era, 2 Esdras is a Jewish apocalypse. It is composed of seven visions set in sixth-century Babylon. The book uses the destruction of the Temple in 587 BCE to discuss the Roman destruction of the Second Temple in 70 CE.³⁷ In 2 Esdras 3:21–27 Adam, not Eve, was blamed for the Fall. The relevance of this story here is that not only is Eve held blameless, but Adam's evil heart alone is at fault.³⁸ This same evil heart was present in all his descendants: "For the first Adam, burdened with an evil heart, transgressed and was overcome, as were also all who were descended from him" (2 Esdras 3:21).

An indirect allusion to Eve is found in 4 Maccabees 18:7–8, in which the righteous woman declared, "I was a pure virgin and did not go outside my father's house; but I guarded the rib from which woman was made. No seducer corrupted me on a desert plain, nor did the destroyer, the deceitful serpent, defile the purity of my virginity." According to Alice Ogden Bellis, the righteous woman's words showed that women are in danger of being seduced by evil spirits. This widespread belief was cited in other pseudepigraphal books such as the Testament of Reuben and Jubilees. It was also mentioned in the non-canonical Book of Enoch. These evil spirits dwelled in the desert and were descendants of the Nephilim (Genesis 6:1–4). The reference implied that the serpent's allure was sexual. Unlike Eve and the women of Genesis 6:1–4 who gave

---

³⁵ Ibid., 103.
³⁶ Yee, Page, Jr., Matthew, and Coomber, 954.
³⁷ Kvam, Schearing, and Ziegler, 55.
³⁸ Peter Hayman, "2 Esdras," in *The Apocrypha: The Oxford Bible Commentary*, ed. Martin Goodman (Oxford: Oxford University Press, 2001), 224.

themselves to the sons of God, the righteous woman protected the rib given to her by man from the serpent and all evil spirits.[39]

In Israelite tradition, Eve was not as important as Christians might think. After all the criticism, blame, and guilt heaped on her in Genesis 1–4, she was not even mentioned in the many Old Testament stories that depicted women as seductresses, liars, weak-minded, ambitious, or duplicitous. She served her purpose as the first woman and her part of the Old Testament narrative was over. In the *Apocrypha*, Eve was revisited and reinterpreted. These stories often made her responsible for bringing sin into the world.

Israelite Women

The Israelite concept of woman is a tapestry woven from many threads. Specific aspects of Torah law reflect women's subordination in terms of patriarchy, slavery, polygamy, and concubinage.[40] Understanding these stories and traditions is important in identifying how Israelite men viewed women and helps to account for the basis of the Christian understanding of women. This chapter examines these disparate threads.

The Woman in the Family

In the Old Testament, men as fathers and/or husbands dominate religious, social, and family life. Women are to submit to men, please them, and help them increase their power and influence.[41] This requirement of enablement fell equally on daughters and wives.

Daughters
Though not as valued as sons, daughters were an asset to an Israelite father. There is ample evidence that fathers loved their daughters,

---

[39] Alice Ogden Bellis, "Eve," in *Woman in Scripture: A Dictionary of Names and Unnamed Women in the Hebrew Bible, the Apocrypha/Deuterocanonical Books, and the New Testament,* eds. Carol Meyers, Toni Craven, Ross S. Kraemer (New York, NY: Houghton Mifflin Harcourt: 2000), 82–83.
[40] Ruether, 48.
[41] Jocelyn Hellig, "Lilith as a Focus of Judaism's Gender Construction," *Dialogue & Alliance* 12, no. 1 (Spring-Summer 1998): 45.

even though their true worth was often employed as a commodity. Men needed wives, and a father with a daughter supplied a need. For an acceptable dowry[42] and bride-price,[43] a man could obtain a wife. Israelite men who wanted to marry did not just need a female, they needed a girl who had never had sex; this was thought to be the only way to ensure a husband's property and wealth stayed in his bloodline. A daughter and her sexuality were therefore under the control of her father. To protect a girl's virginity, a father rarely let his daughter leave home unchaperoned. Exodus 22:16–17 states, "If a man seduces a virgin who is not engaged, and lies with her, he must pay a dowry for her to be his wife. If her father absolutely refuses to give her to him, he shall pay money equal to the dowry for virgins." The father is being compensated for property damage. If a girl is found not to be a virgin, Deuteronomy 22:20–21 says she could be stoned.[44] Protecting a daughter's virginity was protecting an investment. A marriage was a transfer of property, where a father transferred control of a daughter's sexuality to her husband.

Fathers could also use their daughters in other ways. Exodus 21:7 says that a father could sell a daughter into slavery.[45] When Lot was confronted by the people of Sodom who demanded his guests be tossed outside his home to be raped, he offered his two virgin daughters instead (Genesis 19:8). After making a foolish vow to God, Jephthah offered his daughter as a sacrifice (Judges 11–12). It was more important for Jephthah to honor his vow and not bring shame upon himself and his family than to spare his daughter.

In matters of inheritance, the eldest son usually received the largest share. Younger sons received smaller portions. If a family

---

[42] The dowry is a sum of money the bridegroom or his family gives to the father of his bride before he can receive her. In other occasions, the father gave the groom a dowry which took the place of the daughter's inheritance. If the couple divorced, the wife would retain the dowry.

[43] In Israelite society, the groom paid the father of the family an agreed-upon amount of money, property, or service for the woman he is intended to marry. Its purpose is to offset the family's loss of the daughter's economic contribution to the family. It is also a demonstration that the groom cannot financially support his new wife.

[44] Duane L. Christensen, *Deuteronomy* 21:10–34.12 (Nashville, TN: Thomas Nelson, 2002), 520.

[45] Gerda Lerner, 168.

had no son, the inheritance could be given to daughters. The daughters, however, had to marry within their own tribe so the property would remain there (Numbers 22:7–8; 36:6–9).

The Wife

Israelite women were expected to be married and have children. The wife, therefore, had one primary responsibility: to bear her husband's legitimate children. Along with the father, the mother was to be honored by her children. To prevent this problem, husbands could have several wives.[46] Polygamy was common among the patriarchs and Israelite monarchs. Having numerous wives was a sign of a wealthy man. The more wives, the higher his status. Of course, this greatly increased the odds of having more sons.

Men also had concubines or sex slaves. Concubines had no status in the household, so they were easier to dispose. In Judges 19, a Levite threw his concubine out to a crowd of men who wanted to rape him. They raped and killed the concubine, which allowed the Levite to escape.[47] Sometimes concubines, like Hagar (Genesis 16:2), were surrogates for women who could not conceive.[48] King David had at least ten concubines (2 Samuel 15:16) and King Solomon three hundred (1 Kings 11:3).

In Exodus 20:17, the Decalogue lists the wife as a part of the husband's property. "You shall not covet your neighbor's house; you shall not covet your neighbor's wife or his male servant or his female servant or his ox or his donkey or anything that belongs to your neighbor." A husband had the right to give his wife to another man. While in Egypt, when Abraham was afraid he would be attacked by other men because they might desire Sarah, he told her to pretend she was his sister. Pharaoh took notice of her, gave Abraham livestock—perhaps as a bride price—and took her to his palace. God then sent a plague on Egypt, and Pharaoh realized Sarah was Abraham's wife. She was returned to Abraham, and he was permitted to keep both her and the livestock (Genesis 12:10–20). Eight chapters later and fearful once more, he passed Sarah off as his sister again, and she was taken by King Abimelech of Gerar.

---

[46] Ibid., 170.
[47] Trent C. Butler, *Judges* (Nashville, TN: Thomas Nelson, 2009), 424.
[48] Wenham, 7.

He took Sarah but returned her unharmed because her identity was revealed to him in a dream (Genesis 20). Abimelech gave Abraham 1000 pieces of silver for his trouble and the right to reside anywhere in Gerar. In return, Abraham prayed that the king's wives and concubines would be able to bear children. The prayer worked.

Like his father, Isaac pretended that his wife Rebekah was his sister (Genesis 26:1–33). Once again, King Abimelech noticed her. He saw Isaac touching Rebekah in an intimate way. He then warned all men to stay away from Rebekah on the pain of death. The king allowed them to stay in Gerar, where they become wealthy. Since Sarah and Rebekah were property, Abraham and Isaac not only went unpunished but they were financially blessed.

Israelite men could also take women from those they defeated in battle. If one of these men decided he no longer wanted the woman, he could let her go back to her people. He could not, however, sell her as a slave, because she had already been humiliated enough (Deuteronomy 21:10–15).

A woman who had sex outside of her marriage could be put to death for adultery (Leviticus 20:10). If a man had sex with a married woman, he could be put to death. Having sex with a single woman was not considered adultery. Adultery was not about faithfulness; it was protecting a husband's sexual rights and the legitimacy of his children.[49] Prostitution was legal and never condemned in the Old Testament. In Proverbs 7, however, a young man was warned about prostitutes in that he will be led like an "ox to the slaughter" (Proverbs 7:22).

If a husband suspected his wife of adultery, he could force her to endure the *Sotah* ritual, which involved drinking a potion composed of holy water and sweepings from the tabernacle floor (Numbers 5:18–28).

> [18] After the priest has had the woman stand before the Lord, he shall loosen her hair and place in her hands the reminder-offering, the grain offering for jealousy, while he himself holds the bitter water that brings a curse. [19] Then the priest shall put the woman under oath and say to her, "If no other man has had sexual relations

---

[49] Hellig, 39.

with you and you have not gone astray and become impure while married to your husband, may this bitter water that brings a curse not harm you. [20] But if you have gone astray while married to your husband and you have made yourself impure by having sexual relations with a man other than your husband"—[21] here the priest is to put the woman under this curse—"may the Lord cause you to become a curse among your people when he makes your womb miscarry and your abdomen swell. [22] May this water that brings a curse enter your body so that your abdomen swells or your womb miscarries." Then the woman is to say, "Amen. So be it." . . . [27] If she has made herself impure and been unfaithful to her husband, this will be the result: When she is made to drink the water that brings a curse and causes bitter suffering, it will enter her, her abdomen will swell and her womb will miscarry, and she will become a curse. [28] If, however, the woman has not made herself impure, but is clean, she will be cleared of guilt and will be able to have children.

Not surprisingly, in a patriarchal society, a husband could divorce a wife and pay a financial penalty, but a wife could not divorce her husband. The most common reason for divorce was real or perceived adultery, or even when a "[a wife] finds no favor in [a husband's] eyes because he has found some indecency in her" (Deuteronomy 24:1). The husband had to present the wife with an official writ of divorce. They were both then free to marry again. Because the husband was forced to give her official papers and the woman could remarry, the Israelite manner of divorce was kinder than many other ancient Near Eastern religions that did not permit it.

Unlike a daughter who could inherit if she had no brothers, a widow could not inherit. The inheritance went to his deceased brother or nearest kinsmen redeemer (*go'el*). The *go'el* then participated in a levirate marriage (Deuteronomy 25:5–6). He married the widow, and the first son produced from the marriage was considered the deceased husband's heir.[50] In the Old Testament, Tamar

---

[50] Gerda Lerner, 169.

and Onan (Genesis 38) and Ruth and Boaz (Ruth 3:9) had levirate marriages.

Women in Cultic Life

Laws for Women

Many of the law codes state that women are full members of the cultic community (Exodus 21:22–25; 28–31; Leviticus 20:16), but there is little proof to back these assertions. Unlike other ancient Middle Eastern religions, the Israelite religion had no female clergy.[51] Tabernacle and Temple Priests were required to be "Levites" or "sons of Aaron."

The Temple had to be kept clean, and menstruation immediately eliminated women from cultic service, because menstruating women were considered impure.[52] According to Leviticus 15:19, "When a woman has a discharge, if her discharge in her body is blood, she shall continue in her menstrual impurity for seven days; and whoever touches her shall be unclean until evening." After the menses ended, the woman would take a ritual bath and be cleansed. Giving birth also rendered a woman impure.

> ²When a woman gives birth and bears a male *child*, then she shall be unclean for seven days, as in the days of her menstruation she shall be unclean. ³On the eighth day the flesh of his foreskin shall be circumcised. ⁴Then she shall remain in the blood of *her* purification for thirty-three days; she shall not touch any consecrated thing, nor enter the sanctuary until the days of her purification are completed. ⁵But if she bears a female *child*, then she shall be unclean for two weeks, as in her menstruation; and she

---

[51] Women could be servitors at the Tent of Meeting (1 Samuel 2:22). Women could also be prophets. Prominent female prophets were Miriam (Numbers 12:1–8), Deborah (Judges 4:4), Huldah (2 Kings 22:14–16), and the wife of Isaiah (Isaiah 8:3). Women could also participate in sacrificial meals (2 Samuel 1:4), religious festivals (Deuteronomy 12:12; 2 Samuel 6:19), and processionals (1 Samuel 18:6; Psalms 68:24–25).

[52] All seminal discharges were considered unclean. Men were impure after ejaculation (Leviticus 15:18).

shall remain in the blood of *her* purification for sixty-six days. (Leviticus 12:2–5)

Menstruation and childbirth kept women not only from being priests but also limited their activities when visiting the Temple. An impure woman could contaminate the Temple and anything she touched. These standards were not put in place for the good of women but to protect men. Women were also not permitted to take part in the feasts of unleavened bread, harvest, and ingathering (Exodus 23:17).

As demonstrated in the divorce and inheritance stipulations, Old Testament laws were designed to protect the family unit, especially the head of the family. Many laws protected from infringement the honor, authority and property of the *paterfamilias*. Laws showed that women were not equal to men in cultic life or anywhere else. If a woman were raped in the country, she did not have to prove she was raped because if she screamed no one would hear her. If she were raped in a city but did not scream, however, she was convicted of adultery and executed along with the rapist (Deuteronomy 22:23–27). If a woman intervened in a fight between her husband and another man and grabbed the other man's testicles, her hand would be chopped off (Deuteronomy 25:11–12). If a woman made a vow and her father or husband disagreed with it, he could cancel it (Numbers 30:1–8). There is no similar stipulation for men.

A man's word was worth more than that of a woman. Leviticus 27:1–3 states:

> [1] Again, the Lord spoke to Moses, saying, [2] "Speak to the sons of Israel and say to them, 'When a man makes a difficult vow, he *shall be valued* according to your valuation of persons belonging to the Lord. [3] If your valuation is of the male from twenty years even to sixty years old, then your valuation shall be fifty shekels of silver, after the shekel of the sanctuary.

The differing value of an Israelite man or woman's vow determines the value of an Israelite man or woman. In all respects, women did not have the same status as men and were not full members of Israelite society.

Negative Old Testament Stereotypes of Women

When early Christian theologians began to develop a theology of women, Eve took precedence over other Old Testament women. The Apostle Paul's writings ensured it. Other women in the Old Testament, however, add elements to Christian theologians' view of women. Many of these women are unnamed. Others are so famous or infamous that their names have become descriptors.

There are at least six groups of these women. The temptresses used sex to lead men astray, either for their own ends or for the good of Israel.[53] Accidental seducers attracted men without going out of their way to do so. Tricksters deceived men. Difficult wives and the "strange women" of Proverbs are the fourth group. Evil women are personified by Jezebel. The final group is comprised of good women.

The Temptresses

Delilah, Naomi via Ruth, and Solomon's wives are examples of Old Testament temptresses. Everyone knows the story of Samson and the *femme fatale* Delilah. Judges 16 recounts how one of Israel's greatest heroes succumbed to the enticement of a woman. After Samson killed many Philistines, the rulers resolved to rid themselves of him.

> After this it came about that he loved a woman in the valley of Sorek, whose name was Delilah. The lords of the Philistines came up to her and said to her, "Entice him, and see where his great strength *lies* and how we may overpower him that we may bind him to afflict him. Then we will each give you eleven hundred *pieces* of silver" (Judges 16:4–5).

---

[53] In the Book of Esther, Esther used sex to save her people. The man responsible for this potential tragedy, Haman, was hung from the gallows he built for his enemy. Judges 4 describes how Jael seduced and drove a peg through the head of an enemy general who had taken refuge in her home. In the Deuterocanonical book of Judith, Judith seduces the enemy general and cuts off his head. These women killed for Israel and God.

Samson lied to her about his strength three times and killed those sent to kill him. Finally, Samson told her the truth: it was his hair. The Philistines cut off his hair and easily captured him. Judges presents Samson as a man who believed he was invulnerable but proved no match for Delilah. She was sent to entice him and in doing so earn a reward. Delilah serves as an example of a woman using her seductive power for personal gain, a woman's inability to love, and the dangers of foreign women.[54]

The story of Ruth is remembered as a love story between Ruth and her mother-in-law, Naomi. It is a story of loyalty that most people could not even hope to emulate. After a life of difficulty and disappointment, the heroine persevered and married the hero. Dozens—if not hundreds—of books have been written about Ruth.

After the death of all the males in their family and because of her inability to inherit,[55] Naomi was in dire straits. She decided to leave Moab and return to her family in her ancestral home in Judah (Ruth 1:6–7). Naomi's loyal Moabite daughter-in-law, Ruth, accompanied her (Ruth 1:14–17). After arriving in Bethlehem, Ruth met Boaz, a rich relative of Naomi's deceased husband. Though Ruth was a foreigner, Boaz allowed her to glean in one of his fields (Ruth 2:8–9). When asked why she had found favor with Boaz, he told her that he had heard of her loyalty to Naomi and wanted to help them (Ruth 2:11–14). Boaz also provided Ruth and Naomi with food, protected them, and asked Ruth not to glean from anyone else's field (Ruth 2:14–23). Boaz was loyal to his next of kin but also smitten with Ruth.

When Ruth returned home, she told Naomi about Boaz. Naomi recognized Boaz as a relative and that he could be a potential *go'el*, or kinsman-redeemer. Naomi used Boaz's attraction to Ruth to seduce him.[56] She instructed her to bathe, anoint herself, and put on her best clothes (Ruth 3:3). After he had finished eating and drinking, she was to go to the threshing floor, uncover his feet, and lie down (Ruth 3:4).

---

[54] Katharine M. Rogers, *The Troublesome Helpmate: A History of Misogyny in Literature* (Seattle, WA: University of Washington Press, 1966), 5.
[55] Judy Fentress-Williams and Melody D. Knowles, in "Affirming and Contradicting Gender Stereotypes," Gale Yee, ed. (Minneapolis, MN: Fortress Press, 2018), 140.
[56] Bach, 238.

There can be little doubt that Ruth seduced Boaz.[57] The sexual references are rife but whether sex occurred is unclear. "Feet" might be a euphemism for "genitals."[58] When Boaz woke up to see her at his feet, he asked, "Who are you?" She identified herself and said that he was the guardian-redeemer of her family (Ruth 3:9). She then asked Boaz to cover her with his cloak as a symbolic action of engagement (Ruth 3:9). He agreed and eventually married Ruth (Ruth 4:13). The text does not say whether they had sex or not on that fateful night, and it doesn't matter. In the end, Naomi's plan worked, and they now had a *go'el* and, thus, a future. Ruth and Boaz's familial lineage leads to King David (Ruth 4:22) and thus her seduction had a positive result for all of Israel.

Throughout the Old Testament, God warns the Israelites not to marry foreign women. Deuteronomy 7:3–4 forbids it. These women would turn Israelite men to idolatry. Solomon ignored this dictum and in doing so his dedication to Yahweh was weakened.[59]

> [1]Now King Solomon loved many foreign women along with the daughter of Pharaoh: Moabite, Ammonite, Edomite, Sidonian, and Hittite women, [2]from the nations concerning which the Lord had said to the sons of Israel, "You shall not associate with them, nor shall they associate with you, *for* they will surely turn your heart away after their gods. Solomon held fast to these in love. [3]He had seven hundred wives, princesses, and three hundred concubines, and his wives turned his heart away." (1 Kings 11:1–3)

His wives convinced him to make sacrifices to their gods. This did not please God who vowed to tear Solomon's kingdom from him and leave him only with one tribe for the sake of David and Jerusalem.

---

[57] Nehama Aschkenasy, *Eve's Journey: Feminine Image in Hebraic Literary Tradition* (Philadelphia, PA: University of Pennsylvania Press, 1986), 87.
[58] T. J. Wray, *Good Girls, Bad Girls: Enduring Lessons of Twelve Women of the Old Testament* (Lanham: Rowman & Littlefield Publishers, Inc., 2008), 73; Frederick W. Bush, *Ruth, Esther* (Dallas, TX: Word Book Publishers, 1996), 153.
[59] Simon J. DeVries, *1 Kings* (Waco, TX: Word Book Publishers, 1985), 142.

Not even the wise Solomon could withstand these women. His weakness ruined his country. Nehemiah 13:26 stood as a stark reminder, "Did not Solomon king of Israel sin regarding these things? Yet among the many nations there was no king like him, and he was loved by his God. God made him king over all Israel; nevertheless, the foreign women caused even him to sin." Nehemiah clarified the story in 1 Kings 11. Solomon was weak, but it was the women's fault.[60]

The Accidental Seductress

The accidental seducers were so beautiful that men (or angels) simply could not help themselves. The "daughters of humans" in Genesis 6:1–4, Bathsheba, and Tamar are prime examples.

In Israelite tradition, the corruption of humanity begins in Genesis 6:1–4. In this account, the "daughters of humans" were so beautiful that the "sons of God" could not resist them and took them for wives (Genesis 6:2–3). The sons of God are often identified as angels. They are not identified as rebel angels. These illicit unions produced a race of giants known as the Nephilim (Genesis 6:4). This is a physical corruption of God's human creation.[61] God's plan did not include the Nephilim. This unnatural union displeased God, and he determined to destroy humanity, except for Noah and his family. Women, therefore, must be the cause of this evil. The account also provided the Israelites with an explanation for the presence of evil.

In 1 Corinthians 11:10, the Apostle Paul may have been referencing the Nephilim story when he wrote, "Therefore the woman ought to have *a symbol of* authority on her head, because of the angels." Paul demonstrated that the passage concerned a visible sign of women's submission to men. The mentioning of angels, however, seems out of place. If Paul were discussing the danger of women's hair enticing the Nephilim, the pseudepigraphal book of 1 Enoch may have provided him with additional information.[62] First Enoch 7:1–2 recounts,

---
[60] Rogers, 5.
[61] Wenham, 146.
[62] Ruether, 90.

> ¹It happened after the sons of men had multiplied in those days, that daughters were born to them, elegant and beautiful. ²And when the angel, the sons of heaven, beheld them, they became enamored of them, saying to each other, Come, let us select for ourselves wives from the progeny of men, and let us beget children.

Women, therefore, must cover their heads so as not to bewitch angels or Watchers. First Enoch also states that not only did they illicitly reproduce, but the Watchers taught women the art of cosmetics, thus adding to their allure. The angels taught the men how to make metal weapons. More obscure references in the New Testament may include Jude 6, 7, 14 and 2 Peter 2:4.

Perhaps no other woman fits this accidental seducer category better than Bathsheba. Even though David was a man after God's own heart, David's desire for Bathsheba, a beautiful, married woman, led to his committing adultery (very likely rape) and murder.[63] Second Samuel 11:1 tells us that David stayed in Jerusalem instead of leading his army. He then made a fateful mistake. Second Samuel 11:2–15 provides the details.

While walking on his roof, David spotted a beautiful woman bathing (2). He asked about her and was told that she was married to Uriah, who served in his army (3). He sent for her, had sex (whether with or without her consent is unknown), and sent her home (4). Bathsheba is ashamed of what happened and took a ritual bath to cleanse herself (4). She then discovers that she is pregnant (5). To prevent any questions of paternity, David sent for Uriah in the hopes he would come home and have sex with Bathsheba. Since his fellow soldiers were in battle, he refused to sleep with her (6–13). David then sent Uriah to the front line of the battle (14). David then ordered a withdrawal, leaving Uriah alone to be killed (17).[64] The prophet Nathan made this point clear in 2 Samuel 12:1–15. God punished David by killing his son with Bathsheba. For whatever reason, David then married Bathsheba who became quite powerful in her own right. Their second son, Solomon, is remembered as the greatest king of Israel.

---

[63] Rogers, 5.
[64] Kyle P. McCarter, *II Samuel*. The Anchor Yale Bible Commentary Series (New York, NY: Doubleday, 1984), 288.

According to the account, David found Bathsheba's naked body irresistible. As a king, he could take whatever he wanted. Nothing in the text implies that she attempted to seduce him.[65]

Second Samuel 13 tells the story of the half-siblings Amnon and Tamar, who were David's children. Amnon was so obsessed with this half-sister that it made him ill (1–2). Amnon's cousin, Jonadab, arranged to have them find themselves alone together (5). Amnon told Tamar that he was attracted to her, and despite her pleas to marry her rather than force himself on her, Amnon raped her while calling her "sister" (11–14).[66] He further shamed Tamar refusing to marry her and sending her away (17).[67] After raping her, he lost interest in her and never wanted to see her again.[68] Amnon ignored Exodus 22:16 and Deuteronomy 22:28–29 that compels a rapist to marry his victim and make recompense to the father.

David does nothing to avenge his daughter's honor. Absalom, David's son and Tamar's brother, killed Amnon to avenge her (28–29). David then sent Absalom away, and a few years later he led a rebellion against his father (2 Samuel 15–18). Tamar's rape fulfilled Nathan's prophecy given to David. According to 2 Samuel 12:11, "Thus says the Lord, 'Behold, I will raise up evil against you from your own household.'"

Unlike Bathsheba, Tamar becomes neither powerful nor the mother of someone in the Davidic monarchy. Instead, she put on mourning clothes, placed ashes on her head, and cried (19).

---

[65] There have been many people who believed that someone as great as David could not have given into his baser instincts without being purposely enticed. A perfect example is the 1951 film *David and Bathsheba*. In this movie, Bathsheba (Susan Hayward) seduces David (Gregory Peck). She states that she knew he paced the roof at night and took her bath at a time when he would see her. Bathsheba also tells David that she does not love Uriah and has been married to him for only six days and it was an arranged marriage. See Alice Bach, *Women, Seduction, and Betrayal in Biblical Narrative* (Cambridge: Cambridge University Press, 1997), 159.

[66] It should be noted that women also commit sexual crimes in the Old Testament. The story of Lot and his daughters in Genesis 19: 30–38 and of Potiphar's wife in Genesis 39 are prime examples.

[67] Amy Kalmanofsky, *Dangerous Sisters of the Hebrew Bible* (Minneapolis, MN: Augsburg Press, 2014), 108.

[68] Phyllis Trible, *Texts of Terror: Literary-Feminist Readings of Biblical Narratives* (Minneapolis, MN: Fortress Press, 1984), 47.

She remained desolate in Absalom's house (2 Samuel 13:20) and disappeared from the text.

The Tricksters

In most cases, female tricksters have "a low—or relatively lower—social status, prohibiting gain or advancement through means available to others. They have no power of their own, so they employ wit and cunning in devising a plot to achieve their desired end."[69] Representative tricksters are Lot's daughters, Rebekah, and another Tamar.

Genesis 19 is one of the more disturbing chapters in all the Bible. After Lot gave shelter to angels in the guise of handsome men who had just arrived in Sodom, a crowd gathered around his house and demanded that the guests be turned over to them (1–5). Lot offered his virgin daughters instead (8), but the crowd did not want them. The daughters and their plight were so inconsequential to the story that the writer did not even record their names.[70] They were presented as objects.[71] Fortunately, the angels and Lot's family escaped the city before its destruction.

Lot and his family took refuge in a cave in nearby Zoar (21–22). Having witnessed the destruction, Lot's daughters assumed everyone in the world had been killed and that their family line would end (31). To remedy this problem, the daughters devised a horrendous solution. They got their father drunk on two consecutive nights, and each night one of the daughters raped him. Both became pregnant (31–38).

Of all the females in the Old Testament, Rebekah takes enormous initiative, by means of deception, in obeying God. Genesis 25 recounts her deception. After she and Isaac suffer through twenty years without children, she finally became pregnant with twins. She felt the babies moving around in her belly constantly and asked God why this was happening. God replied, "Two nations

---

[69] Melissa A. Jackson, "Lot's Daughters and Tamar as Tricksters and the Patriarchal Narratives as Feminist Theology," *Journal for the Study of the Old Testament* 26, no. 4 (June 2002): 32.
[70] Jackson, 33.
[71] Phyllis Trible, *Texts of Terror*, 74.

are in your womb; And two peoples will be separated from your body; And one people shall be stronger than the other; And the older shall serve the younger" (23). It appeared that she kept this news to herself. Rebekah realized that she had to ensure that her younger son, Jacob, would continue the covenant God made with Abraham.

The twins could not have been more different nor the oracle more precise. As they were being born, Jacob grasped the heel of his brother Esau (26). They looked and acted differently. "Esau became a skillful hunter, a man of the field, but Jacob was a peaceful man, living in tents (27). Now Isaac loved Esau, because he had a taste for game, but Rebekah loved Jacob" (28).

Also a deceiver, Jacob convinced his brother to trade him his birthright for a cup of stew (30–34). The birthright made Jacob the head of the family and due a double inheritance of his father's possessions. Another difference between the brothers was that Jacob, like his mother, was smart and cunning, while Esau, like his father, was gullible.

When Isaac, who had gone blind, realized he was about to die, he told Esau to go hunt, kill, and prepare some wild game for him. Afterward, he would give him his blessing (Genesis 27:1–4). In primitive societies, the blessing was highly desired.[72] Rebekah overheard the discussion and decided to arrange for Jacob to receive the blessing instead. Genesis 27 depicts the elaborate, detailed, and brilliant plan. Rebekah cooked the meal for Isaac, dressed Jacob in Esau's clothes so he would smell like his brother, and even put goat skins on Jacob's hands and neck so that his skin would feel rough, like Esau's (5–17).

Rebekah's scheme worked (27–29). Realizing that Esau would be enraged at being deprived of his blessing, she arranged for Isaac to send him to a safe place. She began to complain that there were no prospective wives for Jacob where they lived and that she could not bear to see him married to a local Hittite (Genesis 27:46 and Genesis 28:1–5). Isaac loved her so much that he blessed Jacob (a second time) and gave him permission to move to Mesopotamia. Rebekah had to be the one to ensure the fulfillment of God's oracle and the

---

[72] John H. Tullock and Mark McEntire, *The Old Testament Story*. 8th ed. (Upper Saddle River, NJ: Pearson, 2009), 57.

continuation of the Abrahamic covenant. She knew Isaac would have chosen Esau.[73] Deception is admirable when accomplished with God's sanction.

The story of Tamar and Judah occurs in Genesis 38. Tamar married Er, one of Judah's sons. God determined that Er was evil and killed him (7). Judah then gave another son, Onan, as Tamar's husband (8). God struck down Onan for spilling his seed on the ground (9). Onan was deliberately attempting to shirk his levirate vow. With children, Tamar could inherit Er's share of Judah's inheritance. If Tamar did not have a child with Onan, the brothers would cut Tamar out of the inheritance.[74] Judah then promised to give his youngest son, Shelah, as Tamar's husband when he came of age (11). He sent her to live with her father as a *grass widow*[75] (11). Judah blamed her for his sons' deaths and did not want to lose another (11).[76] Knowing that Judah had no intention of allowing her to marry Shelah, Genesis 38 recounts an elaborate trick to ensure she had a future without a husband.[77] Tamar learned that the recently widowed Judah was going to Timnah to shear his sheep (13). She veiled herself and waited for Judah at a place she knew he would pass on his way home (14). He assumed she was a prostitute. They then began to negotiate a price for sex (15–16). Judah said he would pay her with a goat but did not have one with him. Tamar shrewdly asked for collateral (17). She asked for his seal and cord (18). Judah's seal and cord were such personal items that everyone would know they belonged to him. They had sex, and she became pregnant (18).

Three months later, Judah was told that Tamar had become pregnant while prostituting herself (24). From Judah's perspective, Tamar had shamed his family by reneging on her vow to wait for Shelah. Judah sent for her so that she could be executed (24). Tamar then revealed her strategy to Judah (25). She returned his seal and

---

[73] Wray, 30.
[74] Phillip F. Esler, *Sex, Wives, and Warriors. Reading Old Testament Narrative with Its Ancient Audience* (London: James Clarke & Co. Ltd., 2011), 94.
[75] A grass widow is a woman whose husband is away often or for a prolonged period.
[76] Rachel Adelman, "Seduction and Recognition in the Story of Judah and Tamar and the Book of Ruth," *Nashim: A Journal of Jewish Women's Studies & Gender Issues* no. 23 (Spring–Fall 2012): 92.
[77] Aschkenasy, 86.

cord in public so he could not deny paternity.[78] Instead of being angry or embarrassed, he said that she was more righteous than he, and said he should have kept his promise to her (26). In this account, Tamar's ruse made it possible for Judah to respect the levirate vow. Tamar gave birth to twins. By navigating patriarchy, one of the twins, Pharez (29), began the familial line of Boaz and David. This might be why this strange encounter within the Joseph account found its way into Genesis, and Tamar is regarded as an admirable person.

Nevertheless, Tamar's story stands as a warning. She used her mind and her body to get what she wanted. Judah learned his lesson and never touched her again (26).

The Nag or Quarrelsome Woman

Additionally, women are portrayed in the wisdom literature as quarrelsome. After Job was afflicted with sores (Job 2:7), his wife tells him to "curse God and die (Job 2:9)." Job calls her a "foolish woman" and tells her that they must accept not only good things from God but also the bad (Job 2:10). Ironically, Job's friends give him similarly poor advice. Proverbs 21:19 warns men to pick a wife carefully because, "It is better to live in a desert land than with a contentious and vexing woman." According to Proverbs 27:15–16, "[15] A constant dripping on a day of steady rain and a contentious woman are alike; [16] He who would restrain her restrains the wind, And grasps oil with his right hand." Proverbs 25:24 even warns, "It is better to live in a corner of the roof than in a house shared with a contentious woman." Ecclesiastes 7:26–28 describes women as having no capacity to love men.

> [26] And I discovered more bitter than death the woman whose heart is snares and nets, whose hands are chains. One who is pleasing to God will escape from her, but the sinner will be captured by her. [27] "Behold, I have discovered this," says the Preacher, adding one thing to another to find an explanation, [28] which I am still seeking

---

[78] Elizabeth A. McCabe, *Women in the Hebrew Bible: A Survey of Old and New Testament Perspectives* (New York, NY: University Press of America, 2011), 6.

but have not found. I have found one man among a thousand, but I have not found a woman among all these.

The Strange Woman of Proverbs

Solomon, the author of Proverbs, did not take his own advice. Interpreted literally, these passages depict a father warning his son about a seductive and treacherous woman. This interpretation has dominated Christian theology. The Strange Woman can be found in Proverbs 2:16–22; 5:1–23; 6:20–35; and 7:1–27. Her proximity to the Woman of Folly in Proverbs 9:13–18 suggests similarities between the two. The Woman of Folly was a prostitute. The Strange Woman was many things—none of them good; her motives and sexual allure were apparent. Proverbs 2:16 asserts that only wisdom would "deliver you from the strange woman, from the adulteress who flatters with her words." Proverbs 5:3–4 warns, "³ For the lips of an adulteress drip honey and smoother than oil is her speech; ⁴ But in the end, she is bitter as wormwood, sharp as a two-edged sword."

The Strange Woman was also seductive. Proverbs 6:23–29 states:

> ²³ For the commandment is a lamp and the teaching is light;
> And reproofs for discipline are the way of life
> ²⁴ To keep you from the evil woman,
> From the smooth tongue of the adulteress.
> ²⁵ Do not desire her beauty in your heart,
> Nor let her capture you with her eyelids.
> ²⁶ For on account of a harlot *one is reduced* to a loaf of bread,
> And an adulteress hunts for the precious life.
> ²⁷ Can a man take fire in his bosom
> And his clothes not be burned?
> ²⁸ Or can a man walk on hot coals
> And his feet not be scorched?
> ²⁹ So is the one who goes in to his neighbor's wife;
> Whoever touches her will not go unpunished.

The Strange Woman was always on the prowl. Proverbs 7:8–12 describes her tactics.

⁸ Passing through the street near her corner;
And he takes the way to her house,
⁹ In the twilight, in the evening,
In the middle of the night and *in* the darkness.
¹⁰ And behold, a woman *comes* to meet him,
Dressed as a harlot and cunning of heart.
¹¹ She is boisterous and rebellious,
Her feet do not remain at home;
¹² *She is* now in the streets, now in the squares,
And lurks by every corner.

The father warned his son not to take his advice lightly. As noted in Proverbs 7:19–20, she was also unfaithful. "¹⁹ For my husband is not at home, he has gone on a long journey; ²⁰ He has taken a bag of money with him, at the full moon he will come home." In Proverbs 7:24–26, the father urges, "²⁴ Now therefore, *my* sons, listen to me, and pay attention to the words of my mouth. ²⁵ Do not let your heart turn aside to her ways, do not stray into her paths. ²⁶ For many are the victims she has cast down, and numerous are all her slain." These passages describe the Strange Woman as a seductive and immoral married woman.[79] She possesses all of the qualities that decent young men should avoid.[80] Ironically, the Strange Woman has many of the same negative characteristics as David, for whom many were slain because of his lust, lies, rape, and murder. David was, however, a man after God's own heart and the King of Israel.

The Evil Woman

Jezebel was denounced as a prostitute, temptress, enemy of God, and murderer. First Kings describes her failures. The daughter of the king of Sidon, Jezebel married Ahab, the king of Israel. This was a political marriage meant to stabilize the relationship between

---

[79] Tova Forti, "The 'Isha Zara' in Proverbs 1–9: Allegory and Allegorization," *Hebrew Studies* 48 (2007): 89.
[80] Christl M. Maier and Nuria Calduch-Benages, eds. *The Writings and Later Wisdom Books: Good and Evil Women in Proverbs and Job, the Emergence of Cultural Stereotypes* (Williston, VT.: Society of Biblical Literature, 2014), 86.

the two countries. Jezebel, therefore, was not an Israelite. She worshipped Baal and Asherah and, unlike Ruth who converted, continued to worship them in Israel. She epitomized the dangerous, foreign woman that so many Old Testament writers feared.

Jezebel led Ahab into idolatry (1 Kings 21:25–26). He later built her a temple to Baal in Samaria (1 Kings 16:31–33). He allowed the 450 prophets of Baal and 400 prophets of Asherah to eat at the royal table (1 Kings 18:19). Jezebel had Yahweh's prophets killed (I Kings 18:13). After Elijah won the showdown with the prophets of Baal at Mount Carmel, he treated the prophets of Baal the same way that Jezebel had treated the Israelite prophets: He had all of them killed (1 Kings 18:38–40). "Then Jezebel sent a messenger to Elijah, saying, 'So may the gods do to me and even more, if I do not make your life as the life of one of them by tomorrow about this time'" (1 Kings 19:2). Even after seeing God's victory at Mount Carmel, Elijah was so terrified that he fled to Mount Horeb. Jezebel also orchestrated the murder and seizure of Naboth's vineyard for her husband who could not secure it for himself (1 Kings 21). Though Ahab was the king, Jezebel was the real power behind the throne.

After the death of Ahab, General Jehu became the new king. In 2 Kings 9:6–7, God instructed him to "strike the house of Ahab your master, that I may avenge the blood of My servants the prophets, and the blood of all the servants of the Lord, at the hand of Jezebel." Before he could become king, Jehu had to defeat King Joram in battle. Before the battle, Joram and Jehu met at the center of the battlefield. When Joram saw Jehu, he said, "Is it peace, Jehu?" And he answered, "What peace, so long as the harlotries of your mother Jezebel and her witchcrafts are so many?" (2 Kings 9:22). From this single verse stems Jezebel's reputation as a witch and a whore. Jehu then killed Joram.

Jehu then traveled to Jezreel to kill Jezebel, who was waiting for him. In preparation, "she painted her eyes and adorned her head and looked out the window" (2 Kings 9:30). This passage has been interpreted as her attempt to seduce Jehu and save her own life. If it was, the ploy failed. He had her thrown from a window and she was eaten by dogs.

The seduction interpretation loses credibility in light of verse 31 "[31]As Jehu entered the gate, she said, "Is it well, Zimri, your master's murderer?" As told in 1 Kings 16, Zimri was the chariot driver for King Elah. He murdered Elah and became king for seven days. By mentioning Zimri, Jezebel is calling Jehu a traitor for the action taken against Joram. Like so many queens who know they will be executed, she may have wanted to die regally.

To Israelites, Jezebel was an immoral interloper who bewitched and seduced the king. She also refused to renounce her religion and accept Israel's god. Jezebel is mentioned in Revelation 2:20, "But I have *this* against you, that you tolerate the woman Jezebel, who calls herself a prophetess, and she teaches and leads My bond-servants astray so that they commit *acts of* immorality and eat things sacrificed to idols." According to Athalya Brenner, the account employs Jezebel as a "catchword for a whoring, non-believing, female adversary."[81] Because of these actions and references, Jezebel has become a moniker for evil women in the Israelite and Christian traditions.

The Good Woman

With the exception of prophetesses such as Miriam and Huldah, women had few opportunities to participate in cultic life. The home was where they made their principal contributions. Courageous women like Deborah, who saved Israel, and matriarchs such as Sarah were uncommon. Few people (man or woman) were as heroic and did as much for the Jewish people as Esther. By rising to the level of Queen, she risked her life by approaching the king to petition him to save her people from annihilation. Indeed, Esther was the rarest of biblical heroines. The women the Old Testament writers valued the most were wives that increased the prestige of their husbands and mothers of legitimate children who were raised to honor God and their parents. These women were trustworthy, loyal, resourceful, family-centered, and virtuous.[82] In the Old Testament, these women were rare. Examples of good women are Ruth, Abigail, and the Worthy Woman of Proverbs 31.

---

[81] *Woman in Scripture: A Dictionary of Names and Unnamed Women in the Hebrew Bible, the Apocrypha/Deuterocanonical Books, and the New Testament.* s.v. "Jezebel 1," by Athalya Brenner.

[82] Thomas P. McCreesh, "Wisdom as Wife: Proverbs 31:10–31," *Revue Biblique* 92, no. 1 (January 1986): 39.

Ruth

Although also described as a seducer, Ruth was a good woman. She may have seduced Boaz at Naomi's instruction, but she exhibited family loyalty by not deserting her mother-in-law. Though Naomi pleaded with Orpah and Ruth to stay in their homeland (Ruth 1:8–13), Ruth chose to relocate with Naomi (Ruth 1:15–16). Orpah chose to stay behind, as was her right (Ruth 1:14). Ruth made the more difficult choice.

Boaz had heard of Ruth's loyalty to her mother-in-law. He knew of the situation Naomi and Ruth faced as widows. He knew that Ruth had left her father and mother and moved to a new land. He praised her for all these actions and rewarded her by allowing her to work in his field (Ruth 2:8–12).

Ruth was resourceful enough to go out on her own to seek grain (Ruth 2:2), to work all day in the fields (Ruth 2:17), and to befriend Boaz (Ruth 2:8). Guided by Naomi, Ruth demonstrated her resourcefulness by seducing Boaz (Ruth 3:3–4) and in doing so found someone to redeem them both.

Ruth also excelled as a wife. After marrying Boaz, she bore a son. The people and elders blessed Ruth who "built up the house of Israel" (4:11). By marrying Boaz, Ruth secured the house of Elimech and helped establish the line of David.[83]

Abigail

The story of Abigail is told in 1 Samuel 25. Abigail was married to Nabal. He is described as rich and evil (3). Abigail, however, is intelligent and beautiful (3). She is the only woman in the Bible described in this way.[84] While David was fleeing from Saul and living as a bandit with the Philistines, he sent word to Nabal that he expected payment for treating his shepherds well and protecting his flock (7–8). The servants went to see Nabal, introduced themselves, stated their purpose, and reminded him that they had come in David's name. Nabal said he had never heard of David,

---

[83] Ibid.
[84] Elisheva Baumgarten, "Charitable like Abigail: The History of an Epitaph," *The Jewish Quarterly Review* 105, no. 3 (Summer 2015): 313.

and called them extortionists (10). When the messengers returned to David and told him what Nabal said, he and his men put on their swords and went to confront Nabal (13).

One of the servants told Abigail what had happened (14). She realized that Nabal had made a grievous error. She instructed her servants to go ahead of her and take food to David as a peace offering (19). Abigail then learned that David planned to kill Nabal and all his men. She bowed to David and apologized for her husband's foolishness (23–25). She praised David, told him he was fighting for the Lord, and glorified his future kingship (26–31). She asked him to take the gifts and ignore her foolish husband. David acquiesced to her request, praised her, and said that if she had not come, he would have killed Nabal and all of his men (32–35).

Abigail returned home to find a drunken Nabal holding a great feast. The next morning when she told him what she had done, "His heart died within him so that he became a stone" (37). Ten days later, he died (38). When David heard of Nabal's death, he took Abigail as his wife. She was a wealthy and intelligent woman, and a marriage to her would help him build support for his future rule.

Abigail was a Good Woman. She was a good wife to Nabal and then to David. She was loyal to Nabal, despite his faults.[85] For David, she kept him from bloodguilt.[86] By riding out to meet David and interceding for her husband, she showed initiative, courage, and intelligence. David admired her enough to marry her. Unlike Bathsheba, Abigail attracted David with her character. Abigail's popularity continued well into the modern era. New England Puritans venerated her as wise and industrious, and many girls were named after her.[87]

The Proverbs 31 Woman (Proverbs 31:10–31)

Written as an acrostic poem with the first letter of each verse being a letter of the Hebrew alphabet, the Proverbs 31 woman is an idealized image of the perfect wife of a wealthy man.

---

[85] Ruether, 65.
[86] Ralph W. Klein, *1 Samuel* (Waco, TX: Word Book Publishers, 1983), 253.
[87] Baumgarten, 330.

This wife made her husband's life easier. Her husband trusted her and she did no evil to him (11–12). Even though she had servants, she worked hard in the home and increased her husband's wealth by purchasing property and planting vineyards (16). She was generous to the poor (20) and she was wise (26). Her husband did not have to worry about the household, so he could sit at the city gate with the other elders (23).[88] Marrying such a woman was a gift from God (Proverbs 18:22; 19:14). Her husband and children praised her. The Proverbs 31 Woman was not sexualized. She was praised for being a wife and mother.

In Actuality

The Old Testament demonstrates the sinfulness of men and women alike. It depicts the patriarchy of ancient culture and the ways women navigated in it. While women were identified in relation to fathers or husbands, as one would expect from a patriarchal culture, women found ways to honor God as noted with Esther's rescue of Israel. The essence of her life as daughter, wife, or mother did not preclude her from thwarting a genocide, as Esther demonstrates.

Because of the perceived uncleanliness of menstruation, pregnancy, and childrearing, women's participation in cultic life was limited. The law stated that she was a member of the community, but there was also evidence of equal communal leadership or participation. Women could not be priests, enter the temple, or participate in certain festivals. Cultural laws and honor codes were equally draconian. A woman could be forced to marry her rapist. A man could offer a woman to a mob to protect his honor. A man could pretend that his wife was his sister. A father could sacrifice his daughter.

Women in the Old Testament, though depicted as seducers, liars, and adulterers, also were bold, courageous, and God-honoring as demonstrated in the examples of Rebecca, Jael, Ruth and others. Old Testament culture described women as devious, but their strategies around patriarchy were often heroic and served as role models and leaders. While culture depicted women as inferior, the Proverbs 31 Woman exceeded expectations for women. She was even honored in the City Gates of Israel.

---

[88] Roland E. Murphy, *Proverbs*. Word Bible Commentary (Nashville, TN: Thomas Nelson, 1998), 247.

CHAPTER TWO

The Greek Concept of Women

Hellenistic philosophy played a major role in how New Testament writers and early and medieval Christian theologians defined women. This chapter examines the place of women in classical Greek (Athenian) life (480 BCE–323 BCE), and in the philosophies of Plato (ca. 429–347 BCE), Aristotle (384 BCE–322 BCE), and the Jewish Hellenistic philosopher, Philo (20 BCE–50 CE).

Greek Women[1]

Greek women lived in a patriarchal society in which they had no more rights than children.[2] Women could not leave the house without a chaperone. Within the home, women were often relegated to certain rooms.[3] They were considered intellectually inferior and, therefore, dependent on their father or husband. Greek women were forbidden to own property and, thus, were not considered citizens.[4]

---

[1] For an excellent description of women in Greek life, see Sue Blundell, *Women in Ancient Greece* (Cambridge, MA: Harvard University Press, 1995).
[2] Little information concerning lower class women or female slaves exists from the classical era of Greek philosophy. The majority of the historical record concerns upper class women and the philosophers who wrote about women most certainly had them in mind. In this section, therefore, women should be understood as those from the upper class.
[3] William J. O'Neal, "The Status of Women in Ancient Athens," *International Social Sciences Review* 68, no. 3 (Summer 1993): 117.
[4] Ute Gerhard, *Debating Women's Equality: Toward a Feminist Theory of law from a European Perspective* (New Brunswick, NJ.: Rutgers University Press, 2001), 35.

Fathers brokered deals with potential suitors to obtain the best possible dowry.[5] A father could take back his daughter, divorce her from her husband, and marry her off again to another man who offered a better dowry.[6] The average bride was fifteen years old and her husband was often twice her age.[7] One of the reasons for the age discrepancy was that an elderly husband could pick his wife's next husband. A father could sell his daughter into slavery if he suspected she was not a virgin. There were no expectations that married men would be monogamous or that single men would remain virgins until marriage. A wife was to have sex only with her husband so that there would be no doubts about her children's paternity. The husband had to divorce his wife if she had sex, consensual or not, with anyone else. The husband also had the right to kill the other man.[8] If the husband refused, he forfeited his citizenship. Women who were raped were blamed for what happened to them. Sons were preferred over daughters, who were often abandoned by their parents soon after birth.[9]

Wives were to be frugal, silent, and hard-working within the home; only prostitutes and women of the lower classes were to be found in the streets.[10] Women rarely participated in public life. If the husband hosted a banquet, normally the wife did not attend unless it was for family.[11] The marital bond between the husband and wife was based on the production of legitimate heirs. A loving relationship was not necessary or expected. Men found intellectual stimulation and camaraderie with other men of their own social class. They also had sexual relationships with men of their own or lower classes and female prostitutes.

---

[5] Julia Annas, "Plato's Republic and Feminism," *Philosophy* 51, no. 197 (July 1976): 317.
[6] Morris Silver, *Wives, Single Women and "Bastards" in the Ancient Greek World: Law and Economics Perspectives* (Barnsley, UK: Oxbow Books, 2018), 108–9.
[7] O'Neal, 118.
[8] J. Roy, "An Alternative Sexual Morality for Classical Athenians," *Greece & Rome* 44, no. 1 (April 1977): 13.
[9] For an excellent introduction on female infant exposure see Cynthia Patterson, "'Not Worth the Rearing:' The Causes of Infant Exposure in Ancient Greece," *Transactions of the American Philological Association* (1974–2014) 115 (1985): 103–123.
[10] Susan Moller Okin, "Philosopher Queens and Private Wives: Plato on Women and the Family," *Philosophy and Public Affairs* vol 6, no. 4 (Summer 1977): 351.
[11] Ibid., 16.

The statesman and orator, Demosthenes (384 BCE-322 BCE) described the station of Greek women in *Against Naera*:

> For this is what living with a woman as one's wife means—to have children by her and to introduce the sons to the members of the clan and of the deme, and to betroth the daughters to husbands as one's own. Mistresses we keep for the sake of pleasure, concubines for the daily care of our persons, but wives to bear us legitimate children and to be faithful guardians of our households.[12]

Plato (429 BCE–347 BCE)[13]

Plato is the most important Greek philosopher. His thought affected not only Greece, but became the basis of Western philosophy. His philosophical system influenced Christian theologians such as Clement of Alexandria (150–215), Origen (184–253), Augustine of Hippo (354–430), and a myriad of others. Plato's impact on Christian theology cannot be overstated.

Plato himself seemed ambivalent about women. On one hand, he promoted a more egalitarian political system that included women in his *Republic*. On the other hand, he made statements in his *Symposium*, *Timaeus* and *Laws* that reflect traditional Athenian misogyny. Over the centuries, philosophers and theologians of many schools have selectively quoted Plato to justify what they already believe.

Plato described the "Just Society" in his *Republic*. In the *Republic*, Socrates was Plato's interlocutor. There were three categories of inhabitants of a Just Society: guardians, auxiliaries, and producers. The guardians were the philosopher-kings. In Book 5, Plato and Socrates discussed whether or not women could be guardians. Plato argued that even though women were not physically as strong as men,[14] they could be guardians. He asserted that the body was

---

[12] Demosthenes, *Private Orations*, Loeb edition, trans. A.T. Murray (Cambridge, MA: Harvard University Press, 1939), 3: 122.
[13] Unless otherwise noted, all quotations from Plato are from Edith Hamilton and Huntington Cairns, eds. *Plato: The Collected Dialogues* (Princeton, NJ: Princeton University Press, 1969).
[14] Plato, *Laws*, 917a4–5.

independent of the soul, which had no gender. The body had no bearing on one's soul and ability to reason. Plato adds:

> And if, I said, the male and female sex appear to differ in their fitness for any art or pursuit, we should say that such pursuit or art ought to be assigned to one or the other of them; but if the difference consists only in women bearing and men begetting children, this does not amount to a proof that a woman differs from a man in respect of the sort of education she should receive; and we shall therefore continue to maintain that our guardians and their wives ought to have the same pursuits.[15]

In Plato's ideal society, all men and women would receive training and education appropriate to whether they were guardians, auxiliaries, or producers. He maintained that it would be a waste for a woman who demonstrated the natural ability to be a guardian to be denied training for that position. For this reason, some feminists have cited Plato as an ally.

Souls in Plato's *Republic* might have been equal but males and females had different responsibilities. Female guardians were mated with male guardians in hopes of breeding even better guardians. Female guardians were to be pregnant throughout their reproductive life. Infants would be taken from their parents and raised by the community. This allowed the parents to concentrate on their duties as guardians. Plato also favored a communal society in which everything, including mates, was shared within the class.

Plato maintained that within the same class and in every task or talent, men were superior to women. Though both men and women could be soldiers, men were physically stronger and thus made better guardians. It was possible, albeit rare, for a woman of the guardian class to be superior to a male guardian. Plato notes, "All the pursuits of men are the pursuits of women also, but in all of them a woman is inferior to a man."[16]

---

[15] Plato, *Republic,* 454e.
[16] Plato, *The Republic,* trans. Benjamin Jowett (Seattle, WA: Amazon Classics, 2017), 428.

The Forms were integral to Plato's philosophy. Borrowing from the Pythagorean table of opposites, Plato began with the dichotomy of the body/soul. He taught that the soul was superior to the body, and the body was a prison for the soul. The Forms were the perfect, nonphysical, and unchangeable essences of all things. Objects perceived by the senses were physical and changeable. Forms, therefore, were the perfect versions of their imperfect earthly copies. Only the soul could know the Forms.[17] The highest of the Forms was the "Good."

Plato believed that devoting oneself to anything that was changeable, physical, or carnal could not lead to genuine knowledge. True knowledge could be found only in the contemplation of the unchanging Forms. Plato's dualism explained how men and women acquired knowledge in different ways. Plato associated women with the body and believed they were interested in more temporal things. Men, in contrast, were much more spiritual and attuned to higher reasoning. Men, therefore, were better at the contemplation of the Good.[18] This concept led Plato to believe that the love of one man for another was more than sexual. It was based on their shared desire for knowledge. As women had less capacity for reason, the love of a man for a woman could be nothing more than physical.[19]

Plato taught that the soul was composed of appetite, spirit, and reason. The appetitive part of the soul is concerned with food, drink, sex, and matters of the flesh. The spirited soul sought to rectify wrongs, take on challenges, and triumph. The rational soul sought to analyze, plan, and find truth and reason. This was the highest part of the soul: the part that contemplated the world of Forms.[20] Plato taught that men were more in touch with the rational soul than women were. Plato described how women were often too emotional to be capable of reason.

---

[17] For instance, I am a human. The Form of human is not limited to me. Billons of people have been and are human. The Form of human is "humanness," which all humans share and yet all are imperfect copies of it. A physical human is an inferior copy of the perfect Form of human.

[18] Elizabeth V. Spellman, "Woman as Body: Ancient and Contemporary View," *Feminist Studies* 8, no. 1 (Spring 1982): 111.

[19] Plato, *Laws*, 837 c-d.

[20] Plato, *Republic*, 442 a-b.

Plato believed that women were secretive and manipulative.[21] "Woman—left without chastening restraint—is not, as you might fancy, merely half the problem; nay, she is a two-fold problem and more than a two-fold problem, in proportion as her native disposition is inferior to man's."[22]

Driven by the appetitive soul, women were hedonistic. In the *Symposium*, Plato placed women above animals—but below men—in the hierarchy of beings. In *Timaeus*, Plato discussed the rebirth of souls. He maintained that when a person died his soul migrated to another being, either a person or an animal. If the deceased had a proper life, the soul could enter a male. If the person had lived a bad life, the soul would be reborn into an animal or a female. Plato held that men "who came into the world, those who were cowards or led unrighteous lives may with reason be supposed to have changed into the nature of women in the second generation."[23] Being born female was how cowardly or immoral men were punished.[24] To become more fully human, women had to become more like men. They must deny their femininity and learn to use their reason.[25]

Aristotle

Aristotle is second to Plato in terms of his influence. His thought had a tremendous impact on Thomas Aquinas (1225–1274) and through him the Roman Catholic Church. Aristotle was much more consistent than Plato and more in line with Athenian tradition. He believed that women were inferior to men. Aristotle based his beliefs based on his knowledge of female biology and women's role in society. He presented his scientific evaluations of women in his *History of Animals* and *Generation of Animals*. Modern scientists have refuted his views on biology, but they influenced medical and theological thought into the seventeenth century.

---

[21] Chandrakala Padia, "Plato, Aristotle, Rousseau and Hegel on Women: A Critique," *The Indian Journal of Political Science* 55, no. 1 (January–March 1994): 28.
[22] Plato, *Laws* VI, 781 b.
[23] Plato, *Timaeus*, 91.
[24] Christine Garside Allen, "Plato on Women," *Feminist Studies* 2/3 (1975): 133.
[25] Chandrakala Padia, "Plato, Aristotle, Rousseau and Hegel on Women: A Critique," 27.

In his *History of Animals,* Aristotle noted that male animals produced more heat than female animals. The hotter the body, the better it metabolized food and converted it into fur and flesh that helped it to achieve its true form.[26] Females did not produce enough heat to do this. Aristotle took this as evidence that males were superior to females. He claimed that heat made male animals larger, more muscular, stronger, and longer-lived. Males could defend themselves with their tusks, horns, and spurs; female animals could not.[27] Aristotle equated upper-body strength in males with honor.[28]

Aristotle believed that the more perfect male animals would use food to build their superior bodies. Anything that was left over was used for hot semen. Because women's bodies were cooler, all they could produce was menstrual fluid.[29] Aristotle observed that men were much bigger and stronger than women than in other animals. This was because women produced more menstrual fluid than other animals he had observed.

Aristotle applied the Pythagorean table of opposites to the relationship between form/soul and matter. Because semen was hot, it could transfer its true form or soul through sex and produce another animal. The male provided the soul and the female contributed the matter.[30]

If the reproductive process went correctly, a male would be produced. A flaw in the process (such as a mother who was too old or too young) would produce a female.[31] As Aristotle noted, "Just as it happened that deformed offspring are produced by deformed parents, and sometimes not, so the offspring produced by a female

---

[26] Elaine Fantham, Helen Peet Foley, Natalie Boymel Kampen, Sarah B. Pomeroy, and H. Alan Shapiro, *Women in the Classical World* (New York, NY: Oxford University Press, 1994), 190.
[27] Aristotle, *History of Animals* 538a22–24 and 538b1–25. Cited in Thompson, D'Arcy. *History of Animals.* Books 1–9 in the *Complete Works of Aristotle,* ed. Jonathan Barnes (Princeton, NJ: Princeton University Press, 1984). Unless noted, all future notations of the *History of Animals* are from Thompson.
[28] Aristotle, *History of Animals,* 538a22–24 and 538b1–25.
[29] Katharine M. Rogers, *The Troublesome Helpmate: A History of Misogyny in Literature* (Seattle, WA: University of Washington Press, 1966), 37.
[30] Cynthia Russett, "All About Eve. What Men Have Thought About Women Thinking," *The American Scholar* 74, no. 2 (Spring 2005): 42.
[31] Ibid., 42.

are sometimes female, sometimes not, but male. The reason is that the female is as it were a deformed male."[32]

Because of this lack of heat, women were physically and intellectually imperfect. Men were unique in their ability to think rationally and make decisions from these abilities. Women did not have these abilities.[33] Consequently, women were "softer in disposition, more mischievous, simpler, more impulsive, and more attentive to the young."[34] Men were "more spirited, more savage, more-simple, and less cunning."[35] They were also more courageous and more helpful to someone in need.

Aristotle used his findings to structure his beliefs on women's roles in society. His *Politics* was a response to Plato's more egalitarian *Republic*.[36] In *Politics*, Aristotle argued that as the soul is superior to the body, the husband is superior to the wife. The father or husband ruled the household. Aristotle maintained that a female's purpose was to carry, give birth, and raise sons who could take their place in society. Aristotle believed that this ideal household should be a microcosm of society, with men in charge.[37]

Philo

Born in Alexandria, Egypt, in the early first century, Philo was a member of its large Jewish population.[38] Alexandria was a city in which Greek philosophy and Judaism flourished. Philo's writings demonstrated that, along with the *Septuagint*, he was influenced by

---

[32] Aristotle, *Generation of Animals*, 737a25–28. A.L. Peck, *Aristotle XIII: Generation of Animals*. Loeb Classical Library. Cambridge: Harvard University Press, 1979. Unless noted, all future notations of the *Generation of Animals* are from Peck.

[33] Elaine Fantham, Helen Peet Foley, Natalie Boymel Kampen, Sarah B. Pomeroy, and H. Alan Shapiro, *Women in the Classical World*, 192.

[34] Aristotle, *History of the Animals*, 608a32–b19.

[35] Ibid.

[36] Rogers, *The Troublesome Helpmate: A History of Misogyny in Literature*, 35.

[37] Aristotle, *Politics*, Book 1:1252a–60b. Beverly Clack, ed. *Misogyny in the Western Philosophical Tradition: A Reader*. London: MacMillan Press, 1999). All future notations of *Politics* are from Clack.

[38] Philo's life also coincides with the life of Christ. His writings are among the earliest to mention Jesus and John the Baptist by name.

Plato, Pythagoras, the Stoics, and perhaps Aristotle.[39] These influences appear in his attempt to synthesize their thought. Philo's allegorical interpretation of the Old Testament that sought hidden meanings was a decisive factor in Alexandrian Christianity's later adoption of this hermeneutic. His thoughts were evident in the writings of Clement of Alexandria, Origen, Ambrose of Milan (340–397), and Augustine. His writings concerning women and their impact on these theologians was equally conspicuous.

Philo's concept of human reproduction and Aristotle's were quite similar.[40] He held that in reproduction the man provided the semen that acted on the passive material provided by the woman. According to Philo, "the material of the female is supplied to the son from what remains over the eruption of blood, while the immediate maker and cause of the son is the male."[41]

He held that each person's mind contained masculine and feminine thoughts. Philo's reliance on Stoicism could be seen in the importance of self-control. Masculine qualities were wisdom, virtue, self-control, and things that were good. Feminine thoughts reflected emotion and a lack of self-control.[42] A woman could strive to be more masculine by dwelling on more masculine thoughts and less on feminine ones. By the same token, men could become more feminine by giving in to feminine thoughts.[43] Having a penis did not necessarily make one male and the lack of one did not necessarily make one female.[44] "Manhood was not a state to be definitively achieved but something always under construction and constantly

---

[39] Lévy, Carlos, "Philo of Alexandria," *The Stanford Encyclopedia of Philosophy*, ed. Edward N. Zalta (Spring 2018 Edition), last modified 5 February 2018, https://plato.stanford.edu/archives/spr2018/entries/philo/.
[40] Sister Prudence Allen, *The Concept of Women: The Early Humanist Reformation, 1250–1500*, Vol. 2 (Grand Rapids, MI: Eerdmans Publishing Company, 2016), 93.
[41] Philo, *Questions and Answers in Genesis*, 3:47, p. 857. Unless further noted, all Philo works are cited from *The Works of Philo: Complete and Unabridged*, trans. C. D. Yonge (Peabody, MA.: Hendrickson Publishers, 1993).
[42] Philo, *Questions and Answers in Genesis*, trans. Ralph Marcus (Cambridge, MA: Harvard University Press, 1963) 4:38, 312–13.
[43] Ibid., 2:49, 830.
[44] D. M. Halperin, Winkler, J. J., & Zeitlin, F. I. *Before Sexuality: The Construction of Erotic Experience in the Ancient Greek World* (Princeton, NJ: Princeton University Press, 1990), 478.

open to scrutiny."⁴⁵ Manhood had to be protected always. For this reason, Philo believed Lot had acted properly at Sodom.⁴⁶

Philo understood the soul in a Platonic manner. He held that men and women differed sharply in the manner of soul. Man identified with the higher aspects of the soul, which he called the *nous*. The *nous* was patterned after God, so women had no part in the *nous*.⁴⁷ He compared women's souls to living quarters. "The woman's quarters are a place where womanly opinions go about and dwell, being followers of the female sex. And the female sex is irrational and akin to bestial passions, fear, sorrow, pleasure, and desire."⁴⁸ This irrational quality was the reason why women aroused men's sexual desire.⁴⁹ Philo cited Potiphar's wife⁵⁰ and the Midianite women of Numbers 25⁵¹ as examples of libidinous women. Philo placed Sarah and Leah in the higher part of the feminine soul and Hagar and Rachel in the lower. Philo believed that Moses was the embodiment of the highest masculine soul. He controlled his passions, communicated well, and displayed a manly spirit.

Philo applied Stoicism to his explanation of how virtue applied to the sexes.⁵² He believed that virtue was displayed in noble deeds, words, self-control, and actions. These are male attributes. Females, with rare exceptions, were considered too passive to be virtuous.⁵³ Because virtue was important in public affairs, he held that only men should be involved in them.⁵⁴ In *On the Special Laws*, Philo stated that women should stay home and not involve themselves in public life.⁵⁵

---

[45] Maud Gleason, *Making Men: Sophists and Self-Representation in Ancient Rome* (Princeton, NJ: Princeton University Press, 1995), 22.
[46] William Loader, *Philo, Josephus, and the Testaments on Sexuality: Attitudes Towards Sexuality in the Writings of Philo and Josephus and in the Testaments of the Twelve Patriarchs* (Grand Rapids, MI: Eerdmans Publishing Co., 2011), 37.
[47] Philo, *On the Creation of the World*, 69, p. 10.
[48] Philo, *Questions and Answers in Genesis*, trans. Ralph Marcus (Cambridge, MA: Harvard University Press, 1963) 4:15, p. 288.
[49] Judith R. Wegner, "The Image of Woman in Philo," *Society of Biblical Literature 1982 Seminar Papers*, ed. Kent Harold Richards (Chico, CA: Scholars Press, 1982), 552.
[50] Philo, *On Joseph*, 41, p. 438–39.
[51] Philo, *Allegorical Interpretations*, 241, p. 78.
[52] Allen, *The Concept of Women: The Early Humanist Reformation*, 96.
[53] Philo, *On Abraham*, 102, p. 420.
[54] Philo, *Questions and Answers in Genesis*, 3:26, p. 796.
[55] Philo, *On the Special Laws*, 3:169, p. 611.

When Philo discussed marriage, he did so in a dismissive manner. Philo held that marriage reunited both elements of the soul. Man functioned better with a woman. A wife's ability to give birth to sons was evidence of her masculine mind.[56] A good wife would serve and obey her husband in all things.[57] Thus, husbands would manage the outside world and wives would manage the home. In *Questions and Answers in Genesis*, he states:

> The union and the plentitude of concord formed by the man and woman is symbolically called a house; but everything is altogether imperfect and destitute of a home, which is deserted by a woman; for to the man the public affairs of the state are committed, but the particular affairs of the house belong to the woman; and a want of the women will be the destruction of the house; but the actual presence of the woman show the regulation of the house.[58]

In praising the Essenes for not marrying, Philo stated that "a woman is a selfish creature and one addicted to jealousy in an immoderate degree, and terribly calculated to agitate and overturn the natural inclinations of the man, and to mislead him by her continual tricks."[59] The husband must always be on guard and be prepared for possible treachery from his wife.

Philo held that there were three phases of a woman's life: menstruation, child-bearing, and menopause.[60] When menstruation began a woman became more sexual. At that time, she had the choice to remain chaste or get married. If chastity were chosen, she had to become an asexual being. Giving up a sex life allowed her to become more male in mind and soul.

Sexual intercourse turned a virgin into a woman and irrationality, lower reason, and emotionality dominated her soul.[61] Sex was

---

[56] Colleen Conway, "Gender and Divine Relativity in Philo of Alexandria," *Journal for Studies of Judaism* 34, no. 4 (2003): 476.
[57] Philo, *Hypothetica*, 7, p. 43.
[58] Philo, *Questions in Genesis*, 3:26, p. 796.
[59] Philo, *Hypothetica*, 11:4–17, p. 746.
[60] Dorothy Isabel Sly, "The Perception of Women in the Writing of Philo of Alexandria" (Ph.D. diss., McMaster University, 1987), 90.
[61] Philo, *On the Cherubim*, 50, p. 85.

only for procreation.⁶² Philo believed that circumcision deterred men from overindulging in sexual intercourse.⁶³ Once a woman reached menopause, she could seek a union with God that would restore the chastity of her soul.⁶⁴ She could then pursue the active, male mind, transcend her sexuality, and became male. A virgin was spiritually equivalent to a man.⁶⁵

Philo believed that some married women in the Bible remained "soul virgins." Because the scriptures did not refer to them "knowing" their husbands, he maintained that God was their father. According to Dorothy Sly, Philo did not interpret their virginity literally. Sly maintains that Philo might have seen these women as examples for other women.⁶⁶ Philo stated that God did not use Sarah (Genesis 18:11) to conceive Isaac until after she had entered menopause, so she had time to be restored as a virgin.⁶⁷ Other married women who bore children but were considered virginal by Philo were Zipporah, Rachel, and Leah.⁶⁸

A woman could also become an ascetic. Philo admired the Therapeutae, elderly virgins. These women were similar to the first Christian monks. They did not own private property and practiced chastity, fasting, and lived solitary lives among other Therapeutae. He praised them for being "indifferent to the pleasures of the body, desiring not a mortal but immortal offspring, which the soul that is attached to God, is alone able to produce by itself and from itself."⁶⁹

Philo believed that Adam and Eve were mythical characters who should be understood in an allegorical manner. He saw them as prototypes, not as historical figures. Philo had no trouble with Genesis having two creation accounts because he believed there had been two creations. He maintained that the first account (Genesis 1:1–2:3) depicted humanity's spiritual creation in the image of an asexual God. This image was the Mind of God. The rational aspect,

---

[62] Loader, *Philo, Josephus, and the Testaments on Sexuality*, 25.
[63] Philo, *Questions and Answers on Genesis*, 3:48, p. 857.
[64] Sly, "The Perception of Women in the Writing of Philo of Alexandria," 86.
[65] Ibid., 109.
[66] Ibid., 89.
[67] Philo, *On the Cherubim*, 60, p. 85.
[68] Ibid., 40, p. 84.
[69] Philo, *On the Contemplative Life*, 68, p. 704.

the Mind, is related to the body, as God relates to the world.[70] In this account, Adam was androgynous.[71] The second account (Genesis 2:2–25) described the physical creation of Adam. When God breathed life into him, Adam received the higher, masculine part of the soul.[72] The dust represented the bodily realm with its senses, emotions, and sexual passions. God then removed the female, material aspects to create the woman while Adam retained the Mind. Both souls were mortal, but "the man who came into existence after the image of God is what one might call an idea, or a genus, or a seal, an object of thought, incorporeal, neither male nor female, but incorruptible."[73]

Philo further explained women's inferior status in terms of Adam's rib. "This was so ordained in the first place, in order that the woman might not be of equal dignity with the man."[74] Man was created in the image of God and, thus, had a rational mind. Having been made from the material aspects of man, the woman did not. Philo maintained that man being first in creation meant that he occupied the superior position in the world.[75]

Philo believed that man was initially happy. Adam's mind was aligned with creation and God. It was not until after the creation of woman that problems began. In *On the Creation*, Philo noted that Adam and Eve immediately recognized their similarities, and desired to procreate. "And this desire caused likewise pleasure to their bodies, which is the beginning of iniquities and transgressions, and it is owing to this that men have exchanged their previously immortal and happy existence for one which is mortal and full of misfortune."[76] With the creation of the material woman came sexual awareness and mortality. It was woman who brought death into the world. Philo noted that Eve was the name Adam chose for the first woman. Eve means life, but she brought Adam's

---

[70] Loader, 12. Baer, 21.
[71] Philo, *On the Creation of the World*, 76, p. 11; Sharon Lea Mattila, "Wisdom, Sense Perception, Nature, and Philo's Gender Gradient," *The Harvard Theological Review* 89, no. 2 (April 1996): 104; Loader, 15.
[72] Philo, *Who Is the Heir,* 56–58, p. 280–81; Loader, 14.
[73] Philo, *On the Creation*, 134, p. 19.
[74] Philo, *Questions and Answers in Genesis*, 1:27, p. 796.
[75] Philo, *On the Creation*, 165, p. 23.
[76] Ibid., 151, p. 21.

death.⁷⁷ Philo found this fitting as life and everything good came from men, while death and everything bad came from women.

Philo explained why the serpent had approached Eve:

> The woman was more accustomed to be deceived than the man. For his counsels as well as his body are of a masculine sort, and competent to disentangle the notions of seduction; but the mind of the woman is more effeminate, so that through her softness she easily yields and is easily caught by the persuasions of falsehood, which imitate the resemblance of truth.⁷⁸

Philo wrote in *Questions and Answers in Genesis*:

> The words used first of all, by their own intrinsic force, assert that it was suitable that immortality and every good thing should be represented as under the power of the man, and death and every evil under that of the woman. But with reference to the mind, the woman, when understood symbolically, is sense, and the man is intellect. Moreover, the outward senses do of necessity touch those things which are perceptible by them; but it is through the medium of the outward senses that things are transmitted to the mind. For the outward senses are influenced by the objects which are presented to them; and the intellect by the outward senses.⁷⁹

Eve was deceived by the serpent. She could not overcome her lower reasoning and desired to know more.⁸⁰

Philo believed Genesis 1–3 allegorically represented the three elements of the soul. Adam represented mind and rationality. Eve characterized sensory perception and irrationality. The serpent symbolized pleasure. Sense perception was valuable, but it needed

---

⁷⁷ Philo, *Who is the Heir?* 52, p. 280.
⁷⁸ Philo, 1:33, p. 798.
⁷⁹ Philo, *Questions and Answers in Genesis*, 1:37, 798–99.
⁸⁰ Ibid., 1:56, 22.

guidance from the rational, masculine mind.[81] Sly notes that Philo blamed the Fall on Adam because Eve was his responsibility. Adam's fault was in following Eve.[82] In other words, he chose passion over God.

Influence on Christian Thought

Athenian society was misogynistic and hierarchical. As Athenians, Plato and Aristotle formulated systems that both reflected this culture and provided intellectual justification. Though Egyptian, Philo was a student of Plato. Plato's view of women was ambivalent; Aristotle and Philo were misogynists. Though Plato, Aristotle, and Philo were not Christians, their philosophies were modified by Christian theologians. Philosophy is often portrayed as the handmaid to theology. This depiction rings true as Greek philosophy and much of its concept of women found a home in Christian theology.

---

[81] Kristen E. Kvam, Linda S. Schearing, and Valerie H. Ziegler, eds. *Eve & Adam: Jewish, Christian, and Muslim Readings on Genesis and Gender* (Bloomington, IN: University of Indiana Press, 1999), 42.
[82] Sly, 125.

CHAPTER THREE

Women in the New Testament

Christianity emerged in Palestine in the first century of the common era. Most of the twenty-seven books that comprise the Christian New Testament were written between 45 and 120 CE. It was a turbulent time for Jews in Palestine. The Jewish people had been oppressed for several hundred years. The Greeks conquered Palestine in 332 BCE and ruled it until 63 BCE when they were defeated by the Romans. The Jews remained in Roman bondage throughout and well beyond the New Testament era. Though Greece had been politically displaced by Rome, Greek philosophy and culture influenced traditional Judaism and its expectations and beliefs about women.

Like the Old Testament, tradition depicts all the New Testament authors as men, although the author of Hebrews remains a mystery. The New Testament, however, does not depict women as heroines, harlots, or seducers. Women were rarely the key actors in a narrative. Rather, the New Testament authors discussed women as figures in men's narratives. Along with customary Jewish teachings, some New Testament authors drew upon Greek concepts in their depictions of women. This chapter examines Roman and Jewish women's lives in the century before and during Jesus' life and how Jesus and the Apostle Paul described women.

Roman Women in the Time of Christ

Little is known about the lives of non-aristocratic women in the first century of the common era. More extant information exists on aristocratic women because of their relationship with their patrician fathers and husbands. In the first century of the common era, Roman women who were not slaves were considered citizens.[1] A woman could also inherit property and initiate divorce. They could not, however, vote, hold political office, or serve in the military.[2] Girls from influential families were expected to remain virgins until marriage.[3] Marriage was facilitated by the *paterfamilias* and the prospective suitor; the goal of the bride's father was to improve his political and/or economic status.[4] When a woman married she became subject to her husband but remained primarily under her father's authority. Wives were expected to have sex only with their husbands, but men were expected to have many sexual partners.[5] Divorce and remarriage were common. During the era of Augustan Reform (27 BCE–4 CE) that sought to increase the aristocratic population, married freeborn mothers of three or more children could administer their own property.[6] Wives could not appear in public without their husband.[7] As husbands were often away conducting business, wives were responsible for managing the household. Single women had influential roles in Roman religion and often served as Vestal Virgins and priestesses.[8] In Paul's ministry, which extended well beyond the Jewish homeland, an understanding of the position of Roman women proved exceedingly important as Christianity began to make inroads throughout the Roman Empire.

---

[1] A. N. Sherwin-White, *Roman Citizenship* (City: Oxford University Press, 1979), 211.
[2] Bruce W. Frier and Thomas A.J. McGinn, *A Casebook on Roman Family Law* (City: American Philological Association, 2004), 31–32.
[3] Lauren Caldwell, *Roman Girlhood and the Fashioning of Femininity* (Cambridge: Cambridge University Press, 2014), 3–4.
[4] Caldwell, 16–107.
[5] Richard Bauman, *Women and Politics in Ancient Rome* (New York, NY: Routledge, 1992), 8, 10, 15, 105.
[6] Sarah Pomeroy, *Goddesses, Whores, Wives, and Slaves: Women in Classical Antiquity* (New York, NY: Schocken, 1995), 166.
[7] Ross Shepard Kraemer and Mary Rose D'Angelo, *Women and Christian Origins* (Oxford: Oxford University Press, 1999), 32.
[8] Phyllis Culham, "Women in the Roman Republic," in *The Cambridge Companion to the Roman Republic* (Cambridge: Cambridge University Press, 2004), 143.

Jewish Women in the Time of Christ

Understanding Jewish women's lives in society, religion, and the family offers valuable insights into their presence in the New Testament. The material, however, is scant as Jewish literature shows little interest in Jewish women.[9] The best sources are the writings of Josephus (37–100 CE), Philo, and the Mishnah.

Josephus stated that women were inferior to men in all things.[10] Women were to obey their husbands and remain in the home, but husbands were to treat wives justly and with kindness.[11] A husband could force a vow on his wife. A husband could divorce his wife, but she could not divorce him.[12] In cultic practices, Jewish women were limited in terms of where they could worship within Herod's Temple. Josephus recorded that women worshipped in an area separated by a partition from the men, and they had their own gate, which led into the women's court.[13]

Philo of Alexandria wrote about the Jewish population of Alexandria. *In Special Laws*, Philo wrote that women should avoid the market, assemblies, and crowds. They should never discuss important issues. She should keep herself busy at home, without venturing beyond the vestibule or outer court. Moreover, unmarried women should remain in the center of the house, behind closed doors.[14]

---

[9] Kraemer and D'Angelo, 51.

[10] Josephus was a historian who first fought for the Jews in the First Jewish-Roman War (66–70 CE) but then joined the Romans and became a Roman citizen.

[11] Josephus, *Against Apion*, 2.25, last accessed 1 May 2021, http://www.earlyjewishwritings.com/text/josephus/apion2.html.

[12] Josephus, *Antiquities of the Jews*, 15.259, in *The Works of Flavius Joseph*, trans. William Whitson, A.M., (Auburn and Buffalo: John E. Beardsley, 1895), last accessed 1 May 2021, http://data.perseus.org/citations/urn:cts:greekLit:tlg0526.tlg001.perseus-eng1:15.259.

[13] Josephus, *The Wars of the Jews*, 5.190, in *The Works of Flavius Joseph*, trans. William Whitson, A.M., (Auburn and Buffalo: John E. Beardsley, 1895), last accessed 1 May 2021, http://data.perseus.org/citations/urn:cts:greekLit:tlg0526.tlg004.perseus-eng1:5.190.

[14] Philo, The Special Laws, III, cited in *The Works of Philo: Complete and Unabridged*, trans. C. D. Yonge (Peabody, MA: Hendrickson Publishers, 1993), 611.

The Mishnah, or Oral Teaching, was a book of Rabbinic regulations and oral traditions collected at the beginning of the third century of the common era. The material dates back to the time of Jesus. It taught that daughters were their fathers' possessions and after marriage, passed to their husbands.[15] In Herod's Temple, women sat in a gallery above the men who were on the floor level and closer to the Holy of Holies.[16]

As the New Testament era dawned, Jewish wives remained subject to their fathers, and when married, subject to their husbands. They were largely relegated to the home.[17] Women's place in Jewish life had changed little.

Jesus

While Jesus spoke with women often, he spoke about women only once. In Mark 13:17 and Matthew 24:19, when prophesying the destruction of the Temple, he stated that those times would be especially difficult for pregnant women and nursing mothers.[18] Jesus' concern for women, however, was apparent in the gospels. There is no record of him belittling or treating women with any less respect than men. Jesus treated women with compassion. He invited them to be his followers, taught them, and honored them by having them witness and announce his resurrection.

Compassion

Jesus put himself in physical danger and at risk of ritual impurity by engaging women in ways that his culture did not. Jesus healed a woman with a bleeding disorder who touched his garment without his permission (Matthew 9:20–22, Mark 5:25–34, Luke 8:43–48).[19]

---

[15] Ketubah, "Marriage Deeds," 4:5, Sefaria, last accessed 1 May 2021, https://www.sefaria.org/Mishnah_Ketubot.4.4?lang=bi.
[16] Middoth, "Measurements," 2:5, Sefaria, last accessed 1 May 2021, https://www.sefaria.org/Mishnah_Middot.2.5?lang=bi.
[17] Shepard and D'Angelo, 36.
[18] Donald Hagner, *Matthew 14–28*, Word Biblical Commentary Series, eds. David Allen Hubbard, Glenn W. Barker, John D. Watts, and Ralph P. Martin (Dallas, TX: Word Book Publishers, 1995), 701.
[19] Joseph Martos and Pierre Hégy, *Gender in the Origins of Christianity: Jewish Hopes and Imperial Exigencies* (Toronto: University of Toronto Press, 1998), 33; Ulrich Luz,

Ignoring the Levitical blood law (Leviticus 15:19–25), Jesus did not admonish the woman for potentially making him ritually unclean but called her "daughter."[20] Jesus also broke Sabbath law by healing a woman who had been bent double for eighteen years (Luke 13:10–17).

After a synagogue leader admonished him for healing on the Sabbath, Jesus rebuked him, saying, "Should this daughter of Abraham not be healed on the Sabbath (Luke 13:16)?"

Jesus extended forgiveness and charity to women. Despite his disciples' criticism, he spoke to the Samaritan woman at the well (John 4:1–42). In this encounter, Jesus violated Jewish religious law in several ways. Men were not supposed to talk to women in public.[21] A rabbi did not teach theology to women, but not only does Jesus do it on this occasion, but also to Mary and Martha in a separate incident (Luke 10:38–42). Though she had been married five times, Jesus did not shun a woman whom many would have viewed as impure (John 4). Moreover, if Jesus' breaking of Jewish law was not enough, the woman was a Samaritan, so Jews considered her inferior to them. Jesus saw value in her and she became one of the followers who proclaimed him in Samaria.[22]

Jesus was concerned about widows. A widow who did not have a son to take care of her was in a vulnerable position. In Mark 12:38–40, Jesus condemned scribes who attempted to steal from widows instead of protecting them.

Jesus defended a woman caught in adultery whose fate, under the Law of Moses, was death by stoning (John 8:1–11).[23] He then told those who had not sinned to cast the first stone. The crowd

---

Matthew 8–20. Hermeneia Commentary Series on the Bible, ed. Helmut Koester (Philadelphia, PA: Fortress Press, 2001), 42.

[20] Mark Guelich, *Mark 1–8:26*, Word Biblical Commentary Series, eds. David Allen Hubbard, Glenn W. Barker, John D. Watts, and Ralph P. Martin (Dallas, TX: Word Book Publishers, 1989), 296, 299.

[21] George R. Beasley-Murray, *John*, Word Biblical Commentary Series, eds. David Allen Hubbard, Glenn W. Barker, John D. Watts, and Ralph P. Martin. (Waco, TX: Word Book Publishers, 1987), 62.

[22] Barbara MacHaffie, *Her Story: Women in the Christian Tradition*, 2nd ed. (Minneapolis, MN: Fortress Press, 2006), 5.

[23] Raymond E. Brown, *The Gospel According to John* (i–xii), The Anchor Yale Bible Commentary Series (New York, NY: Doubleday, 1966), 333.

that gathered slowly dispersed. Jesus forgave her and told her to sin no more.

At a dinner hosted by a Pharisee, Jesus allowed a woman identified as a sinner to anoint him with expensive perfume, as priests did for kings of Israel (Luke 7:36–50).[24] She cried at his feet, wiped them with her hair, and then poured the perfume on them. The host complained that if Jesus were a true prophet, he would have known the type of woman who had touched him. Jesus explained that though her debt had been great so was her forgiveness. Similar stories appear in Matthew 26:6–13,[25] Mark 14:3–9, and John 12:1–8.

Jesus showed great empathy for married Jewish women. He contradicted the law of Moses by stating that men could not divorce their wives for any reason other than adultery (Matthew 19:9). This gave the wife a better standing within the marriage.

Followers

Jesus traveled with at least twelve named women. By allowing them in his presence, Jesus demonstrated that he did not see women as a sexual threat, either to his male followers or to himself.[26] Women such as Mary Magdalene, Joanna, and Susanna supported Jesus and his ministry by sponsoring him and his disciples (Mark 15:40–41; Luke 8:1–3). They provided money and care (Luke 8:1–3). While not calling women his disciples, Jesus taught them the scriptures. In Luke 10:38–42, Jesus defended Mary's right to sit at his feet with the men and learn from him.[27] Women were also the only followers brave enough to attend his crucifixion (Matthew 27:55–56, Mark 15:40, Luke 23:49, John 19:25).

Honor and Praise

Jesus praised the poor widow who gave two copper coins to the Temple (Mark 12:41–44, Luke 21:1–4). While wealthy people gave

---

[24] Mary Daly, *The Church and the Second Sex: With a New Feminist Post Christian Introduction by the Author* (New York, NY: Harper and Row, 1975), 80.
[25] Hagner, 758.
[26] Kraemer and D'Angelo, 42.
[27] Mary T. Malone, *Women and Christianity: The First Thousand Years, Vol. 1.* (Maryknoll, NY: Orbis Books, 2000), 46.

from their abundance, the widow made a true financial sacrifice.[28] Jesus also made women the primary characters in many of his parables. When he described his ministry in the parable of the lost coin (Luke 15:8–10), he compared his ministry to a woman who searched for one lost coin even though she had nine others.[29] In the parables of the leaven and the dough (Mathew 13:33) and the parable of the wise and foolish virgins (Matthew 25:1–13), Jesus compared traditional women's work and actions to the arrival of the Kingdom of God.[30] By assigning these roles to women, Jesus demonstrated women's value as disciples and their worthiness for inclusion in his new covenant people.

Jesus honored his mother by performing the miracle at Canaan (John 2:1–11) and ensuring her care while on the cross (John 19:25–27). Mary, the mother of Jesus, Mary Magdalene, and Mary the mother of James and Joseph were present at his crucifixion (Matthew 27:55; Mark 15:40–41; Luke 23:49; John 19:25). For attending to his suffering,[31] Jesus allowed them to be the first witnesses to the resurrection and to inform the Apostles (Mark 16:1–6, Matthew 28:1–9, Luke 24:1–12, John 20:1–2).[32] In this sense, women were the first evangelists. This might have been their greatest honor.

The Apostle Paul

The Apostle Paul was a Roman citizen and former Pharisee (Philippians 3:5). After his dramatic conversion to Christianity, Paul's main emphasis was the new life in Christ (Galatians 3:28). He also established that women could serve as his coworkers in the Gospel (Romans 16:1–3, Philippians 4:3) and plant churches in their homes in cities like Corinth, Ephesus, and Philippi (Acts 18:1–17; 24–26; Acts 16:13–14, 40.

---

[28] Craig A. Evans, *Mark 8:27–16:20*, Word Biblical Commentary Series, eds. David Allen Hubbard, Glenn W. Barker, John D. Watts, and Ralph P. Martin (Nashville, TN: Thomas Nelson, 2000), 282.
[29] Ben Witherington, *Women and the Genesis of Christianity* (Cambridge: Cambridge University Press, 1990), 54.
[30] Ibid., 56–7.
[31] Luz, 337.
[32] Hagner, 855. Mary Magdalene may have been the leader of this group as she is the only person mentioned in each account.

Paul did not write gospels or histories. He wrote letters to congregations with which he had an affiliation. Paul wrote Romans, 1 and 2 Corinthians, Galatians, Philippians, 1 Thessalonians, and Philemon. Other than Philemon, these letters are responses to congregations that asked for his advice.[33] According to current knowledge, none of the first letters sent to Paul to which he was responding have survived. Therefore, interpreters cannot determine Paul's meaning when he answered a question because the question is unknown. Moreover, many scholars believe that Paul did not write Second Thessalonians, Ephesians, and Colossians; one of his disciples did.[34] These scholars denote this disciple as Deutero-Paul. Many scholars do not hold that Paul wrote the Pastoral Epistles (First Timothy, Second Timothy, and Titus).[35] These unknown authors are identified as pseudonymous.[36] Whether these books are authentic, Deutero, or pseudonymous, most Christians have accepted them as Pauline for more than 1700 years.

While Jesus said little about women, Paul said quite a bit more but still not a great deal. Women were less important than other themes, and he paid them only passing attention. Paul's statements about women fall into five categories: newness in Christ, marriage and virginity, veiling and the image of God, headship, and women's leadership in Christian work.

Pauline Writings
Galatians 3:27–29

Galatia was a region in central Asia Minor that became a Roman province in 25 BCE. The inhabitants were known for their fidelity to Rome. Ancyra, the capital, was home to a temple dedicated to Augustus Caesar, the *Augusteum*. The Galatians also venerated the

---

[33] Kraemer and D'Angelo, 223. Paul to Philemon concerning the slave, Onesimus.
[34] Ibid., 242.
[35] Bart Ehrman, *The New Testament: A Historical Introduction to the Early Christian Writings*, 6th ed. (Oxford: Oxford University Press, 2016), 336.
[36] Winsome Munro, "Patriarchy and Charismatic Community in Paul," in *Women and Religious Paper for Working Groups on Women and Religion*, 1972–73, rev. ed., eds. Judith Plaskow and Joan Arnold Romero (Missoula, MT: Scholars Press, 1974), 189.

mother goddess, Cybele. Paul's letter to the Galatian church was written early in his theological development.[37] As Paul founded this church, he defended his interpretation of Christ's gospel from Judaizers. He stressed the importance of justification by faith and the new freedom found in the spirit after baptism.

In this passage, Paul emphasized that the Galatians did not need to listen to the Judaizers who were attempting to convince them to follow Jewish law to become Christians (Galatians 2:4).[38] As ones baptized in the Spirit, they wore Christ like a cloak (27). The law was irrelevant to salvation. Because of their baptism, they were now equal in Christ's new kingdom. In the family of God, there was no difference between Jew or Greek, slave or free, male or female (28).[39] As Christ's return appeared imminent,[40] Paul stressed all Christians were equal. The verse did not stress the necessity of marriage and allowed the individual to remain celibate if they were so gifted (1 Corinthians 7:34).[41] Paul recognized gender differences but not the gender barriers between men and women[42] (1 Corinthians 11:2–16). Many scholars believe Galatians 3:28 predates Paul and was a common baptismal formula employed by early Christians.[43]

1 Corinthians

Corinth was the largest city in Roman Greece, with an approximate population of eighty thousand. Philo wrote that Corinth

---

[37] Gary M. Burge and Gene L. Green, *The New Testament in Antiquity: A Survey of the New Testament Within Its Cultural Contexts.* 2 ed. (Nashville, TN: Zondervan Academic, 2020), 332.

[38] Richard N. Longenecker, *Galatians*, Word Biblical Commentary Series, eds. David Allen Hubbard, Glenn W. Barker, John D. Watts, and Ralph P. Martin (Dallas, TX: Word Book Publishers, 1990), 156.

[39] J. Louis Martyn, *Galatians*, The Anchor Yale Bible Commentary Series (New York, NY: Doubleday, 1997), 376–77.

[40] Constance F. Parvey, "The Theology and Leadership of Women in the New Testament," in *Religion and Sexism: Images of Woman in the Jewish and Christian Traditions*, ed. Rosemary Radford Ruether (Eugene, OR: Wipf and Stock Publishers, 1998), 133.

[41] Witherington, 164.

[42] Ruether, 134.

[43] Malone, 30; Martyn, 374.

was a Diaspora city with a large Jewish population.[44] Just inside the city wall was an Asclepius temple where the injured and sick would seek divine healing.[45] Corinth had a long history of Dionysius worship and cultic prostitution. Women were prominent in the Dionysian cult and often spoke while performing the rites.[46] Paul wrote to this congregation about solutions to their personal problems, ethical issues, and proper decorum within worship.[47]

1 Corinthians 7:1–9

In First Corinthians 7:1–9, the Apostle Paul discussed sex, marriage, and virginity. Paul began with a puzzling statement. "Now concerning the things about which you wrote, it is good for a man not to touch a woman" (1). Is Paul answering the congregation's question about celibacy within marriage? Is Paul relaying his belief "that it is good for a man not to touch a woman" or is he repeating the question asked by the Corinthians?[48] There is no clear answer. Some biblical translations such as the New International Version place this phrase in quotations in the belief that Paul was restating the question. Arguably, this phrase demonstrated that the question of celibacy was coming from men. It also provided context for Paul's response. Paul and the Corinthians believed they were living in the last days before the return of Christ (1 Corinthians 7:29–31). In preparation, some spouses were abstaining from sexual relations with their partners to spend more time in prayer and spiritual discipline.

Paul began by stating that marriage was between a wife and her husband (2). For Paul, sex was limited to a monogamous marriage.[49] The husband's body belonged to the wife, and vice versa. In this respect, he took a position of sexual equality within

---

[44] Philo Leg. Gai, 281–82. S. J. Hafemann, "Letters to the Corinthians," in *Dictionary of Paul and His Letters* (Downers Grove, IL: InterVarsity Press, 1993), 173.
[45] Karen Jo Torjesen, *When Women Were Priests: Women's Leadership in the Early Church and the Scandal of their Subordination in the Rise of Christianity* (San Francisco, CA: HarperCollins, 1993), 21.
[46] Witherington, 174.
[47] Ehrman, 369.
[48] Witherington, 126.
[49] Ibid., 208.

marriage.[50] Moreover, the spouses were to perform their sexual duties and not deprive the other unless briefly for prayer (3–5).[51] Paul castigated married couples who did not have sex because Satan would use their pent-up passions to tempt them to lose self-control (5). Withholding sex could lead the other partner to have sex outside of marriage. Sex within marriage is meant to be a barrier against extramarital sex.[52] Paul did not describe the joys of marital sex. Marriage was merely a container for lust (6). Using himself as an example, he stated that he wished all men could remain unmarried, but many people did not have this gift (7). This was the first passage that stipulated the superiority of celibacy to marriage that many Patristic fathers and monks adopted.[53] Celibacy, however, was a gift that all did not possess. Marriage was an indulgence for those without the gift. Paul concluded by stating that if a person was unmarried or a widow, it was better to remain so, but if a couple had no self-control they should marry. It was better than burning with passion (8–9). Paul made celibacy an option for both men and women irrespective of age.[54] For celibate women, this passage removed them from the hierarchal structure and provided some manner of individual freedom. As the eschaton was imminent, Paul encouraged the Corinthians to spend their brief time in preparation rather than changing their marital status.[55] This could be why he did not discuss the importance of procreation. In this passage, Paul presented marriage as nothing more than a protection against the sin of lust while people waited for Christ's return.[56]

---

[50] Jouette M. Bassler, "1 Corinthians," in *Women's Bible Commentary with Apocrypha: Extended Edition*, eds. Carol A. Newsome and Sharon H. Ringe (Louisville, KY: Westminster John Knox Press, 1992), 413.
[51] Hans Conzelmann, *1 Corinthians*, Hermeneia Commentary Series on the Bible, ed. Helmut Koester (Philadelphia, PA: Fortress Press, 1976), 117.
[52] April D. DeConick, *Holy Misogyny: Why the Sex and Gender Conflicts of the Early Church Still Matter* (New York, NY: Bloomsbury, 2011), 54.
[53] Elizabeth Castelli, "Virginity and Its Meaning for Woman's Sexuality in Early Christianity," *Journal of Feminist Studies in Religion*. vol 2. no. 1 (Spring 1986): 68.
[54] Kraemer and D'Angelo, 212.
[55] Ehrman, 465.
[56] Katharine M. Rogers, *The Troublesome Helpmate: A History of Misogyny in Literature* (Seattle, WA: University of Washington Press, 1966), 9.

1 Corinthians 11:2–16

In First Corinthians 11:2–16, Paul discussed the veiling of women and the image of God. In this passage, Paul addressed a group of recent converts in Corinth, Greece, who were having problems in their worship services. These believers had left their former gods and practices behind and now embraced Christ but still needed instruction on how to behave during worship services.

Paul began by stating that Christ is the head of man and man is the head of woman (3). He based this view by interpreting Genesis 1:27 and Genesis 2:22–23 in a two-part sequence.[57] God created man first and in his image (7). God then created woman second in man's image. As man was in God's image, men should not cover their heads while prophesying (4). Paul explained that God created woman for man, and women did not reflect the image of God (9). They reflected the glory of man. For this reason, a woman should cover her head as a sign of authority over her own head (10).[58] Veiling was a widespread practice in Judaism. A veiled woman was assumed to be modest and holy. It was unbecoming for a Jewish woman to appear in public without a veil.[59] Not veiling could reflect a woman's social status, wealth, her city's culture, or her immorality. Women in the Dionysius cult did not veil themselves.[60] Paul appeared to be attempting to move women away from the pagan religions that dominated in Corinth to those more in line with Judaism and Christianity.

Paul also mentioned the angels as a reason for women to cover their heads (10).[61] This might be a reference to the story of the fallen angels in Genesis 6 and 1 Enoch 7.[62] The New Testament writers knew these stories, as noted in Jude 6 and 7 and 2 Peter 2:4. The 1 Enoch 7 passage held that women should cover their heads so the angels would not lust after them and create another race of giants similar to the Nephilim. Paul may have shared this fear.[63]

---

[57] Walter F. Orr Walter and James Arthur Walther, *1 Corinthians*. The Anchor Yale Bible Commentary Series (New York, NY: Doubleday, 1976), 263.
[58] Ibid., 264.
[59] DeConick, 58.
[60] Burge and Green, 382.
[61] Conzelmann, 189.
[62] J.A. Phillips, *The History of an Idea: Eve* (New York, NY: Harper and Row, 1984), 124.
[63] Rogers, 11.

Paul then stated that, in God, men and women depended on each other (11). Referencing Genesis 2:22–23, Paul stated that men and women originated from God. He then stated there was no universal custom concerning head coverings while prophesying, so women were free to make their own choices (13). However, she must respect propriety and not offend others (16). If she was attending a church where women cover their heads while prophesying, then she should cover her head; if women did not cover their heads, then she should not.[64] Nowhere in the passage does Paul state that women may not prophesy. The question was whether women had to cover their heads when doing so. Galatians 3:28 proclaimed there were no longer males nor females in Christ's family, but there were still important differences between the sexes.[65] Paul told the Corinthians that a man with long hair dishonored himself, but a woman's long hair was a glory to her because it was her covering (14–15).

1 Corinthians 14:34–35

Much of 1 Corinthians 14 (1 Corinthians 14:5, 6, 9, 16, 19, 23, 26–31) offered instruction in how to maintain order in worship services. Even people with spiritual gifts were to be in control of themselves when prophesying. With this background, Paul made a statement that contradicted what he had said in 1 Corinthians 11. Although he had not previously objected to women prophesying, he now made his first revision[66] and declared that women had to remain silent.[67] Paul began by insisting women must be silent in the churches (34). The plural form of churches (*ekklesiai*) implies that this was not just for the Corinth church, but rather a universal prohibition. If a married woman had a question, she should wait until the service was

---

[64] Conzelmann, 191.
[65] Kraemer and D'Angelo, 215.
[66] Malone, 77.
[67] There is confusion on whether verses 34 and 35 belong in chapter 14. In the Eastern texts these are between verses 33 and 36. The Western texts, however, place them after verse 40. The passage, therefore, moved directly from verse 33 to 36. With the text located after verse 40, the passage flows more smoothly. Alice Matthews, *Gender Roles and the People of God: Rethinking What We were Taught about Men and Women in the Church* (Grand Rapids, MI: Zondervan, 2017), 108–9; Newsome and Ringe, 418. An interpolator may have added these verses later because there were no Old Testament laws, as Paul would have known, forbidding women to speak or to bring this passage more into agreement with Paul in 1 Timothy 2:12.

over and ask her husband when they had returned home (35). This verse assumed that all the women addressed were there with their husbands, and some of them were disturbing the service by talking.[68] Paul continued by referring to the laws governing the synagogue by stating that a woman speaking in church was disgraceful (35). Paul again contradicted his statement in Ephesians 5:19, in which he stated congregants should be "speaking to one another in psalms and hymns and spiritual songs, singing and making melody with your heart to the Lord."

Ephesians 5:22–33

In his letter to the Ephesians, Paul spoke to a community living in one of the most important Mediterranean port cities. At this time, the population was approximately 250,000, making it the fourth-largest city in the world. Ephesus was known for its trade and commerce. It was quite cosmopolitan, with its large amphitheater, and was known for Artemis worship.[69] Paul wrote this letter to remind his Gentile readers that they were no longer alienated from God and his people, Israel, but were now one with Christ.[70]

In this section, Paul discussed household codes. He understood the Aristotelean household codes[71] and did not want to cause trouble for the new church by offending the Ephesians.[72] Aristotle wrote:

> Of household management we have seen that there are three parts—one is the rule of the master over slaves, which has been discussed already, another of the father, and the third of a husband. A husband and father, we saw, rules over wife and children, both free, but the rule differs, the rule over his children being a royal, over his wife a constitutional rule. For although there may be exceptions to the order of nature, the male is by nature fitter

---

[68] Malone, 77.
[69] Mitchell Reddish, "Ephesus," in *Holman Bible Dictionary*.
[70] Ehrman, 446.
[71] Torjesen, 40.
[72] Andrew T. Lincoln, *Ephesians*, Word Biblical Commentary Series, eds. David Allen Hubbard, Glenn W. Barker, John D. Watts, and Ralph P. Martin. (Waco, TX: Word Book Publishers, 1990), 367.

for command than the female, just as the elder and full-grown is superior to the younger and more immature.[73]

After telling Christ's followers to be filled with the Spirit (Ephesians 5:18) and to submit to one another (Ephesians 5:21), Paul explained the importance of marital submission.[74] Paul began by stating that wives should submit to their husbands just as believers submit to the Lord (22). The older manuscripts, however, do not contain the word "submit." This "submit" appeared only in later editions. In the earlier manuscripts, the text implies a continuation of the mutual submission as noted in verse 21.[75] Translating this verse is a major point of contention between scholars. Some scholars maintain that, though not present, the verb submit should be understood as implied and, thus, maintain that wives must submit to their husbands. Other scholars hold that the verb is not present and the mutual submission as depicted in verse 21 is the most literal translation.[76] Paul then described how marriage was based on Christ, the head of the church, and was formed by Christ's sacrificial and salvific actions.[77] The church was now the family of God—Christ's body (23). The husband, however, could not be his wife's savior. The similarities between Christ and the husband, therefore, must be based on their self-sacrifice because men have the most authority in culture as Christ has as God-incarnate. Therefore, those with the most cultural authority are those Paul calls to sacrifice themselves. Paul stated that as the church/body submits to Christ, husbands and wives should submit to Christ, and all Christians should be known by their mutual submission (Ephesians 5:24). Husbands are to love their wives as Christ loved the church, by dying for her. Love must now be the burden of husbands who love as Christ did, with empathy—a quality uncommon in power-based relationships such as those between men and women in antiquity.

---

[73] Aristotle, *Politics*, I.12.1259a–b, *The Basic Works of Aristotle*, trans. Richard McKeon (New York, NY: Random House, 1941), 1143.
[74] Markus Barth, *Ephesians: Translation and Commentary on Chapters 4–6*, The Anchor Yale Bible Commentary Series (New York, NY: Doubleday, 1974), 610.
[75] Lincoln, 367.
[76] Craig S. Keener, *Paul, Women, & Wives: Marriage and Women's Ministry in the of Paul* (Peabody, MA.: Hendrickson Publishers, 1992), 169.
[77] Ibid., 368.

Paul thus described how men should love their wives through self-sacrifice and empathy. A husband must love his wife as Christ loved the church (25). It is a love that mirrored Christ's love for the church/body. Christ could then sanctify the church through water and word (spiritual baptism) and in doing so purify the church (26–27). The husband was to love his wife as he loved his own body. When loving his wife, the husband was also loving himself (Ephesians 5:28). As no one hated his own flesh, but rather loved it as he loved himself, a husband should care for and nurture his wife just as Christ loved the church and its members (5:28–30). The use of flesh rather than body referred to the spiritual union of marriage when the two became one as described in Genesis 2:24, the same union of the church to Christ. This new manner of Christian marriage reversed the body-head metaphor so that unlike the emperor of Rome who as head demanded obedience and sacrifice of the empire—his body, Christ as head of the church sacrificed himself for the church—his body, in which those with power follow Christ's self-sacrifice. Paul quoted Genesis 2:24 and explained that through marriage the couple gained a new identity. The head and the body became unified in one flesh (31).[78] The completeness of the unity displayed in marriage was difficult to comprehend, especially when used to depict Christ and the church (32).

Paul concluded by commanding husbands to love their wives as they love themselves and wives to respect and honor their husbands (33). Whereas before Paul used emotional terms to depict how the man should love his wife, he commanded the husband to act on his love for his wife. He also commanded the wife to respect her husband.

Colossians 3:18–19

Colossae was a small Roman city in southern Asia Minor, roughly nine miles from its more prosperous neighbor, Laodicea, and one hundred miles from Ephesus. The city was a mercantile center known with a large Greek and Roman population.[79] There was also a sizable Jewish population. In matters of religion, it was very

---

[78] Matthews, 126.

[79] Josephus stated that Antiochus III settled 2000 Jewish families into the region in the second century B.C.E.

cosmopolitan. It contained Gentile shrines dedicated to Nike, Artemis, Dionysus, Isis, and Athena.[80] The Jewish inhabitants had at least one synagogue. There was also a cult dedicated to the Archangel Michael.[81] Because of these diverse religions, Paul wrote to the Colossians to encourage them to ignore all other religious teachers.[82]

Colossians 3:18–19 was Paul's first section of a larger household code (Colossians 3:18–25). The hierarchal code was similar to but shorter than the code found in Ephesians 5:21–33 (husbands and wives, parents and children, masters and slaves). Paul began by informing wives to submit to their husbands, but the statement was not as forceful a statement as "children obey their parents" (Colossians 3:20). Paul insisted that the wife should voluntarily submit to her husband. Paul reminded the reader that the wife's submission was what the Lord desired (18). This verse was addressed only to married couples.[83] He did not state that women must submit to men outside the confines of marriage.

Paul then turned to husbands and instructed them to love their wives (19). He chose *agape* as his term for love. This type of love was that of cherishing, affection, and care.[84] A husband could not abuse his wife.[85] He was to love her with an unselfish heart.

1 Timothy 2:11–15

Paul addressed this letter to Timothy—his close friend and traveling companion. His purpose was to encourage Timothy, to correct false teachings, to bring order to the church, and to appoint qualified leaders.[86]

In this passage, Paul began by telling women to dress modestly. They should not wear gold or pearl jewelry or expensive clothes (1 Timothy 2:9) so as not to offend their neighbors. Modest dress in worship was a virtue extolled in both Roman and Christian

---

[80] Burge and Green, 427.
[81] F.F. Bruce, *New Testament History* (New York, NY: Galilee-Doubleday, 1969), 415f.
[82] Ehrman, 443.
[83] Witherington, 150.
[84] Peter O'Brien, Colossians, *Philemon*, Word Biblical Commentary Series, eds. David Allen Hubbard, Glenn W. Barker, John D. Watts, and Ralph P. Martin (Waco, TX: Word Book Publishers, 1982), 223.
[85] Ibid., 223.
[86] Ehrman, 450.

worship.[87] Instead, good works were the proper ornamentation for women (1 Timothy 2:10).[88] As in 1 Corinthians 14:34–35, Paul instructed women to be silent and, presumably, to become better students to learn correct theology before teaching error. However, if they learn in silence as students of Rabbis do, they can become able teachers. Paul, then, provided a theological reason for this necessity by citing the second creation story and the Fall.[89] After not appearing in the Old Testament beyond the first chapters of Genesis, Eve reappeared. God gave Adam the rules of Eden: do not eat the forbidden fruit. However, just as Eve was deceived by the serpent, so, too, women at Ephesus were deceived by false teachers. Verse 15 did not refer to the consequence of sin placed on Eve in Genesis 3:15—labor pains, but rather the blessing of bearing children as her seed brought forth the one who overcame the tempter—Christ.[90]

Titus 2:3–5

Titus was the pastor of a church in Crete. He was one of Paul's converts and a trusted friend who delivered his second letter to the church in Corinth. Paul mentioned Titus by name in Galatians and Second Corinthians. Paul wrote Titus to encourage him to teach sound doctrine and refute the false teachers who appeared to have incorporated myths from other religions into his teachings.[91]

In Titus 2:3–5, Paul instructed older women how to live a life consecrated to God. Titus was to teach these older women not to gossip or drink to excess.[92] These women could then be proper models for younger women (3). The older women could teach decorum to younger women. Paul then stressed that older women must urge the younger women to love their husbands and children (4). Unlike in 1 Corinthians 7, celibacy was not an option. He stressed

---

[87] Lucinda A. Brown, "1 Timothy 2:9–15," in *Women in Scripture: A Dictionary of Named and Unnamed Women in the Hebrew Bible, the Apocryphal/Deuterocanonical Books, and the New Testament*, ed. Carol Myer (Grand Rapids, MI: Eerdmans Publishing Company, 2000), 487.
[88] Martin Dibelius, *The Pastoral Epistles*, Hermeneia Commentary Series on the Bible, ed. Helmut Koester (Philadelphia, PA: Fortress Press, 1972), 46.
[89] Kraemer and D'Angelo, 246.
[90] Witherington, 195.
[91] Ehrman, 452.
[92] Jerome Quinn, *The Letter to Titus*, The Anchor Yale Bible Commentary Series (New York, NY: Doubleday, 1990), 119.

that the older women teach the younger women that their sphere of work and influence was in the home.[93] They must also continue to observe subordinate status to their husbands, just as the passage called slaves to obey their masters (Titus 2:9), so society could not complain about Christians not following cultural and current social norms (Titus 2:5).

Women in Paul's Churches

The Pauline Corpus in its totality includes a female deacon and the only woman holding a church office, Phoebe, cited in Romans 16:1–2. Phoebe also carried Paul's most theological letter to Rome, where, as a letter carrier, she explained its contents. Paul also cites Junia, a woman who was prominent among the apostles (Romans 16:7). Women were called to learn in silence as the Rabbis did when engaged in studying the texts (1 Timothy 2:11–12). Further, in addressing false teachers in Ephesus, Paul calls women not to usurp authority over men because as false teachers they are deceived like Eve. Yet, Paul worked beside one of the most gifted church planters and teachers, his coworker Priscilla, who taught one of the most gifted teachers in the New Testament, Apollos (Acts 18:26). As Timothy was struggling to address false teachers in the church at Ephesus, Paul sends Priscilla back to help out, most likely as a teacher (2 Timothy 4:19). Women are valued not only as wives and mothers but, like men, as church planters, prophets, teachers, and apostles.

For the Future of Christian Women

As the biblical era ended and the Patristic era began, the Pauline letters had more to say about women. The early Church Fathers rarely considered Christ's compassion and treatment of women in their writings. Rather, their theology concerning women was based on Greek dualism that demeaned women as ontological inferiors and this was the lens through which they read the Eve stories in Genesis, the Pauline corpus, and Greek philosophy's more misogynistic interpretations of women.

---

[93] Lea and Griffith, Jr., 300–301.

CHAPTER FOUR

The Perception of Women in the Patristic Era

The major theologians of the Patristic era whose writings addressed women wrote from approximately 150 CE to the establishment of a defined papacy in 590 CE. To varying degrees, these Church Fathers relied on Greek philosophy when reading Paul's writings, Philo's allegorical hermeneutic, and the writings of Judaism. Moreover, most of these men were celibate clerics and thus rarely wrote from their own experience. Their task was to promote the gospel in a Greco-Roman world that viewed women as inferior to men. This was the background of their theological interpretation of women. The areas in which the Church Fathers commented on women were the creation stories; original sin; wives' submission in marriage; women's effect on men; female chastity; and ministry and teaching. The Church Fathers whose thoughts contributed to future Christian views of women were Clement of Alexandria (150–215), Tertullian of Carthage (ca. 144–ca. 220), Jerome (342–420), John Chrysostom (347–407) and Augustine (354–430).[1]

Local synods, ecumenical councils, and writings shaped the hierarchy of the growing church. Many of the canons sought to identify the conditions under which women could or could not

---

[1] All quotations and references from these Church Fathers are from either *The Ante-Nicene Fathers*, eds. Alexander Roberts and James Donaldson, 10 vols. 1885–1887 (Peabody, MA: Hendrickson, 1994), hereafter cited as *ANF*; or *The Nicene and Post-Nicene Fathers*, First Series, ed. Philip Schaff, 14 vols. 1886–1889 (Reprint, Peabody, MA: Hendrickson, 1940), hereafter cited as *NPNF*; or *Patrologiae Cursus Completus*, series *Graeca*, ed. Jacques Paul Migne (Paris, 1857–1866), hereafter cited as *PG*; or Series *Latina*, hereafter cited as *PL*.

serve in the clergy. The representative writings, councils, and synods include the *Apostolic Tradition* (215), *Didascalia Apostolorum* (ca. 225), Council of Nicaea (325), Council of Laodicea (363), *Apostolic Constitutions* (375–380), bishop of Rome Siricius' (384–399) decree on clerical celibacy (384–389), Synod of Carthage (390), Synod of Nimes (394), Synod of Orange (441), bishop of Rome Gelasius'(492–496) letter concerning women at the altar, (517) Council of Epon (517), Second Synod of Orleans (553), and the Council of Macon (585).

Clement of Alexandria

Clement of Alexandria was the director of its Christian catechetical school in Alexandria. Born into a pagan family in Athens, he became a Christian and settled in Alexandria, Egypt. He knew Judaism, Philo's writings, and the Christian scriptures very well. He was also well-schooled in Greco-Roman literature, and his philosophy demonstrates a heavy reliance on Platonism and Stoicism. He believed that there was truth in pagan philosophy that could be useful to Christianity. His theological writings reflect his intellectual background. The *Logos*, its incarnation in Christ, and its role in the Trinity are the heart of his system. Clement's goal was to provide the church with an alternative to the Gnosticism that had taken root in Alexandria.

Clement held that in Genesis 1:26–27 the term *Anthropos* (Adam) meant human and included both men and women. Adam, therefore, had no gender. Clement's understanding of the image of God is Christocentric, meaning that Christ is the image of God, humans are the image of Christ, and thus, the *Anthropos* is the image of God.[2] The *Anthropos* became separate entities when God created Eve from Adam's side. Both man and woman retained the image of God. They were equally capable of being trained as philosophers and living a life of virtue and perfection as emulated in the "Instructor," Christ.[3]

Though both sexes shared the image of God, Clement recognized their biological differences. These differences were part of God's initial plan, not a result of the Fall, and would not exist in the

---

[2] Janet Martin Soskice, *Feminism and Theology* (Oxford: Oxford University Press, 2003), 51.
[3] Clement of Alexandria, *The Instructor*, bk. 1.11, *ANF*, 2:234.

world predicted in Galatians 3:28. Men's bodies were designed for physical work outside the home. Women's bodies were designed for childbearing.[4] Clement writes:

> For God wished women to be smooth, and rejoice in their locks alone growing spontaneously, as a horse in his mane; but has adorned man, like the lions, with a beard, and endowed him, as an attribute of manhood, with shaggy breasts,—a sign this of strength and rule. So also cocks, which fight in defense of the hens, he has decked with combs, as it were helmets; and so high a value does God set on these locks, that He orders them to make their appearance on men simultaneously with discretion, and delighted with a venerable look, has honored gravity of countenance with grey hairs. But wisdom, and discriminating judgments that are hoary with wisdom, attain maturity with time, and by the vigor of long experience give strength to old age, producing grey hairs, the admirable flower of venerable wisdom, conciliating confidence. This, then, the mark of the man, the beard, by which he is seen to be a man, is older than Eve, and is the token of the superior nature.[5]

Clement drew on Platonism in separating the soul from the body. Clement held that the soul—whether in a male or in a female—consisted of three parts. The higher soul was associated with reasoning, spirituality, and apprehension. As the creator of the *Logos* and the principle of rationality, God's likeness was found on this level.[6] The lower soul was composed of the bestial.[7] To grow in the likeness of Christ, one must cultivate the qualities of the higher soul.

Clement did not believe that the body was a prison for the soul. He held that to have a healthy soul one must discipline the

---

[4] Ibid., bk. 3.10, *ANF*, 2:283.
[5] Ibid., 3.3, *ANF*, 2:274.
[6] Soskice, *Feminism and Theology*, 327.
[7] Michel Desjardins, "Why Women Should Cover Their Heads and Veil Their Faces: Clement of Alexandria's Understanding of the Body and His Rhetorical Strategies in the *Paedagogus*," *Scriptura*, no. 90 (2005): 704.

body and control the instincts found in the lower soul. These baser instincts were associated with women. This higher soul was identified as masculine but women were capable of having one. They should seek it, but it was more trying for them because they had more difficulty controlling themselves.[8] At the same time, women were more passive than men. For women to achieve this higher level, they must transcend their femininity and become masculine by controlling their feminine passions. Women could then achieve a life of perfection.[9]

Clement stressed the Stoic tenet of self-control. "And in this way, is not woman translated into man, having become equally unwomanish and masculine and perfect?"[10] In the same way, men who did not cultivate the higher soul could become more effeminate, and move away from the likeness of God. Certain female aspects, therefore, were not congruous with the likeness of God. The image of God must be obtained through the masculinization of the lower, feminine soul.[11] Clement's description appears to constitute an intermediate gender where women are neither female nor male.

Many second-century Christian sects held that a chaste or celibate life was preferable to a married life. The Encratites were Clement's foil in his discussions concerning marriage. One Encratite, Tatian of Assyria (120–180), believed that sex was fornication taught by the devil to the first couple.[12] Clement disagreed; marriage helped men and women bear each other's burdens and he noted that Peter and Phillip were married and had children.[13] He maintained that sexual differences predated the Fall; therefore, God intended for men and women to procreate.[14] Sexual desire and sexual differentiation were nonexistent in heaven.[15]

Citing the Fall, Clement believed that uncontrolled sexual desire could be dangerous. In the Fall narrative, Adam embraced pleasure

---

[8] Clement of Alexandria, *Stromata*, bk. 3.7, *ANF*, 2:389–391.
[9] Ibid., 4.9, *ANF*, 2:432.
[10] Ibid., *Stromata* bk. 6.12, *ANF*, 2:503.
[11] Benjamin H. Dunning, *Specters of Paul: Sexual Difference in Early Christian Thought* (Philadelphia, PA: University of Pennsylvania Press, 2011), 52.
[12] Clement of Alexandria, *Stromata*, bk. 3.12, *ANF*, 2:396.
[13] Ibid., bk. 3.6, *ANF*, 2:390; Norris, 180.
[14] Ibid., bk. 2.23, *ANF*, 2:377.
[15] Clement of Alexandria, *The Instructor*, bk. 1.4, *ANF*, 2:211.

in the form of the serpent, and his desire overtook him. Eve was implicitly the object of his desire. Although sexual desire was not mentioned, it was implied.[16] Consequently, Adam fell because the serpent used Eve. According to Ruether,[17] Clement applies Jeremiah 20:14 "no blessing on the day my mother bore me," Psalm 51:5 "in sin did my mother conceive me," and Job 14:4 "who can bring a clean thing out of an unclean," to tie every birth to this first sin. Every birth brought sin. Sexual relations, therefore, were an expected part of being a human couple, but it must be done without desire or pleasure. The first couple did not sin by having sex in the Garden of Eden, but rather by having sex before God told them to do so.

Clement says:

> But if nature led them [Adam and Eve], like the irrational animals, to procreation, yet they were impelled to do it more quickly than was proper because they were still young and had been led away by deceit. Thus, God's judgment against them was just because they did not wait for his will. But birth is holy. By it were made the world, the existences, the natures, the angels, powers, souls, the commandments, the law, the gospel, the knowledge of God.[18]

Clement believed that the failure to procreate was disobedience to God's command to be fruitful and multiply. Moreover, when a man had sex with a woman, he cooperated with God in creating another person. Sex within marriage may have been in God's original plan, but only for procreation. In Stoic fashion, Clement taught that humans must control their sexual passions:

> For nature, just as in the case of eating, has permitted to us that which is proper and useful and fitting for lawful marriages, and thus has permitted us to yearn for procreation.

---

[16] Clement of Alexandria, *Stromata*, bk. 3.17, *ANF*, 2:400.
[17] Rosemary Radford Ruether, ed., *Religion and Sexism: Images of Woman in the Jewish and Christian Traditions* (Eugene, OR: Wipf and Stock Publishers, 1998), 102.
[18] Clement of Alexandria, *Stromata*, bk. 3.17, *ANF*, 2:400.

> But those who pursue excess sin against nature, (are) hurting themselves through lawless intercourse.[19]

Sexual relations that did not take place during a woman's fertile period or that had no chance of resulting in pregnancy, such as oral or anal sex, were forbidden. If a couple no longer wanted or were incapable of producing children, their relationship should be more like that of a brother and sister.[20] This allowed the marriage to remain intact in anticipation of the resurrected life.[21]

Because God made biological differences between men and women before the Fall, Clement assigned gender roles to Adam and Eve.[22] Using 1 Corinthians and the household codes, Clement maintained that the husband was head of the household.[23] The wife was the helper.[24] She was to stay home and attend to domestic responsibilities.[25] She must "never do anything against his will, with the exception of what is contributing to virtue and salvation."[26] She had no formal, ministerial role in the church but was capable of being martyred.[27]

Clement also believed that women could lead men astray. For this reason, women were to dress modestly. Outside the home, women should be fully covered and veiled. Clement noted, "that style of a dress is grave, and protects from being gazed at. And she will never fall, who puts before her eyes modesty and her shawl; nor will she invite another to fall into sin by uncovering her face. For this is the wish of the Word (I Cor. 11:5), since it is becoming for her to pray veiled."[28] A purple veil, however, should be avoided as it causes men to lust.[29]

---

[19] Clement of Alexandria, *The Instructor*, bk. 2.10, *ANF*, 2:260.
[20] Dunning, 65.
[21] Ibid., 65.
[22] Ibid., 54.
[23] Donald Kinder, "Clement of Alexandria: Conflicting Views on Women," *The Second Century Journal: A Journal of Early Christian Studies* 7, no. 4 (Winter 1989–90): 215–216.
[24] Dunning, 63.
[25] Clement of Alexandria, *The Instructor*, bk. 3.10, *ANF*, 2:283.
[26] Clement of Alexandria, *Stromata*, bk. 4.19, *ANF*, 2:432.
[27] Ibid., bk. 4.8, *ANF*, 2:420–21.
[28] Clement of Alexandria, *The Instructor*, bk. 3.11, *ANF*, 2:290.
[29] Ibid., bk. 2.11, *ANF*, 2:266–67.

Clement referenced 1 Enoch 7 when he discussed women's power to tempt even the angels. He maintained that women's beauty was so great that angels chose to leave heaven to be with them. These angels then taught women the secrets of ornamentation.[30] When discussing jewelry, Clement referred to Eve and the serpent:

> But now women are not ashamed to wear the most manifest badges of the evil one. For as the serpent deceived Eve, so also has ornament of gold maddened other women to vicious practices, using as a bait the form of the serpent, and by fashioning lampreys and serpents for decoration. Accordingly, the comic poet Nicostratus says, "Chains, collars; rings, bracelets, serpents, anklets, earrings."[31]

Tertullian

Tertullian (155–240) was an early Christian apologist and defender of orthodoxy from Carthage in the Roman Province of Africa. A voluminous author, he was the first major theologian to write in Latin and was the first known to use the term "trinity." A legalist, Tertullian was conservative in his theology and later joined the strict Montanist sect. Tertullian was one of the few Church Fathers who rejected the use of Greek philosophy, declaring, "What indeed has Athens to do with Jerusalem? What concord is there between the Academy and the Church?"[32] He wrote critically of women and is sexist if not misogynistic.

Tertullian held that God created Adam's body from the soil and then breathed his soul into him.[33] He saw these elements as related to the man's sperm which provided both the body and soul.[34] Adam and Eve were the prototypes for all humanity. Since God created

---

[30] Ibid., bk. 5.1, *ANF*, 2:446; Rosemary Radford Ruether, ed. *Religion and Sexism: Images of Woman in the Jewish and Christian Traditions* (Eugene, OR: Wipf and Stock Publishers, 1998), 101.
[31] Clement of Alexandria, *The Instructor*, bk. 2.13, *ANF*, 2:269.
[32] Tertullian, *Prescription Against the Heretics*, *ANF*, 3:246.
[33] Tertullian, *A Treatise on the Soul*, *ANF*, 3:208.
[34] Ibid., 208.

Adam first and then formed Eve from Adam, Eve was second to Adam but not subordinate. Unlike the Platonists and Aristotelians, Tertullian followed the medical theories of the Greek physician, Soranus (ca. second century CE), who believed in the simultaneous formation of the body and soul at conception. Gender was also determined at this time. The man provided both body and soul through the sperm.

> Certainly, in this view we have an attestation of the method of the first two formations, when the male was molded and tempered in a completer way, for Adam was first formed; and the woman came far behind him, for Eve was the later formed. So that her flesh was for a long time without specific form (such as she afterwards assumed when taken out of Adam's side); but she was even then herself a living being, because I should regard her at that time in soul as even a portion of Adam. Besides, God's afflatus would have animated her too, if there had not been in the woman a transmission from Adam of his soul also as well as of his flesh.[35]

Tertullian believed Adam was the father of the human race and more complete than Eve. Tertullian did not claim Eve's unworthiness to receive her soul directly from God, but rather there was no reason for God to do it again. Eve and women, therefore, were second in the order of creation but shared equality in soul. Nowhere in this account did Tertullian state that Eve was inferior to Adam. Moreover, as the body, soul, and gender originated simultaneously, no external factors determined the gender as they did in Greek philosophies such as Aristotelianism.[36]

Because the body and soul were created at the same time, Tertullian rejected the Platonist theory that the body was inferior to the soul. To be human, one required both elements—each of which was good. Flesh, therefore, could not be associated solely with women.

---

[35] Ibid., 217.
[36] *De generatione animalium*, 766a35–767b5, cited in A.L. Peck, *Aristotle XIII: Generation of Animals* (Cambridge, MA: Harvard University Press, 1979).

Concerning the image of God, Tertullian cited Genesis 1:26. He held that the image of God referred to Christ's human nature and his flesh. As the prototype of the image of God, Adam passed this image on to Eve because her soul came from him.[37] All those who possessed human flesh were therefore in the image of God.

Tertullian had much to say about Eve's, and by extension all women's, role in the Fall.[38]

> No one of you at all, best beloved sisters, from the time that [Eve] had first known the Lord and learned (the truth) concerning her own (that is, woman's) condition, would have desired too gladsome (not to say too ostentatious) a style of dress; so as not rather to go about in humble garb, and rather to affect meanness of appearance, walking about as Eve mourning and repentant, in order that by every garb of penitence she might the more fully expiate that which she derives from Eve—the ignominy, I mean, of the first sin, and the odium (attaching to her as the cause) of human perdition. "In pains and anxieties dost thou bear (children), woman; and toward thine husband (is) thy inclination, and he lords it over thee." And do you not know that you are (each) an Eve? The sentence of God on this sex of yours lives in this age: the guilt must of necessity live too. You are the devil's gateway; you are the unsealer of that (forbidden) tree: you are the first deserter of the divine law: you are she who persuaded him whom the devil was not valiant enough to attack. You destroy so easily God's image, man. On account of your desert—that is, death—even the Son of God had to die.[39]

In this account, Tertullian laid the blame squarely at Eve's feet. Women should feel so guilty that they should dress modestly and live in permanent penance. In other accounts, Tertullian blamed

---

[37] F. Forrester Church, "Sex and Salvation in Tertullian," *The Harvard Theological Review* 68, no. 2 (April 1975): 91; *De anima* 36.4.
[38] Beverly Clack, ed. *Misogyny in the Western Philosophical Tradition: A Reader* (London: MacMillan Press, 1999), 49.
[39] Tertullian, *On the Apparel of Women*, bk. 1.1, *ANF*, 1:14.

Adam or Adam and Eve for the Fall.[40] As a traducianist, he held that inherited sin originated from Adam.[41] In this regard, he was not consistent. Tertullian continues:

> Woman is at once condemned to bring forth in sorrow, and to serve her husband, Genesis 3:16, although before she had heard without pain the increase of her race proclaimed with the blessing, *increase and multiply*, and although she had been destined to be a help and not a slave to her male partner.[42]

He maintained that while being married was not a sin, renouncing marriage was the higher calling. After becoming a Montanist, he viewed his marriage as a mistake. Citing Paul in 1 Corinthians 11, he claimed that marriage was for those who could not control their sexual urges, and sex was the greatest impediment to salvation.[43] He considered marriage a lesser evil.[44] Marriage dulled the senses and dampened the spiritual life.[45] Moreover, women had ulterior motives for marriage such as lust and the desire to control their husband's estate. Even if a woman's primary desire was motherhood, children were a distraction from preparing for the second coming.[46] He also opposed widows remarrying. It could hurt the churches' reputation, shame her,[47] and it was nothing more than giving herself over to depravity once again.[48] If some were compelled to marry, Tertullian believed that they should when the couple was young to impede any rumors concerning Christian women's weak sexual mores.[49]

---

[40] Tertullian, *An Exhortation to Chastity*, ch. 2, *ANF*, 4:50–51; Tertullian, *On Fasting*, ch.3, *ANF*, 4:103.
[41] Tertullian, *A Testimony on the Soul*, ch. 3, *ANF*, 3:177.
[42] Tertullian, *Against Marcion*, bk. 2, *ANF*, 3:306.
[43] F. Forrester Church, "Sex and Salvation in Tertullian," 96.
[44] Tertullian, *On Monogamy*, ch. 3, *ANF*, 3:60.
[45] Tertullian, *An Exhortation to Chastity*, ch. 11, *ANF*, 4:56.
[46] Tertullian, *To His Wife*, ch. 5, *ANF*, 4:42.
[47] April DeConick, *Holy Misogyny: Why the Sex and Gender Conflicts of the Early Church Still Matter* (New York, NY: Bloomsbury, 2011), 112.
[48] Tertullian, *An Exhortation to Chastity*, *ANF*, 4:50, 52.
[49] April D. DeConick, *Holy Misogyny: Why the Sex and Gender Conflicts of the Early Church Still Matter* (New York, NY: Bloomsbury, 2011), 114.

Tertullian valued female chastity. By refraining from sexual activity, a woman becomes more spiritual but remains a woman.[50] He identified three types of chastity: those who chose it, married couples who renounced sex, and widows who refused remarriage.[51] All virgins were wed to Christ and they "walk[ed] in accordance to the will of [their] Espoused."[52] These chaste women already belonged to the angelic family[53] and were living in the resurrected state.[54] Tertullian may be the first person to equate consecrated virgins with brides of Christ.[55]

Tertullian spoke often and strongly about veiling. Virgins who wore the veil did a service to their gender and demonstrated their submission to Christ.[56] He maintained that in 1 Corinthians 11 Paul meant for all women to wear a veil at all times. All women, therefore, were under submission to either Christ and/or their husbands.

> You do well in falsely assuming the married character, if you veil your head; nay, you do not seem to assume it *falsely*, for you *are* wedded to Christ: to Him you have surrendered your body; act as becomes your Husband's discipline.[57]

Another reason Tertullian gave women for wearing a veil was because of their seductive beauty. "But why are we a [source of] danger to our neighbor? Why do we import concupiscence into our neighbor? Which concupiscence, if God, in amplifying the law, does not dissociate in [the way of] penalty from the actual commission of fornication..."[58] Her beauty was something to be feared and

---

[50] Ibid., 111.
[51] Lisa M. Bitel and Felice Lifshitz, eds. *Gender and Christianity in Medieval Europe: New Perspectives* (Philadelphia, PA: University of Pennsylvania Press, 2008), 21.
[52] Tertullian, *On the Veiling of Virgins*, ch. 16, *ANF*, 4:36.
[53] Bitel and Lifshitz, eds. *Gender and Christianity in Medieval Europe*, 22.
[54] Tertullian, *On the Resurrection of the Flesh*, ch. 61, *ANF*, 3:593.
[55] Bitel and Lifshitz, eds. *Gender and Christianity in Medieval Europe*, 17.
[56] Ibid., 17.
[57] Tertullian, *On Prayer*, *ANF*, 3:689.
[58] Tertullian, *On the Apparel of Women*, bk. 2.2, *ANF*, 4:19.

necessarily controlled.[59] A beautiful woman was the "sword that destroys him."[60]

Tertullian also believed that women could seduce angels, citing Genesis 6:1–4. He also referenced 1 Enoch 7. In this account, these angels, or "sons of heaven" not only reproduced with women but taught them the secrets of ornamentation and cosmetics.[61] The veil, therefore, not only signaled women's submission but also warded off lustful angels.[62]

The Virgin Mary served as an example of obedience. Tertullian presented her as the antithesis to Eve. Eve was a virgin before she believed the serpent. Immediately after the Fall, she gave up her Edenic state of virginity and gave birth to a devil (Cain) who murdered his brother. The Virgin Mary believed Gabriel and bore Christ who brought life. Mary was obedient and preserved her virginity.[63] One virgin made amends for the other.[64] Unlike other Church Fathers, Tertullian did not believe that Mary remained a perpetual virgin as she had married Joseph, and Jesus had brothers and sisters.[65] Mary, therefore, served as an example to all women, especially mothers.

Tertullian limited women's roles in the church. Using Genesis 3:16 and 1 Corinthians 14:34–35 as his rationale, he claims, "It is not permitted for a woman to speak in the church; but neither (is it permitted her) to teach, nor baptize, nor offer, nor to claim to herself a lot in any manly function, to say (in any) sacerdotal office."[66] He held that women who performed these functions were heretics and belonged to sects such as the Marcionites. They were performing rites reserved for men. "The very women of these heretics, how wanton they are! For they are bold enough to teach, to dispute, to enact exorcisms, to undertake cures—maybe even to baptize."[67]

---

[59] Katharine M. Rogers, *The Troublesome Helpmate: A History of Misogyny in Literature* (Seattle, WA: University of Washington Press, 1966), 15.
[60] Tertullian, *On the Apparel of Women*, bk. 2.2, ANF, 4:19.
[61] Beverly Clack, ed., *Misogyny in the Western Philosophical Tradition*, 51.
[62] Bitel and Lifshitz, eds. *Gender and Christianity in Medieval Europe*, 18, 24.
[63] J.A. Phillips, *The History of an Idea: Eve* (New York, NY: Harper and Row, 1984).
[64] Tertullian, *On the Flesh of Christ*, ch. 17, ANF, 3: 536.
[65] Tertullian, *On the Flesh of Christ*, ch. 7, ANF, 3:526; Tertullian, *Against Marcion*, book 4, ch. 19. ANF, 3:377–78.
[66] Tertullian, *On the Veiling of Virgins*, ch. 9, ANF, 4:36.
[67] Tertullian, *Prescription Against the Heretics*, ch. 41, ANF, 3:263.

In some ways, however, Tertullian believed women could assist the church. As a Montanist who believed in the elevated importance of the Holy Spirit, Tertullian followed Paul and allowed women to prophesy if their heads were covered. He praised a female Montanist prophet named Prisca stating, "[T]hrough the holy prophetess Prisca the Gospel is thus preached, that the holy minister knows how to minister sanctity. 'For purity,' says she, 'is harmonious, and they see visions; and, turning their face downward, they even hear manifest voices, as salutary as they are withal secret.'"[68]

Tertullian listed widows and virgins as official church orders.[69] He held widows in high regard. Women could become widows if they met the criteria in 1 Timothy 5:10, but he did not describe their role or activity. As attested in his many writings discussing them, Tertullian greatly admired women who dedicated their lives to virginity. For him, they were the spouses of Christ who served the church as living examples of the resurrected age to come.

Tertullian, like many early Christians, greatly admired martyrs, whether male or female. Female martyrs were held in especially high esteem. Concerning female martyrs, Fox notes, "The most excellent Christians in the early Church were neither virgins nor the visionaries. They were the Christians whom pagans put to death."[70]

Perpetua of Carthage was one of the most celebrated female martyrs. She kept a diary. Because of her many prophecies, Tertullian probably edited it and gave it the title *The Passion of Perpetua*. In *The Passion*, she turned down the pleas of her father to recant her Christianity, symbolically separated from her son, and embraced her fate. In this manner, she showed courage, fortitude, and spiritual development, meaning that she transcended her female nature and became a male. Perpetua wrote, "I was stripped, and became a man (*facta sum masculus*)."[71] The idea of a virtuous woman who spiritually developed to the point that she surpassed her feminine weaknesses and became a man in terms of spirituality was a common characteristic in many of the Church Fathers.[72]

---

[68] Tertullian, *An Exhortation to Chastity*, ch. 10, ANF, 4:56.
[69] Tertullian, *Prescription Against the Heretics*, ch. 3, ANF, 3:244.
[70] R. L. Fox, *Pagans and Christians* (New York: Harper, 1988), 419.
[71] Tertullian, *The Passion of Perpetua and Felicitas*, ch. 3, ANF, 3:702.
[72] Barbara J. MacHaffie, *Her Story: Women in the Christian Tradition*, 2nd ed. (Minneapolis, MN: Fortress Press, 2006), 28.

John Chrysostom

Known as the "golden mouthed" for his excellent preaching, John Chrysostom was a priest in Antioch and later the archbishop of Constantinople. He was an advocate of asceticism and an opponent of political corruption. His major concern was for the welfare of his church and its congregants.

Chrysostom held that man and woman were created equal and had the same ontology. They both shared in equal honor and were to be co-rulers of creation.[73] They possessed free will, freedom from irrational passion, and a lack of need.[74] He maintained that being in the image of God granted humanity authority over all creation. The likeness of God conferred the potential to take on God's attributes.[75]

> You have heard that God created the human being in his image. And we have said that the meaning of this "in his image and likeness" does not mean [to be] identically alike in essence, but alike in rule. The said "likeness" means gentle and kind and the ability for us to liken ourselves to God according to the sermon of virtues, where Christ says. "Become like my Father who is in Heaven." For exactly as on this wide and spacious earth some animals are more irrational, and others more wild, so in this way in the breadth of our souls, some of our thoughts are irrational and beastly, and others are savage and wild. Therefore, we must rule over them, greatly conquer them, and surrender them to reason.[76]

According to Clark,[77] Chrysostom read Genesis 1 through the lens of 1 Corinthians 11. This interpretation made man the only one

---

[73] Maria-Fotin Polidoulis Kapaslis, "Image as authority in the writings of John Chrysostom" (PhD Dissertation: University of St. Michael's College, 2001), 54.
[74] Valerie Karras, "Male Domination of Women in the Writings of Saint John Chrysostom," *The Greek Orthodox Theological Review* 36, no. 2:132.
[75] Maria-Fotini Polidoulis Kapsalis, 59.
[76] Chrysostom, *Sermons on Genesis*, 3, PG, 54.
[77] Elizabeth A. Clark, "Ideology, History, and the Construction of 'Woman' in Late Ancient Christianity," *Journal of Early Christian Studies* 2 (1994): 176.

to enjoy God's full image utilizing authority.[78] As God had complete authority, only the male had complete authority over creation. "Like God in the heavens, so the male on earth has no superior and rules over all beings."[79] Chrysostom gave Eve a high honor but a higher honor to Adam.[80]

Chrysostom maintained that though man and woman were created equal, the man was first among equals.[81] Adding Genesis 3 to the interpretation, he held that Eve was created to be his helpmate.[82] She was made from Adam and for Adam.[83]

> And since he taught him with all that, that he consists between the two natures and that he is the most honored of all creatures, and that none could be found among such a great multitude of creatures equal to him, then he created woman. Honoring him with this manner again and making it evident that she was formed for him, as Paul says, "For man was not formed for woman, but woman for the man."[84]

Therefore, Chrysostom placed Eve only slightly under Adam in the original hierarchy. This arrangement changed with the original sin. Chrysostom believed the serpent approached Eve because she was weaker than Adam and would be easier to deceive.[85] As a superior creature to the serpent, Eve should have been able to resist.[86]

---

[78] Korinna Zamfir, "The Quest for the 'Eternal Feminine:' An Essay on the Effective History of Genesis 1–3 with Respect to Women," *Annali Di Storia Dell-Essegessi* 24, no. 2 (2007): 514.
[79] Chrysostom, *Sermons on Genesis*, 2, *PG*, 54.
[80] Mary Daly, *The Church and the Second Sex: With a New Feminist PostChristian Introduction by the Author* (New York, NY: Harper and Row, 1975), 86.
[81] Maria-Fotini Polidoulis Kapsalis, 190.
[82] Chrysostom, *Sermons on Genesis*, 4.1, *PG*, 54.
[83] Maria-Fotini Polidoulis Kapsalis, 134.
[84] Chrysostom, *Sermons on Genesis*, 4.1, *PG*, 54.
[85] Kristen E. Kvam, Linda S. Schearing, and Valerie H. Ziegler, eds. *Eve & Adam: Jewish, Christian, a Muslim Readings on Genesis and Gender* (Bloomington, IN: University of Indiana Press, 1999), 141.
[86] Korinna Zamfir, "The Quest for the 'Eternal Feminine:' An Essay on the Effective History of Gen. 1–3 with Respect to Women," *Annali Di Storia Dell-Essegessi* 24, no. 2

Out of a desire to be greater than what God intended, she abandoned her reason.

> Do you see how the devil led her captive? Handicapped her reasoning and caused her to set her thoughts on goals beyond her real capabilities, in order that she might be puffed up with empty hopes and lose her hold on the advantages already accorded her?[87]

Chrysostom believed that Adam was also culpable. He defined Adam as the head and Eve as the body. The head must always lead the body. As the head, Adam should not have obeyed his wife.[88]

> After all, you are head of your wife, and she has been created for your sake; but you have inverted the proper order: not only have you failed to keep her on the straight and narrow but you have been dragged down with her, and whereas the rest of the body should follow the head, the contrary has in fact occurred, the head following the rest of the body, turning things upside down.[89]

Original sin destroyed the natural hierarchy at creation. As punishment, Chrysostom held that Eve was subordinated to Adam.

> In the beginning I created you equal in esteem to your husband, and my intention was that in everything you would share with him as an equal, and as I entrusted control of everything to your husband, so did I to you; but you abused your equality of status. Hence, I subject you to your husband.[90]

Chrysostom believed that Adam and Eve did not have sexual intercourse before the Fall but would have reproduced in a sinless

---

(2007): 517; Valerie Karras, "Male Domination of Woman in the Writings of Saint John Chrysostom," *The Greek Orthodox Theological Review* 36, no. 2 (1991): 136–137.

[87] Chrysostom, *Homilies on Genesis*, 16, *PG*, 53.

[88] Maria-Fotini Polidoulis Kapsalis, 141.

[89] Chrysostom, *Homilies on Genesis*, 17.18, *PG*, 53.

[90] Ibid.

manner.⁹¹ Immediately after falling into sin the first couple's desires and passions took control of them and they had sex.⁹² Death then entered the world, and sexual intercourse became necessary for procreation. Chrysostom maintained that marriage became a necessary measure to enforce monogamy.⁹³

He believed that marriage was good. Eve was created from Adam's flesh, so she was more like a sister than a wife. Men and women needed each other for companionship and to procreate. Women and men could not be self-sufficient.⁹⁴ Marriage, therefore, was the closest possible union between two people.

> And indeed, from the beginning, God appears to have made special provision for this union, and discoursing of the two as one, He said thus, "Male and female created He them," and again, "There is neither male nor female." For there is no relationship between man and man so close as that between man and wife, if they be joined together as they should be … For there is a certain love deeply seated in our nature, which imperceptibly to ourselves knits together these bodies of ours. Thus, even from the very beginning, from man sprang woman, and afterwards from man and woman sprang both man and woman.⁹⁵

He held that sexual intercourse was only permissible within marriage. It was a God-ordained outlet for procreation and to keep people from falling into fornication.⁹⁶ He maintained that marital sex "preserves the believer's chastity."⁹⁷ Children were a blessing that bound the couple together.

> And the child is a sort of bridge, so that the three become one flesh, the child connecting each other on either side. For as two cities, which a river divides through, become

---

[91] Maria-Fotini Polidoulis Kapsalis, 195.
[92] Chrysostom, *Homilies on Genesis*, 18.12, *PG*, 53.
[93] Chrysostom, *On Virginity*, 2.14, *PG*, 48.
[94] Chrysostom, *On Ephesians*, Homily 20.1, *NPNF*, 13:143.
[95] Ibid.
[96] Chrysostom, *On Titus*, Homily 3, *PG*, 62; *NPNF* 13:530.
[97] Chrysostom, *On Hebrews*, Homily 33, *NPNF* 14:516.

one city if a bridge connects them on both sides, so is it in this case; and yet more, since the very bridge here is formed from the substance of each side.[98]

Chrysostom believed that there was both unity and submission in marriage. In the prelapsarian state, the man's station was to be honorary and not one of rigid hierarchy. It was similar to the relationship between the Father and the Son.[99] The term "head," however, has different spiritual and temporal meanings. If the headship applied identically to the Father and Son and to men and women, the Son would be subordinate to the Father. God was the head of Christ and the Son freely gave obedience to him in a more intimate way than did husbands and wives. Christ recognized himself as the Father's begotten son and under his father's authority.[100] This clarification demonstrated his desire to remain true to Nicaean Trinitarianism. Nonetheless, Chrysostom appears to maintain that the Son was subordinated to the Father:[101]

> Thou art the head of the woman; then let the head regulate the rest of the body. Dost not thou see that it is not so much above the rest of the body in situation, as in forethought, directing like a steersman the whole of it? For in the head are the eyes both of the body and of the soul, and hence both the faculty of seeing, and the power of directing. And the rest of the body is appointed for service, but this is set to command.[102]

The original relationship between the husband and wife became stricter because Eve abused her position in the Garden of Eden. She was to be a helper, but instead submitted to the serpent and brought

---

[98] Chrysostom, *On Colossians*, Homily 12, *NPNF*, 13:319.
[99] David C. Ford, *Women and Men in the Early Church: The Vision of John Chrysostom* (South Canaan, PA: St. Tikhon's Monastery Press, 2017), 90.
[100] Maria-Fotin Polidoulis Kapaslis, 126.
[101] Chrysostom, *On St. John*, Homily 39, *NPNF*, 14:137; Valerie Karras. "Male Domination of Woman in the Writings of Saint John Chrysostom," *The Greek Orthodox Theological Review* 36, no. 2 (1991): 134.
[102] Chrysostom, *On II Thessalonians*, Homily 5, *NPNF*, 13:397.

Adam into sin. Eve is warned that henceforth, "your turning shall be to your husband."[103]

Chrysostom provided several rationales for women's submission to men.

> The first being, that Christ is the head of us, and we of the woman; a second, that we are the glory of God, but the woman of us; a third, that we are not of the woman, but she of us; a fourth, that we are not for her, but she for us.[104]

Chrysostom also noted that the male would balk at a woman's attempt to assert authority because of her role in the Fall and this would lead to marital strife.[105]

The wife's obedience to her husband was total but he should not abuse his authority. If done properly, the wife's submission was no burden. However, not all husbands were kind to their wives. Chrysostom disagreed with domestic violence, but wives still had to obey their husbands.[106] Under no circumstance could she divorce him.[107] Rather, he praised the courage and spiritual strength of abused women's souls, because it reflected badly on their abusers.[108]

Chrysostom believed that a woman should always cover her head. A veil was required in worship, and when not in worship, she should show her hair.[109] He contended that women who did not veil themselves were showing a desire to take on men's role.[110]

> This is again another cause. "Not only," so he speaks, "because he has Christ to be his Head, ought he not to cover the head, but because also he rules over the

---

[103] Chrysostom, *On First Corinthians*, Homily 26, *NPNF*, 12:151.
[104] Ibid., 153.
[105] Karras, "Male Domination of Woman in the Writings of Saint John Chrysostom," 135.
[106] Leslie Dossey, "Wife Beating and Manliness in Late Antiquity," *Past and Present*, no. 199 (May 2008): 8.
[107] Chrysostom, *On I Corinthians*, Homily 26. *NPNF* 12:156–57.
[108] Chrysostomus Bauer, *John Chrysostom and His Time*, trans. Sr. M. Gonzaga, 2 vols. (Westminster, MD: The Newman Press, 1959), 2:375–376.
[109] Chrysostom, *On First Corinthians*, Homily 26, *NPNF*, 12:152–53.
[110] Ibid., 152.

woman." For the ruler, when he comes before the king, ought to have the symbol of his rule. As therefore no ruler, without military girdle and cloak, would venture to appear before him that has the diadem: so neither do you without the symbols of your rule, (one of which is not being covered.) pray before God, lest you insult both yourself, and Him that has honored you. And the same thing likewise one may say regarding the woman. For to her also it is a reproach, the not having the symbols of her subjection. "But the woman is the glory of the man." Therefore, the rule of the man is natural.[111]

God had ordained separate spheres for men and women. Men were to participate in government, military, business matters, and other public affairs. Women did not have the skills to participate in this world. They were to raise children and manage the household. By taking on this role, wives alleviated their husband's concerns.[112]

Chrysostom did not believe that women should be priests or instruct men. A priest asserted authority and leadership over a congregation. The male was created first; the female was created for him. Moreover, when a woman was allowed to lead, she led men into sin and now she is subject to them.[113] Women, therefore, did not have the authority to lead men. Eve's sin moved women into the permanent ranks of congregational learners. They also talked too much about frivolous things and were "weak and fickle."[114] When looking for someone to guide the church, "and be entrusted with the care of so many souls, the whole female sex must retire before the magnitude of the task."[115] Chrysostom was critical of women who overstepped their bounds.

> The divine law indeed has excluded women from the ministry, but they endeavor to thrust themselves into it. And since they can affect nothing of themselves, they

---

[111] Ibid., 153.
[112] Stephen Dray, "Women in Church History: An Examination of pre-Reformation Convictions and Practice," *Evangel* 21, no. 1 (Spring 2003): 22.
[113] Chrysostom, *On the Letter of 1 Timothy*, Homily 9, *NPNF*, 13:435–36.
[114] Ibid., 436.
[115] Chrysostom, *On the Priesthood*, *NPNF*, 9:40.

do all through the agency of others. In this way they have become invested with so much power that they can appoint or eject priests at their will. Things in fact are turned upside down, and the proverbial saying may be seen realized—"Those being guided are leading the guides." One would wish that it were men who were giving such guidance, rather than women who have not received a commission to give instruction in church. Why do I say "give instruction?" The blessed Paul did not suffer them even to speak with authority in the church. But I have heard someone say that they have obtained such a large privilege of free speech as even to rebuke the prelates of the churches and censure them more severely than masters do their own domestics.[116]

However, Chrysostom did allow women to serve as deaconesses. There were many deaconesses in Antioch and Constantinople.[117] They were responsible for reprimanding women for inappropriate behavior, caring for sick women, enforcing decorum during services, and anointing other women.[118] He also allowed for the non-ordained position of widow and virgin. He credited widows with great power of prayer[119] and virgins as uplifting the entire community with their angelic presence.[120] He did, however, see widows as troublesome.

> For widows are a class who, both on account of their poverty, their age and natural disposition, indulge in unlimited freedom of speech (so I had best call it); and they make an unseasonable clamor and idle complaints and lamentations about matters for which they ought to be

---

[116] Chrysostom, *On the Priesthood*, 3, *NPNF*, 9:49.
[117] Maria-Fotini Polidoulis Kapsalis, 263.
[118] Chrysostomus Bauer, *John Chrysostom and His Time*, trans. Sr. M. Gonzaga (Westminster, MD: The Newman Press, 1959), 1:155.
[119] Chrysostom, *On St. John*, Homily 70.3, *PG*, 59.
[120] David Carlton Ford, "Misogynist or Advocate? St. John Chrysostom and His Views on Women." PhD Dissertation: Drew University, 1989, 268; Chrysostom, *On the Necessity of Guarding Virginity*, 9, *PG*, 48.

grateful, and bring accusations concerning things which they ought contentedly to accept.[121]

Chrysostom did not object to women's second marriages but believed they were not the best way to honor God. A widow, especially young, should dedicate the remainder of her life to chastity and prayer.[122] Chrysostom also permitted women to prophesy and pray in communal worship.[123]

For Chrysostom, Galatians 3:28 applied to two distinct worlds. After baptism, women attained the Holy Spirit and became children of God but remained subject to men. When a woman attained the heavenly world there were no gender differences in terms of superiority. Chrysostom held that the heavenly world was a new creation entered by baptism[124] where all would be one in Christ.[125]

> There is not heard, "In the sweat of thy face thou shalt eat your bread," nor "thorns and thistles" [Gen. 3:18–19]; no longer, "In sorrow thou shalt bring forth children, and to thy husband shall be thy desire and he shall rule over thee" [Gen. 3:16]. All is peace, joy, gladness, pleasure, goodness, gentleness.[126]

Chrysostom spent several years as an ascetic and it engrained in him a strong belief in the celibate life. He saw nothing "sweeter, more beautiful, more brilliant, than virginity."[127] He believed in virginity for both men and women but spoke more often of the female virginal joys. Virginal women were married to Christ.[128] It was the pinnacle of the life one could lead while on earth.

---

[121] Chrysostom, *On the Priesthood*, 3.16, NPNF, 9:55–56.

[122] Marie-Henry Keane, "Woman in the Theological Anthropology of the Early Fathers," *Journal of Theology for Southern Africa* 62, (March 1988): 8.

[123] Stephen Dray, "Women in Church History: An Examination of pre-Reformation Convictions and Practice," *Evangel* 21, no. 1 (Spring 2003): 22; Valerie Karras, "Male Domination of Woman in the Writings of Saint John Chrysostom," *The Greek Orthodox Theological Review* 36, no. 2 (1991): 138.

[124] Chrysostom, *On Colossians*, Homily 6, NPNF, 13:287.

[125] Chrysostom, *On Galatians*, Homily 3, PG, 61, NPNF, 13:30.

[126] Chrysostom, *On Hebrews*, Homily 6.10, NPNF, 14:397.

[127] Chrysostom, *On Virginity*, 48.

[128] Ibid., 48.

Like many other Church Fathers, Chrysostom considered virginity far superior to marriage.[129]

> But mankind, inferior in its nature to blessed spirits, strains beyond its capacity and, in so far as it can, vies eagerly to equal the angels. How does it do that? Angels neither marry nor are given in marriage; this is true of the virgin. The angels have stood continuously by God and serve him; so does the virgin. Accordingly, Paul has removed all cares from virgins "to promote what is good, what will help you to devote yourselves entirely to God." If they are unable for a time to ascend to heaven as the angels can because their flesh holds them back, even in this world they have much consolation since they receive the Master of the heavens, if they are holy in body and spirit. Do you grasp the value of virginity? That it makes those who spend time on earth live like the angels dwelling in heaven? It does not allow those endowed with bodies to be inferior to the incorporeal powers and spurs all men to rival the angels.[130]

Women who dedicated themselves to chastity did not have to submit to a husband. Those who married were bound by a "chain" to submit to their husbands and their marital duties.[131] If the wife married a cruel or overbearing husband, her life was intolerable.[132] Virgins could avoid the pain of childbirth and the burden of childrearing.[133] Sexual intercourse clouded one's mind with passion and damaged prayer life.[134] The virgin was spared all these things.

No one exemplified the celibate life more than his friend and confidante, Olympias (ca. 368–408). She was a rich widow from Constantinople who was ordained a deaconess and paid for the construction of a convent near the city's main church. She dedicated the remainder of her life to celibacy and leading the convent.

---

[129] Ibid.
[130] Chrysostom, *On Virginity*, 11, *PG*, 48.
[131] Ibid., 48.
[132] Ibid.
[133] Ibid.
[134] Ibid.

A staunch supporter and disciple of Chrysostom, Olympias used her own money to fund his endeavors. Chrysostom believed that her dedication to chastity was so complete that she should no longer be considered a female. He wrote of her, "Don't say woman, but what a man! Because this is a man, despite her physical appearance."[135]

When Chrysostom discussed women, much of his rhetoric was caustic and typical of men in his era. When discussing the teaching ministry, he stated that women were too weak-minded and gullible for such an important task.[136] Women were too talkative in church and prone to gossip.[137] They wore clothes that were fitting only to attract male attention.[138] Women were contemptuous and arrogant, which made them difficult to control when angry. "When women have many pretexts for being contemptuous, there is nothing to hold them back. They are like a flame igniting a piece of wood; they are carried away by an unheard off arrogance. They overturn the order of things, making everything upside down."[139] And of course, women ensnared men with their beauty and drew them into fornication.[140] It is also important to note that much of Chrysostom's most disparaging writings about women were written during his feud with Empress Eudoxia (d. 404) who had exiled him several times for criticizing her imperial excesses and her belief that he accepted Origen's heretical teachings.[141]

Jerome

Jerome was born in 347 to wealthy Christian parents in Stridon, Dalmatia. He moved to Rome when he was twelve years old and received an excellent education in the Latin classics and Christian

---

[135] *Life of Olympias*, cited in Karen Jo Torjesen, *When Women Were Priests: Women's Leadership in the Early Church & the Scandal of their Subordination in the Rise of Christianity* (San Francisco, CA: HarperCollins, 1993), 211.
[136] Chrysostom, *On First Corinthians*, Homily 37, *NPNF*, 12:222.
[137] Chrysostom, *On I Timothy*, Homily 9, *PG*, 62, *NPNF*, 13:435.
[138] Ibid., 422.
[139] Chrysostom, *On Virginity*, 53, *PG*, 48.
[140] Chrysostom, *On the Statues*, Homily 15, *NPNF*, 9:442.
[141] Joseph Early, *A History of Christianity: An Introductory Survey* (Nashville, TN: Broadman and Holman, 2015), 99, 100.

literature. He developed an interest in asceticism and became a hermetic monk living near Chalcis, Syria. His strict ascetic practices damaged his health, so he left the desert and was ordained a priest at Antioch. His commitment to strict asceticism, however, never waned. He briefly relocated to Constantinople (380–81) where he studied under Gregory of Nazianzus (329–390) and in 382 moved to Rome. He became assistant to Damasus (366–384), the bishop of Rome, and was charged with revising the Latin Bible. Known as the Vulgate, Jerome's edition became popular and the Council of Trent (1545–1563) adopted it as the Catholic Church's official Latin version. Jerome moved to Bethlehem around 386 with several aristocratic women whom he taught asceticism and celibacy. He remained in Bethlehem working on the Vulgate, writing commentaries on the Bible, and participating in theological debates until he died in 420.

Jerome wrote some of the most misogynistic material since the Latin poet Juvenal's (ca. 55–60—ca. 127 CE) Satire VI. Like Juvenal, Jerome often used satire in this when discussing women. He quoted Juvenal and other ancient Roman writers such as Cicero (106 BCE–34 BCE) and Horace (65 BCE–8 BCE).[142] He is also remembered for having close female friends whom he mentored in asceticism. Jerome praised these women and even dedicated books to them.

Unlike many of the Church Fathers, Jerome appears to have had sexual experience and the memories of it made it difficult for him to remain celibate.[143] While living in the Syrian desert for three years mortifying his flesh and learning Hebrew, he was tormented by visions of women and dancing girls. "I often found myself amid bevies of girls. My face was pale and my frame chilled with fasting; yet my mind was burning with desire, and the fires of lust kept bubbling up before me when my flesh was as good as dead."[144] He fought these visions and came to the belief that asceticism was the truest proof of devotion.[145]

---

[142] Elizabeth Clark and Herbert Richardson, eds. *Women and Religion: A Feminist Sourcebook of Christian Thought* (San Francisco, CA: HarperCollins, 1977), 54.

[143] Jane Barr, "The Influence of Saint Jerome on Medieval Attitudes to Women," in Janet Martin Soskice, *After Eve: Women, Theology, and the Christian Tradition* (London: Collins Religious Division, 1990), 90.

[144] Jerome, *Letter* 22.7, *NPNF*, 6:22–41.

[145] Elaine Pagels, *Adam, Eve, and the Serpent* (New York: Random House, 1988), 90; David Gilmore, *Misogyny: The Male Malady* (Philadelphia, PA: University of

Jerome believed women, in general, were weak, fickle, and prone to complain. They were seductive and libidinous. They deliberately dressed in ways to entice men. He noted,

> Your very dress, cheap and somber as it is, is an index of your secret feelings. For it has no creases and trails along the ground to make you appear taller than you are. Your vest is purposely ripped asunder to show what is beneath and while hiding what is repulsive, to reveal what is fair. As you walk, the very creaking of your black and shiny shoes attracts the notice of the young men. You wear stays to keep your breasts in place, and a heaving girdle closely confines your chest. Your hair covers either your forehead or your ears. Sometimes too you let your shawl drop so as to lay bare your white shoulders.[146]

According to Jerome, women's temptation was strong. "A woman's love in general is accused of ever being insatiable; put it out, it bursts into flame; give it plenty, it is again in need; it enervates a man's mind, and engrosses all thought except for the passion which it feeds."[147] He asked if someone as great as David capitulated to Bathsheba, what chance did lesser a man have?[148]

Women were also prone to follow heresy.[149] They were the assistant to some of the greatest heresies the church had faced. Jerome believed:

> It was with the help of the harlot Helena that Simon Magus founded his sect ... and Arius intent on leading the world astray began by misleading the Emperor's sister. The resources of Lucilla helped Donatus to defile with his polluting baptism many unhappy persons throughout Africa.[150]

Pennsylvania Press, 2001), 87.
[146] Jerome, *Letter 117*, *NPNF*, 6:218.
[147] Jerome, *Against Jovian*, bk 1.28, *NPNF*, 6:367.
[148] Jerome, *Letter 22*, *NPNF*, 6:26.
[149] Marie Henry Keane, "Woman in the Theological Anthropology of the Early Fathers," *Journal of Theology for Southern Africa* 62, (March 1988): 8.
[150] Jerome, *Letter 133.4*, *NPNF*, 6:275; Soskice, *After Eve*, 99.

For Jerome, women were the principal reason for sin in the world.[151]

Jerome's writings displayed a staunch belief in virginity, celibacy, and a corresponding negative view of marriage.[152] Many of these works appeared in times of controversy. Among the most virulent were written by a monk named Jovian (d. 405). In the late fourth century, Jovian argued that virgins, widows, and married women, even remarried women, were of equal merit in the Christian community. This idea went against all of Jerome's beliefs and he attacked Jovian without relent.

Jerome held that the first couple had intercourse only after they sinned and were cast out of Paradise.[153] "Eve in Paradise was a virgin: it was only after she put on a garment of skins that her married life began."[154] Jerome held that the "garment of skins" was a metaphor for intercourse. Procreation would have occurred in some non-sexual manner. Virginity, therefore, was the Edenic state and thus, superior to marriage and sex and Jovian's beliefs. "Now paradise is your home too. Keep therefore your birthright and say: 'Return unto your rest, O my soul.'"[155] Jerome was the only Church Father who maintained that virginity was the natural state for both men and women.[156]

Eve was the reason for the Fall.[157] Adam was the first in creation and intellectually superior to Eve. Therefore, the devil sought out Eve.

> Adam was first made, then the woman out of his rib; and that the Devil could not seduce Adam, but did seduce Eve; and that after displeasing God she was immediately subjected to the man, and began to turn to her husband;

---

[151] David D. Gilmore, *Misogyny: The Male Malady* (Philadelphia, PA: University of Pennsylvania Press, 2001), 87.
[152] Jane Barr, "The Influence of Saint Jerome on Medieval Attitudes to Women," in Soskice, *After Eve*, 89.
[153] Jerome, *Against Jovian*, bk. 1.16, *NPNF*, 6:359.
[154] Jerome, *Letter 22, NPNF*, 6:29.
[155] Ibid.
[156] Castelli, "Virginity and Its Meaning for Woman's Sexuality in Early Christianity," 75.
[157] Jerome, *Letter 22, NPNF*, 6:30.

and he points out that she who was once tied with the bonds of marriage and was reduced to the condition of Eve, might blot out the old transgression by the procreation of children: provided, however, that she bring up the children themselves in the faith and love of Christ, and in sanctification and chastity; for we must not adopt the faulty reading of the Latin texts, *sobrietas*, but *castitas*, that is, σωφροσύνη.[158]

Jerome was willing to interpret scripture in a manner that confirmed what he already believed. He added a second step to Paul's 1 Timothy 2:15 statement that "women will be saved through childbearing." Childbearing did not save women alone but mothers must also teach their children chastity so they could remain in the Edenic state of virginity.

None of the Church Fathers considered marriage a sin, but Jerome believed that as marriage was not a part of God's original creation it could not be a part of the image of God.[159] The only justification that Jerome gave for a man entering marriage was to prevent fornication. He depicted it as choosing an inferior food to avoid eating "cow dung."[160] He sarcastically claimed to approve of marriage just because it provided him with more virgins. When asked if he disparaged marriage, he said,

> Someone may say, Do you dare detract from wedlock, which is a state blessed by God? I do not detract from wedlock when I set virginity before it. No one compares a bad thing with a good. Wedded women may congratulate themselves that they come next to virgins. Be fruitful, God says, and multiply, and replenish the earth (Genesis 1:28). He who desires to replenish the earth may increase and multiply if he will. But the train to which you belong is not on earth, but in heaven. The command to increase and multiply first finds fulfillment after the expulsion from paradise, after the nakedness and the fig-leaves which

---

[158] Jerome, *Against Jovian*, bk. 1.27, *NPNF*, 6:366.
[159] Jerome, *Against Jovian*, bk. 1.16, *NPNF*, 6:359.
[160] Ibid., 350.

speak of sexual passion. Let them marry and be given in marriage who eat their bread in the sweat of their brow; whose land brings forth to them thorns and thistles, Genesis 3:18–19 and whose crops are choked with briars. My seed produces fruit a hundredfold. All men cannot receive God's saying, but they to whom it is given.[161]

Jerome also ridiculed marital and family life. When he attempted to convince young women to choose chastity, he constantly told them of the travails of having a difficult husband, the demands of children, and the unrewarding life of taking care of the home. In his infamous *Letter to Eustochium*, he writes:

> Then come the prattling of infants, the noisy household, children watching for her word and waiting for her kiss, the reckoning up of expenses, the preparation to meet the outlay. On one side you will see a company of cooks, girded for the onslaught and attacking the meat. There you may hear the hum of a multitude of weavers. Meanwhile a message is delivered that the husband and his friends have arrived. The wife, like a swallow, flies all over the house. "She has to see to everything. Is the sofa smooth? Is the pavement swept? Are the flowers in the cups? Is dinner ready?" Tell me, pray, where amid all this is there room for the thought of God? Are these happy homes? Where there is the beating of drums, the noise and clatter of pipe and lute, the clanging of cymbals, can any fear of God be found? The parasite is snubbed and feels proud of the honor.[162]

Jerome did not explicitly forbid a widow to remarry, but he warned against it. He insisted that a widow would remarry because she craved intercourse, and compared her to a dog returning to its vomit.[163] A widow did not lose her salvation for marrying again

---

[161] Jerome, *Letter 22*, NPNF, 6:29.
[162] Jerome, *On the Perpetual Virginity of Mary: Against Helvidius*, 22, NPNF, 6:345.
[163] Jerome, *Against Jovian*, bk. 1.16, NPNF, 6:359.

but her status was lowered like those of the unclean animals on the Ark.[164]

He did not see men benefiting from marriage either. When he read 1 Corinthians 11, "better for a man to not touch a woman," in light of Proverbs 6, 7, and 9 that warned men of women who "touch," he concluded that a man should never touch a woman. If touching was bad, then marital intercourse was even worse.[165] In *Against Jovian* book 1 chapter 47, he complained that wives were obsessed with costly things and kept their husbands from studying. The husband was burdened with the care of a sick wife and would not have any time to spend with his friends. Wives were jealous of other women and insecure about their appearance. Jerome believed that a homely wife would be more faithful than a pretty one. If a husband was just looking for someone to manage his house it was better to own a good and faithful slave.

Jerome also rejected Jovian's assumption that the human race would die out if everyone became celibate. Jerome assured him that virginity is a difficult task that not all women wanted. His answer to Jovian was:

> You are afraid that if the desire for virginity were general there would be no prostitutes, no adulteresses, no wailing infants in town or country. Every day the blood of adulterers is shed, adulterers are condemned, and lust is raging and rampant in the very presence of the laws and the symbols of authority and the courts of justice.[166]

As harshly as Jerome denigrated marriage, he praised virginity. If a woman chose marriage, she had chosen to live in the post-Edenic state where life was difficult. She was only preparing herself for earthly life. If she chose virginity, she was already living the heavenly life.

---

[164] Jerome, *Letter 123.9*, *NPNF*, 6:233.
[165] Jerome, *Against Jovian*, bk. 1.7, *NPNF*, 6:350; Elizabeth Clark, "Ideology, History, and the Construction of 'Woman' in Late Ancient Christianity," *Journal of Early Christian Studies* 2, (1994): 177.
[166] Jerome, *Against Jovian*, bk. 1.36, *NPNF*, 6:373.

> In the resurrection of the dead they will neither marry nor be given in marriage, but will be like the angels. What others will hereafter be in heaven, that virgins begin to be on earth. If likeness to the angels is promised us (and there is no difference of sex among the angels), we shall either be of no sex as are the angels, or at all events which is clearly proved, though we rise from the dead in our own sex, we shall not perform the functions of sex.[167]

Jerome believed virgins had overcome their female nature to the point that they were equal with men.[168] "Let paleness and squalor be henceforth your jewels. Do not pamper your youthful limbs with a bed of down or kindle your young blood with hot baths."[169] He believed that husbands and wives could practice marital celibacy and the wife be rewarded. By neglecting the flesh, the wife's soul became male. In this way, "You have with you one who was once your partner in the flesh, but is now your partner in the spirit, once your wife but now your sister, once a woman but now a man, once an inferior but now an equal."[170]

Jerome's contempt for women was evident in his translation and interpretation of the Old and New Testaments. He freely translated scripture to overstate women's subjugation, inferior intellect, and odious nature. These writings were popular and became a staple in the Middle Ages and did much to promote the era's significant misogyny.[171]

Jerome either misinterpreted or deliberately mistranslated Genesis 39. He translated the story of Joseph and Potiphar's wife to vilify women. The Hebrew translation said that after Potiphar's wife told Joseph to lie with her, "He refused." Jerome translated the passage to "by no means agreeing to this wicked deed." According to Barr, Jerome believed scripture did not sufficiently emphasize a woman's wickedness, so he had to.[172]

---

[167] Ibid., 373.
[168] Mary T. Malone, *Women and Christianity: The First Thousand Years*, (Maryknoll, NY: Orbis Books, 2000), 1: 161.
[169] Jerome, *Letter 79*, 7–9, *NPNF*, 6: 166.
[170] Ibid., 153.
[171] Mary T. Malone, *Women and Christianity*, 166.
[172] Ibid., 15–16.

Jerome maintained that women's sexual insatiability was a distraction to men.[173] He accused wives of nagging, talking too much, and being argumentative. It was better to live in the desert or on the roof than with such a wife (Proverbs 21:9, 25:24). He then asked his male readers, why take a chance on finding a good wife when you are more likely to find one who will make your life miserable? If you want peace and quiet, don't get married.[174]

Jerome manipulated numbers to argue for celibacy. In the Parable of the Sower (Matthew 13:1–23, Mark 4:1–20, and Luke 8:4–15), he determined that the 100-fold represented virginity, the 60-fold represented widowhood, 30-fold represented single marriage. Second marriages were among the thorns.[175] He also ascertained that there was something wrong with the number two. "We are meant to understand that there was something not good in the number two, separating us as it did from unity, and prefiguring the marriage-tie. Just as in the account of Noah's ark, all the animals that entered by twos were unclean, but those of which an uneven number was taken were clean."[176]

Barr noted several instances in which Jerome interpreted scripture in a manner that allowed him to make his point.[177] He maintained that since Christ only went to one marriage a person should only be married once.[178] John was a virgin so his gospel was better.[179] Moses unlatched his sandal because a latched sandal signified marriage.[180]

Jerome was, predictably, a strong believer in Mary's perpetual virginity.[181] Unlike Eve who surrendered her virginity and brought death, Mary retained her virginity and brought life.[182] She was the

---

[173] Jerome, *Against Jovian*, bk. 1.28, *NPNF*, 6:367.
[174] Ibid.
[175] Ibid., 1.3, *NPNF*, 6:347.
[176] Jerome, *Letter 48*, *NPNF*, 6:77.
[177] Barr, "The Vulgate Genesis and Jerome's Attitudes to Women," 7.
[178] Jerome, *Against Jovian*, bk. 1:40, *NPNF*, 6:379.
[179] Ibid., 65–66.
[180] Ibid., 361.
[181] Elizabeth Clark and Herbert Richardson, eds. *Women and Religion: A Feminist l Sourcebook of Women in Christian Thought* (San Francisco, CA: HarperCollins, 1977), 42.
[182] Jerome, *Letter 22.21*, *NPNF*, 6:30.

embodiment of virginity. Jerome dedicated much of his *Against Helvidius* to Mary. Helvidius believed that after giving birth to Jesus that she and Joseph had sexual relations just like other married couples. He noted that scripture mentioned that Jesus had brothers and sisters. Jerome countered that Helvidius should not interpret those passages so literally.[183] Jerome turned Jesus' brothers and sisters into relatives.[184]

Jerome's thoughts on women were deplorable, but he had a circle of wealthy female patrons that he met while in Rome. He taught them Hebrew and biblical exegesis and encouraged them in their celibacy. Jerome insisted they dress in rags, rarely bathe, and mortify their flesh. Jerome considered them living saints. One of the women, Blæsilla (d. ca. 384), starved herself to death.[185] Many blamed Jerome for the death of Blaesilla, and there were rumors that he might have been having sexual relations with his female disciples. Soon after, Jerome left Rome for Bethlehem, and they followed him. These wealthy ascetics paid the passage and for the construction of a monastery and convent in Bethlehem.[186]

Jerome was closest to Paula (347–404), Blaesilla's mother. She was a member of one of Rome's richest and most influential senatorial families. At the age of 32, Paula was left a widow with five children. She remained close to her family but accepted a strict ascetic lifestyle. She took care of the virgins in Bethlehem, studied the scriptures, fasted, and mourned. Jerome noted that she "was squalid with dirt; her eyes were dim with weeping… The Psalms were her only songs; the gospel her whole speech; continence her own indulgence; fasting the staple of her life."[187] He praised Paula when she was leaving for Bethlehem because she did not even look back to the shore where she had left her son and daughter. "She knew herself no more as a mother, that she might approve herself a handmaid of Christ."[188] Paula was Jerome's platonic soulmate and

---

[183] Katherine M. Rogers, *The Troublesome Helpmate: A History of Misogyny in Literature* (Seattle, WA: University of Washington Press, 1966), 19.
[184] Jerome, *On the Perpetual Virginity of Mary: Against Helvidius*, 19, NPNF, 6:343.
[185] Jerome, *Letter 39.6*, NPNF, 6:53; Soskice, *After Eve*, 91.
[186] Jane Barr in Soskice, *After Eve*, 91.
[187] Jerome, *Letter 45.3*, NPNF, 6:59.
[188] Ibid., 197.

his ideal virtuous woman. Jerome honored Paula, and her daughter, Eustochium, as follows:

> There are people, O Paula and Eustochium, who take offense at seeing your names at the beginning of my works. These people do not know that Olda prophesied when the men were mute; that, while Barak trembled, Deborah saved Israel; that Judith and Esther delivered from supreme peril the children of God. I pass over in silence Anna and Elizabeth and the other holy women of the Gospel, but humble stars when compared with the luminary, Mary. Shall I speak now of the illustrious women among the heathen? ... Was it not to women that our Lord appeared after His resurrection? Yes, and the men could then blush for not having sought what women had found.[189]

Augustine

Born in North Africa to a Christian mother and pagan father, Augustine was the most influential theologian of the late Patristic and early medieval eras. His mother, Monica (332–387), was a devout Christian. To her son, Monica was the perfect woman. She constantly prayed for his and his father's conversion to Christianity. His father, Patricius (fl. 354) accepted baptism on his deathbed. Unlike many theologians of his era, Augustine wrote a detailed autobiography in his *Confessions*, which also traced his theological development. Augustine had been trained as a philosopher. He initially gravitated to Manicheanism, which taught a radical dualism between the good and the bad, the spiritual and the material. While in Milan in 387, Augustine was captivated by Bishop Ambrose's (340–397) teachings. He then abandoned Manicheanism for Christianity. He became the bishop of Hippo in 395, a position that he held until his death. Augustine's voluminous theological writings, many of them controversial, concerned free will, predestination, original sin, the Trinity, and sacramental integrity. Augustine's writings and thoughts still have a central role in Catholic and Protestant theology.

---

[189] Jerome, *Preface to Commentary on Zephaniah, PL*, 25:1337ff.

Augustine's thoughts on women must be interpreted in light of his relationship with his mother and his satisfying sex life. He had a close relationship with his mother. She constantly prayed for his soul and warned him not to take part in extramarital sexual intercourse. After his conversion, she became the only woman in his life and his ideal of what all women should be. Ruether[190] and Dodds[191] are two scholars who see Augustine's relationship with his mother as unhealthy.

As a young man, Augustine had a fifteen-year relationship with a woman who lived with him and bore his son. He was loyal to her but claimed that his love for her was based on lust. Monica arranged a more suitable marriage for her son in the hope that it would advance his career. With great sadness, he ended his relationship with his son's mother but kept their child. Since his fiancée was not of legal age to marry, he started another relationship.

> But I, unhappy one, who could not imitate a woman, impatient of delay, since it was not until two years' time I was to obtain her I sought—being not so much a lover of marriage as a slave to lust—procured another (not a wife, though), that so by the bondage of a lasting habit the disease of my soul might be nursed up.[192]

Augustine did not marry his fiancée but continued to satisfy his sexual desires. He began to listen to Ambrose's sermons, read biblical texts, and considered accepting Christianity. He realized, however, that his sexual habits were impeding his conversion. In a famous passage, he summed up his frustration, "Grant me chastity and continency, but not yet."[193] After his conversion, he decided to become a celibate monk. Memories of his earlier relationships, however, continued to haunt him.

---

[190] Rosemary Radford Ruether, "Misogynism and Virginal Feminism in the Fathers of the Church," in *Women and Sexism: Images of Woman in the Jewish and Christian Traditions* (New York, NY: Simon and Schuster, 1974), 12.
[191] E.R. Dodds, "Augustine's Confessions: A Study of Spiritual Maladjustment," *The Hibbert Journal* 26, (1927): 466.
[192] Augustine, *Confessions*, 6, *NPNF*, 1:100.
[193] Ibid., 124.

> But there still exist in my memory—of which I have spoken much—the images of such things as my habits had fixed there; and these rush into my thoughts, though strengthless, when I am awake; but in sleep they do so not only so as to give pleasure, but even to obtain consent, and what very nearly resembles reality. Yea, to such an extent prevails the illusion of the image, both in my soul and in my flesh, that the false persuade me, when sleeping, unto that which the true are not able when waking.[194]

Based on his Platonism and Paul's writings, Augustine maintained there was one creation account of humanity that occurred in two stages. Genesis 1:26–27 states, "let us make mankind in our image," so God alone did not create Adam; the Trinity did.[195] The nature of humanity, therefore, is Trinitarian. In this first stage, the designation "Adam" encompassed both man and woman.[196] The "Adam" had a spiritual form, a rational mind, an asexual soul, but no physical body. They were equal in all ways and created in the image of God. They received their corporal bodies in the second stage, Genesis 2:7, 21—Adam from the dust of the earth and Eve from Adam's side.[197] The initial unity of the first human was split.[198] The female came from Adam's rib. Augustine platonically discerned that it made her more closely tied to passion and, thus, weaker. She represented corporal nature and had a lower mind, "*Scientia*," tied to sense perception.[199] Thus, women were more passionate, petty, and argumentative.[200] The male retained all the masculine attributes and a higher mind, "*Sapientia*," that was transcendent and

---

[194] Augustine, *Confessions*, 10.30.2, *NPNF*, 1:153.
[195] Augustine, *On the Trinity*, 12.6.6, *NPNF*, 3:157.
[196] Alan D. Fitzgerald, *Augustine: Through the Ages* (Grand Rapids, MI: Eerdmans Publishing, 1999), 6.
[197] John O'Meara, "Saint Augustine's Understanding of the Creation and Fall," *The Maynooth Review* 10, (May 1984): 55.
[198] Augustine, *On the Trinity*, 12.3.3, *NPNF*, 3:156.
[199] A. Kent Hieatt, "Eve as Reason in a Tradition of Allegorical Interpretation of the Fall," *Journal of the Warburg and Courtland Institutes* 43, (1980): 221.
[200] Thomas Bokenkotter, *A Concise History of the Catholic Church* (New York, NY: Doubleday, 2005), 465–466.

pure. He could observe invisible truths.[201] Because of the order of creation, her designation was as a "helper mate." Adam, the male, was supposed to rule Eve, the female.[202] In this manner, the woman was subordinate to the man from the moment of their corporal creation.[203] There would be no subordination in the life to come or in the resurrection. Because women were created before the Fall and were considered good, they would still be distinguished by their sex in the resurrection.[204]

Augustine's understanding of the image of God was based on his interpretation of the second creation account and 1 Corinthians 11:7. The image of God did not relate to the physical body but of man's nature grounded in physical sexuality that engendered intellect and reason. These higher male qualities of reason were meant to rule the lower qualities, represented by the female.[205] Action without reason was not a part of the image of God. The woman had a rational, asexual soul that was in the image of God,[206] but she was still inferior to the man based on her physical sexuality and assigned role as his helpmate. Augustine maintained that the woman could not be in the full image of God until she married.

> But we must notice how that which the apostle says, that not the woman but the man is the image of God, is not contrary to that which is written in Genesis, 'God created man: in the image of God created him; male and female created He them.' ... For this text says that human nature itself, which is complete [only] in both sexes, was made in the image of God; and it does not separate the woman from the image of God which it signifies ... The woman together with her own husband is the image of God, so that the whole substance may be one image; but when

---

[201] Hieatt, "Eve as Reason in a Tradition of Allegorical Interpretation of the Fall," 223.
[202] Rosemary Radford Ruether, *Women and Redemption: A Theological History* (Minneapolis, MN: Fortress Press, 1998), 72.
[203] Jane Dempsey Douglass, *Women, Freedom, and Calvin* (Philadelphia, PA: The Westminster Press, 1985), 74; Malone, *Women and Christianity: The First Thousand Years*, 1:167.
[204] Douglass, *Women, Freedom, and Calvin*, 74–75.
[205] Ruether, *Women and Redemption*, 73.
[206] Douglass, *Women, Freedom, and Calvin*, 74.

she is referred to separately in her quality of helpmate, which regards the woman herself alone, then she is not the image of God; but as regards the man alone, he is the image of God as fully and completely as when the woman too is joined with him.[207]

Women wore a veil because they were not the reflection of God but of man.[208] By covering their heads, women covered the part of the body that because of its *Scientia*, must submit to the man's wisdom.[209]

Eve's lower reasoning also explained her role in original sin.[210] The serpent knew he could not tempt the more rational male, so he approached the less rational female. By attacking the woman, the serpent hoped she would do what he could not: convince Adam.[211] After capitulating to the serpent, she convinced Adam to sin. Because of her lower reason, Eve's sin was not as bad as Adam's. He had a transcendent mind and received the command not to eat of the tree from God but disobeyed.[212] The lower aspects of reason were usurped by the higher. All three characters were to blame. For Augustine, the serpent represented suggestion and persuasion, Eve the desire for pleasure, and Adam rational consent.[213] Adam was the one who should have known better.[214]

Augustine then explained that Adam knew that Eve had sinned. He knew the consequences. He could not bear to be separated from her, so he chose to sin too.

---

[207] Augustine, *On the Trinity*, 12.7.10, NPNF, 3:158–159.
[208] Fitzgerald, *Augustine: Through the Ages*, 888.
[209] Augustine, *Against the Manichees* 2.26.40, cited in Augustine, *Two Books on Genesis against the Manichees and On the Literal Interpretation of Genesis: An Unfinished Book* (Washington, D.C.: Catholic University of America, 2001), 136–37.
[210] Ruether, *Women and Redemption*, 73.
[211] Augustine, *City of God*, 12.7.12, NPNF, 2:272.
[212] Hieatt, 223.
[213] Pierre J. Payer, *The Fall, Original Sin, and Concupiscence* (Toronto: University of Toronto Press, 1993), 43.
[214] Hieatt, "Eve as Reason in a Tradition of Allegorical Interpretation of the Fall," 221.

> So we cannot believe that Adam was deceived, and supposed the devil's word to be truth, and therefore transgressed God's law, but that he by the drawings of kindred yielded to the woman, the husband to the wife, the one human being to the only other human being. For not without significance did the apostle say, and Adam was not deceived, but the woman being deceived was in the transgression; 1 Timothy 2:14 but he speaks thus, because the woman accepted as true what the serpent told her, but the man could not bear to be severed from his only companion, even though this involved a partnership in sin. He was not on this account less culpable, but sinned with his eyes open.[215]

The consequences of the Fall were serious. Augustine held that not only would Adam have to toil the land, but his sin also brought death to himself and his descendants. The couple's free will became the inability not to sin.[216] Their moral freedom was gone. Eve's punishment condemned her to pain in birth and to be under the authority of her husband. Augustine saw Adam as the representative of all humanity with federal headship. Through Adam's federal headship, free will was lost and all humans were born with original sin.

Augustine believed Adam and Eve would have had sex even if the Fall had not occurred. Why else would God have told them "to be fruitful and multiply?"[217] If they had not sinned, their sexual relationship would be without desire. Lust would not have aroused the sexual organs.[218] Sex would have occurred by will and reason. The sexual organs would have activated in the same way as other parts of the body.[219] Intercourse would be like a handshake. Marriage and sexual intercourse, therefore, were not God's afterthought and not a

---

[215] Augustine, *The City of God*, 14.11.2, NPNF 2:272.
[216] Pagels, *Adam, Eve, and the Serpent*, xxvi.
[217] Augustine, *Two Books on Genesis Against the Manichees*, 1.19.3, cited in Augustine, *Two Books on Genesis against the Manicheans and On the Literal Interpretation of Genesis: An Unfinished Book* (Washington, D.C.: Catholic University of America Press, 2001), 77.
[218] Augustine, *City of God*, 14, NPNF, 2:276.
[219] Ibid., 281–82.

result of the Fall. Moreover, if sex had not been a part of the original plan, God would not have created the woman. God would have created another man instead.[220] "A male helper would be better, and the same could be said of the comfort of another's presence if perhaps weary of solitude. How much more agreeably could two male friends, rather than a man and woman, enjoy companionship and conversation in a life shared together."[221] Sexual relations existed for one reason: procreation.[222]

No sooner had the first couple sinned than their carnal desires took over. For this reason, Augustine held that they covered themselves with fig leaves.[223] They were ashamed. God then banished them from Eden.

Through the uncontrolled passion of Adam and Eve, humanity inherited original sin. All humans born by the combination of passion and sexual intercourse were Adam's offspring.[224] Augustine noted that no one could overcome this passion.

> And this lust not only takes possession of the whole body and outward members, but also makes itself felt within, and moves the whole man with a passion in which mental emotion is mingled with bodily appetite, so that the pleasure which results is the greatest of all bodily pleasures. So possessing indeed is this pleasure, that at the moment of time in which it is consummated, all mental activity is suspended.[225]

No sexual act took place without lust. Even married couples gave in to lust whenever they had sex.[226] Every child born through

---

[220] Ruether, *Women and Redemption*, 76.
[221] Augustine, *The Literal Interpretation of Genesis*, 9.5.6, cited in *Ancient Christian Commentary on Scripture, Genesis 1–11*, eds. Andrew Louth and Thomas C. Oden (Downers Grove, IL: InterVarsity Press, 2001), 1:68.
[222] Ruether, ed., *Religion and Sexism*, 156.
[223] Augustine, *City of God*, 13, *NPNF*, 2:251.
[224] Michael Dauphinais, Barry David, and Matthew Levering, eds., *Aquinas the Augustinian* (Washington D.C.: Catholic University Press of America, 2007), 151.
[225] Augustine, *City of God*, 14, *NPNF*, 2:275.
[226] Dauphinais, David, and Levering, eds., *Aquinas the Augustinian*, 151.

intercourse was born of sin and in need of redemption.²²⁷ The lust that led to sexual intercourse became the basis for original sin which was passed down from the first man. Baptism was the only escape. Because of infant mortality rates in Augustine's era, infant baptisms became customary practice.²²⁸

Original sin had an important Christological aspect.²²⁹ Eve's sin brought death into the world, but she made amends through childbirth. For sinless Christ to enter the world, he had to be conceived without sexual intercourse. "He only was born without sin whom a virgin conceived without the embrace of a husband, not by the concupiscence of the flesh, but by chaste submission of her mind. She alone was able to give birth to the One who should heal our wound, who brought forth the germ of a pure offspring without the wound of sin."²³⁰ Eve's sin was born in curiosity and weakness. Mary rejected sensuality and in doing so remained a virgin and provided a way for Christ to be born without original sin. Augustine noted that women participated in humanity's redemption.

> Women might have despaired of themselves, as mindful of their first sin, because by a woman was the first man deceived, and would have thought that they had no hope in Christ … The poison to deceive man was presented to him by a woman, through woman let salvation for man's recovery be presented; so let the woman make amends for the sin by which she deceived the man, by giving birth to Christ.²³¹

---

[227] Michael Jordan, *The Historical Mary: Revealing the Pagan Identity of the Virgin Mother* (Berkeley, CA: Seastone, 2004), 201.
[228] Fitzgerald, *Augustine: Through the Ages*, 608.
[229] Ibid., 607.
[230] Augustine, *On the Merits and Forgiveness of Sin*, ch. 57, Orthodox Church Fathers, ed. C.J.S. Hayward, last accessed 1 May 2021, https://orthodoxchurchfathers.com/fathers/npnf105/npnf1010.htm#P645_429414.
[231] Augustine, *Sermons on Selected Lessons of the New Testament*, 1.3, NPNF, 6:245.

Like Jerome, Augustine believed that Mary remained a virgin. He disagreed with Jovian's assertion[232] that she had sexual relations with Joseph after Christ's birth. Augustine not only praised her for remaining chaste but also for being able to control her sexual desire. Mary's body and soul were in balance and undivided.[233] Because of Mary's unwavering dedication to celibacy, Augustine made her the ideal woman. It was, however, a model that no woman could fully emulate.[234]

Since Augustine held this concept of original sin and praise of the Virgin Mary, it should come as no surprise that he was a strong advocate of celibacy. "The chastity of celibacy is superior to the chastity of marriage."[235] He did not condemn marriage, but it was not as good as celibacy.[236] He maintained that celibacy was the closest a person could live in this world to the spiritual world to come.[237] Virginity also allowed a woman to escape being subordinate to a man.[238] Augustine held that if a virgin was raped, she still maintained her virginity.[239] Purity was a virtue of the soul. Virginity was more a state of mind than a physical condition.[240]

Though a distant second to celibacy, Augustine saw the benefits of marriage:

> Wherefore I admonish both men and women who follow after perpetual continence and holy virginity, that they so set their own good before marriage, as that they judge not marriage an evil: and that they understand that it was in no way of deceit, but of plain truth that it was said by the Apostle, whoever gives in marriage does well; and whoever gives not in marriage, does better; and, if

---

[232] Jovian was excommunicated for his teachings against asceticism at a synod convened in Rome under Bishop Siricius in 390. He was also condemned by a synod held in Milan by St. Ambrose in 393.
[233] Malone, *Women and Christianity: The First Thousand Years*, 1:162.
[234] Michael Jordan, *The Historical Mary*, 200.
[235] Augustine, *The Excellence of Marriage*, 23.28.
[236] Clark and Richardson, eds., *Women and Religion*, 71.
[237] Douglass, *Women, Freedom, and Calvin*, 75.
[238] Augustine, *On Holy Virginity*, 2.2, *NPNF*, 3:424.
[239] Augustine, *City of God*, 1.25, *NPNF*, 2:17.
[240] Ibid., 1.18, *NPNF*, 2:12–13.

you shall have taken a wife, you have not sinned; and, if a virgin shall have been married, she sins not; and a little after, but she will be more blessed, if she shall have continued so, according to my judgment ... Whoever therefore shall be willing to abide without marriage, let them not flee from marriage as a pitfall of sin; but let them surmount it as a hill of the lesser good, in order that they may rest in the mountain of the greater, continence.[241]

He maintained that there are three reasons for marriage: procreation, the satisfaction of sexual needs, and permanence. In *Against the Manicheans*, he attacked his former religion's strictures against procreation. In its place, he argued for the idea of procreative sex within marriage. The patriarchs who were in polygamous marriages were held to this standard. They only had sex to increase the Hebrew population.[242] "A good Christian is found in one and the same woman to love the creature of God whom he desires to be transformed and renewed, but to hate in her the corruptible and mortal conjugal connection, sexual intercourse and all that pertains to her as a wife."[243] Moreover, original sin still passed to the infant.

In addition, marriage offered a sexual release outlet for sexual desire. The wife should be passive and submissive while performing the act. Even while releasing sexual tension, the potential for pregnancy must not be eliminated.[244] Neither member should deny the other conjugality.

Finally, marriage was a source of unity and permanence.[245]

> And as the twain is one flesh in the case of male and female, so in the mind one nature embraces our intellect and action, or our counsel and performance, or our reason and rational appetite, or whatever other more significant terms there may be by which to express them; so that, as

---

[241] Augustine, *On Holy Virginity*, 18, *NPNF*, 3:422.
[242] Augustine, *On Marriage and Concupiscence*, 1.9, *NPNF*, 5, New Advent, rev., ed. Kevin Knight, last accessed 1 May 2021, http://www.newadvent.org/fathers/15071.htm.
[243] Augustine, *Sermon on the Mount*, 15.41, *NPNF*, 6:18.
[244] DeConick, *Holy Misogyny*, 127.
[245] Ruether, ed., *Religion and Sexism*, 167.

it was said of the former, "And they two shall be in one flesh," it may be said of these, they two are in one mind.[246]

The reunification of the mind allowed woman to be fully in the image of God.

Augustine did not allow for divorce for any reason; adultery was grounds for separation.[247] Even if the wife was infertile, the husband must remain with her. He often praised his mother for enduring beatings from his father. Monica admonished other abused wives to endure and not to provoke their husbands.[248] Widows should not remarry, but instead dedicate themselves to the service of God.[249]

Augustine believed in the submission of wives. The natural hierarchal order deems that man submitted to God and the woman submitted to the man. "For the man is the head of the woman in perfect order when Christ who is the Wisdom of God is the head of the man."[250] Moreover, "nor can it be doubted that it is more consonant with the order of nature that men should bear rule over women than women over men. It is with this principle in view that the apostle says, 'The head of the woman is the man;' and, 'Wives, submit yourselves to your own husbands.'"[251] The woman is the man's helper and she was created for him. He rules and she obeys. Together they are to raise spiritual children.[252] Like Jerome, Augustine held that Galatians 3:28 made all people equal in faith but it

---

[246] Augustine, *On the Trinity*, 12, NPNF, 3:156.
[247] Augustine, *The Excellence of Marriage*, 7.7, NPNF, 3:402.
[248] Augustine, *Confessions*, 9.9, NPNF, 1:136.
[249] Augustine, *The Excellence of Widowhood*, 6, NPNF, 3:443.
[250] Augustine, *Against The Manichaeans*, 2.12.16, cited in Augustine, *Two Books on Genesis against the Manichees and On the Literal Interpretation of Genesis: An Unfinished Book* (Washington, D.C.: Catholic University of America, 2001), 113.
[251] Augustine, *On Marriage and Concupiscence*, 1.9.10, in "Why It Was Sometimes Permitted That a Man Should Have Several Wives, Yet No Woman Was Ever Allowed to Have More Than One Husband. Nature," BibleHub, last accessed 1 May 2021, https://biblehub.com/library/augustine/anti-pelagian_writings/chapter_10_ix_why_it_was.htm.
[252] Augustine, *Two Books On Genesis Against The Manichaeans. 2.11.15*, cited in Augustine, *Two Books on Genesis against the Manichees and On the Literal Interpretation of Genesis: An Unfinished Book* (Washington, D.C.: Catholic University of America, 2001), 111.

would take place in heaven and in the world to come. Nothing has changed in our current world. "The orders of this life they persist. So we walk this path in a way that the name and doctrines of God will not be blasphemed."[253]

Augustine believed men were superior to women and worked better together. He refused to entertain the thought that women could be equal companions to men. Augustine blamed women for his sexual frustration. All women were like Eve. Men must be constantly on guard.[254] Women's beauty was so great that it captivated the Genesis 6 Sons of God who gave into their desires and procreated with them.[255] He found it even more difficult for a celibate man to be around women. Even a touch caused his mind to move to carnal thoughts. "How vile, how detestable, how shameful, how dreadful" was "the embrace of a woman." There is "nothing which brings the manly mind down from heights more than a woman's caresses and the joining of bodies without which one cannot have a wife."[256] Marriage could serve more than one good, but the reason for marriage was procreation.

Counsels, Synods, and Books of Church Order

As Christianity became the official religion of the Roman Empire, Christian leaders began to gather in synods and councils to determine doctrine. They concerned themselves with the preservation and promotion of church order and practices of what they determined had been handed down to them by the Apostles.

Written by Hippolytus (170–235)[257] around 215, the *Apostolic Tradition* was a document that attempted to regulate liturgy and develop a hierarchal church organization.[258] The *Apostolic Tradition* identified the church offices that required ordination such as

---

[253] Augustine, *Epistle to the Galatians*, 3.28–29.
[254] Augustine, Sermon 242. Augustine did not believe the sons of God were angels, but men who had fallen into concupiscence.
[255] Augustine, *City of God*, 15, *NPNF*, 2:303; Bitel and Lifshitz, eds., *Gender and Christianity in Medieval Europe*, 30.
[256] Thomas F. Gilligan, ed., *The Soliloquies of Saint Augustine* (New York, NY: Cosmopolitan Science & Art Service Co., 1943), 376.
[257] Hippolytus allowed himself to be set up as rival bishop in Rome to Bishop Zephyrinus whom he accused of modalism.
[258] Madigan and Osiek, *Ordained Women*, 153–54.

a bishop, priest, or deacon. Widows and virgins were appointed but not ordained, so they could not conduct the liturgy. Hippolytus appeared to have some apprehensions about recent widows.

> When a widow is appointed, she shall not be ordained but she shall be appointed by the name. If her husband has been long dead, she may be appointed [without delay]. But if her husband has died recently, she shall not be trusted; even if she is aged she must be tested by time, for often the passions grow old in those who yield to them. The widow shall be appointed by the word alone, and [so] she shall be associated with the other widows; hands shall not be laid upon her because she does not offer the oblation nor has she a sacred ministry. Ordination is for the clergy on account of their ministry, but the widow is appointed for prayer, and prayer is the duty of all.[259]

Though the document claims to be written by the Apostles at the Jerusalem Conference in Act 15, the *Didascalia Apostolorum* was a third-century (ca. 225) pastoral treatise written in northern Syria. The *Didascalia Apostolorum* had a great deal to say about the roles of women in church leadership. The deaconess was given a high place of honor, ordained, and stood in the Holy Spirit's place in the church hierarchy. "Let [the bishop] be honored by you as God, for the bishop sits for you in the place of God almighty. But the deacon stands in the place of Christ; and you must love him. The deaconess shall be honored by you in the place of the Holy Spirit."[260] Deaconesses should baptize women but never men. "For if it were lawful to be baptized by a woman, our Lord and Teacher himself would have been baptized by Mary his mother, whereas he was baptized by John, like others of the people."[261] The deaconess had important roles that proper comportment required that only a female could do, such as visiting sick women and bathing them.[262]

---

[259] Hippolytus, *Apostolic Tradition*, 10, cited in Hippolytus, *Apostolic Tradition*, trans. Burton Scott Easton (Cambridge: Cambridge University Press, 1934), 40.
[260] *Didascalia Apostolorum*, trans. R. Hugh Connolly (Oxford: Clarendon Press, 1929), 34.
[261] Ibid., 58.
[262] Ibid., 61.

Like the *Apostolic Tradition*, the *Didascalia Apostolorum* had strong reservations about widows, motives, and actions. They were instructed not to be troublemakers.[263] They were described as running about asking questions and believing that they were wiser than presbyters or bishops.[264] They should also never teach or attempt to explain doctrine to outsiders. Though women traveled with Christ and his apostles, none were sent to teach. If women were supposed to teach, Christ would have made it explicit.[265] They were instructed to stay in their homes. With such a withering depiction of the actions and motives of many widows, it is no surprise that they were not ordained.

The *Didascalia Apostolorum* also provided specific instructions to women and wives. They were to please and honor their husbands and work in their homes. Within the home, wives were to be quiet and not quarrelsome with their husbands. They should never bathe with men nor dress provocatively. The man was the head and the woman submissive to him in all things.[266] The document also discussed the eucharist and menstruating women. Because of the Levitical codes concerning menstruating women, some men considered them unclean and forbade them to approach the altar. Dionysius of Alexandria (d. 264) forbade menstruating women to touch the altar in his Second Canon.[267]

The *Didascalia Apostolorum* was rather gracious and stated the baptismal cleansing replaced any need for further purification. Women could approach the altar and their husbands should be kind to them in their "courses."

> For this cause therefore do you approach without restraint to those who are at rest, and hold them not unclean. In like manner also you shall not separate those (women) who are in the wonted courses; for she also who had the flow of blood was not chidden when she touched the

---

[263] Ibid., 56.
[264] Ibid., 57–58.
[265] Ibid., 56.
[266] Ibid., 9.
[267] Dionysius Archbishop of Alexandria, Canon 2; William E Phipps, "The Menstrual Taboo in the Judeo-Christian Tradition," *Journal of Religion and Health* 19, no. 4 (Winter 1980): 300.

skirt of our Savior's cloak, but was even vouchsafed the forgiveness of all her sins [Mt 9.20–22]. And when (your wives) suffer those issues which are according to nature, have a care that, in a manner that is right, you cleave to them; for you know that they are your members, and do you love them as your soul.[268]

The Council of Nicaea of 325 was the first great ecumenical council. Though it was called to discuss the Arian controversy, the attendees passed canons concerning women. The Council accepted deaconesses, but they were not ordained.[269] The Council also stressed clerical celibacy. Bishops, priests, and deacons were instructed not to live with women or be familiar with them even if they were "ugly" or under the pretext of bringing them up as orphans. The temptation was too great. "For the devil with such arms slays religious, bishops, presbyters, and deacons, and incites them to the fires of desire." An elderly woman or relative could live in their home.[270] The bishop was not to allow a man to leave his wife because she had a bad temper.[271]

The Synod of Gangra in the province of Galatia was held in 340. Called to confront Manichean practices in the church, the canons demonstrated the actions of women also demanded attention.[272] Canon 13 stated, "If any women under pretense of asceticism, shall change her apparel and instead of a woman's accustomed clothing, shall put on that of a man, let her be anathema."[273] Women were not to wear monk's clothing. Canon 17 explicitly reminded women of the obedience due to their husbands. "If any woman from pretended asceticism shall cut off her hair, which God gave her as the reminder of her subjection, thus annulling it as it were the ordinance of subjection, let her be anathema."[274]

---

[268] *Didascalia Apostolorum*, 100.
[269] Council of Nicaea, Canon 19, *NPNF*, 14:40. Unless further noted, all notations from the Council of Nicaea are from this work.
[270] Ibid., Canon 4, *NPNF*, 14:46.
[271] Ibid., Canon 51, *NPNF*, 14:48.
[272] Joseph Martos and Pierre Hégy, eds., *Equal at the Creation: Sexism, Society, and Christian Thought* (Toronto: University of Toronto Press, 1998), 62.
[273] Synod of Gangra, Canon 13, *NPNF*, 14:97.
[274] Ibid., Canon 17, *NPNF*, 14:99.

The Council of Laodicea was a regional synod held in 363 in Laodicea, Asia Minor. Canon 11 stated that "presbytides" or "female presidents" were no longer to be ordained.[275] It appeared that presbytides were deaconesses. Canon 44 stated, "women may not go to the altar." Alongside a consideration of canon 11, cannon 44 must mean that women had no role in the oblation.[276]

The *Apostolic Constitutions* were written in northern Syria between 375 and 380. The *Constitutions* borrowed heavily from the *Didascalia Apostolorum*. The deaconess was held in higher regard than in most previous synods. The bishop was compared to God, the male deacon to Christ, and the deaconess to the Holy Spirit.[277] Deaconesses were to be ordained. They were considered to be necessary for proper decorum in the baptism of women and other ministries to women.[278] Following the *Didascalia Apostolorum*, the *Apostolic Constitutions* declared that deaconesses were not to perform the baptism.

> For if baptism were to be administered by women, certainly our Lord would have been baptized by His own mother, and not by John; or when He sent us to baptize, He would have sent along with us women also for this purpose. But now He has nowhere, either by constitution or by writing, delivered to us any such thing; as knowing the order of nature, and the decency of the action; as being the creator of nature, and the Legislator of the constitution.[279]

Like deacons, deaconesses were responsible for carrying messages and serving wherever needed. The deaconess was to be honored in the Assembly.[280] She assigned the places where women will sit or stand[281] and welcomed female strangers.[282]

---

[275] Council of Laodicea, Canon 11, *NPNF*, 2:14.
[276] Ibid., Canon 44, *NPNF*, 2:14.
[277] *Apostolic Constitutions*, 2.16, *ANF*, 7:410
[278] Ibid., 3.2, *ANF*, 7:431.
[279] Ibid., 2.9, *ANF*, 7:429
[280] Ibid., 2.57, *ANF*, 7:421.
[281] Ibid.
[282] Ibid., 2.58, *ANF*, 7:422.

The *Apostolic Constitutions* placed strict limitations on the office of widow. They must be sixty years old to ensure that they would not remarry.[283] Perhaps as a result of previous behavior, the widows were given very precise directions on how they must conduct themselves. "Let every widow be meek, quiet, gentle, sincere, free from anger, not talkative, not clamorous, not hasty of speech, not given to evil-speaking, not captious, not double-tongued, not a busybody."[284] They must be obedient to their bishop.[285] Under no circumstances should widows teach. Those who do were:

> ... gadders and impudent: they do not make their feet to rest in one place, because they are not widows, but purses ready to receive, triflers, evil-speakers, counsellors of strife, without shame, impudent, who being such, are not worthy of Him that called them. For they do not come to the common station of the congregation on the Lord's day, as those that are watchful; but either they slumber, or trifle, or allure men, or beg, or ensnare others, bringing them to the evil one; not suffering them to be watchful in the Lord, but taking care that they go out as vain as they came in, because they do not hear the word of the Lord either taught or read.[286]

Women could not be priests. It went against the order of creation since the man was the head of the woman. The woman came from rib of the man and was created for the man so she was subject to him. Because of the Fall, man was to rule over women. Ordaining women to the priesthood was "one of the ignorant practices of Gentile atheism, to ordain women priests to the female deities, not one of the constitutions of Christ."[287]

The *Apostolic Constitutions* offered guidance on how to treat menstruating women. "For neither lawful mixture, nor childbearing, nor the menstrual purgation, nor nocturnal pollution, can defile

---

[283] Ibid., 3.1, *ANF*, 7:426. By 390 Civil Law decreed that deaconesses had to be at least 60 and dispose of all their property; Malone, *Women and Christianity: The First Thousand Years*, 1:127.
[284] Ibid., 3.5, *ANF*, 7:428.
[285] Ibid., 3.7, *ANF*, 7:429.
[286] Ibid., 3.6, *ANF*, 7:428.
[287] Ibid., 3.9, *ANF*, 7:429.

the nature of a man, or separate the Holy Spirit from him. Nothing but impiety and unlawful practice can do that. For the Holy Spirit always abides with those that are possessed of it, so long as they are worthy."[288] Because of the emphasis placed on nocturnal emissions by several Church Fathers, it is surprising that it did not bar men from the altar. Husbands and wives should not have sex while the wife is menstruating. It was assumed that conception was impossible, so the act would not be procreative.[289]

In 385, Deacon Siricius of Rome left his wife and became the bishop of Rome (384–399). With the power and influence of the Roman See growing, he declared that priests were no longer to have sexual relations with their wives. Two years later, he made celibacy mandatory for taking holy orders.[290] Though this decree concerned the ordained clergy, it treated women as a distraction to consecrated work.

> Therefore, also the Lord Jesus, when He had enlightened us by His coming, testifies in the Gospel, that he came to fulfill the law, not to destroy it (Matthew 5:17). And so He has wished the beauty of the Church, whose spouse He is, to radiate with the splendor of chastity, so that on the day of judgment, when He will have come again, He may be able to find her without spot or wrinkle (Ephesians 5:27) as He instituted her through His Apostle. All priests and Levites are bound by the indissoluble law of these sanctions, so that from the day of our ordination, we give up both our hearts and our bodies to continence and chastity … have been cast out of every ecclesiastical office, which they have used unworthily, nor can they ever touch the sacred mysteries, of which they themselves had deprived themselves, so long as they give heed to impure desires.[291]

Following bishop Siricius of Rome, the Synod of Carthage met in 390 and determined that bishops, presbyters, and deacons were

---

[288] Ibid., 6.27, *ANF*, 7:462.
[289] Ibid., 6.27, *ANF* 7:463.
[290] Jordan, *The Historical Mary*, 248.
[291] DS Denzinger-Schoenmetzer, *Enchiridion Symbolorum*, ed. 34 (Feiburg im Breisgau, Germany: Herder, 1967), 252.

not to have sexual intercourse with their wives.[292] Sexual relations defiled the cleric going to the altar.

At the 394 Synod of Nimes, canon 2 barred women from being deacons. This canon was enacted in response to heretical Priscillianists allowing women to serve as priests.[293]

Canon 26 at the 441 Synod of Orange prohibited women from being ordained as deaconesses. Deaconesses should stand with the laity and bow their heads. Previously ordained deaconesses were no longer considered part of the ordained clergy.[294]

In 494, Bishop Gelasius of Rome (492–496) wrote a scathing letter to the bishops in Lucania, Bruttium, and Sicilia in response to reports that women were serving at the altar. "Nevertheless, we have heard to our annoyance that divine affairs have come to such a low state that women are encouraged to officiate at the sacred altars, and to take part in all matters imputed to the offices of the male sex, to which they do not belong." Gelasius' letter demonstrated that the practice of allowing women to attend the altar continued in some regions.[295]

In 517 at the Council of Epon, in southeastern France, the delegates determined in canon 22 that widows and deaconesses were no longer permitted to be consecrated. Only the blessing of penance could be given. In 553, the Second Synod of Orleans reiterated the findings of the Council of Epon in canon 18 by decreeing, "that from now on the diaconal ordination should not be imparted to any woman, because of the weakness of her condition." These councils marked the end of the female diaconate in the West.[296]

In 585 at a council held at Macon, Burgundy, forty-three bishops and twenty bishop's deputies supposedly argued over whether women had souls.[297] No canon mentions this subject, so the debate

---

[292] Council of Carthage 390, Canon 3, *NPNF*, 14:444.
[293] Canons of the Synod of Nîmes, *Women Deacons*, Wijngaards Institute for Catholic Research, trans. John Wijngaards, last accessed 1 May 2021, https://www.women-deacons.org/minwest-canons-of-nimes/.
[294] Canons of the 441 Synod of Orange, Canon 26, *NPNF*, 14:41.
[295] Kevin Madigan and Carolyn Osiek, eds., *Ordained Women in the Early Church: A Documentary History* (Baltimore, MD: Johns Hopkins University Press, 2005), 186.
[296] Ibid., 146–147.
[297] Michael Nolan, "The Mysterious Affair at Macon: The Bishops and the Souls of Women," *New Blackfriars* 74, no. 876 (November 1993): 501–507.

may be apocryphal. The earliest source for the debate was Gregory of Tours (538–594). While noting the date but not the city, he wrote:

> There came forward at this Council a certain bishop who maintained that woman could not be included under the term "man." However, he accepted the reasoning of the other bishops and did not press his case, for the holy book of the Old Testament tells us that in the beginning, when God created man, "Male and female he created them and called their name Adam," which means earthly man; even so, he called the woman Eve, yet of both he used the word man.[298]

No official record of the debate can be found. The supposed council appeared in the sixteenth century when Protestants attempted to use it to sway Catholic women to their cause.[299]

The Patristic Past Is Medieval Prologue

By the late third century, women had lost much of their egalitarian status within Christianity. Although local synods condemned women for serving in ecclesial roles, the affair had not yet been settled. The Church Fathers had much to do with this decline in status. They believed that women were created in the image of God, but they had few other positive things to say about them. Their writings demonstrated a belief that women were to blame for Adam's fall, and impossible to live with. The only way for a woman to overcome her nature was to dedicate herself to virginity or marriage. Following the strictures found in the Pauline Epistles, the Fathers insisted that wives be subservient to their husbands in all things. The Fathers held that beyond the office of deaconess, virgin, and widow, women should hold no position in the church. The idea of allowing the ordination of women was literally anathema to them. The councils, synods, and books of church order echoed the Church Fathers' words. The need for declarations and canons condemning

---

[298] Gregory of Tours, *The History of the Franks*, trans. Lewis Thorpe (Harmondsworth: Penguin Books, 1974), 452.
[299] Douglass, *Women, Freedom, and Calvin*, 72.

women's ordination, however, demonstrated that women were being ordained throughout much of the Patristic era. Rather than the Bible, the Church Fathers' teachings and the canons of councils and synods served as the starting point for many medieval theologians' beliefs about women.

CHAPTER FIVE

Women in the Middle Ages

The Middle Ages began with the fall of the western Roman Empire in 476 and ended with the onset of the modern era (ca. 1500). This very long era may be segmented into the Low Middle Ages (476-ca.–1000), the High Middle Ages (ca. 1000–1250), and the Late Middle Ages (ca. 1250–1500). In matters of the Catholic Church, however, I date the beginning of the Middle Ages to the pontificate of Gregory I (590–604). He was the first bishop of Rome who could truly speak to all Christendom, most Christians obeyed his dictums, and could accurately be called the first Pope.

After the fall of the Roman Empire in the late fifth century, western Europe lost its political cohesiveness. In the Early Middle Ages, the Catholic Church and papacy filled this void, provided stability, and became the most powerful institution of the era. Monasticism grew and became organized; the great ecumenical councils defined the Christian faith, and the papacy continued to accumulate power and prestige.

The late Middle Ages saw wars, famine, and the Black Death (1346–1353) which killed two-thirds of the European population. The Catholic Church, however, remained powerful. Popes bent kings to their will and sent Christian armies to conquer the Holy Land. The last of Europe was Christianized in the late eleventh century, and the Mendicant Orders were established. Churchmen were trained in Scholasticism in the great cathedral schools and universities. Though weakened by the 1054 schism and the Avignon Papacy, or Babylonian Captivity (1309–1376), and the Investiture Controversy of the eleventh and twelfth centuries, the Catholic

Church and its teachings remained largely unchallenged until the sixteenth-century Protestant Reformation.

Women's Life in the Middle Ages

The Middle Ages was a time of hierarchal and feudalistic society in which everyone had their designated place in a sacred order. No matter the station of a woman's father or husband, women were secondary to men. Women were expected to be content with their lot and not attempt to move beyond their appointed station as wife or mother. If a woman attempted to do so, she was seen as prideful and endangered the sacred balance of power.[1] Even in noble homes, girls received less formal education than boys and instead received a practical education from their mothers.[2] In the countryside, girls often took positions as servants.

Many marriages, especially in the nobility, were arranged. Consent of the future husband and wife was not required until the Fourth Lateran Council of 1215.[3] Arranged marriages were not as common among poor families. Whether high born or peasant, a woman remained subject to her father or husband. A husband could beat his wife and children, but not to the point of permanent injury.[4] Most girls were married by age thirteen or fourteen[5] and lived in their husband's home.[6] Wives were often much younger than their husbands and could expect to be widowed and remarried several times.[7] If the family was of means, the marriage contract often specified dower lands to provide for the widow.[8] She could not sell the land but rather was expected to hold onto it for

---

[1] Mary T. Malone, *Women and Christianity: From 1000 to the Reformation* (Maryknoll, MY: Orbis Books, 2001), 2:26.
[2] Sandy Bardsley, *Women's Roles in the Middle Ages* (Westport, CT: Greenwood Publishing Group, 2007), 94.
[3] Ibid., 147.
[4] Ibid., 147.
[5] R.W. Southern, *Western Society and the Church in the Middle Ages* (London: Penguin Books, 1970), 309.
[6] Christopher Brooke, *A General History of Europe: Europe in the Central Middle Ages, 962–1154* (Essex, England: Longman Group Limited, 1975), 122.
[7] Bardsley, 103.
[8] Ibid., 118.

her children or her husband's family.⁹ Peasant women who had lost their husbands were in desperate straits if they did not remarry. By age forty, many women had spent half their lives pregnant.

Other than women of the highest castes, women had little to no place in the public arena. They could not serve in public office, the military, and only rarely in town councils or assemblies.¹⁰ Women were believed to lack the intelligence and capacity to do anything outside the home.¹¹ Some rare women of privilege did inherit fiefs and ran feudal assemblies.¹² In the eyes of the law, women were little different from children.¹³ They were to be obedient, subservient, submissive, and modest.¹⁴

Women and the Church in the Early Middle Ages

The early Middle Ages were, in many respects, a continuation of the values developed in the Patristic era and inherited many of the era's beliefs concerning women.¹⁵ This allowed women two options. She could be an obedient wife and mother or dedicate herself to the church.¹⁶ The church continued to regard virginity as the highest calling. Women were prohibited from partaking in formal cultic roles. Jerome's and Augustine's works concerning women were often quoted by male clerics who added their own beliefs to the nature, role, and purpose of women.¹⁷ Ecclesiastical law that limited the rights of women based on the order of creation and original sin was well-established and provided the foundation for the development of further canon law.¹⁸ Menses continued to trouble church leaders and much ink was spilled in attempts to find

---

⁹ Ibid., 152.
¹⁰ Shulamith Shahar, *The Fourth Estate: A History of Women in the Middle Ages*, rev. ed., (London: Routledge, Taylor, and Francis Group, 2003), 11–12.
¹¹ Malone, 25.
¹² Shahar, 14.
¹³ Bardsley, 130.
¹⁴ Malone, 62.
¹⁵ Katharine M. Rogers, *The Troublesome Helpmate: A History of Misogyny in Literature* (Seattle, WA: University of Washington Press, 1966), 56.
¹⁶ Rosemary Radford Ruether, ed., *Religion and Sexism: Images of Woman in the Jewish and Christian Traditions* (Eugene, OR: Wipf and Stock Publishers, 1998), 231.
¹⁷ Malone, 23.
¹⁸ Shahar, 11.

a solution to whether it should keep women from[19] partaking in the Eucharist.[20] As in the Patristic era, the church continued to find women of secondary importance.

Creation

In the Early Middle Ages, the church's understanding of creation had changed little from the Patristic era. Women were considered to have been created in the image of God. The order of creation meant women were expected to be subservient. Most accepted Neoplatonism's dichotomies of body and soul and male and female with all its implications of superiority and inferiority.[21] This interpretation of creation remained unchanged until the ideas of Thomas Aquinas (1225–1274) emerged in the thirteenth century.

Aquinas was a Dominican scholar, an advocate of Scholasticism, and an architect of much Catholic theology. Unlike scholars who embraced Platonism or Neoplatonism, Aquinas' theology was Aristotelian. His greatest work was *Summa Theologica*.

Unlike Chrysostom and Augustine, Aquinas had no relationships with women.[22] His depictions of women were drawn from philosophy and theology. He held that woman was created by God and so had a place in the world. Man, however, was created first. "First, in order thus to give the first man a certain dignity consisting in this, that as God is the principle of the whole universe, so the first man, in likeness to God, was the principle of the whole human race. Wherefore Paul says that 'God made the whole human race from one'"

---

[19] Marie Anne Mayeski, "Excluded by Logic of Control: Women in Medieval Society and Scholastic Theology," in *Equal at Creation: Sexism, Society, and Christian Thought*, eds. Joseph Martos and Pierre Hégy (Toronto: University of Toronto Press, 1998), 79.
[20] Joan Young Gregg, *Devils, Women, and Jews: Reflections of the Other in Medieval Sermon Stories* (Albany, NY: State University of New York Press, 1997), 90–91.
[21] Marie Anne Mayeski, "Excluded by Logic of Control: Women in Medieval Society and Scholastic Theology," in Martos and Hégy, eds., 79.
[22] Elizabeth Clark and Herbert Richardson, eds., *Women and Religion: The Original Sourcebook of Women in Christian Thought* (San Francisco, CA: HarperCollins, 1996), 79.

(Acts 17:26).[23] She, therefore, was endowed with less intelligence than her male counterpart and was more apt to make immoral decisions. Females, therefore, were a lesser grade of perfection and this allowed for the presence of evil in the world.[24] Aquinas followed Aristotle's biology to the letter. From creation, men had active souls and superior bodies and minds (and thus greater intelligence) than women. The female was defective because of her passive soul, body, mind, and limited intelligence.[25] Unlike Aristotle, Aquinas did not believe that the male provided the soul, rather it was God that provided it. The male exerted the force that prepared female matter to accept the soul.[26]

Aquinas believed humanity in its perfection was male and that the female was an accident.[27]

> As regards to the individual nature, woman is defective and misbegotten, for the active force in the male seed tends to the production of a perfect likeness in the masculine sex; while the production of woman comes from defect in the active force or from some material indisposition, or even from some external influence; such as that of a south wind, which is moist, as the Philosopher observes (*De Gener. Animal.* iv, 2).[28]

Aside from circumstances beyond his control, the male was generally at fault for the creation of a female. His semen was not strong enough.

---

[23] Aquinas, "The Production of the Woman," *Summa Theologica*, I, 92.2, Summa Theologiae, last accessed 1 May 2021, http://summa-theologiae.org/question/09202.htm.

[24] Aquinas, "Of the Condition of the Offspring as to the Body," *ST*, I, 99.2, Summa Theologiae, last accessed 1 May 2021, http://summa-theologiae.org/question/09902.htm.

[25] Aquinas, "Of Incontinence," *ST*, II-II, 156.1, ad 1, Summae Theologiae, last accessed 1 May 2021, http://summa-theologiae.org/question/38901.htm.

[26] Aquinas, "The Order of Charity," *ST*, II-II, 26, 10. ob. 1, 2nd rev. ed., trans. Fathers of the English Dominican Province, in New Advent, ed. Kevin Knight, last modified 2017, https://www.newadvent.org/summa/3026.htm#article10.

[27] Collen McCluskey, "An Unequal Relationship between Equals: Thomas Aquinas on Marriage," *History of Philosophy Quarterly* 24, no. 1 (January 2007): 2.

[28] Aquinas, "The Production of the Woman," *ST*, I, 92, ob. 1, Summa Theologiae, last accessed 1 May 2022, http://summa-theologiae.org/question/09201.htm.

Like Augustine, Aquinas believed that women's primary purpose was for bearing and raising children.[29] "As regards [to] human nature in general, woman is not misbegotten, but is included in nature's intention as directed to the work of generation."[30] In all other circumstances, a man would be a more suitable partner.[31] Men, therefore, were more noble and male leadership was a divine and biological necessity.[32]

> Father and mother are loved as principles of our natural origin. Not that the father is principle in a more excellent way than the mother, because he is the active principle, while the mother is a passive, and material principle. Consequently, strictly speaking, the father is to be loved more.[33]

As the first woman, Eve passed on her inferiorities and defects to her daughters.[34] Because his teachings were honored and accepted at the Council of Trent (1545–1563), Aquinas' "misbegotten" biology not only promoted misogyny in his era but allowed it to continue well into the twenty-first century.[35]

Image of God

The belief that only men were created in the image of God was held by most theologians at the end of the Patristic era and maintained

---

[29] Thomas Petri, *Aquinas and the Theology of the Body: The Thomist Foundations of John Paul II's Anthropology* (Washington, D.C.: Catholic University of American Press, 2016), 106.
[30] Aquinas, "The Production of the Woman," *ST*, I, 92, ob. 1, Summa Theologiae, last accessed 1 May 2022, http://summa-theologiae.org/question/09201.htm.
[31] Collen McCluskey, "An Unequal Relationship between Equals: Thomas Aquinas on Marriage," 5.
[32] Rosemary Radford Ruether, *Women and Redemption: A Theological History* (Minneapolis, MN: Fortress Press, 1998), 95.
[33] Aquinas, "Of the Order of Charity," *ST*, II-II, 26, 10, Summae Theologiae, last accessed 1 May 2022, http://summa-theologiae.org/question/25910.htm.
[34] Beverly Clack, ed., *Misogyny in the Western Philosophical Tradition: A Reader* (London: MacMillan Press, 1999), 75.
[35] Cynthia Russett, "All About Eve. What Men Have Thought About Women Thinking," *The American Scholar* 74, no. 2 (Spring 2005): 43.

throughout the Middle Ages. Farley posited that early in the Middle Ages the church determined that women were not only excluded from God's image but were perceived as evil.[36] Saint Bonaventure (1221–1274) held that women identify with the inferior aspects of the soul and men with the superior.[37] Peter Abelard (1079–1142), however, believed that woman was the superior creation because she alone was formed inside paradise.[38] He did do damage to women, however, by maintaining, "Certainly man according to the Apostle, is in the image of God and not the woman (1 Cor. 11:7). Just as man is in the image of God, so woman is to be in the image of man."[39] Anslem of Canterbury (1033–1109) was one of the few theologians to believe that men and women were both created in the image of God.[40]

As with many medieval theological discussions, Aquinas' interpretations were held in high regard. He maintained that both men and women were created to know God, had a rational soul,[41] and were in the image of God but to different degrees. While Augustine claimed that women were created in God's image only when married, Aquinas saw women as less in soul and reason.[42] He depicted the image of God as active, formulative, and perfect. These divine attributes were presumably male. Aquinas defined the presence of the image of God in man as humanity's ability to love and

---

[36] Farley, "Sources of Sexual Inequality in the History of Christian Thought," 168.

[37] Mary Daly, *The Church and the Second Sex: With a New Feminist PostChristian Introduction by the Author* (New York, NY: Harper and Row, 1975), 91.

[38] Dyan Elliott, "Gender and the Christian Traditions," in *The Oxford Handbook of Women & Gender in Medieval Europe*, eds. Judith M. Bennett and Ruth Mazo Karras (Oxford: Oxford University Press 2013), 32.

[39] Peter Abelard, *Introdcutio ad theologiam*, cited in Maryanne Cline Horowitz, "The Image of God: Is Woman Included?" *The Harvard Theological Review* 72, no. 3–4 (July–October 1979): 179.

[40] Maryanne Cline Horowitz, "The Image of God: Is Woman Included?" *The Harvard Theological Review* 72, no. 3–4 (July–October 1979): 180.

[41] Kari Elisabeth Børresen, *Subordination et Equivalence. Nature et rôle de la femme d'aprés Augustin et Thomas d'Aquinas* (Paris: Maison Mame, 1963): 136.

[42] Margaret A. Farley, "Sources of Sexual Inequality in the History of Christian Thought," *Journal of Religion* 2, (1976): 168.

comprehend God. To have the image of God completed, the person must realize and respond to this image.[43]

Following Aristotle, Aquinas perceived the body and soul as a unit. Men had a superior body, which made them more rational and capable of making moral decisions. Thus, men possessed a high degree of the image of God. Women had inferior bodies, were passive, corporal, and less perfect. Their inferior bodies limited their intelligence and clouded moral decision-making.[44] Women, therefore, were inferior to men in the image of God.

Aquinas also relied on biblical exegesis. By using Genesis 1: 26–27 as his primary argument and 1 Corinthians 11:7–9 as secondary, he noted:

> The image of God, in its principal signification, namely the intellectual nature, is found both in man and in woman. Hence after the words, "To the image of God He created him," it is added, "Male and female He created them" (Genesis. 1:27). Moreover, it is said "them" in the plural, as Augustine (Genesis ad lit. iii, 22) remarks, lest it should be thought that both sexes were united in one individual. But in a secondary sense the image of God is found in man, and not in woman: for man is the beginning and end of woman; as God is the beginning and end of every creature. So when the Apostle had said that "man is the image and glory of God, but woman is the glory of man," he adds his reason for saying this: "For man is not of woman, but woman of man; and man was not created for woman, but woman for man."[45]

Women would gain the full image of God and equality with man only in the resurrection. Unlike Augustine, who believed all souls would be asexual in paradise, Aquinas maintained there

---

[43] Aquinas, "The End of Term of the Production of Man," *ST*, II.I, 93, art. 4, Summa Theologiae, last accessed 1 June 2021, http://summa-theologiae.org/question/09304.htm.
[44] Børresen, 143.
[45] Aquinas, "The End of Term of the Production of Man," *ST*, I, q. 93, art. 4, ad 1, Summa Theologiae, last accessed 1 June 2021, http://summa-theologiae.org/question/09304.htm.

would be both males and females in the resurrection.[46] Genitals, however, would no longer be of use.[47]

The Fall

As in the Patristic era, the Middle Ages theologians often blamed humanity's Fall on Eve. Aquinas' interpretation differed only slightly from that of his predecessors. Since Adam held the greater reason, body, and moral superiority, she was subordinate to him. The serpent approached Eve because she was weak-minded and inferior to Adam.[48] As Adam possessed higher reason, he held the higher degree of the image of God and was in charge of the first family; the Fall occurred only after Eve led Adam astray.

Aquinas had a different interpretation of sin. He did not believe in original sin but in original guilt. It was a privation of original righteousness and transmitted corruption. "Original sin is not the sin of this person, except inasmuch as this person receives his nature from his first parent, for which reason it is called the 'sin of nature,' according to Ephesians 2:3: 'We … were by nature children of wrath.'"[49]

Adam and Eve were motivated to sin. Eve gave in to the serpent because she was weak-minded, prideful, and wanted to be like God. Aquinas held that Eve was guiltier than Adam because she not only sinned but also convinced Adam to sin.[50] Adam's motivation to sin was to be more like God and to remain with his wife. He did not believe

---

[46] Aquinas, "Of the Quality of Those Who Rise Again," *ST*, Supp., q. 81, a. 3, Summa Theologiae, last accessed 1 June 2021, http://summa-theologiae.org/question/59303.htm.

[47] Aquinas, "Of the Integrity of the Bodies in the Resurrection," *ST*, Supp., q. 80, a.1, Summa Theologiae, last accessed 1 June 2021, http://summa-theologiae.org/question/59201.htm.

[48] Aquinas, "Of Our Parents' First Temptation," *ST*, II-II, 165.2, a.1, Summa Theologiae, last accessed 1 June 2021, http://summa-theologiae.org/question/39802.htm; Aquinas, "Of the First Man's Sin," *ST*, II-II, 163, a.4, Summa Theologiae, last accessed 1 June 2021, http://summa-theologiae.org/question/39604.htm.

[49] Aquinas, "Of the Cause of Sin, On the Part of Man," *ST*, II.I, q. 81, ob. 5, Summa Theologiae, last accessed 1 June 2021, http://summa-theologiae.org/question/20001.htm.

[50] Aquinas, "Of the First Man's Sin," *ST*, II-II, 163.4.c, last accessed 1 June 2021, http://summa-theologiae.org/question/39604.htm.

the serpent.⁵¹ Adam was more culpable because he was more intelligent than his wife. As the head of the family, if Adam had not joined Eve in sin, the couple would not have been expelled from Paradise.

Submission

Aquinas believed that the first couple's punishments corresponded with their designated roles as depicted in creation. Adam must now acquire food by the sweat of his brow. Eve's reason for existence, childbirth, was now painful.⁵² She was now economically and socially subject to the man in a manner that reflected Aristotelian household ethics.⁵³

> Subjection is twofold. One is servile, by virtue of which a superior makes use of a subject for his own benefit; and this kind of subjection began after sin. There is another kind of subjection which is called economic or civil, whereby the superior makes use of his subjects for their own benefit and good; and this kind of subjection existed even before sin. For good order would have been wanting in the human family if some were not governed by others wiser than themselves. So by such a kind of subjection woman is naturally subject to man, because in man the discretion of reason predominates.⁵⁴

Aquinas differed little from Patristic and Early Middle Age theologians in his rationalization of women's inferiority. Adam was created first and was the founder of the human race. Woman was

---

⁵¹ Aquinas, "Of Our Parents' First Temptation," *ST*, II-II, 165.2, a.1, Summa Theologiae, last accessed 1 June 2021, http://summa-theologiae.org/question/39802.htm.
⁵² Aquinas, "Of the First Man's Sin," *ST*, II-II, 163, a. 4, Summa Theologiae, last accessed 1 June 2021, http://summa-theologiae.org/question/39604.htm.
⁵³ Daniel Mark Cere, "Marriage, Subordination, and the Development of Christian Doctrine," in *Does Christianity Teach Male Headship: The Equal-Regard Marriage and Its Critics*, eds. David Blankenhorn and Don Browning, and Mary Stewart Van Leeuwen (Grand Rapids, MI: Eerdmans Publishing, 2004), 103.
⁵⁴ Aquinas, "The Production of the Woman," *ST*, I, q. 92, a.1, Reply to Objection 2, Summa Theologiae, last accessed 1 June 2021, http://summa-theologiae.org/question/09201.htm.

created from and for man. Woman was less intelligent, more inclined to sin, and, thus, for the sake of the family, required male leadership.[55] His synthesis of Genesis 2 and Ephesians 5 required it. He did add one significant aspect to the church's perception of women; his belief that women were naturally defective dealt another blow to women's standing in Christendom.

Marriage

From the third to the sixteenth century, the Catholic Church regarded marriage as secondary to chastity.[56] Almost all the Church Fathers treated marriage as little more than a container for lust.[57] Though it was not stated as directly as in the Patristic era, women were perceived as the more lustful gender. They were also held to be morally weaker and, thus, more prone to give in to their physical desires. Medieval canon law demeaned marriage and exalted virginity.[58] Unlike many other beliefs inherited from the Patristic era, beliefs of marriage began to alter as the church changed its teachings in the eighth century and marriage began to be viewed as a sacrament.[59] Chaste marriage, however, was forbidden out of the fear that the wife might seduce the husband.[60]

The woman's purpose was to give birth to as many children as possible. This not only provided a future workforce, but it also allowed women to atone for Eve's sin and gain salvation.[61] Mothers were responsible for the education of their children to such a degree that it was almost a religious task.[62] The wife also ran the household and the household economy. Old Testament women such as

---

[55] Børresen, 199.
[56] Joanne Carlson Brown and Carole R. Bohn, eds., *Christianity, Patriarchy, and Abuse: A Feminist Critique* (Cleveland, OH: Pilgrim Press, 1989), 34.
[57] Steven Ozment, *When Fathers Rule: Family Life in Reformation Europe* (Cambridge, MA: Harvard University Press, 1983), 10.
[58] Ibid., 12.
[59] Shahar, 66.
[60] Barbara J. MacHaffie, *Her Story: Women in the Christian Tradition*, 2nd ed. (Minneapolis, MN: Fortress Press, 2006), 52.
[61] Malone, 66.
[62] Marie Anne Mayeski, "Excluded by Logic of Control: Women in Medieval Society and Scholastic Theology," in Martos and Hégy, eds., 74.

Sarah and the Virgin Mary were held up as ideal women. From these exemplary women, wives were to learn chastity (once beyond childbearing age), obedience, and devotion.[63]

Even though marriage was becoming a sacrament, the patriarchal nature of marriage did not change. Following the Pauline scriptures, the wife remained subjugated to her husband. One area in which both had equal authority was conjugal rights.[64] Neither should deny the other sexual intercourse unless both agreed to it for a season of prayer. Married women, of course, were held to more stipulations than their husbands. They were expected to be available for sex whenever the husband desired. The "debt of her body" was often written into the marriage contract. The woman should be submissive to her husband in bed and perform the act with the least amount of passion possible.[65] The wife's sexual availability was assumed to be a deterrent to her husband's infidelity.[66] Even within marriage, sex was often perceived as giving into the sin of lust, and it was to happen only with the goal of procreation.[67]

In the Middle Ages, the husband could physically punish a disobedient or disappointing wife. The English jurist and cleric, Henry Bracton (1210–1268) declared that the wife must obey the husband in all respects unless he commanded her to do something against divine law.[68] He was to make sure she behaved properly. She, however, must not mention his faults.[69] The most common complaints men had against their wives, and women in general, were disobedience, insubordination, nagging, or needing constant correction.[70] Aquinas believed that no matter what the situation, a wife could never leave her husband.[71] Canon law allowed separations and annulments. There were two grounds for legal separation: entrance into the religious life or adultery. Later canonists allowed separation

---

[63] Malone, 64.
[64] Blankenhorn, Browning, and Stewart Van Leeuwen, 100.
[65] Vern L. Bullough and James A. Brundage., eds., *Handbook of Medieval Sexuality* (New York, NY: Routledge, 2000), 87.
[66] Malone, 65.
[67] Brown and Bohn, 39.
[68] Shahar, 89.
[69] Malone, 65.
[70] Brown and Bohn, 35.
[71] Aquinas, *Summa Contra Gentiles*, III, 123. Hereafter cited as *SCG*. See also *ST*, II-I, L154, 8, ad 3.

on the grounds of cruelty, female frigidity, or male impotence.[72] Annulments were rare.

Aquinas held that procreation followed by the female raising of children were the primary reasons for marriage. This allowed men to have a family but be free from many family duties and allow them more time for intellectual pursuits.[73] They each had their sphere of influence. She worked in the home and he in the public sphere. The man, however, was the patriarchal head of the family, and the wife's weaknesses required his direction. This led him to believe that fathers should educate their children.[74] The woman was weak-minded and did not have the authority to ensure success.[75] Marriage was also a monogamous relationship. Polygamy was forbidden because it led to strife within the home, the man could not sexually service several women,[76] and it made the woman little more than a slave.[77]

Aquinas saw marriage as a sacrament that stabilized the home. The monogamous nature of the marriage sacrament gave the man peace of mind as he felt confident he was the child's father. He believed the sacramentality of marriage symbolized the union of Christ and conferred grace so it neutralized the sinful elements of sex.[78] Sex for procreation within marriage was not a sin.[79] Aquinas maintained that the availability of prostitutes kept single men from committing adultery with married women.[80]

---

[72] Sara McDougall, "Women and Gender in Canon Law," in Bennett and Karras, 173–175.
[73] Rogers, 66.
[74] McCluskey, "An Unequal Relationship between Equals: Thomas Aquinas on Marriage," 5.
[75] Aquinas, "Natural Law and Conscience," *Summa Contra Gentiles*, III, 122, last accessed 1 June 2021, https://www.natural-law-and-conscience.org/aquinas-summa-contra-gentiles-book111-chapter-122/. Hereafter cited as *SCG*.
[76] Aquinas, "Of Plurality of Wives," *ST*, Supp., q. 65, ob. 9, Summae Theologiae, last accessed 1 June 2021, http://summa-theologiae.org/question/57701.htm.
[77] McCluskey, "An Unequal Relationship between Equals: Thomas Aquinas on Marriage," 6.
[78] Aquinas, *ST*, Supp., 42, Summae Theologiae, last accessed 1 June 2021, http://summa-theologiae.org/question/57701.htm.
[79] Since marriage was now a sacrament, Aquinas eschewed the emergence of courtly love. Ruether, ed., *Religion and Sexism*, 258.
[80] Aquinas, "Unbelief in General," *ST*, II-II, q. 10, art. II, ob. 3, 2nd rev. ed., trans. Fathers of the English Dominican Province, in New Advent, ed. Kevin Knight, last modified 2017, https://www.newadvent.org/summa/3010.htm.

In 1215, the Fourth Lateran Council made marriage a sacrament. Later councils reaffirmed the decision. The 1439 Council of Florence determined that marriage served a triple good—procreation, monogamous covenant, and indissolubility.[81] Marriage also signified the permanence of the bond between Christ and his church and conferred a blessing on the couple.[82]

Sex

As in the Patristic era, sex in the Early Middle Ages was perceived as sinful because it involved passion.[83] Even within marriage, intercourse was to be avoided. In the High Middle Ages, however, marriage was moving closer to sacramental status, and the church wanted to regulate marital sex. It had to be for procreation only. The male always had to be on top of and facing the female. Homosexuality was sinful under all circumstances. Anal and oral sex were forbidden because they did not lead to conception. Men could not approach the female from behind, as animals did.[84] Gratian (d. ca. 1155), a canonist from Bologna, however, surprisingly held that masturbation was not a mortal sin. In the High and Late Middle Ages, courtly love became a problem for the church as noblemen and knights perceived married women as sexual objects. It was therefore necessary to keep a close eye on them. In many cases, a child's paternity rested on it.[85]

Aquinas believed that sex and procreation were a part of God's original plan for humanity.[86] This prelapsarian sex would be innocent and dominated by reason. Like Augustine, Aquinas believed that sex in paradise would be passionless and both partners would remain virginal. Female defloration happened only after the Fall.[87]

---

[81] David C. Steinmetz, "Theological Reflections on the Reformation and the Status of Women," *Duke Divinity School Review* 41, (1976): 198.
[82] Ruether, ed., *Religion and Sexism*, 222.
[83] Ozment, 10.
[84] Bullough and Brundage, 41.
[85] Brown and Bohn, 38.
[86] Aquinas, *ST*, I, q. 99, art. 2; Petri, 221.
[87] Børresen, 153.

In addition, prelapsarian sex would be better.[88] Because sex was necessary for procreation, he determined that marriage was an office of nature before it was a sacrament.[89] Married intercourse was not evil, but Aquinas always viewed it with suspicion. He saw sex done out of passion as a venial sin.[90] He maintained that no one should take the Eucharist after having sex. He believed menstruating women should not even enter the church.[91]

Aquinas separated love from sex. All love must be directed at God. Continence allowed one to stay in control of the rational faculties. Women were more likely to disregard the constraints imposed by the church. Women did not have the strength of mind to resist "concupiscence,"[92] and, thus, became a danger to men.[93]

Virginity

Women who dedicated themselves to chastity predate institutionalized monasticism.[94] They were praised for giving up their desires, living the angelic life, and emulating the Virgin Mary. Little changed as the church entered the Middle Ages. Chaste life overrode all other social and religious categories. Virgins were above widows and married women.

The life of the consecrated virgin was lived out of public view. A virgin was often the target of unscrupulous men. Moreover,

---

[88] Aquinas, "Of the Preservation of the Species," *ST*, I, q. 98, a. 2, ad 3, Summa Theologiae, last accessed 1 June 2021, http://summa-theologiae.org/question/09801.htm.
[89] Petri, 281.
[90] John Giles Milhaven, "Thomas Aquinas on Sexual Pleasure," *The Journal of Religious Ethics* 5, no. 2 (Fall 1977): 159.
[91] Ruether, ed., *Religion and Sexism*, 229.
[92] Aquinas, "Of Sobriety," *ST*, II-II. q. 149, a. 4, last accessed 1 June 2021, http://summa-theologiae.org/question/38204.htm.
[93] Aquinas notes that some effeminate men may not be in control of their sexual urges and some particularly strong women may be blessed with more fortitude. See "Of the Vices Opposed to Perseverance," *ST*, II-II, q. 138, a. 1, 24, Summae Theologiae, last accessed 1 June 2021, http://summa-theologiae.org/question/37101.htm; "Of Sobriety," *ST*, II-II, q. 149, a. 4, Summae Theologiae, last accessed 1 June 2021, http://summa-theologiae.org/question/38204.htm.
[94] Shahar, 28.

a virgin might accidentally seduce a man, even a cleric.[95] These fears led to the cloistering of virgins.[96] Virgins enjoyed a special relationship with God. If, however, the virgin broke her vows, the punishment was severe. Bernard of Clairvaux (1090–1153) warned:

> But if you allow the Divine fire burning in your heart to be extinguished, you may be sure that there will be nothing for you but the fire which will never die out. Permit the fire of the Divine spirit to extinguish the lust of the flesh, for if, Heaven forbid, your sacred aspirations which beat in your heart die down because of the lust of the flesh, you will thus consign yourself into the fires of Hell.[97]

Concerning the Virgin Mary, Aquinas did not deviate far from the teachings of the Patristic era and the Early Middle Ages. She remained the perfect role model. "The mother of the Lord being both espoused and a virgin, both virginity and wedlock are honored in the person, in contradiction to those heretics who disparaged one or the other."[98] Virginity mirrored the life of Christ and Paul. It was "directed to the good of the soul" and "directed to the good of the body." Moreover, "venereal pleasures above all debauch a man's mind." Quoting Augustine, he stated, "that nothing so casts down the manly mind from its height as the fondling of a woman."[99]

Nuns and Orders

Women had been living together and practicing a celibate religious life since the early Patristic era.[100] They were often supported by prominent men who lived monastic lives. Pachomius (292–348), the

---

[95] Marie Anne Mayeski, "Excluded by Logic of Control: Women in Medieval Society and Scholastic Theology," in Martos and Hégy, eds., 79.
[96] Gregg, 93.
[97] Bernard of Clairvaux, *Opera*, vol. I, *Epistola* CXIII, p. 121.
[98] Aquinas, "Of the Espousals of the Mother of God," *ST*, III, q. 29, a. 1, Summae Theologiae, last accessed 1 June 2021, http://summa-theologiae.org/question/45101.htm.
[99] Aquinas, "Lust," *ST*, II-II, q. 153, art. 1, 2, 2nd rev. ed., trans. Fathers of the English Dominican Province, in New Advent, ed. Kevin Knight, last modified 2017, https://www.newadvent.org/summa/3153.htm.
[100] Nuns were not required to be virgins but were now celibate.

father of Coenobitic monasticism, built female monasteries with his sister. Jerome founded the monastery of St. Paula in Bethlehem. Augustine formulated rules for nuns to follow. By the end of the eighth century, there were female monasteries in Rome, Italy, Gaul, and Spain.

During the Middle Ages, women joined monastic orders for a variety of reasons. Some wanted to serve God. Some families wanted to get rid of unmarriageable daughters. Since the church had told them sex was bad, some women joined to avoid marriage altogether.[101] Reformed sinners often followed a belief/tradition which held that after her experience with Jesus, Mary Magdalene dedicated her life to penitence.[102] Others joined to avoid male subordination and have a sense of female autonomy under an abbess.[103]

In the early Middle Ages, female monasteries were often created and supported by wealthy women. This allowed wealthy widows the right to control their wealth. Southern noted that this explains why there were so many foundations for nuns in the Early Middle Ages.[104]

Female monasteries were often situated near a monastery in the same order. These joint monasteries existed since the fourth century. The monks and nuns lived in separate houses but shared a monastery. The nuns took care of the cooking and cleaning. Ordained monks or priests administered the sacraments.[105] Precautions were taken to ensure that male and female monastics did not spend too much time in others' social and sacred spaces.[106] The abbot and abbess shared administrative responsibilities.[107] Some monasteries, however, were led by an abbess to whom both monks and nuns were subordinate. The Whitby Abbey, North Yorkshire, England, headed by Abbess Hilda (614–680) is an example. By the tenth century, bishops were complaining that double monasteries would lead to moral

---

[101] Michael Jordan, *The Historical Mary: Revealing the Pagan Identity of the Virgin Mother* (Berkeley, CA: Seastone, 2004), 247.
[102] Gregg, 103.
[103] Southern, 309.
[104] Ibid., 309.
[105] Ibid., 309–10.
[106] Albrecht Diem, "The Gender of the Religious: Wo/Men and the Invention of Monasticism," in Bennett and Karras, 435.
[107] Malone, 220.

laxity. Church councils and papal decrees banned their creation and attempted to disband those that existed. Despite these efforts, double monasteries survived until the end of the Middle Ages.[108]

The most popular monastic orders for women in the Early Middle Ages were the Benedictines and Premonstratensians. Since the sixth century and throughout the Middle Ages, the Benedictines attracted the largest number of women. Their popularity among women stemmed from the Rule of Saint Benedict. Under his rule, the Abbesses ruled their house. Though not as large as the Benedictines, the Premonstratensian order was initially welcoming. A Premonstratensian canon of Laon reported that in 1150 there were as many as ten thousand women in the order.[109] By the thirteenth century, however, the Premonstratensians had closed their female chapters. It was feared that the nuns might endanger men's souls. The Premonstratensian Abbot, Conrad of Marchtal (fl. 1200), was succinct.

> Recognizing that the wickedness of women is greater than all the other wickedness of the world, and that there is no anger like that of women, and that the poison of asps and dragons is more curable and less dangerous to men than the familiarity of women [we] have unanimously decreed for the safety of our souls, no less than that of our bodies and goods, that we will on no account receive any more sisters to the increase of our perdition.[110]

Other orders severed ties with their affiliated nunneries. The Cistercians had no legal link to the nunneries that adopted the rules of the Cistercian Order.[111] They did not believe that women had the ability to keep the Benedictine Rule. Their disdain was apparent as they were mandated not to have contact with women or bless a nun.[112] Because nuns were not ordained, ordained monks and priests

---

[108] Shahar, 31. The Premonstratensian Order banned all double monasteries in 1137.
[109] Erens, "Les sœurs dans l'ordre de Prémontré," *Analecta Praemonstratensia*, 1929, 6–26, cited in Southern, 314.
[110] E.L. Hugo, *Annales Praemonstratenses*, 2, 147, cited in Southern, 314.
[111] Shahar, 35.
[112] *Constitutiones antiquae ordinis fratrum Paraedicatorum* (1215–1237), ed. A.H. Thomas (Louvain, 1965), cited in Edward Tracy Brett, *Humbert of Romans: His Life*

had to enter the female monastery to administer the sacraments. Bernard of Clairvaux agreed that there was a danger of allowing monks to associate with women. "To be always with a woman and not to have intercourse with her is more difficult than to raise the dead. You cannot do the less difficult: do you think I will believe that you can do what is more difficult?"[113]

The eleventh century was marked by the church's push to impose celibacy on the priesthood. It was a particularly difficult time for priests' wives. Peter Damian (1007–1073) stated, "The priests that touch the body and blood of Christ must not have touched the genitals of a whore."[114] He continued:

> I speak to you, O charmers of the clergy, appetizing flesh of the devil, that castaway from paradise, poison of the minds, death of souls, companions of the very stuff of sin, the cause of your ruin. You, I say, I exhort you women of the ancient enemy, you bitches, sows, screech-owls, night-owls, blood-suckers, she-wolves … come now, hear me, harlots, prostitutes, with your lascivious kisses, you wallowing places for fat pigs, couches for unclean spirits …[115]

The eleventh century was also the era of Gregorian Reform. Primarily concerned with the Investiture Controversy, Pope Gregory VII (1073–1085) also pressed the issue of celibacy. His reforms associated women with sexual promiscuity. To protect priests' and monks' celibacy, he sought to deny clerical marriage. This forced many women married to clerics to leave their homes. In 1074 Gregory suspended all married priests and instructed the laity to reject them. Between 1075 and 1082, he deposed fifteen bishops and four archbishops for defying his decree.[116] After the Second Lateran Council of 1139, priests' wives were declared concubines and

---

and Views of Thirteenth-Century Society (Toronto, 1984), 59.

[113] Bernard of Clairvaux, *Sermones in Cantica*, Lxv, cited in Southern, 314.

[114] Peter Damian, *De celibatu sacerdotum*, PL, 145.385, cited in Anne Llewellyn Barstow, *Married Priests and the Reforming Papacy: The Eleventh Century Debates* (New York: The Edwin Mellen Press, 1982), 60.

[115] Peter Damian, *De celibatu sacerdotum*, PL, 145.410, cited in Barstow, 60.

[116] Between 1075 and 1082 Gregory VII deposed fifteen bishops and four archbishops. Malone, 48–50.

their children bastards.[117] Many clerics took mistresses and fathered numerous children.[118] Clerical celibacy became official in 1298 when Pope Boniface VIII (1294–1303) issued the bull *Periculoso*.[119]

The Gregorian Reform's attempt to purge the church of women's leadership affected female monastics. Though Boniface VIII did not mandate it until 1298, nuns were now cloistered.[120] The only men they saw were the priests who administered the sacraments. Abbesses lost much of their authority to the local bishop.[121] The orders that had once accepted women were now refusing to take them. The number of patrons who supported nunneries decreased. The cost of cloistering became too high. The church favored ordained monks who could administer the sacraments and hold special intercessory masses. As a result, the number of men's houses continued to grow, and there were not enough female monasteries to house all of the women who wanted to join.[122]

In the twelfth and thirteenth centuries, aspiring nuns sought homes in the new Mendicant orders.[123] The teachings of the founders of the Dominican and Franciscan orders appealed to many women. The papacy affirmed women's chapters in these orders because they did not want women's religious communities existing outside of male supervision.[124] The first Dominican Nunnery was organized in Prouille, France, in 1207. The neighboring male monasteries were spiritually and financially responsible for them. Under pressure for the Order's leadership in 1228, Pope Gregory IV (1227–1241) absolved the Dominicans of their fiscal responsibility to the nunneries. In 1267, the Dominicans were made responsible for a nun's education and held jurisdiction over these houses, but had no financial

---

[117] Ibid., 47.
[118] Jacqueline Murray and Konrad Eisenbichler, eds., *Desire and Discipline: Sex and Sexuality in the Premodern West* (Toronto: University of Toronto Press, 1996), 25.
[119] Merry E. Wiesner-Hanks, *Women and Gender in Early Modern Europe* (Cambridge: Cambridge University Press, 2008), 210.
[120] Southern, 41.
[121] Marie Anne Mayeski, "Excluded by Logic of Control: Women in Medieval Society and Scholastic Theology," in Martos and Hégy, eds., 81.
[122] Mary Skinner, "Benedictine Life for Women in Central France 850–1100: A Feminist Revival" in *Medieval Religious Women, Distant Echoes*, eds. John A. Nichols and Lillian Thomas Shank (Kalamazoo, MI: Publisher, 1984), 1:87–113.
[123] Shahar, 30.
[124] Bennett and Karras, 484.

commitment to them.[125] Headed by Clare of Assisi (1194–1253), the Poor Clares were affiliated with the Franciscans.[126] Though Francis (1182–1226) and Clare were close friends, Francis cloistered the nuns which kept them from preaching and ministering to the poor. Francis did not approve of the creation of more nunneries. "God has taken our wives from us, and now Satan has given us sisters."[127]

The Church's message to women was that they were a threat to monks and priests. They were viewed as competing with God for their souls. No matter how devout they were, their ecclesiastical service was no longer needed. Clerical celibacy soon bled over into lay marriage. Celibate priests began to express contempt for marriage. In effect, clerical celibacy supported misogyny within the church.[128]

Beguines

The Beguines appeared in the late twelfth century as an alternative to the traditional female orders. They were various groups of ascetics, celibate, normally poor, women living together who were not under permanent vows, a specific rule, or beholden to any order. Thus, they were a religious organization, not an ecclesiastical one[129] that had sought authorization from the papacy. They were not cloistered. They embraced poverty and performed good works. Often, they had their own independent houses and chapters. Southern believes they appeared as a "series of reactions to the conditions of urban life and commercial wealth, combined with disillusionment about elaborate structures of government and systems of theoretical perfection."[130]

The Catholic Church's patriarchal establishment could not imagine a place for the Beguines.[131] They were lay-led by women,

---

[125] Shahar, 35.
[126] Ibid.
[127] J. Moorman, *The Franciscan Order from its Origins to the Year 1517* (Oxford: 1968), 35.
[128] Marie Anne Mayeski, "Excluded by Logic of Control: Women in Medieval Society and Scholastic Theology," in Martos and Hégy, eds., 80.
[129] Shahar, 53.
[130] Cited in Malone, 130.
[131] Ibid., 132.

not attached to any established order, taught Bible and theology to other women, were involved in mysticism, and had not sought the papacy's permission to organize. For these reasons, they were often accused of heresy and insubordination.

Bruno, bishop of Olmütz, (1205-ca. 1281) was among the first to oppose the Beguines in 1273. The "religion of the Beguines had not been approved by the Holy See, that the women used their liberty as a veil of wickedness in order to escape the yoke of obedience to their priests and the coercion of marital bonds."[132] At the Council of Lyons in 1274, the Beguine movement was declared illegal for not having papal permission to organize. The proceedings stated they "have not obtained papal confirmation, are forever prohibited and quashed, no matter how far they have progressed."[133] Soon after, persecution began. In June 1310, a Beguine mystic named Marguerite Porete was burned at the stake for heresy in Paris.[134] In 1317 four more Beguines were burned at the stake in Narbonne.

The Beguines were condemned at the Council of Vienne in 1312. The Council stated:

> We have been told that certain women commonly called Beguines, afflicted by a kind of madness, discuss the Holy Trinity and the divine essence, and express opinions on matters of faith and sacraments contrary to the catholic faith, deceiving many simple people. Since these women promise no obedience to anyone and do not renounce their property or profess an approved Rule, they are certainly not 'religious,' although they wear a habit and are associated with such religious orders as they find congenial ... We have therefore decided and decreed with the approval of the Council that their way of life is to be permanently forbidden and altogether excluded from the Church of God.[135]

---

[132] Cited in Southern, 329.
[133] Malone, 131.
[134] Ibid.
[135] Cited in Southern, 330.

The Beguines were persecuted by the Inquisition.[136] By the fifteenth century, however, the Beguines received limited toleration, but by this time many of its members had joined the established orders.

Forbidden Roles Within the Church

Despite earlier Councils and Conferences that forbade women to take Holy Orders or administer the sacraments, Richard Miller noted that women still performed limited liturgical and administrative roles in the early Middle Ages. They celebrated Mass, distributed communion, heard confessions, and preached. Following the birth of the Carolingian Dynasty in the eighth century, these roles diminished. These women were possibly married to the priest but, nonetheless, living with him caused great embarrassment.[137] That women performed these sacerdotal acts was verified in 747 by Frankish authorities who asked Pope Zachary (741–752) if women could read the gospel or sing at Mass. In no uncertain terms, he told them "no," adding, "Nevertheless, as we have heard to our dismay, divine worship has fallen into such disdain that women have presumed to serve at the sacred altars, and that the female sex, to whom it does not belong, perform all the things that are assigned exclusively to men."[138]

The 829 Council of Paris decreed that not only could women not administer the sacraments, but they could not even touch sacred vessels, ring bells, or light candles for the remembrance of the dead. This decree stemmed from the fear that menstruating women were unclean. Pope Gregory the Great (590–604), in his 597 Letter to Augustine of Canterbury (d. 604), determined that menstruating women could receive the Eucharist. Gregory noted, "Therefore, if that woman who, in her infirmity, touched our Lord's garment was justified in her boldness, why is it that what was permitted to one was not permitted to all women who are afflicted through the weakness

---

[136] Shahar, 55.
[137] Richard W. Miller, *Woman and the Shaping of Catholicism: Women Through the Ages* (Liguori, MO: Liguori Publications, 2009), 59–60.
[138] Translation in Ute Eisen, *Women Officeholders in Early Christianity: Epigraphical and Literary Studies* (Collegeville, MN: Liturgical Press, 2000), 133–34.

of their natures?"[139] This fear continued well into the thirteenth century. An Italian prelate and historian, Sicard of Cremona (1155–1215) stated that out of reverence, menstruating women should not attend church or make offerings. Canonist William Durandus (d. 1296) stated that women who were about to go into labor should not enter the church. Echoing Leviticus 12, Pope Honorius III (1216–1227) decreed women who had recently given birth were not clean enough to enter the church. If a woman gave birth to a girl, the waiting purification period was longer than if she had given birth to a boy.[140]

Gratian's *Decretum* and the *Codex Iuris Canonici*

In 1147, Gratian issued his *Concordia discordantium canonum* or *Concordantia discordantium canonum*, better known as the *Decretum*. It consists of three sections, each based on the opinions of popes, councils, and Church Fathers. The first section concerned distinctions on finer points of canon law. The second contained thirty-six causes concerning ecclesiastical administration and the sacraments, marriage, and penance. The third treated the sacraments and sacred objects. Later editions were made by St. Raymond of Pennaforf (1175–1275) and became known as the *Liber Extravagantium*, endorsed by Pope Gregory IX (1227–1241) in 1234. It served as the basis for the *Codex Iuris Canonici* that remained canon law until 1916. Gratian included works that were later proven to be forgeries. He cited an unidentified author known as Ambroister, whom Gratian believed to be either Augustine or Ambrose. Ambroister was the *Decretum's* authoritative source on women.

The *Decretum* depicted women as having weaker minds than men.

> But if someone were to object that in that case no more is allowed to a husband than to a wife if the husband is unfaithful, he must know that Ambrose does not call him "man" on account of his male sex, but by the strength of

---

[139] Bede, *Ecclesiastical History of the English People*, ed. and trans. Bertram Colgrave and R. A. B. Mynors (Oxford, 1969), 94–95.
[140] Peter Biller, "Christians and Heretics," in *The Cambridge History of Christianity: Christianity in Western Europe c. 1100–1500*, Miri Rubin and Walter Simmons, (New York, NY: Cambridge University Press, 2009), 191.

the soul; and he should realize that "woman" is not called so because of the sex of her body but because the weakness of her mind.[141]

Despite the teaching of Genesis 1:26–29, it was argued that women were not created in the image of God.

> As Augustine[142] says: This is the likeness of God in man [the male], that he is created as the only being, from whom the others have come, and that he possesses, as it were, the dominion of God as his representative, since he bears in himself the image of the one God. So woman is not created in the image of God; that is what [scripture] says: "And God created man [the male], according to the image of God he created him;" and therefore the Apostle also says: "Man certainly must not cover his head, because he is image and reflection of God, but woman must cover her head because she is neither the reflection nor the image of God." And Jerome says: "Since the man is the head of the woman, while the head of the man is Christ, any wife who does not subordinate herself to her husband as her head is as guilty as a man who does not subordinate himself to Christ"... And Ambrose[143] says: "A woman must cover her head because she is not the likeness of God; in order that she may appear submissive ... she must wear this sign ..."

The *Decretum* taught that both the man and woman had to freely consent to marriage. Yet, within marriage, husbands had complete authority. The wife was essentially her husband's servant. A wife could not take a vow of abstinence without his permission. "But in everything else the husband is the head of his wife, and the wife is the body of her husband, so that a wife may make a vow of abstinence if her husband allows her to, but which she may not fulfill

---

[141] *Decretum Gratiani*, Causa 32, question 7, chapter 18, cited in *Corpus Juris Canonici*, ed. A. Friedberg (Leipzig 1879–1881; reprint Graz 1955), vol. 1, col. 1145.
[142] Falsely attributed to Augustine. Pseudo-Augustine is the author.
[143] Falsely attributed to Ambrose. Ambroister is the author.

if her husband forbids her to." "And this is, as I have said before, because of her state of servitude through which she has to be subject to her husband in everything." He then listed ten Church Fathers as his precedent.[144]

Women must be submissive due to original sin.

> Ambrosius[145] says: Women must cover their heads because they are not the image of God. They must do this as a sign of their subjection to authority and because sin came into the world through them. Their heads must be covered in church in order to honor the bishop. In like manner they have no authority to speak because the bishop is the embodiment of Christ. They must thus act before the bishop as before Christ, the judge, since the bishop is the representative of the Lord. Because of original sin they must show themselves submissive.[146]

The ordination of women was forbidden. "What kind of female priest we should accept, the Council of Laodicea shows when it says: 'Those women who are called *presbyterae* by the Greeks but by us are called widows, senior women, *univirae* and *matricuriae*, may not be installed in the church as ordained persons.'"[147] Moreover, women were removed from any sacerdotal task by Causa 2, question 7, princ. "Women cannot, however, be promoted to the priesthood or even the diaconate and for this reason they may not raise a complaint or give testimony against priests in court."[148]

Women could not serve communion.

> It has come to our notice that certain priests despise the Divine Mysteries to such an extent that they hand over the sacred Body of the Lord to a lay person or a woman, in order for them to take them to the sick. The

---

[144] *Decretum Gratiani*, Causa 33, question 5, chapter 11, cited in *Corpus Juris Canonici*, vol. 1, col. 1254–1256.
[145] Falsely attributed to Ambrosius. Ambrosiaster is the author.
[146] *Decretum Gratiani*, Causa 33, question 5, chapter 19, cited in *Corpus Juris Canonici*, vol. 1, col. 1255–1256.
[147] Ibid., Distinction 2 de cons., Chapter 29, cited in *Corpus Juris Canonici*, vol. 1, col. 1323–1324.
[148] Ibid., Causa 2, question 7, princ., cited in *Corpus Juris Canonici*, vol. 1, col. 750–751.

most Blessed Sacrament is therefore entrusted to those people whom it is forbidden to enter the sanctuary or to approach the altar! All people who fear God will understand that this is a terrible and despicable practice. Therefore, the Synod prohibits this in the most strong terms, in order that such irresponsible and repulsive behavior will not happen again. In every single case the priest should himself bring holy communion to the sick. If anyone acts in contrary fashion, he incurs the risk to be demoted.[149]

Women could not teach or baptize.

About baptizing by women we want you to know that those who presume to baptize bring themselves into no small danger. So we do not advise it, for it is dangerous, yes, even forbidden and godless. That is to say, if man is the head of woman and he is promoted to the priesthood, it militates against divine justice to disturb the arrangement of the Creator by degrading man from the preeminence granted to him to the lowest place. For woman is the body of man, has come from his rib and is placed in subjection to him, for which reason also she has been chosen to bear children. The Lord says, 'He will rule over her.' Man has lordship over the woman, since he is also her head. But if we have already forbidden women to preach, how would anyone want to permit them to enter the priesthood? It would be unnatural. For women to be priests is an error of heathen godlessness but not of Christ's way. But if women are permitted to baptize, then Christ would surely have been baptized by his mother and not by John and he would have sent women with us to baptize also, when he sent us out to baptize. But now the Lord never made any such arrangements nor left us with any such scriptural admonition, since he as creator

---

[149] Ibid., Distinction 2 de cons., Chapter 29, cited in *Corpus Juris Canonici*, vol. 1, col. 1323–1324.

of nature and founder of its order knew the gradations of nature and what is proper.[150]

Women could not touch sacred objects, vessels, or vestments.

> "Consecrated women are forbidden to touch the sacred vessels and altar cloths and to carry incense round the altar."[151] Wherefore (Pope) Soter[152] wrote to the bishops of Italy: "It has come to the notice of the apostolic See that consecrated women or nuns among you touch sacred vessels or palls and carry incense round the altar. No one in his senses doubts that this behavior deserves condemnation and correction. Therefore, we command you on the basis on the authority of this Holy See, that you put an end to this behavior thoroughly and as soon as possible. And in order that this kind of plague will not proliferate further in other provinces, we order that the practice be discontinued as soon as possible."[153] Moreover, "The Holy See decrees that the consecrated vessels may be handled only by holy men ordained to the Lord's service and by no others, in order that the Lord in his anger may not punish his people with calamity, in which those who have not sinned may be also destroyed, since it often happens that the righteous suffer for the ungodly."[154] "Women cannot touch or wear sacred vestments. The vestments may not be touched or offered except by consecrated men."[155]

Building on the beliefs of the Patristic Era, Middle Ages theologians, councils, and canon law reinforced the rationale that women could not participate in any churchly function that required

---

[150] Ibid., Distinction 32, Chapter 19, cited in *Corpus Juris Canonici*, vol. 1, col. 122.
[151] Ibid., Distinction 23, Chapter 25, cited in *Corpus Juris Canonici*, vol. 1, col. 85.
[152] This is a false [forged] letter found in the 'False Decretals.'
[153] Ibid., Distinction 23, Chapter 25, cited in *Corpus Juris Canonici*, vol. 1, col. 85.
[154] Ibid., Section III, Distinction 1 de cons., Chapter 41, cited in *Corpus Juris Canonici*, vol. 1, col. 1304–1305.
[155] Ibid., Section III, Distinction 1 de cons., Chapter 42, cited in *Corpus Juris Canonici*, vol. 1, col. 1305.

ordination.[156] Women were viewed as misbegotten men, intellectually and physically defective, and prone to moral failure. Seeing a woman in such an ecclesiastical role could lead men to lust over them. It was argued that women were not in the full image of God unless married. Thus, only men expressed the full image of God. Because Christ was the perfect human, a woman could not represent him in the New Adam's headship or authority.[157] Though Christ consistently referred to himself as son of *anthropos* (human) not son of male (*aner*), because Christ was male, so must his priests be. Moreover, Christ called only men to be his apostles. In 1210, Pope Innocent III (1198–1216) noted, "No matter whether the most blessed Virgin Mary stands higher, and is also more illustrious, than all the apostles together, it was still not to her, but to them, that the Lord entrusted the keys to the Kingdom of Heaven."[158] Women were also in subjection to man in both her pre- and postlapsarian states.[159] As Christ was in subjection to no one and Christ was present in the Eucharist, one under subjection could not serve it. Only men, therefore, could act as extensions of Christ's humanity and represent him as priests. To ensure a male-only priesthood at the turn of the thirteenth century, the church determined that only men could attend universities and be trained for ministry.[160]

Church-Approved Female Role Models

Mary Magdalene

Though Pope Gregory the Great had conflated Mary of Bethany and the unnamed sinful woman who anointed Jesus' feet in Luke 7:36–39 into Mary Magdalene, the repentant prostitute, she became someone to emulate for married women in the Middle Ages.[161] Before following

---

[156] The volume of dictums, however, implies that as late as the twelfth century women were being ordained and serving the sacraments.
[157] Brown and Bohn, eds., 32.
[158] Innocent III, Epistle, 11 December 1210, cited in Arlene Swidler & Leonard Swidler, eds., *Women Priests* (Mahwah, NJ: Paulist Press, 1977), 145–151.
[159] Marie Anne Mayeski, "Excluded by Logic of Control: Women in Medieval Society and Scholastic Theology," in Martos and Hégy, eds., 90.
[160] Ibid., 86.
[161] For more information see Susan Haskins, *Mary Magdalene: Myth and Metaphor* (San Francisco, CA: HarperCollins, 1993).

Christ, she was often represented as wearing jewelry, cosmetics, and sexually alluring clothing. After her repentance, one tradition dictates that she lived the remainder of her life as a penitent and miracle worker in Marseille, France.[162] Her change allowed the church to hold her as a more apt role model for married women than the Virgin Mary.

The Virgin Mary

The Virgin Mary was the greatest role model for women in the Middle Ages.[163] A significant step in her growing stature occurred at the third ecumenical council at Ephesus in 431. At this council she was deemed *Theotokos*, meaning "god-bearer." Mary, therefore, did not give birth only to Christ's physical body but also his divinity. This finding undergirded the eleventh- and twelfth-century belief in the Immaculate Conception that taught since Mary had borne divinity she had to have been born without original sin. Some medieval theologians, such as Aquinas, did not believe in the Immaculate Conception. If she had not been born in original sin, Christ could not be her savior.

> And thus, in whatever manner the Blessed Virgin would have been sanctified before animation, she could never have incurred the stain of original sin: and, thus, she would not have needed redemption and salvation which is by Christ, of whom it is written (Matthew 1:21): "He shall save His people from their sins." But this is unfitting, through implying that Christ is not the "Saviour of all men," as He is called (1 Timothy 4:10). It remains, therefore, that the Blessed Virgin was sanctified after animation.[164]

---

[162] Jacobus De Voragine, *The Golden Legend Book: Readings on the Saints*, trans. William Granger Ryan (Princeton, N.J.: Princeton University Press, 2012), 374–383; Miri Rubin, "Cult of Saints," in Bennett and Karras, eds., 488.

[163] For a more in-depth examination of the development of Mariology see Michael Jordan, *The Historical Mary: Revealing the Pagan Identity of the Virgin Mother* (Berkeley, CA: Seastone, 2004).

[164] Aquinas, "The Sanctification of the Blessed Virgin," *ST*, III, q. 27, a. 2, 2nd rev. ed., trans. Fathers of the English Dominican Province, in New Advent, ed. Kevin Knight, last modified 2017, https://www.newadvent.org/summa/4027.htm.

The Immaculate Conception was used to impose celibacy upon the clergy and monastic orders. It was placed on the liturgical calendar in 1476.

In 553 at the fifth ecumenical council in Constantinople, the decrees enshrined what many Church Fathers had been teaching for centuries: Mary was a lifelong virgin.

> If anyone shall not confess that the Word of God has two nativities, the one from all eternity of the Father, without time and without body; the other in these last days, coming down from heaven and being made flesh of the holy and glorious Mary, Mother of God and always a virgin, and born of her: let him be anathema.[165]

At the Lateran Synod of 649, Pope Martin I (649–655) declared,

> If anyone does not properly and truly confess in accord with the holy Fathers, that the holy Mother of God and ever Virgin and immaculate Mary in the earliest of the ages conceived of the Holy Spirit without seed, namely, God the Word Himself specifically and truly, who was born of God the Father before all ages, and that she incorruptibly bore Him, her virginity remaining indestructible even after His birth, let him be condemned.[166]

By the eighth century, the belief in the Assumption of Mary was well known. Mary, like Elijah, did not die but was taken to heaven immediately after her earthly life was over. According to Pius XII (1939–1958) in 1950, she was given this honor as the New Eve because of her unity with her son.[167] Though Mary's lack of original sin and physical assumption were not declared Catholic

---

[165] "Fifth Ecumenical Council in Constantinople," *Catholic Book*, last accessed 1 June 2021, http://www.catholicbook.com/AgredaCD/Ecumenical_Councils/Constantinople2.htm.
[166] "Canons of the Lateran Council of 649," *Classical Christianity*, last modified 25 March 2012, https://classicalchristianity.com/2012/03/25/canons-of-the-lateran-council-of-649/.
[167] W.N. Kerr, "Mary, Assumption of," in Walter A. Elwell, ed., *Evangelical Dictionary of Theology* (Grand Rapids, MI: Baker Academic, 2001), 746.

dogma until much later,[168] these four teachings known as the "Marian Dogmas" became engrained in the Middle Ages and served as a model for virgins and celibate clerics.

The Eve-Mary antithesis remained a prominent theological construct in the Middle Ages. Anselm of Canterbury (1033–1109) agreed. "Just as the sin which was the source of our loss originated in woman, so too the father of our righteousness and our salvation was born to a woman."[169] Aquinas added his own Aristotelian interpretation to Mary's importance: She was necessary to ensure the universality of redemption. Christ represented the men; Mary represented women and their proper role. As she was an auxiliary to Christ, women were to serve as an auxiliary to men.[170] She was a sexually undefiled woman whom virgins should emulate.

From the fourth century onward, Mary was depicted in many ways, each of which glorified her.[171] One of her most significant roles was that of intercessor. As the mother of Jesus, she had a relationship with her son that allowed her to intervene on behalf of a penitent. She also advocated for the poor, women, and others who found themselves in crisis.[172] Bernard of Clairvaux[173] and Peter Damian[174] wrote sermons and prayers about her. St. Bernard called her the mediator to the mediator.[175] By the tenth century, there were many Marian festivals, four major feasts, and hundreds of churches dedicated to her. Mary was perceived as a woman of virginal virtue. This led to the eleventh-century belief that Mary's body was incorruptible and almost more than human.[176] By the end

---

[168] The Assumption of Mary was declared dogma by Pius XII (1939–1958) in 1950. Mary's lack of original sin was defined by Pope Pius IX (1846–1878) in 1854.
[169] Anselm of Canterbury, *Cur Deus Homo*, PL vol. CLVIII, col. 364.
[170] Ruether, ed., *Religion and Sexism*, 249.
[171] Gregg, 105.
[172] MacHaffie, 63.
[173] S. J. Eales, trans. and J. Mabillon, ed., *The Life and Works of St. Bernard of Clairvaux* (London: Hodges, 1896), 3: 293, 299, 315–316; Roberta Anderson and Dominic Aiden, eds., *Medieval Religion: A Sourcebook* (New York, NY: Routledge, 2007), 7–9.
[174] A Word in Season: Monastic lectionary for the divine office, pt iv, Santoral (1991) pp. 161–162, cited in Roberta Anderson and Dominic Aiden, eds., *Medieval Religion: A Sourcebook* (New York, NY: Routledge, 2007), 6.
[175] Eales and Mabillon, 3:293, 299, 315–316; Anderson and Dominic Aiden, 7–9.
[176] Gregg, 105.

of the thirteenth century, Mary was an intercessor for women, a source of womanly compassion, and the idealized virgin.[177]

While Mary added a feminizing element to the Middle Ages, her depiction still supported an androcentric bias and Christian misogyny. First, she had no real female personhood. She never suffered from sexual temptations. She was depicted as a traditional mother and wife and had no active part in Jesus' ministry. Mary was impossible for women to emulate. Her attributes and the four Marian dogmas were based solely on her role as the mother of Jesus.[178] Mary balanced Eve but owed everything to her son.

Mysticism

The cloistering of many female monastics and their inability to serve in ordained roles led women to seek God in other ways. Mysticism was one of the few avenues open to them in the High Middle Ages. These women had visions of events from the Bible in which Christ's humanity was on display. The most frequent visions were of the Nativity, Christ's Passion, the Annunciation, the Virgin Mary, and God appearing as light. The worshipper was meant to imagine herself present at the event and to suffer or rejoice as it unfolded.[179] Catherine of Siena (1347–1380) claimed to suffer along with Christ on the cross to the point that she received the stigmata. Other mystics' visions, often depicted in erotic terms, were of their union and spiritual marriage to Christ. The visions often involved highly emotional, mental, and often physical religious experiences. Sometimes these experiences led to mental and physical suffering. After many years of effort, some mystics claimed to have directly encountered God.[180] This encounter placed the mystic in union with God.[181] All the female mystics described God as loving and compassionate.

---

[177] Malone, 263.
[178] Ruether, ed., *Religion and Sexism*, 246.
[179] John H. Arnold, *The Oxford Handbook of Medieval Christianity* (Oxford: Oxford University Press, 2014), 398–99.
[180] MacHaffie, 71.
[181] Arnold, 396.

When she recovered from her experience, she described it to another sister who wrote it down for their sisters and other women.[182]

The great mystics such as Hildegard of Bingen (1098–1179), Catherine of Siena, Julian of Norwich (1342–ca.1416), Margery Kempe (1342–1416), Teresa of Avila (1515–1582), and others were held in high regard within Christendom.[183] Monks, such as Bernard of Clairvaux, accepted the validity of their experience, special status, and influence. In a letter to Hildegard of Bingen, he wrote, "We bless the divine grace which resides in you … How can I aspire to instruct you and advise you, who have attained hidden knowledge, and in whom the influence of Christ's anointing still lives."[184] Her visions were also recognized by Pope Eugenius III (1145–1153), King Henry II of England (1154–1189) and his wife Eleanor of Aquitaine (1122–1204).

Catherine of Siena was another influential mystic. She helped to convince Pope Gregory XI (1371–1378) to leave Avignon, France, and return the papacy to Rome.

The Church compared female mystics to the female prophets of the Old and New Testaments (Exodus 15:20, Judges 4–5, 2 Kings 22:14, Acts 21:9).[185] Their sanctity was not tied to their position or title. Aquinas claimed:

> Prophecy is not a sacrament but a gift of God. Wherefore there it is not the signification, but only the thing which is necessary. And since in matters pertaining to the soul woman does not differ from man as to the thing (for sometimes a woman is found to be better than many men as regards the soul), it follows that she can receive the gift of prophecy and the like, but not the sacrament of orders.[186]

---

[182] Malone, 99.
[183] Shahar, 56. Catherine of Siena and Hildegard of Bingen were also active in the secular world.
[184] Saint Bernard, *Opera, Epistola* 266, 1:331, cited in Shulamith Shahar, 56.
[185] Shahar, 56.
[186] Aquinas, "Of the Impediments to This Sacrament," *ST*, Supp. 3, q. 39, art. 1, Summa Theologiae, last accessed 1 June 2021, http://summa-theologiae.org/question/55101.htm.

Hildegard of Bingen wrote, "When God saw man, he saw that he was very good for man was made in his image. But in creating woman, God was aided by man … Therefore woman is the creation of man … Man symbolizes the divinity of the Son of God and woman his humanity. Therefore, man presides in the courts of the world since he rules all creatures, while woman is under his rule and submits to him."[187] Moreover, she did not believe women should be priests.[188] In this regard, the female mystics accepted church teachings.

Even with this support, the church did not accept all of their visions. Because some mystics claimed intimate access to God, it was feared that they might believe or teach that they did not need a priest to petition God or take the eucharist. This challenged the church's hierarchal and ecclesiastical authority. Lay religion, especially when led by weak women who could be easily deceived by Satan, was dangerous and could lead to heresy. The Beguine mystic Marguerite Porete was burned at the stake in Paris in 1310. In her book, *Le Mirouer*, she wrote that after one reached the highest level of divine grace, the person no longer required sermons, sacraments, or the Church. Catherine of Siena and Margery Kempe were both charged with heresy but escaped punishment because they had powerful patrons and never challenged the ecclesiastical hierarchy.[189] Other mystics who lost their political support, such as Joan of Arc (1412–1431), were often executed for witchcraft.

Some scholars have tried to explain these mystical experiences. For many women, mysticism was an outlet for their religious expression and for a more intimate relationship with God. Cloistered women had more time for meditation and prayer, which were conducive to mystical experiences.[190] It was also a form of penance for women who blamed themselves as the source of sin and gateway to the devil. This led some women to yearn to be more closely

---

[187] Hildegard of Bingen, *Liber Divinorum Operum Simplicas Hominis*, PL, vol. 197, col. 885, cited in Shahar, 57.
[188] Hildegard of Bingen, *Liver Scivias*, PL, II, visio 6, 545–546, cited in Shahar, 57.
[189] Chris Wickham, *Medieval Europe: From the Breakup of the Western Roman Empire to the Reformation* (New Haven, CT: Yale University Press, 2016), 189.
[190] Elizabeth Petroff, *Body and Soul: Essays on Women and Mysticism* (New York, NY: Oxford University Press, 1994), 3–24.

tied to Christ and to suffer his passions. Because these women followed such strict ascetic practices, the constant mental and physical strain may have led them to have visions.[191] It could also have been a response to the patriarchal church.

Stereotypes

During the Patristic era, church leaders accused women of being, among other things, lascivious, weak-minded, Eve's daughters in sin, and gossips. These labels continued into the Middle Ages.

Following the Gregorian Reform, celibate clergy began to suspect that women were trying to ruin them. Their writings depicted women as the personification of evil. The bishop of Le Mans Hildebert of Lavardin (1055–1133) wrote, "Woman is treacherous, woman is sordid, worthy of fetters. Her mind is evil, inconstant, impious, full of poison."[192] The French canon and bishop of Acre Jacques de Vitry (ca. 1160/70–1240) believed that woman was "a virtuoso artist, as they say; because she has one skill—that is, in the way of deceiving—more than the devil."[193]

Women were also sexual threats. Canonists taught that women were sexually insatiable. Some held that women's overactive libido was because without the moisturizing effect of sperm the uterus would dry up.[194] Because of their weaker minds and sexual desire women were vulnerable to demonic temptation. If a man merely saw a woman, even at Mass, he could fall under her spell. Women who danced or even looked out a window were often perceived as seductresses. The fourteenth-century Dominican John Bromyard (d. ca. 1352) said that women dressed provocatively to capture men's souls.

> In the woman wantonly adorned to capture souls, the garland upon her head is as a single coal or firebrand of Hell

---

[191] Arnold, 407.
[192] Cited in Cynthia Stewart, *Medieval Heresies and Women's Freedoms* (PhD Dissertation, Vanderbilt University, 2001).
[193] Jacques de Vitry, Sermon 66 in Sermones Vulgares, cited in Alcuin Blamires, ed., *Women Defamed and Women Defended* (Oxford: Oxford University Press, 1992), 147.
[194] Ozment, 11.

to kindle men with that fire; so too the horns of another, so the bare neck, so the brooch upon the breast, so with all the curious finery of the whole of their body. What else does it seem or could be said of it save that each is a spark breathing out hell-fire, which this wretched incendiary of the Devil breathes so effectually ... that, in a single day, by her dancing or her perambulation through the town, she inflames with the fire of lust—it may be—twenty of those who behold her, damning the souls whom God has created and redeemed at such a cost for their salvation. For this very purpose the Devil thus adorns these females, sending them forth through the town as his apostles, replete with every iniquity, malice, fornication.[195]

Women were viewed also as dangerously curious. They wanted more for their lives than the church merited them. This led to the assumption that women were irrational and needed to stay home. Sewing was viewed not only as a needed skill, but it also kept their hands and eyes occupied so they could not get into trouble. The church also saw women as too talkative. Women were created to bear children and to work within the home. Their work was to be done in silence. When women left the home, they congregated with other women. Men believed these women were gossiping and causing problems in the community.[196]

Many male monastics saw women as filthy. Composed by an Augustinian canon in the thirteenth century, the *Ancrene Riwle* described women as follows:

> There cometh out of a vessel such things as it contains. What cometh out of the vessel of thy flesh? Doth the smell of spices or of sweet balsam come thereof? [...] Man, what fruit doth thy flesh bear in all its apertures? Amidst the greatest ornament of thy face; that is, the fairest part between the taste of mouth and smell of nose, hast thou not two holes, as if they were two privy holes? Art thou

---

[195] Cited in Gerald R. Owst, *Literature and Pulpit in Medieval England* (Cambridge: Cambridge University Press, 1933), 384.
[196] Malone, 58–61.

not formed of foul slime? Art thou not always full of uncleanness? Shalt thou not be food for worms?[197]

Albertus Magnus (1200–1280) believed that woman was a natural liar. "What she cannot get, she seeks to obtain through lying and diabolical deceptions. And so, to put it briefly, one must be on one's guard with every woman, as if she were a poisonous snake and the horned devil. [...] Thus, in evil and perverse doings woman is cleverer, that is, slyer, than man. Her feelings drive woman toward every evil, just as reason impels man toward all good."[198]

Witchcraft

Christianity has a long history of supernatural beings using their power and influence against God. In this realm, the witch stood second only to Satan and his demons. Witches and sorcerers appeared as evil beings in the Old and New Testaments. They were condemned in Exodus 22:18 and Deuteronomy 18:10. In 1 Samuel 28:7–25, Saul entreated the Witch of Endor for advice concerning a Philistine threat. In the New Testament, Galatians 5:20 warned against sorcery. In the Patristic era, Tertullian[199] and Augustine[200] believed in witchcraft. Hippolytus and John of Chrysostom did not. Witchcraft was not a concern in the early church.[201]

Prior to the eleventh century, witchcraft was often confused with traditional pagan practices and medicine. The first witches were often women who understood nature and herbal medicine. These "wise women" provided natural cures that could not be explained by approved medical practitioners. As long as these healers were believed to be using their power for good, they were left alone.

---

[197] James Morton, ed. and trans., *The Ancren Riwle* (London: Camden Society [LVII], 1853), 59, 277.

[198] Albert the Great, *Quaestiones super de animalibus* 15.11, 265, 62–266, 6 (QDA, 454), cited in Stan Goff, *The Misbegotten Man: Reflections on War, Sex, and Church* (London: Lutterworth Press, 2015), 67.

[199] Tertullian, *Apology* 22, ANF, 3:36.

[200] Augustine, *City of God*, 21.6, NPNF, 2:17.

[201] F. L. Cross and E. A. Livingstone, eds., *The Oxford Dictionary of the Christian Church*, 3rd ed. (Oxford: Oxford University Press, 2005), 1757–1758.

Emperor of the Romans, Charlemagne (800–814) protected them and ordered the death penalty for anyone who killed a witch.[202]

To evangelize Europe, the church banned nature worship. The church viewed its practitioners as lunatics or as pagans.[203] In the eyes of the church, the worship of spirits that inhabited trees and streams was ignorant but not heretical. According to the *Canon Episcopi* (ca. 900), witchcraft did not exist and therefore had no effect. *Canon Episcopi* deemed them either dreaming or mad. However, if it was believed the devil was involved, these beliefs demanded immediate action. "Bishops and their officials must labor with all their strength to uproot thoroughly from their parishes the pernicious art of sorcery and *malfeasance* invented by the devil, and if they find a man or woman follower of this wickedness to eject them foully disgraced from the parishes."[204]

The Church of the Middle Ages was suspicious and fearful of lay religion. When the importance of the priest, sacraments, confession, and patriarchal hierarchy were challenged, it became heretical. Lay movements, such as the Waldensians and Cathars, that allowed women to take prominent roles in their cultic rites attracted particular scrutiny.[205] The first witch hunts in the late twelfth century were actually waves of persecutions of Waldensian heretics. The Catholic Church charged the Waldensians and Cathars with heresies which included worshipping the devil. Because women preached and participated in all their cultic rites, they were accused of having given their allegiance to the devil. However, as late as 1258 Pope Alexander IV (1185–1261) forbade the Inquisition to persecute witches unless they were charged with heresy.

From the thirteenth century, witchcraft was associated with the devil. By the fourteenth century, witches were considered the devil's accomplices.[206] The Franciscans and Dominicans argued that witchcraft was heresy because it involved making a pact with the

---

[202] Clark and Richardson, 116.
[203] Ibid.
[204] Marc Carlson, "Canon," *Marc Carlson*, last accessed 1 June 2021, http://www.personal.utulsa.edu/~marc-carlson/witch/canon.html.
[205] Julia O'Faolain and Lauren Martines, eds., *Not in God's Image* (New York, NY: Harper and Row, 1973), 207.
[206] Shahar, 270.

devil. In 1398, the Inquisition was given jurisdiction over witchcraft cases.[207]

During the Middle Ages, women were accused of witchcraft four times more than men.[208] Women were midwives at a time when infant mortality rates were high, and these deaths were often attributed to witchcraft.[209] The extraordinarily high number of women being accused of witchcraft was the direct result of the church's belief system.[210]

The Black Death of the fourteenth century killed up to two-thirds of Europe's population. The Hundred Years' War between England and France brought atrocities. Islamic warriors were slowly closing in on the remnants of the Eastern Empire. In the following century, the "Little Ice Age" brought crop failures, mass starvation, and crime. With the rise of commercialization, trade, and the middle class, women began to join guilds and the workforce. Their economic status improved. After commercialization came regional migration. These newcomers were often seen as outsiders. If the community suddenly suffered adversity, the outsiders were blamed. Moreover, the rising middle class disrupted the traditional economic structure. These changes did not sit well with those whose livelihoods depended on the status quo. These changes shook medieval society to its foundation. With no clear answer to these disastrous events and traditional norms being challenged, a scapegoat was needed: it had to be witches.

In the late fifteenth century, a Dominican friar named Heinrich Kramer (1430–1505) petitioned Pope Innocent VIII (1484–1492) to allow the Inquisition to investigate rumors of witchcraft in Germany. In response, Innocent issued the *Summis desiderantes* on December 5, 1484:

> It has recently come to our ears, not without great pain to us, that in some parts of upper Germany, [...] Mainz, Köln, Trier, Salzburg, and Bremen, many persons of both sexes, heedless of their own salvation and

---

[207] Cross and Livingstone, 1757–1758.
[208] MacHaffie, 66.
[209] Wiesner-Hanks, 260.
[210] Kathleen M. Crowther, *Adam and Eve in the Protestant Reformation* (Cambridge: Cambridge University Press, 2010), 48.

forsaking the catholic faith, give themselves over to devils male and female, and by their incantations, charms, and conjurings, and by other abominable superstitions and sortileges, offences, crimes, and misdeeds, ruin and cause to perish the offspring of women, the foal of animals, the products of the earth, the grapes of vines, and the fruits of trees, as well as men and women, cattle and flocks and herds and animals of every kind, vineyards also and orchards, meadows, pastures, harvests, grains and other fruits of the earth.[211]

Innocent then gave his approval to the Inquisition.

We therefore, desiring […] to remove all impediments by which in any way the said inquisitors are hindered in the exercise of their office, and to prevent the taint of heretical pravity and of other like evils from spreading their infection to the ruin of others who are innocent … do hereby decree, by virtue of our apostolic authority, that it shall be permitted to the said inquisitors in these regions to exercise their office of inquisition and to proceed to the correction, imprisonment, and punishment of the aforesaid persons for their said offences and crimes, in all respects and altogether precisely as if the […] places, persons, and offences aforesaid were expressly named in the said letter. And [with assistants] […] may exercise against all persons, of whatsoever condition and rank, the said office of inquisition, correcting, imprisoning, punishing and chastising […] those persons whom they shall find guilty as aforesaid.[212]

Kramer and James Sprenger (ca. 1435–1495) wrote the *Malleus Maleficarum* (Hammer of Witches) in 1486 and included *Summis desiderantes* in the introduction. This was the most authoritative

---

[211] Pope Innocent VIII, *Summis desiderantes*, cited in Henrich Kramer and James Sprenger, *Malleus Maleficarum*, trans. Montague Summers (New York, NY: Dover Publications, Inc., 1971, ed.), xliii.
[212] Pope Innocent VIII, *Summis desiderantes*, cited in Kramer and Sprenger, *Malleus Maleficarum*, xliii.

book on witchcraft produced by the Church. No book did more to associate witchcraft with women and promoted the witch hysteria of the sixteenth and seventeenth centuries. Kramer cited Church Fathers, Old and New Testament scriptures, as well as Cato and Seneca. It also contained generalized attacks on women. The *Malleus* explained why women were more likely to practice witchcraft than men.

> When a woman thinks alone, she thinks evil [...] I have found a woman more bitter than death, and a good woman subject to carnal lust. They are more impressionable than men and more ready to receive the influence of a disembodied spirit [...] They have slippery tongues [...] Since they are weak, they find an easy and secret manner of vindicating themselves in witchcraft. They are feebler both in mind and body. It is not surprising that they should come more under the spell of witchcraft. As regarding intellect or the understanding of spiritual things, they seem to be of a different nature than men [...] Women are intellectually like children [...] And it should be noted that there was a defect in the formation of the first woman, since she was formed from a bent rib, the rib of the breast which is bent in the contrary direction to a man [...] And since through the first defect in their intelligence, they are always more prone to abjure the faith, so through their second defect of inordinate passions, they search for, brood over and inflict various vengeances, either by witchcraft or some other means. Wherefore it is no wonder that so great a number of witches exist in this sex [...] Women have weaker memories, and it is a natural vice in them not to be disciplined, but to follow their own impulses without any sense of what is due [...] She is a liar by nature [...] Let us consider her gait, posture and habit, in which she is vanity of vanities [...] Woman is a wheedling and secret enemy. For the sake of fulfilling their lusts they consort even with devils.[213]

---

[213] Kramer and Sprenger, 41–47.

Sprenger brought a millennium's worth of religious misogyny to the *Malleus*. J. A. Phillips summarizes his arguments.

> [Woman] is more carnal than a man, as is clear from her many carnal abominations.' She is deceitful, with a 'slippery tongue,' 'a liar by nature.' She is naturally credulous and impressionable, therefore, 'quicker to waver in her faith, and consequently quicker to abjure the faith, which is the root of all witchcraft.' Since women are 'feebler both in mind and body,' they have weak memories, are undisciplined, impulsive, and particularly dangerous when given authority over anything. The authors' conclusion is a testimony to the strength and tenacity of the blending of the stories of Eve and Pandora: 'Beautiful to look upon, contaminating to the touch, and deadly to keep;' 'a wheedling and secret enemy.[214]

The *Malleus* linked women's sexuality and witchcraft to devil worship.[215] Witchcraft had its basis in carnal lust.[216] The devil could take on a form that was sexually attractive to women.[217] Eve succumbing to the serpent served as the *Malleus's* evidence. Men were largely immune from the temptations of witchcraft because Christ came to earth as a male.[218] Many women were so lustful that they were not strong enough to allay his advances and became Satan's lover and worshipped him. The *Malleus* then stated that these witches had power over men via sex. Witches could make men potent, impotent, or even sex them to death. Another belief was that a demon would take on the form of a woman, have sex with a man, and collect his semen. The demon would then take the form of a man and impregnate the witch. The child of this illicit act was a demon.[219]

---

[214] J.A. Phillips, *The History of an Idea: Eve* (New York, NY: Harper and Row, 1984), 70; Kramer and Sprenger, 41–47.
[215] Clack, ed., 83.
[216] Kramer and Sprenger, 47.
[217] Belief that demons could have sex with humans is found in early Jewish thought and taken over by Christians.
[218] Clark and Richardson, 118.
[219] Kramer and Sprenger, 21–28.

Scholars estimate that as many as eighty-five percent of those accused of witchcraft were women.[220] The accused tended to be marginalized women such as widows, eccentrics, the poor, and those living on the outskirts of the community.[221] They were blamed for spoiled food, bad harvests, and dead livestock.[222] Midwives also fell under scrutiny. As so many children died at or shortly after birth, the *Malleus* accused midwives of using witchcraft to kill babies. If a child was born with a physical deformity, a midwife's pact with the Devil was often to blame.[223]

In regions where the Inquisition held sway, people accused of witchcraft were forced to confess under torture. Torture had been a part of the Inquisition since the end of the thirteenth century. Angela of Toulouse (1230–1275) was accused of having sex with an incubus and producing a baby that was part wolf and snake. After being tortured, she was burned at the stake.[224]

An accused witch would first be stripped and shaved so that her body could be examined. If she had any birthmark, mole, or blemish, it was considered a witch's teat. Confession, however, was sought to eliminate any doubt. Under physical duress, the accused would describe the witch's sabbath, black masses, shriveling penises, night flying, and casting spells.[225] If the accused refused to confess, it was believed she had help from the Devil and was often drowned.[226]

In Europe, the persecution of witches was at its height from the mid-sixteenth to the end of the seventeenth century. The largest witch hunts took place in the Holy Roman Empire, Switzerland, and eastern France. The Spanish, Roman, and Portuguese Inquisitions rejected the *Malleus*. They were more concerned with heretics and conversos. England and Scotland participated in witch hunts but did not permit torture. They used witch trials instead.[227]

---

[220] Clark and Richardson, 119.
[221] Brown and Bohn, eds., 36.
[222] Wiesner-Hanks, 258.
[223] Kramer and Sprenger, 140.
[224] Malone, 216.
[225] Ibid., 218.
[226] Brown and Bohn, eds., 37.
[227] Wiesner-Hanks, 268–69.

The persecutions often ended when men or prominent citizens were accused.[228]

The witch hunts were not limited to the Catholic Church. Martin Luther (1483–1546) and John Calvin (1509–1564) believed that witches should be burned as heretics. While it is doubtful that he believed it, Henry VIII of England (1509–1547) accused Anne Boleyn (1501–1536) of witchcraft.[229] A strong believer in witchcraft, King James VI of Scotland (later King James I of England (1603–1625) wrote *Daemonologie* in 1597.[230] The Salem Witch Trials of 1692 helped define the intolerance of New England Puritanism. The scientific revolution and then the Enlightenment, with its emphasis on reason and anticlericalism, helped bring the witch hunts to an end. The last known burning of a witch was in Switzerland in 1782. According to one estimate, between 1450 and 1750 between fifty thousand and one million accused witches, most of whom were women, were put to death.[231]

Conclusion

As in the Patristic era, there were women leaders like Hilda, Hildegard, Catherine, Theresa, the Beguines, and others who served the Medieval Church wisely and sacrificially overcame the limitations placed on their gender. Yet with the aid of Aquinas' teachings, the church's misogyny was institutionalized.[232] Women were misbegotten men whose only purpose was to bear children. Women had no leadership in the church other than the convent, and even they were viewed with some suspicion. Women were no longer merely a detriment to society because they were weaker in all respects to men, but they could now be a witch in league with the devil. The Virgin Mary provided some succor, but even she was a faint light in the darkness. As the Middle Ages faded into the Enlightenment, the Church's hostility to women continued.

---

[228] Brown and Bohn, 36.
[229] Clark and Richardson, 124.
[230] James was the King of Scotland at the time. With his ascension to the English throne in 1603 England became more aggressive in persecuting accused witches.
[231] Clark and Richardson, 116.
[232] In 1879 Pope Leo XIII declared that Aquinas' teaching normative for the church.

CHAPTER SIX

Women in the Reformation

The Renaissance (ca. 1300–1650) began in a highly religious time, between the scholasticism of the Late Middle Ages and the Protestant Reformation. This rebirth of learning encompassed the arts, literature, exploration, architecture, and science. It asserted the value of the individual, and the ability to forge one's own way.[1] Christian humanists stressed the principles of classical learning for studying the Bible in its original languages, understanding the importance of the individual conscience and human dignity, and the belief that all humans are created in the image of God. By these means, they sought spiritual renewal and institutional reform of Christian society. Women of means participated in the artistic Renaissance. They included the poet Marguerite D'Angoulême (1492–1549), Queen of Navarre, and the Court of Ferrara's literary critic and philosophy lecturer, Olympia Morata (1526–1555). Elisabetta Gonzaga (1471–1526), the wife of Duke Guidobaldo of Urbino (1482–1508), was the patron of writers, artists, and scholars who attended her court. Due to his position and desire for them, Thomas More's (1476–1535) daughters were among the few women who acquired a classical education. Women of the lower classes did not have the opportunity for formal education.[2] Unless they served

---

[1] Bard Thompson, *Humanists and Reformers: A History of the Renaissance and Reformation* (Grand Rapids, MI: William B. Eerdmans Publishing Company, 1996), 3.
[2] John D. Woodbridge and Frank A. James III, *Church History, Volume Two: From Pre-Reformation to the Present Day* (Grand Rapids, MI: Zondervan Academic, 2013), 103.

as a muse or model for an artist, women had only a slight impact on the explosion of the arts, scientific inquiry, exploration, and literature that swept Europe.

The Renaissance also promoted the reading of Greek and Roman classics in their original languages. Because of their stress on *ad fontes*, humanism played a significant role in the Reformer's insistence on *sola scriptura*, which allowed for new insight. Unlike the Renaissance, which was limited to the educated elite, the Reformation affected all of society.[3] When Martin Luther (1483–1546) posted his 95 Theses on the door of the Wittenberg Cathedral on October 31, 1517, the Reformation began in earnest and the all-encompassing and powerful Catholic Church began to splinter. Soon others such as Ulrich Zwingli (1484–1531), John Calvin (1509–1564), and other Radical Reformers began to redefine Christianity by discussing *sola scriptura*, the rejection of papal supremacy, and justification by faith.[4] In England, Henry VIII's (1509–1547) desire for a male heir led to a break from the Catholic Church and the birth of the Anglican Church and the rise of Puritanism and Separatism. Women were not at the forefront of the Reformer's new ideas, but they were not ignored.

Desiderius Erasmus (1466–1536)

Desiderius Erasmus was one of the most influential scholars of the sixteenth century. The "Prince of Humanism" prepared a new edition of the Greek New Testament in 1516 and brought to light many errors found in the Vulgate. His secular writings challenged medieval thinking. *In Praise of Folly* (1511), a satirical attack on Catholic superstition, was one of the most significant books of the Renaissance and played an important role in the beginnings of Reformation thought.

Erasmus also wrote a great deal about women and their role in the church, family, and society. The first eleven chapters of *On Disdaining the World* (1521) were a paean to monasticism. In the

---

[3] Thompson, 372.
[4] Willis P. DeBoer, "The Role of Women," in *Exploring the Heritage of John Calvin: Essays in Honor of John Bratt*, ed. David E. Holwerda (Grand Rapids, MI: Baker Book House, 1976), 238.

twelfth chapter, which was written much later, he turned against it. Many convents had lost their direction as parents placed their daughters in cloisters either because they could not afford a dowry or find them a suitable husband.[5] Erasmus bemoaned these actions, complaining that "most monasteries are in the midst of worldly affairs."[6] He maintained that unless one enters the monastic life freely and with pure intentions, the monasteries are just as worldly as anything outside of its gates. He held no regard for superstitious parents who believed having a daughter who was dedicated to the church would provide some manner of spiritual blessing.[7] As a result of his 1523 edition of *Colloquies*, representatives of the Catholic Church accused Erasmus of deprecating monasticism and challenging the superiority of celibacy over marriage. Erasmus defended his beliefs in the *1526 Usefulness of Colloquies*.

> I denounce who, despite the opposition of parents, lure boys and girls into a monastery, playing upon their innocence or their superstitiousness, persuading them there is no hope of salvation outside a monastery. If the world is not full of such fishermen; if countless happy natures, which had been chosen vessels of the Lord had they sensibly taken up a career suited to their natural talents, are not most miserably buried alive by these creatures—then I have been wrong in my warning. But if ever I am compelled to speak my mind plainly on this topic, I will give such a description of those kidnappers, and the magnitude of their mischief, that all will agree I had plenty of reason to utter these warnings. I wrote politely, however, to avoid giving malevolent men occasion for making trouble.[8]

---

[5] Erika Rummel, ed. *Erasmus on Women* (Toronto: University of Toronto Press, 1996), 23.
[6] In *The Collected Works of Erasmus*, trans. R. A. B. Mynors and D. F. S. Thomson; ann. W. K. Ferguson (Toronto: University of Toronto Press, 1974), 66:173. Hereafter cited as *CWE*.
[7] Rummel, 26.
[8] Ibid.

Erasmus' assertion that marriage was part of God's plan for humanity in his *In Praise of Marriage* (1518) attracted the wrath of many theologians.

> If we seek the author of marriage, we discover that it was founded and instituted not by Lycurgus, or Moses, Solon, but by the sovereign maker of all things, and from the same it received praise, and by the same it was made honorable and holy. In the beginning, when he created man out of clay, God realized that man's life would be thoroughly unhappy and unpleasant unless he joined Eve to him as a companion. Therefore, he did not bring man's wife out of clay from which he had brought man, but out of Adam's ribs, so that we might clearly understand that nothing should be dearer to us, nothing more closely joined, nothing more tightly glued to us than a wife.[9]

Erasmus was attacked by Catholic theologians who believed it was nothing more than a covert attack on celibacy. He responded with *Apologia for the Declamation of Marriage* (1519) in which he claimed *In Praise of Marriage* was merely a rhetorical exercise. Whatever his intent, Erasmus made a strong case for marriage.

While Erasmus railed against mandatory celibacy, he often extolled virginity.[10] He viewed it as praiseworthy as long as it was not imposed on the majority of humanity.[11] Marital sex should be rare.

> If you are married, consider how worthy of respect is an unsullied marriage-bed and make every effort possible that your marriage imitate the hallowed wedding of Christ and the Church, of which your marriage is a reflection, and therefore should be as free as possible of all immorality and filled with fecundity. In no state of life is it not a most base thing to serve lust.[12]

---

[9] Erasmus, *In Praise of Marriage*, cited in Rummel, 59.
[10] Alan W. Reese, "Learning Virginity: Erasmus' Ideal of Christian Marriage," *Bibliotheque d'Humanisme et Renaissance* 57, no. 3 (1995): 552.
[11] Erasmus, *The Institution of Marriage*, cited in Rummel, 67.
[12] Erasmus, *Enchiridion*, CWE, 66:117.

There was less danger in marital abstinence than in being unmarried. If the desires of the flesh overtook a married couple, they could give in to each other. Women should be taught the chaste life but not all are capable of learning it. Celibacy, therefore, could not be mandatory. Erasmus compared virginity to matrimony. "The marriage I praise is very similar to virginity, a marriage in which one has a wife for the production of offspring, not the satisfaction of lust."[13]

In 1525, Martin Luther had married and in doing so invited further debates on the merits of marriage and celibacy. The following year, Erasmus penned *The Institution of Marriage*. He did not fail to pick up on the irony of a celibate man writing about marriage. "Perhaps my remarks may seem as inept … as those of the philosopher whom Hannibal considered foolish for disputing about war when he had never taken part in one."[14]

Erasmus rejected forced or arranged marriages. Ignoring hundreds of years of tradition and teaching, he then cited scripture to prove the superiority of marriage. God's first command was to be fruitful and multiply.[15] Christ's first miracle occurred at a wedding.[16] The Patriarchs had many wives and were not superior to them.[17] When discussing why Jesus did not marry if marriage was superior to celibacy, Erasmus noted that Jesus was special. "As if indeed there were not very many aspects of Christ's life that should excite our wonder rather than our imitation. He was born without a father, was given birth without pain to his mother, and came forth from a sealed sepulcher."[18] Moreover, he opposed mandatory celibacy for priests and monks.[19] In a letter to Parisian theologian Noel Bead (1470–1537), he wrote that clerics who had already taken their vows and were desirous of marriage should be released from their vows of celibacy.[20] Marriage was a gift for all.

---

[13] *CWE*, 71:93.
[14] P.S. Allen, ed., *Opus Epistolarum Erasmi Roterodami* (Oxford, 1906–58), Ep. 1715:7–9. Hereafter cited as Allen.
[15] Erasmus, *In The Institution of Marriage*, cited in Rummel, 59.
[16] Ibid., 58.
[17] Ibid., 65.
[18] Ibid., 60.
[19] Reese, 551.
[20] Erasmus, *Private Correspondence to Noel Bead*, Allen, Ep. 1620:52.

Erasmus also rejected the idea that grace was confirmed *ex opera operato*[21] at the consummation of a marriage. Grace came when the couple persevered. If the couple divorced or separated, a true union had not taken place and "God had not brought it together."[22] Divorce, therefore, was permitted for reasons other than adultery. For sacramental grace to occur, the marriage had to endure.

The Institution of Marriage also demonstrated Erasmus's belief that the wife was to be subjugated to her husband at home and in society. This subjugation should be kind not as a "farmer drives his cattle, but as the spirit rules the body."[23] Citing Ephesians 5:22–26, he suggested that husbands were superior to wives and, as such, wives must be obedient.[24] This obedience was not because of her feminine weakness, but rather she was being obedient as Christ was obedient to his death. Husbands, however, must treat their wives with love and kindness. They were to "bestow on them with that love that Christ has bestowed and continues to bestow on his church. So far was he from repudiating her as adulterous and rebellious that he surrendered himself to death to purchase her salvation."[25] The wife was not equal in rank with her husband, but she was equal in merit. Citing Galatians 3:26, Erasmus held that before Christ all were equal.

> [Christ] made us equal in so many ways. He redeemed us by the same death, he washed us in the same blood, he justified us with the same faith, he refreshes us with the same Spirit, he strengthens us with the same sacraments, he honors us with the same name, calling us his brothers and the children of God, and he has summoned us all to share the same inheritance of heavenly life.[26]

---

[21] The merit of the sacrament did not depend on the merits of the minister or recipient.

[22] Anton G. Weiler, G. Barker and J. Barker, "Desiderius Erasmus of Rotterdam on Marriage and Divorce," *Dutch Review of History*, no. 84 (2004): 155.

[23] Erasmus, *The Institution of Marriage*, cited in Erika Rummel, 100.

[24] CWE, 69:340.

[25] Ibid., 69:397–9.

[26] Ibid., 99:362.

Erasmus often made contradictory statements about women. On the one hand, he praised their abilities as caregivers, in prayer, and for diligence in running a home. A wife helped her husband become a better person by submitting to him and ministering to his needs.[27] He especially praised women who raised daughters who could run an orderly home. Women who had learned this skill would never have difficulty finding a husband.[28]

On the other hand, in his 1523 *Manual for Women*, he noted that women needed firm control by men. Young widows, therefore, should remarry because their lives would be useless otherwise. He often compared women to children and wrote that they were gossips, superstitious, and slanderers.[29] A housewife was to be kept busy in the home or "her thoughts turn inevitably towards evil."[30] He did not view them as seducers or prone to practicing witchcraft.[31] They were just more simple-minded and emotional than men.

Erasmus also held that women should receive an education.[32] In a letter to Guillaume Budé (1467–1540) he wrote that reading and studying were the "occupations that best protect the mind from dangerous idleness […] the mind trained is attracted to virtue […] nothing is more intractable than ignorance." Moreover, educated women were more interesting. "One can really enjoy their society. I differ profoundly from those who keep a wife for no purpose except physical satisfaction, for which half-witted females are better fitted."[33]

Erasmus' positions on women were difficult to discern because he often took the role of devil's advocate. His theology was in transition. He accepted some of the misogyny of the Medieval Church and adopted some of the progressive ideas that prefigured the Reformation. He also derided the belief that celibacy was superior to marriage. He held that priests should be permitted to marry if they wanted. He spoke out against forced marriages that always proved

---

[27] *Conjugium*, in Erasmus, *The Colloquies of Erasmus*, trans. Craig R. Thompson (Chicago and London: The University of Chicago Press, 1965), 123–124.
[28] Rummel, 3.
[29] *CWE*, 167, 491–2, C; *CWE*, 29:276, 283.
[30] Erasmus, *The Institution of Marriage*, cited in Rummel, 85.
[31] Rummel, 8.
[32] Ibid., 3.
[33] *CWE*, 1233:112–15.

more damaging to the wife than to the husband. By advocating for divorce, he permitted unhappy married women (and men) to escape a life of disappointment. Even if it was to keep women out of trouble and to entertain men who wanted more than sex from their wives, he believed that women should have an education.

Martin Luther

Martin Luther affected Christianity more than any other person in the sixteenth century. His key concepts of justification by faith and the priesthood of all believers went against traditional Catholicism. Luther's writings primarily concerned these key theological aspects and other issues that set him apart from the Catholic Church.

Luther changed Christianity forever, but he was initially a Catholic Augustinian friar with a doctoral degree in theology. He was well-schooled in canon law, the teachings of the Church Fathers and Medieval scholastics, and other writings.

Luther's understanding of the creation account changed after 1525.[34] When he wrote *Lectures on Genesis* (1523–1524),[35] he accepted late medieval thought as taught by the Catholic Church. The first creation account detailed the spiritual birth of humanity, and the second recorded the creation of their physical bodies. Luther held that both Adam and Eve were made in the image of God, but Adam was the archetype. Eve was a lesser being but not an afterthought. "Just as Adam was created in accordance with a well-considered counsel, so [...] Eve (was) created according to a definite plan."[36]

In the second account, Luther highlighted the importance of Adam being created first. The order of creation signified rank and this meant that Eve must be subordinate to Adam.[37] Because woman came from man's side, she was to be his assistant or "helpmeet."[38]

---

[34] Mickey L. Mattox, "Luther on Eve, Women, and the Church," *Lutheran Quarterly Review* 17, no. 4 (Winter 2003):456–74.
[35] First published in 1527.
[36] *Luther's Works*, eds. J. Pelican and H.T. Lehmann, 55 vols., (Philadelphia, PA: Fortress, 1958ff.), 1:115. Hereafter cited as *LW*.
[37] Douglass, 60.
[38] Kathleen M. Crowther, *Adam and Eve in the Protestant Reformation* (Cambridge: Cambridge University Press, 2010), 111.

Moreover, because Eve's substance was derived from Adam, women took the name of their husbands at marriage.

When discussing the soul, Luther was a Neoplatonist. The male, Adam, was wiser, stronger, and had a more rational soul. Eve was weaker and her soul was less rational, so she gave in more easily to the pleasures of the flesh.[39] For this reason, the man should be in charge and make all major decisions.

Luther believed that God had designed separate roles for men and women. Adam was to work the land. Eve was to tend the home. They were also commanded to be "fruitful and multiply." Following Augustine, Luther believed sex in the Garden of Eden would have been painless and without lust or shame. The couple would be very fertile and birth simple. In *Lectures on Genesis*, he wrote, "How blessed was the state of man in which the begetting of offspring was linked to the highest respect and wisdom, indeed with the knowledge of God. Now the flesh is so overwhelmed by the leprosy of lust that in the act of procreation the body becomes downright brutish and cannot beget in the knowledge of God."[40]

When Luther wrote *Enarrationes on Genesis*[41] in 1525 his views on creation had changed. He wrote that, before the Fall, Eve had been equal to Adam. They were both entrusted with equal shares of ruling God's creation. Eve, however, remained subordinate to Adam in the area of preaching. God entrusted Adam with his order concerning the Tree of Life. Luther held that the tree was "Adam's church, altar, and pulpit."[42]

Luther stated that woman was physically weaker and thus inferior to man.[43] Eve, however, was still created in the image of God, but it was a lesser image.

> For the woman appears to be somewhat different from the man, having different members and a much weaker nature. Although Eve was a most extraordinary creature—similar to Adam so far as the image of God is

---

[39] *LW*, 1:66–69.
[40] Ibid., 1:71.
[41] Luther's classroom lectures were given between 1525 and 1535.
[42] *LW*, 1:95.
[43] Mattox, 463.

concerned; that is, in justice, wisdom and happiness—she was nevertheless a woman. For as the sun is more excellent than the moon (although the moon, too, is a very excellent body), so the women, although she was a most beautiful work of God, nevertheless was not the equal of the male in glory and prestige.[44]

God placed Adam and Eve into the perfect Garden of Eden. God provided for all their needs. Then, the serpent appeared. Prior to 1525, Luther believed the serpent was a product of fallen angels.[45] The serpent was either Satan or one of his minions.

Because Adam was the perfect image of God, the serpent did not approach him. Eve was prone to flattery and gullible.[46] The serpent, therefore, approached Eve when Adam was off tending the garden.[47] He offered her godlike knowledge if she ate from the forbidden tree. Immediately, the woman engaged the serpent and believed his words. Luther held that Eve passed on her flaws to all future women. She took the fruit, ate it, and then gave some to Adam, who also ate. Because Eve gave the fruit to Adam, Luther held her more responsible.[48] Adam, however, should have known better. "He makes the sin all the heavier and more gruesome. She was a fool, easy to lead astray, did not know any better. But he had God's word before him. He knew it well and should have punished her."[49]

Young Luther (pre-1525) believed that Eve sinned because she resented her husband's superior status and his authority over her.[50] She did not look to Adam when Satan approached her about the tree. She was secondary in rank to her husband, and he had more information about the tree as God spoke directly to him about it. As Adam was not given to emotional decisions, he

---

[44] *LW*, 1:68–69.
[45] Kathleen M. Crowther, 46.
[46] *Luthers Werkes, Tischreden*, 12 vols. (Weimar: Verlag Hermann Böhlaus Nachfolger, 1912–21), 9:334. Hereafter cited as *WA*.
[47] Mary Hayter, *The New Eve in Christ: The Use and Abuse of the Bible in the Debate about Women in the Church* (Grand Rapids, MI: Eerdmans Publishing House, 1987), 104.
[48] *LW*, 8:115–18.
[49] *WA*, 24:82.
[50] J. A. Phillips, *The History of an Idea: Eve* (New York, NY: Harper and Row, 1984), 105.

would not have believed the serpent's lies.[51] Eve's failure to obey God and consult Adam led to the Fall and a change in the primordial couple's relationship.[52] Before the Fall, Eve's subjugation was more in the manner of second among equals. Now her situation was forever altered. Her subjugation was more punitive. She was to be obedient. All Eve's posterity were under the same punishment for her act.[53] The couple immediately realized they were naked and their innocence was lost. Lust took over, and they had sex. From this point forward, humanity's lower elements dominated the act of procreation. Lust now overcame reason.[54]

The older Luther (post-1525) believed that before the Fall, Eve was wise and engaged the serpent because she realized it was one of the creatures that she and Adam held in dominion.[55] The Fall occurred because the first couple did not believe God's command concerning the tree. Her subordination occurred when God handed down her punishment.[56] In comparison to her husband, Eve was now an inferior creature.[57] Luther's marriage to Katherine Von Bora (1499–1552) in 1525, his love for her and the six children she bore may have been responsible for his reevaluation of Eve.[58]

The Catholic Church held that because of Eve's role in the Fall women should disavow their sexuality. If Eve had not led Adam into sin, procreation would have taken place without lust. Adam and Eve were virgins before the Fall and embracing that state should be the goal of all Christians. Marriage, therefore, was an inferior state to virginity. It was a concession for those who could not control their lust. Luther did not agree. He believed that virginity was a gift for those who had no sexual desire. It should not be required

---

[51] Mattox, 460.
[52] Rosemary Radford Ruether, *Women and Redemption: A Theological History* (Minneapolis, MN: Fortress Press, 1998), 124.
[53] Classen and Tanya Amber Settle, "Women in Martin Luther's Life and Theology," *German Studies Review* 14, no. 2 (May 1991): 237.
[54] *WA*, 24:102.
[55] Barbara J. MacHaffie, *Her Story: Women in the Christian Tradition*, 2nd ed. (Minneapolis, MN: Fortress Press, 2006), 93.
[56] *WA*, 42:138; *LW*, 1:185.
[57] Joanne Carlson Brown and Carole R. Bohn, eds., *Christianity, Patriarchy, and Abuse: A Feminist Critique* (Cleveland, OH: Pilgrim Press, 1989), 33.
[58] Mattox, 462.

for clergy.⁵⁹ There was no reason why a pastor, who only differed from the laity in vocation, should not be permitted to have a family. Many clergy members were already having illicit relationships with women, and marriage would give their wives and children some legal rights and security.⁶⁰ Moreover, he believed that allowing ministers to marry would help create a Christian society.⁶¹ Marriage was the natural state of humanity and he encouraged nuns to break their vows of celibacy and marry.⁶² He did not believe sex was sinful or that women used it to lead men into immorality.⁶³ Those who chose celibacy were ignoring God's mandate of Genesis 1:28. "After God had made man and woman he blessed them, 'Be fruitful and multiply.' From this passage, we may be assured that man and woman should and must come together in order to multiply."⁶⁴ Luther disagreed with those who believed marriage was a necessary evil and noted, "I shall die as one who loves and lauds marriage."⁶⁵ Luther also berated the Catholic Church's hypocrisy for declaring marriage a sacrament in 1184 and then demeaning it as secondary to virginity.

Many people took religious vows to avoid time in Purgatory. They believed that working for God gave them a spiritual advantage over the laity. The laity was not as close to God as the priests or monastics and could not approach him and seek forgiveness. Luther employed justification by faith and the priesthood of all believers to level the playing field between the clergy and laity. Justification by faith taught that Christ alone saved; works were of no aid. The clergy, therefore, could not merit salvation through celibacy. Saving faith was equally available to the clergy, laymen, and women.⁶⁶ The priesthood of all believers ended the need for a priest to mediate for lay people when petitioning God for forgiveness. All believers, including women, were their own priests and could approach God

---

[59] David C. Steinmetz, "Theological Reflections on the Reformation and the Status of Women," *Duke Divinity School Review* 41, (1976): 201.
[60] MacHaffie, 91.
[61] Steinmetz, 202.
[62] Crowther, 108.
[63] MacHaffie, 91.
[64] *LW*, 45:18.
[65] *WA*, 1:174.
[66] *LW*, 11:10.

directly. Luther believed that no one who wanted to follow God's mandate to be "fruitful and multiply" should take a vow of celibacy.

> Therefore, priests, monks, and nuns are duty-bound to forsake their vows whenever they find that God's ordinance to produce seed and to multiply is powerful and strong within them. They have no power by any authority, law, command, or vow to hinder this which God has created within them. If they do hinder it, however, you may be sure that they will not remain pure but inevitably besmirch themselves with secret sins or fornication. For they are simply incapable of resisting the word and ordinance of God within them. Matters will take their course as God has ordained.[67]

For Luther, the husband and wife were far better models for Christian life than the monk and the nun. "[Monks and nuns] cannot boast that what they do is pleasing in God's sight, as can the woman in childbirth even if her child is born out of wedlock."[68] Luther knew that many members of the clergy were involved with women and having children out of wedlock.

> There was in Austria, at Nieuburg, a convent of nuns, who, by reason of their licentious doings, were removed from it, and placed elsewhere, and their convent filled with Franciscans. These monks, wishing to enlarge the building, foundations were dug, and in excavating there found twelve great pots, in each of which was the carcass of an infant. How much better to let these people marry, than, by prohibition thereof, to cause the murder of so many innocent creatures.[69]

Luther believed that marriage, genuine love, and the importance of familial relationships were essential. The man who loved

---

[67] Ibid., 45:19.
[68] Ibid., 45:41.
[69] Martin Luther, *Table Talk*, trans. William Hazlitt (London: HarperCollins Publishers, 1995), 354. Hereafter cited at *TT*.

and cared for his family was more of a saint than a priest or monk. "The legends or stories of the saints which we have in the papacy are not written according to the norm of Holy Scripture. For it is nothing to wear a hood, fast, or undertake other hard works of that sort in comparison with those troubles which family life brings, and the saints [e.g., the patriarchs] bore them and lived in patience."[70]

He believed that everyone should marry if possible. Those who did not marry were fighting their sex drive and ignoring God's dictum to procreate.[71] Like other men of his era, he also feared that women who were not under the control of a man could prove a danger to herself or society.[72] In certain situations, he even maintained that polygamy was permitted.[73]

Luther maintained that God created a well-ordered world where the man was in charge. Before the Fall, there had been two orders or estates: the ecclesiastical and the domestic (*oeconomia*). After the Fall, a third estate, the *politia*, became necessary.[74] Reading Genesis through Ephesians, Luther believed that Eve must now submit to Adam in all three estates.[75] Women were now subjugated to men in the home, church, and society. Women did not gain a new social or theological position if they became Christians. Women were to accept their punishment. Woman's subservience was based on order and God's punishment due to original sin. He made this point clear in *Lectures in Genesis*.

> This punishment, too, springs from original sin; and the woman bears it just as unwillingly as she bears those pains and inconveniences that have been placed upon her flesh. The rule remains with the husband, and the wife is compelled to obey him by God's command. He rules the home and the state, wages wars, defends his

---

[70] *WA*, 42:55.
[71] *Encyclopedia of the Renaissance and Reformation*, s.v. "Women," 4:291.
[72] Scott Hendrix, "Masculinity and Patriarchy in Reformation Germany," *Journal of the History of Ideas* 56, no. 2 (April 1995): 178.
[73] John L. Thompson, "Patriarchs, Polygamy, and Private Resistance: John Calvin and Other on Breaking God's Rules," *The Sixteenth Century Journal* 25, no. 1 (Spring 1994): 10.
[74] *WA*, 24:102.
[75] Phillips, 104.

possessions, tills the soil, builds, plants, etc. The woman, on the other hand, is like a nail driven into the wall [...] The wife should stay at home and look after the affairs of the household, as one who has been deprived of the ability of administering those affairs that are outside and that concern the state.[76]

Luther once told his wife, Katie, "You make me do what you will; you have full sovereignty here and I award you, with all my heart, the command in all household matters, reserving my rights in other points."[77] The wife's primary vocation was to bear and raise children. He advised mothers:

If a mother of a family wishes to please and serve God, let her not do what the papists are accustomed to doing: running to churches, fasting, counting prayers, etc. But let her care for the family, let her educate and teach her children, let her do her task in the kitchen [...] If she does these things in faith in the Son of God, and hopes that she pleases God on account of Christ, she is holy and blessed.[78]

Luther's comments about the role of mothers were unforgiving. "Women are created for no other purpose than to serve men and be their helpers. And even if they bear themselves weary—or ultimately bear themselves out—that does not hurt. Let them bear themselves out. This is the purpose for which they exist."[79] "If women grow weary or even die while bearing children, that doesn't harm anything. Let them bear children to death; they are created for that."[80]

Women were to be silent in the *ecclesia* estate. This dictum was founded in the creation when Adam was told by God to give Eve his message concerning the tree. Referencing 1 Corinthians 14, Luther insisted that women could not receive ordination. She could preach or baptize if a male was not available.[81] If it was an infrequent

---

[76] *LW*, 1:202–3.
[77] *TT*, 335.
[78] *WA*, 43:20, 31–36.
[79] *LW*, 45:46.
[80] Merry E. Wiesner-Hanks, "Women."
[81] *LW*, 30:135; 39:234.

outpouring of the spirit, women could prophesy.[82] The priesthood of all believers allowed for women to speak about Christ, but in the home. Luther did create a new office for women. Since ministers could now marry, the role of the pastor's wife became a coveted position.[83] The pastor's wife was expected to set an example.

As Luther's teachings began to spread, many convents closed. Some nuns were forced to leave the convent. For many, the cloister was a more attractive option than marriage.[84] They despaired that they could no longer dedicate their lives to Christ and be leaders in their own world. They had sacrificed themselves in their desire to emulate the Virgin Mary and it was no longer an option.[85] Women were restricted to the role of helpmate.[86] Moreover, the cloister was safer than joining Luther's movement.[87] Rather than find husbands as Luther had hoped, many women moved back home with their families or chose to live with others in a religious community not tied to the church.[88] Closing some convents left women homeless, destitute, and with no means to integrate into this new society.[89]

Luther believed that women should not participate in the estate. He was not a misogynist, but he believed women were like children and should remain in the home under the close control of their husbands.[90] Women were more than capable in the home, but the outside world was that of men.

> But when they talk about matters other than those pertaining to the household, they are not competent. Although they have words enough, they are lacking in

---

[82] *WA*, 13:111.

[83] Wendy Fletcher-Marsh, "Towards a Single Anthropology: Developments in Modern Protestantism," in *Equal at the Creation: Sexism, Society, and Christian Thought*, 2nd ed., eds. Joseph Martos and Pierre Hégy (Toronto: University of Toronto Press, 1998), 134.

[84] Steven Ozment, *When Fathers Ruled: Family Life in Reformation Europe* (Cambridge, MA: Harvard University Press, 1983), 15.

[85] Ann Braude, *Sisters and Saints: Women and American Religion* (Oxford: Oxford University Press, 2008), 11.

[86] MacHaffie, 93.

[87] Classen and Settle, 232.

[88] *Encyclopedia of the Renaissance and Reformation*, s.v. "Women," 4:294.

[89] Martos and Hégy, 132.

[90] *WA*, 1:17; 1:26.

substance, which they do not understand. For that reason, they speak foolishly, without order, and wildly, mixing things together without moderation. It appears from this that woman was created for housekeeping but man for keeping order, governing worldly affairs, fighting, and dealing with justice—[things that pertain to] administering and leading.[91]

Luther removed marriage as a sacrament and made it a favored status as commanded by God. By removing its sacramental status, however, divorce became a possibility.[92] Divorces could be granted for impotence, adultery, or failure to fulfill marital duties.[93]

Luther's concept of the Virgin Mary changed after 1517. Before 1517, he accepted the traditional Marian Catholic teachings (*Theotokos*, Immaculate Conception, and perpetual virginity).[94] After 1517, he no longer held to her Immaculate Conception or role as intercessor.[95] He maintained, however, that Mary lived a sinless life of perpetual virginity. In his 1521 *Commentary on the Magnificat*, he stressed God's grace bestowed on Mary and her obedience to God.[96]

Luther and the Protestant Reformation had a profound effect on women. His doctrine of the priesthood of all believers and justification by faith was often applied in gender-specific ways. For men, these doctrines granted freedom from Catholicism but not as much for women. Women were ontologically the same as men and had equal access to God as men did, but they were still subjugated to men. Single women were viewed with suspicion. Moreover, Luther never advocated for woman's equality. His belief that women should not have any leadership roles other than wife and mother did little to elevate women; especially those who may have found fulfillment in convents.

---

[91] Ibid., 1:1054.531–32.
[92] MacHaffie, 89–91.
[93] Classen and Settle, 234.
[94] Remigius Bäumer and Leo Scheffczyk, eds., *Marienlexikon* (Regensburg: Institutum Marianum, 1994), 190.
[95] Ibid., 191.
[96] H. George Anderson, J. Francis Stafford, and Joseph A. Burgess, eds. (1992). *The One Mediator, The Saints, and Mary: Lutherans and Catholics in Dialogue*, (Minneapolis, MN: Augsburg, 1992), 7:239, 381; Crowther, 33.

Luther's teaching on the superiority of marriage not only lifted the status of marriage but also of women. Within the constraints of marriage, women were partners to be cherished. Justification by faith and the priesthood of all believers were meant to eliminate the stranglehold the clergy held on access to God and provide the laity with a closer relationship to God. In later years, Luther's teachings limited gender-based discrimination in theology and social practice. Luther, therefore, helped remove the stigma of Eve's sin and provided an avenue for equality in many Protestant denominations.

John Calvin

John Calvin was a French reformer and pastor in Geneva, Switzerland. Calvin had been trained as a lawyer in France. He broke with the Catholic Church in 1530 and became a Protestant in 1533. In 1535, he fled Catholic persecution to Basel, Switzerland, where he penned the first draft of his influential *Institutes of the Christian Religion*. Further editions appeared in 1539, 1543, 1550, and 1559. This text became a handbook for the Protestant Reformation. In it, Calvin's dependence on Augustine was manifested in his own strong belief in predestination and the absolute sovereignty of God.

Calvin settled in Geneva in 1541 where he ruled most city affairs and implemented his theological system. The majority of Calvin's writings on women were not found in the *Institutes*,[97] but rather in his *Commentaries*.[98]

Calvin held that in Genesis 1 God created Adam and Eve as rational beings, which made them equal in every way and endowed with complete free will. This state of equality, however, changed in Genesis 2 when they received their bodies. Adam and Eve remained equal but Adam's position was first among equals. Because Adam was created first,[99] he was already the governor of the world before the woman first appeared.[100] Eve was created

---

[97] John Calvin, *Institutes of the Christian Religion* (1559), ed. and trans. Henry Beveridge (Grand Rapids, MI: Eerdmans, 1953).
[98] Quotations from Calvin's *Commentaries* are from the *Calvin's Commentaries*, 22 vols. (Grand Rapids, MI: Baker, 1999). Hereafter cited as *CC*.
[99] Douglass, 60.
[100] Ibid.

as a companion and helpmate.[101] The woman came from the man and was an accessory, like a branch comes from a tree trunk. God, therefore, "forever established the man above the woman."[102] As an accessory or appendage, the woman should obey the man.[103] The woman was to complete the man. Calvin averred that even if the Fall had not taken place, Eve's subordination to Adam would not have changed.[104] God planned this cosmic order for humanity to be permanent. Calvin believed that both men and women were created in the image of God, but there was a difference based on honor.[105] Women were not marked with the image of God in the same manner as men.[106] Women were equal regarding moral perfection related to the mind and heart. Yet, "Men are preferred to females in the human race. We know that God constituted man as the head and gave him a dignity and preeminence above that of the woman […] It is true that the image of God is imprinted on all; but the woman is inferior to man."[107] The woman's inferiority was in respect to the domestic, political, social, and ecclesiastical order.[108] Subjugation in these realms was due to woman's secondary place in creation.[109]

In spiritual matters, women were in the image of God.[110] When discussing 1 Corinthians 11, Calvin affirmed that Christ is the head of both men and women. "To be a child of God, ruled by his Holy Spirit and a participant in inheriting the Kingdom of Heaven, to pray to God, to be baptized, to come to the Lord's Supper—in none of these things are we permitted to distinguish between males and females […] This is what we must note concerning Paul's words

---

[101] Willis P. DeBoer, "The Role of Women," in *Exploring the Heritage of John Calvin*, 240.
[102] John Calvin, *Sermon on 1 Corinthians 11:4–10*, *Calvini Opera*, eds. William Baum, Edward Cunitz, and Edward Reuss, trans. David E. Holwerda, 59 Vols. (Brunswick: Schwestche, 1863–1900), 49:728–29. Hereafter cited as *CO*.
[103] Calvin, *Commentary on 1 Timothy 2:13*, *CC*, 11:69.
[104] Willis P. DeBoer, "The Role of Women," in *Exploring the Heritage of John Calvin*, 241.
[105] Mary Potter, "Gender Equality and Gender Hierarchy in Calvin's Theology," *Signs* 11, no. 4 (Summer 1986): 727.
[106] Douglas, 33.
[107] Calvin, *Sermon on Genesis*, *CO*, 146.
[108] John L. Thompson, "Creata ad Imaginem Dei, Licet Secundo Gradu: Woman as the Image of God According to John Calvin," *Harvard Theological Review* 81, no. 2 (April 1998): 136.
[109] Rosemary Radford Ruether, *Women and Redemption*, 126.
[110] Willis P. DeBoer, "The Role of Women," in Holwerda, 253.

that the head of the man is Jesus Christ. He is very much the head of men and women in those things I have just mentioned."[111] Moreover, when he discussed the image of God in Ephesians, he wrote:

> This also certainly has to apply to all women. If they are not in the church, they have no hope of the promised salvation. But we know that there is this sure foundation: God has sent Jesus Christ, who has gathered us to himself in such a way that the image of God which had been destroyed through Adam's sin is restored. Certainly, this image belongs to women just as much as to men. Therefore, St. Paul, when he writes to the Ephesians about the hope of salvation, does not speak exclusively to the men. He does not select one sex to the exclusion of the other. Rather he calls without distinction, the men as much as the women, to become involved in becoming like him who created them, even (to use Paul's words) in all holiness. Now can it be required only of men that they develop this holiness, while women live any way they please? Obviously, the opposite is the case.[112]

Calvin rejected the belief that Eve seduced Adam. Instead, he praised her for initially resisting the serpent. Calvin maintained that Eve capitulated because she wanted to be like God. Adam followed her in sin because he too wanted to be like God. He did not hold Eve solely responsible for the Fall. Moreover, Eve was almost absent from the story.[113] In his *Commentary on 1 Timothy*, he admitted the text stated that Eve alone was deceived and that Adam wrongly submitted to her. Calvin reiterated that Timothy spoke of Eve as the origin of sin. Adam was the parent to humanity and the closest to the image of God. It was through Adam, therefore, that sin entered the world as noted by Paul in Romans 5:12.[114]

---

[111] Calvin, *Sermon on 1 Corinthians 11:2, 3, CO*, 49:718–19.
[112] Ibid., 11:4–10, CO 49:726.
[113] Calvin, *1536 Institutes of Christian Religion, Calvini opera selecta*, ed. Peter Barth and William Niesel, 5 vols. (Munich: Christian Kaiser Verlag, 1974), 1:49, 50–51. Hereafter cited as *OS*; Douglas, 46.
[114] Kristen E. Kvam, Linda S. Schearing, and Valerie H. Ziegler, eds. *Eve & Adam: Jewish, Christian, and Muslim Readings on Genesis and Gender* (Bloomington, IN: University of Indiana Press, 1999), 254.

Prior to the Fall, Eve was subject to her husband but her subjection was benign.[115] After the Fall, the subjection became akin to bondage. As Calvin explained, "Thus, the woman, who had perversely exceeded her proper bounds, is forced back to her own position. She had, indeed, previously been subject to her husband, but that was a liberal and gentle subjugation; now, however, she is cast into servitude."[116]

The Fall also disrupted the natural order. While Calvin emphasized the importance of mutual submission in marriage, the husband now exercised a stauncher headship. A firmer hand in the home would help reestablish proper societal order. When women did not submit to their husbands it discouraged men.[117] Women must respect the divinely appointed order because it pleased God for the man to take precedence.[118] If the wife graciously submitted to her husband in the home, men would take the lead in society, and their contribution would benefit women.[119]

Unlike Luther, Calvin showed little interest in sex in the Garden of Eden. He noted that procreation was part of God's original plan. "It is not good that the man should be alone." Human beings required companionship. Prelapsarian sexual relations would have been chaste. Now it was based purely on lust.[120] Sexual relationships between husband and wife, therefore, were still meant for procreation and to control lust. The conjugal nature of marriage was how God chose to propagate humanity. Man and woman were complete only when the two become one.[121] If a person was born with no sexual desire, chastity was a gift but not superior to marriage.[122]

---

[115] Jane Dempsey Douglass, "Woman and the Continental Reformation," in *Religion and Sexism: Images of Woman in the Jewish and Christian Traditions*, ed. Rosemary Radford Ruether (Eugene, OR: Wipf and Stock Publishers, 1998), 299.
[116] Calvin, *Commentary on Genesis 3:16, CC*, 1:172.
[117] Rosemary Radford Ruether, 123.
[118] Calvin, *Sermon on 1 Timothy 2:12–14*, trans. L.T. (London: Bishop and Woodcoke, 1579), 214–15.
[119] Douglass, *Women, Freedom, and Calvin*, 35.
[120] John Calvin, *Institutes of the Christian Religion*, ed. John T. McNeil (Philadelphia, PA: Westminster Press, 1960), 2.13.3.
[121] Calvin, *Commentary on Genesis, CO*, 23, 28.
[122] MacHaffie, 90.

Calvin believed that marriage was humanity's better state, and, thus, women were not a necessary evil.[123] Rather, she was to assist the man to live well. She was not created for him merely to satisfy his lust but to be his companion.[124] They were bound together by mutual service. "The male sex has the superiority over the female, but on this condition, that they ought to be bound together in mutual good will; the one cannot get on without the other […] Let them then be tied to each other by the bond of mutual duty."[125]

Interpreting Genesis 1–3 through Ephesians 5, Calvin did not think that marriage elevated women. Marriage was the way that the headship of the man was expressed over the woman.[126] Women were completely subjugated to their husbands.[127] Husbands were meant to rule the home.[128] The husband, however, should not abuse his authority over his wife.

> Let the husbands think on their duty […] They are advanced to that honor of superiority on a certain condition, namely, that they should not be cruel towards their wives, or think all things that they please to be permissible and lawful, for their authority should rather be a companionship than a kingship. For there is no question that the husband is not the wife's head to oppress her or to make no account of her. But let him understand that the authority he has puts him so much the more under obligation to her. For seeing he is the head, he must have discretion in himself to guide his wife and his household. And what is the way to bring that to pass but to use kindness and mildness, and discreetly to support his wife in respect of the frailty which he knows to be in her, even as St. Peter warns us (I Peter 3:7). You see then that husbands must require obedience from their wives while at the same time they themselves must also do their own duty; and let them consider that they will not be upheld

---

[123] Rosemary Radford Ruether, 123.
[124] Calvin, *Commentary on Genesis 2:18*, CC 1:130.
[125] Calvin, *Commentary on 1 Corinthians 11:11*, CC, 20:359–360.
[126] Willis P. DeBoer, "The Role of Women," in *Exploring the Heritage of John Calvin*, 250.
[127] Phillips, 104.
[128] Ozment, 50.

before God, if they give occasion to their wives to rise against them.[129]

Calvin believed Matthew 19:9 gave both men and women the right to divorce.[130] He allowed Geneva's pastors to place it in the city's 1547 Marriage Ordinances.[131] Few divorces, however, were granted in Geneva, often to the detriment of the wife. No matter the cruelty, the wife must be obedient to her husband and subjugate herself to him. God saw her pain and would judge the husband for misusing his authority as the head of the family. Unless a wife was in danger of losing her life, she must remain with her husband.[132]

> We have a special sympathy for poor women who are evilly and roughly treated by their husbands, because of the roughness and cruelty of the tyranny and captivity which is their lot. We do not find ourselves permitted by the Word of God, however, to advise a woman to leave her husband, except by force of necessity; and we do not understand this force to be operative when a husband behaves roughly and uses threats to his wife, nor even when he beats her, but when there is imminent peril to her life, whether from persecution by the husband or by his conspiring with the enemies of the truth, or from some other source […] we exhort her […] to bear with patience the cross which God has seen fit to place upon her; and meanwhile not to deviate from the duty which she has before God to please her husband, but to be faithful whatever happens.[133]

Calvin believed that God decreed a cosmic order that set the universe into motion and laws that hold it in place. He also created

---

[129] Calvin, *Sermon on Ephesians 5:22–26*, (Edinburgh: Banner of Truth Trust, 1974), 569–570.
[130] Douglass, 61–62.
[131] *The Register of the Company of Pastors of Geneva in the Time of Calvin*, ed. and trans. Philip E. Hughes (Grand Rapids, MI: Eerdmans, 1966), 77, 79.
[132] Calvin, *Sermon on Ephesians 5:22–26*, (Banner of Truth Trust, 1974), 569–70.
[133] *CO*, 17:539.

a political order that organized the family, society, civil state, and the church. In this order, God had placed men over women.[134]

Calvin held that women's freedom in Christ was separate from the temporal world. Galatians 3:28 spoke of things to come in the heavenly world. For now, women, both married and unmarried, should not hold a leadership position in society.[135] Men should be rulers.[136] Women rulers went against decorum and tradition. The natural order as affirmed by God demanded that women submit to men.[137] He maintained that 1 Corinthians 14:34 and 1 Timothy 2 demonstrated that women should have no role in public leadership. "And unquestionably, wherever even natural propriety has been maintained, women have in all ages been excluded from the public management of affairs. It is the dictate of common sense, that female government is improper and unseemly."[138] Moreover, a woman should stay out of public leadership roles as it would take her away from the home. It would distract her from her duties as wife and mother.[139]

Calvin lived in the age of Queen Mary (1553–1558) and Queen Elizabeth (1558–1603) of England, and Queen Mary (1542–1567) of Scotland. He held that God permitted women to lead or reign when he was seeking to punish a people or to call to attention that no qualified man had stepped forward.[140] Calvin spoke highly of the Protestant Elizabeth[141] but not the Catholic Mary Tudor. Mary and other lesser female monarchs must be obeyed and tolerated much as a disobedient Israel was forced to receive women rulers (Isaiah 3:12).[142] Though Calvin objected to female rulers, he was much more open to the idea than were Luther and John Knox (1514–1572).

Calvin believed in the priesthood of all believers, but he did not believe women should hold church office. A woman minister

---

[134] Douglass, 24.
[135] Potter, "Gender Equality and Gender Hierarchy in Calvin's Theology," 725.
[136] Willis P. DeBoer, "The Role of Women," in *Exploring the Heritage of John Calvin*, 244.
[137] Calvin, *Sermon on 1 Timothy 2:12–14*, in *Sermons of M. John Calvin on the Epistles of St Paul to Timothy and Titus*, trans. L.T (London: Bishop and Woodcoke, 1579), 212.
[138] Calvin, *Commentary on 1 Corinthians 14:34*, CC, 20:468.
[139] Ozment, 68.
[140] John L. Thompson, "Creata ad Imaginem Dei, Licet Secundo Gradu," 137.
[141] Willis P. DeBoer, "The Role of Women," in *Exploring the Heritage of John Calvin*, 261.
[142] Douglass, 96.

would subvert the natural order.¹⁴³ Women should not preach, teach, be ordained, or serve on any governing bodies. Women could prophesy as this was a spiritual gift. Calvin never explained why women could not serve as deacons. DeBoer maintained that Calvin believed the office was only for men and Paul must have been referring to widows.¹⁴⁴ As in the political sphere, women could lead for no other reason than to shame the men.¹⁴⁵

Calvin viewed Paul's admonition to female silence as a teaching determined by a local custom or tradition and not as a commandment.¹⁴⁶ Concerning 1 Corinthians 14:35–36, Calvin believed Paul was telling women to stop interrupting the service.¹⁴⁷ Advice such as Paul's should not be taken lightly, but only Christ's commands and doctrine were binding. Church governance based on tradition, therefore, could be changed if it did not damage propriety, decorum, and proper order.¹⁴⁸ The same could be said of women not covering their heads while praying.¹⁴⁹ The church should be sensitive to forms of worship and respectful of cultural differences. Calvin, therefore, believed that in the future women could take greater roles in worship. The Reformation had disrupted Europe. The time for change was in the future. These customs and potential changes, however, did not change the natural order.¹⁵⁰

When God used women like Deborah in an unusual way, it was because no men were available. God was chastising men.¹⁵¹ This was why women were the first to witness the angel at Christ's resurrection. "It may be thought strange, however, that he does not produce more competent witnesses; for he begins with a woman [...] and I consider this was done by way of reproach, because [the disciples were] so tardy and sluggish to believe. And, indeed, they deserve not only to have women for their teachers, but even

---

¹⁴³ Calvin, *Commentary on 1 Timothy 2:12*, CC, 11:69.
¹⁴⁴ Willis P. DeBoer, "Calvin on the Role of Women," 268.
¹⁴⁵ MacHaffie, 94.
¹⁴⁶ Calvin, *Commentary on 1 Corinthians 14:37*, CC, 20:472; Jane Dempsey Douglass, *Women, Freedom, and Calvin* (Philadelphia, PA: The Westminster Press, 1985), 62–63.
¹⁴⁷ Ibid., 20:471–72.
¹⁴⁸ *Encyclopedia of the Renaissance and Reformation*, s.v. "Women," 4:291.
¹⁴⁹ John Calvin, OS, 1:255–58.
¹⁵⁰ Thompson, "Creata ad Imaginem Dei, Licet Secundo Gradu," 140.
¹⁵¹ Calvin, *Sermon on 1 Timothy*, CO, 53:221–22; *Commentary* on 2 Timothy, CO, 52:276.

oxen and asses."[152] In his attempt to shame men, Calvin avoids praising women.

Calvin was no misogynist, but he did believe that women were morally weaker than men and required male dominance.[153] Women were more prone to vanity, curiosity, and immodesty. He also presented them as being more apt to sexual sins.[154]

> Talkativeness is a disease of woman and it is increased by old age. To this is added, that women think that they are eloquent enough, if they are not given to prattling and slander—if they do not attack the characters of all. The consequence is, that old women, by their slanderous talkativeness, as by a lighted torch, frequently sent on fire many houses. Many are also given to drinking so that, forgetting modesty and gravity, they indulge in unbecoming wantonness.[155]

Calvin held that women were not as culpable as men who professed good deeds. He made this clear when discussing 1 Timothy 2:10.[156] "True it is, that this belongs to men and women: but let us mark, that when St. Paul speaks here of women, he binds men much more to such declarations of their faith: for if there were any excuse to be had, no doubt it belongs to women rather than to men, because of their infirmity. And indeed, these creatures are to be born withal."[157]

Calvin's belief that Eve was not solely responsible for the Fall, that women were spiritually equal to men, and wives were not a necessary evil was a slight improvement in the view of women. Like Luther, he permitted divorce, but only for adultery and under the gravest situations. His greatest achievement was his teaching that

---

[152] Calvin, *Commentary on John 20:1–17, CC,* 18:217, 260.

[153] David D. Gilmore, *Misogyny: The Male Malady* (Philadelphia, PA: University of Pennsylvania Press, 2001), 86.

[154] *CO,* 53:197–98; 54:234.

[155] Calvin, *Commentary on Titus 2:3, CC,* 11:311–312.

[156] Willis P. DeBoer, "The Role of Women," in *Exploring the Heritage of John Calvin,* 249.

[157] Calvin, *Sermon on 1 Timothy 2:9–11,* cited in David E. Holwerda, *Exploring the Heritage of John Calvin: Essays in Honor of John Bratt* (Grand Rapids, MI: Baker Book House, 1976), 249.

several of the Pauline passages that silenced women in the church should be read in a cultural context. By doing so, Calvin, perhaps unwittingly, made it possible for women to improve their position in church and even perhaps become a pastor.

The English Reformation

In continental Europe, the Protestant Reformers such as Luther and Calvin built their efforts on the people whose religious life had become burdensome under the Catholic Church. The evangelical Reformers often sought support from civil magistrates in their effort to correct the churches under their jurisdiction.

The English Reformation unfolded differently. King Henry VIII (1509–1547) needed a male heir, and Pope Clement VII (1523–1534) would not allow him to divorce his first wife Catherine of Aragon (1509–1533) who had borne him a daughter. The king's solution required severing the English Church from Rome. Thus, a marital problem that led to a political problem sparked the Reformation in his realm.

In the late Middle Ages, most of the population in England were Catholic. There were more than 138 convents in England, most of which were Benedictine or Cistercian. Although priests administered the sacraments, abbesses ruled the convents. In the convents, nuns had some freedom from the direct control of men. Beguines were particularly active in Norwich.[158] Some women found more equality within the Lollard movement which allowed them to speak and even preach.[159] Aside from nuns and the occasional patroness and parish church warden, women held no recognized church positions. Many wives and mothers enjoyed some practical religious leadership in the home as they supervised and prepared their families for fasts, feasts, and holy days. Women's roles in English society and Catholic life differed little from that on the continent.

Despite being named a "Defender of the Faith" for his denunciation of Luther's idea of justification by faith, Henry made himself the head of the Catholic Church in England. His initial reforms retained the primary doctrines of the medieval church such as

---

[158] Patricia Crawford, *Women and Religion in England, 1500–1720* (New York, NY: Routledge, 1993), 22–23.
[159] Ibid., 25.

transubstantiation and clerical celibacy. Nevertheless, he appointed the bishops who freed him from his second marriage to his second wife, Anne Boleyn (1533–1536). Following the advice of his archbishop Thomas Cranmer (1533–1555) and chief minister, Thomas Cromwell (1534–1540), Henry solidified his control over the church by confiscating the convents and monasteries throughout his realm.

Henry VIII's son and only male heir, Edward VI (1547–1553) was raised Protestant. In 1549, he pressured Parliament to allow clerical marriage, which many of the clergy halfheartedly accepted.[160] Archbishop Cranmer himself was married.[161]

In 1547, Edward's "A State of Matrimony" was published and read twice a year to all English congregations. It stressed that wives must be obedient to their husbands in accordance with biblical commands, avoid strife, and acknowledge their faults. It also noted that a woman was "a weak creature […] more prone to all weak affections and dispositions of the mind […] than men be; and lighter […] and more vain in their phantasies and opinions."[162] In a sermon preached before Edward by Hugh Latimer (1487–1555), he warned of how difficult it was for a man to rule his wife.

> For a woman is frail, and has a proclivity to all evils: a woman is a weak vessel, and may soon deceive a man and bring him into evil. Many examples we have in scripture. Adam had but one wife […] and how soon had she brought him to consent unto evil, and to come to destruction! How did wicked Jezebel pervert king Ahab's heart from God and all godliness and finally unto destruction![163]

With the death of Edward in 1553, Henry VIII's elder daughter, Mary Tudor (1553–1558), came to the throne. The daughter of Catherine of Aragon, she had been raised a devout Roman Catholic. She reinstituted Catholicism and hundreds of Protestants fled to the

---

[160] Eric Josef Carlson, "Clerical Marriage and the English Reformation," *Journal of British Studies* 31, no. 1 (January 1992): 1–31.
[161] MacCullough, 628.
[162] Doris Mary Stenton, *The English Woman in History* (London: George Allen and Unwin, 1957), 104–106.
[163] Hugh Latimer, *Works*, ed. G. E. Corrie, 2 vols. (Cambridge: Cambridge University Press, 1844–45), 1:94.

continent. Many of these "Marian exiles" ended up in Geneva where they became disciples of Calvin. Anglican priests were forced to divorce their wives. Many women and men remaining in England refused to accept Roman Catholicism and fifty-four of these women paid for their faith with martyrdom.[164]

Following the death of Mary Tudor, Henry VIII's younger daughter, Elizabeth (1558–1603), became Queen of England. She had been raised Protestant but realized that England faced religious strife at home and something had to be done before the country tore itself apart. She determined the Church of England would follow a *via media*. It would be a Protestant church in doctrine but retain some Catholic traditions. To avoid controversy in worship, she did not alter Mary's decree that priests could not marry, but rather she chose not to punish those who had married. Concerning the lives of women, little changed. The *Homily on the State of Matrimony* (1562) reminded wives to:

> Be in subjection to obey your own husbands. To obey is another thing than to control or command; which yet they may do to their children, and to their family; but as for husbands, must they obey, and cease from commanding, and perform subjection [...] Let women be subject to their husbands, as to the Lord: for the husband is the head of the woman as Christ is the Head of the church. Here you understand that God hath commanded that ye should acknowledge the authority of the husband, and refer to him in honor and obedience.[165]

Despite the Reformation principle of spiritual equality, women remained inferior to men and were required to be in submission. There were no ministerial roles open to women within the Anglican Church.[166]

---

[164] Arthur Geoffrey Dickens, *English Reformation*, rev. ed., (London: Collins/Fontana, 1967), 364–65.
[165] *Certain Sermons or Homilies Appointed to be Read in Churches in the Time of Queen Elizabeth* (1908), 539–40.
[166] Crawford, 39.

When Elizabeth became queen, the Marian exiles returned to England in jubilation. These returned Exiles stressed the need for a personal encounter with the Holy Spirit that led to the awareness of one's election and a conversion experience. This experience typically took place by hearing a sermon ending in the inward call to faith by the Holy Spirit. They would then enter into a covenant of grace with God. They followed the soteriological teachings of John Calvin and stressed the importance of predestination. Morality was an important aspect of their lives. Strict Sunday Sabbath observance held a high priority. They emphasized the importance of family as a "Little Commonwealth" and a means of teaching godly behavior.[167] Many hoped for a glorious age under Elizabeth and wanted to make the Church of England thoroughly Protestant.

Upon their return to England, some exiles immediately rejected the Church of England's *via media*, or middle way. Their idea of a true church did not include retaining traditional liturgies, vestments, sermons that did not have salvation as their focus, written prayers in the *Prayer Book*, and other such practices. Therefore, they determined to purify the Church of England from any Catholic elements and became known as "Puritans."

Puritan husbands still expected their wives to be obedient and pious. They upheld a rigid Old Testament patriarchy, which they believed the Apostle Paul taught. They promoted marriage and eschewed asceticism. They also allowed for divorce if one partner committed adultery.[168] The wife was spiritually equal to her husband, but she remained in subjection to him.[169] If she obeyed him, took care of the children, and lived a pious life, she was deemed a good woman. Women, however, were dangerous. Puritan Divine Richard Greenham (1535–1594) believed that even women who proved gifted wives must be subject to their husbands" [or] they are nothing […] if she be not obedient, she cannot be saved."[170] Puritan

---

[167] Paul S. Seaver, *Wallington's World: A Puritan Artisan in Seventeenth-Century London* (Stanford, CA: Stanford University Press, 1985), 183–4.

[168] Charles H. George and Katherine George, *The English Protestant and the Family* (Princeton, NJ: Princeton University Press, 1961), 271.

[169] Katharine M. Rogers, *The Troublesome Helpmate: A History of Misogyny in Literature* (Seattle, WA: University of Washington Press, 1966), 135.

[170] Richard Greenham, *The Workes of the Reverend Richard Greenham*, ed. Henry Holland (London, 1612), 742.

Preacher Henry Smith (ca. 1560–1591) warned husbands to control their wives. "Such furies do haunt some men […] as though the devil had put a sword into their hands to kill themselves; therefore, choose whom thou mayest enjoy, or live alone still, and thou shalt not repent thee of thy bargain." He provided examples of the fate of men who did not keep their wives in check. Job's wife exacerbated his plight when she told him to curse God and die. Samson was ruined by Delilah, and David was mocked by Michal. "This is the quality of that sex, to overthwart, and upbraid, and sue the preeminence of the husbands, therefore, the philosophers could not tell how to define a wife, but called her the contrary to a husband, as though nothing were so cross and contrary to a man as a wife."[171]

In Scotland, John Knox (1514–1572) had been involved in an attempt to reform the Church of Scotland. His earlier efforts at reform had incurred the wrath of Scotland's Catholic regent, Mary of Guise (1554–1560). He found favor with King Edward VI of England in 1550. When Mary Tudor became queen, however, he was among the Marian exiles in Geneva. He returned to Scotland in 1559 and founded the Presbyterian Church of Scotland.

John Knox held that women were spiritually equal to men. Women, however, were meant to serve. Their temporal subordination included even monarchs. In this regard, he disagreed with Calvin who held that a female ruler was occasionally necessary. In 1558, Knox published *The First Blast of the Trumpet Against the Monstrous Regiment of Women* in which he declared female monarchs repugnant and against biblical order.

> For who can deny that it is repugnant to nature, that the blind shall be appointed to lead and conduct as they see fit? That weak, sick and impotent people shall be in charge of the whole and strong, and finally, that the foolish, mad and frenetic shall govern the discreet and give counsel to the sober of mind? And such be all women, in comparison with men who bear the authority. For their sight in civil regiment is but blindness: their strength is weakness:

---

[171] Henry Smith, *The Works*, ed. T. Fuller (Edinburgh: James Nichol, 1866), 1:12–13, 21, 30.

their advice: foolishness: and judgement: frantic, if it be rightly considered.[172]

The targets of his book were most certainly Mary Tudor of England and Scottish regent, Mary of Guise, and her daughter Mary Stuart (1542–1587). Mary Tudor's death brought the Protestant Elizabeth I (1558–1603) to the throne. Elizabeth still banned Knox from entering England. Knox's comments referenced the Bible, Tertullian and other Church Fathers, and Aristotle. His popularity in Scotland made him impossible to ignore. Mary Stuart had spent her youth in France where she had been married to the Dauphin. Upon his death, she returned to Scotland in 1561 to assume the throne. Knox caused her great anguish, and she accused him of leading an insurrection against her. On at least one occasion, his words brought her to tears.[173] Otherwise, they had no effect.

King James of Scotland assumed the English throne in 1603. James had been raised in the Church of Scotland. The Puritans, who were primarily Presbyterians, had high hopes for James and the Protestantization of the Church of England. James, however, preferred bishops to presbyteries, and the Anglican Church was not altered along Puritan lines.

Anglican ministers, such as William Gouge (1575–1653) in his 1622 *On Domestical Duties*, stated that the wife was only slightly above the children, and she should treat the husband like a king.[174] Thomas Gataker (1574–1654) maintained that even if the wife was more talented than her husband, she must obey him, because "the husband is superior, and the wife the inferior […] the husband is the head, the wife the body."[175] Poet-turned-cleric John Donne (1572–1631) shared Augustine's belief that two men living together was more peaceful. Donne claimed that Eve was created second and made to be Adam's helper. She was not assigned by God to aid

---

[172] John Knox, *The First Blast of the Trumpet Against the Monstrous Regiment of Women*, ed. Edward Arber, 15 August 1878, last accessed 1 May 2022, https://www.amherst.edu/system/files/media/0104/Knox%2C%20Monstrous%20Regiment%20Excerpts.htm. The modern English wording is by this author.

[173] John Guy, *My Heart is my Own: The Life of Mary Queen of Scots* (London: Fourth Estate, 2004), 176.

[174] Crawford, 39.

[175] Thomas Gataker, *Marriage Duties* (1637), 188.

Adam in naming the animals. She was taken from man's side and in so doing man became weaker. She should be chaste, sober, and truthful. There was no reason for a woman to be educated. Eve was also responsible for the Fall.

> Even before there was any Man in the world, to solicit, to tempt her chastity, she could find another way to be false and treacherous to her husband: both the husband, and the wife offended God, but the husband offended not towards his wife, but eate the apple [...] lest by refusing to eate, when she had done so, he should deject her into a desperate sense of sinne.[176]

Adam did not want Eve to be alone in her sin and dejection, and therefore, he joined in the sin. Adams' desire for Eve not to be alone became a prominent theme.

With a king, the Puritans had no reason to attack women rulers. They still disagreed vehemently with the Anglican establishment and argued that priests should be permitted to marry. The manner of seating in church also angered Puritans. The Anglican church continued to seat men and women separately. Because of the value placed on the family, the Puritans believed families should sit together.[177] The Puritans continued to stress a hierarchy based on the order of creation. The good wife was a godly matron, obedient to her husband, and pious.[178] The home was the designated sphere where she could shape the religious life of her family.[179] If a woman did not do so, she could be accused of witchcraft. Puritan divines such as William Perkins (1558–1602) continued to stress that women could not serve as ministers or administer the sacraments.[180] Henry Ainsworth (1571–1622) warned that women must be watched

---

[176] John Donne, *Sermons*, eds. George Potter and Evelyn Simpson, 10 Vols. (Oakland, CA: University of California Press, 1953–1962), 2:339, 343–46; 5:114–15.

[177] Michael J. Braddick and Phil Withington, eds., *Gender, Agency, and Religious Change in Early Stuart England* (Suffolk, England: Boydell Press, 2017), 147.

[178] Brown and Bohn, 39.

[179] R. C. Richardson, *Puritanism in North-West England: A Regional Study of the Diocese of Chester to 1642* (Manchester: Manchester University Press, 1972), 109–110.

[180] George and George, *The English Protestant and the Family*, 288.

closely as heresy comes "under the figure of a foolish woman."[181] Robert Bolton (1572–1631) added:

> The husband by the benefit of a more manly body; tempered with natural fitness for the soul to work more nobly in; doth, or ought ordinarily out go the wife in largeness of understanding, height of courage [...] moderation of his passions, dexterity to manage businesses, and other natural inclinations and abilities to do more excellently.[182]

During the reigns of James and his son Charles I (1625–1649) many Puritans were persecuted for not following Anglican Church mandates. Charles proved particularly difficult as he demanded rigid conformity to the Church of England's *Prayer Book*. Many Puritans fled to Amsterdam while others decided to start fresh in New England. Some Puritans concluded the Anglican Church was beyond repair. They became known as "Separatists."

In regard to spiritual matters and the church, little changed for Anglican and Puritan women. The English Reformers did not perceive the plight of women and a desire to elevate their status in the home, church, and society as a primary concern. They were still subject to their husbands, could not serve in an ecclesiastical role, and were considered weak-minded and often shrewish. The Puritan woman was just as constrained as the Anglican woman, but she began to take on a new role as a pious leader in the establishment of her family's "Little Commonwealth." Catholic women suffered the most. They were no longer able to venerate the Virgin Mary, could no longer seek spiritual freedom in a convent, and wives' roles in preparing the home and family for feasts and festivals ended.

Conclusion

The Protestant concept of justification by faith and priesthood of all believers provided an avenue to personal faith rather than dependence on a priestly class. Men and women were told that they now

---

[181] Hendrik Niclas, *An Epistle sent unto Two Daughters of Warwick ... With a Refutation ... by Henry Ainsworth* (Amsterdam, 1608), 13.
[182] Robert Bolton, *Works*, IV:245, cited in George and George, *The English Protestant and the Family*, 261.

had equal access to God. The Bible stood at the center of Protestantism and the ability to hear it read in one's own language was paramount. This led to the belief that everyone, including women, should be educated at least enough to be able to read the Bible. The Reformers taught that marriage was a part of God's plan, and it was superior to celibacy. Women, therefore, were no longer considered a necessary evil but rather companions and partners. Since Protestants no longer considered marriage a sacrament, divorce became an option in which women had equal rights to as men. Since priests could now marry, their wives were able to serve God alongside their husbands. Though women were not permitted any ecclesiastical role, Calvin's belief that certain teachings such as "head coverings" were cultural and local practices, not doctrinal prescripts, opened the door to future opportunities.

For Catholic women living in a Protestant territory, the closing of convents removed one of the few places where women had some autonomy. The loss of the cult of the Virgin Mary hurt women's spiritual comfort as they lost the ability to petition another female for help in trying circumstances. Catholic women also lost their ability to lead their families in home devotion since many feasts, festivals, and holy days had diminished roles as good works for salvation.

Protestant women gained more ground than Catholic women did, but they still remained subservient to men. Wives were expected to remain subject to their husbands in all respects. Women were spiritually equal to men, but not in everyday life. Women did not have official roles in society or government. Protestantism without any religious orders provided women with no opportunities to serve the church in any ecclesial capacity. A woman's sphere remained the home, where she was to care for her husband and rear children. All the major Reformers and Puritan divines considered women weak-minded and prone to frivolities that required men to watch over them closely. Misogyny had lessened, but negative stereotypes, such as the woman as a shrew or manipulator, persisted. Overall, the Reformation helped women in a few ways, but, largely, their status did not change.

CHAPTER SEVEN

Women in Seventeenth and Eighteenth-Century England and America

During the first half of the seventeenth century, thousands of people fled England and flocked to the New World in search of a home where they could practice their faith without fear of persecution. Christians included Congregationalist Puritans, Separatists, Baptists, Quakers, Roman Catholics, and a myriad of other sects. Each group brought its own theological beliefs concerning the nature, role, and purpose of women.

New England

Congregationalists, better known as Puritans, were the most influential Protestant religious group in early colonial America. Congregationalism significantly influenced other denominations. These New England Puritans were like Puritans in old England in terms of soteriology, ecclesiology, and other aspects of their faith. They did maintain the importance of the good woman even with her mental weakness, need for personal piety, and perpetual relationship to Eve. As the century developed, the Puritan concept of women began to mirror ideas and movements that led to the birth of the United States.[1]

---

[1] Laurel Thatcher Ulrich, *Good Wives: Image and Reality in the Livzes of Women in Northern New England, 1650–1750* (New York, NY: Random House, 1980), 99.

Jocelyn M. Boryczka maintains that the New England Puritan interpretation of women came from the story of Eve.[2] The first New England Puritans held the traditional belief that Eve could not stand up to Satan's persuasions and then compounded her error by luring Adam into her sin.[3] She was the epitome of original sin. Eve's sin, however, was to be expected. Her weakness also made all her female descendants dangerous. Eve's nature was also demonstrated in her temptation of Adam. Marriage, and the subjugation of a husband, was the best way to restrain women's sexual impulses.[4] Because of these inherent feminine qualities, Puritans realized the importance that women be under the supervision of a man, but they rarely berated women for Eve's role in the Fall.

Cotton Mather (1663–1728), an influential Puritan minister, believed that Eve was represented in all women. She was still culpable in the Fall, but women were not the personification of original sin nor the reason for the presence of evil in the world. Mather commented, "It is indeed a Piece of great injustice, that every woman should be so far an Eve, as her depravation should be imputed unto all the sex."[5] Mather also praised women's role in building a Puritan society as they gave birth to souls who would join their ranks.

> The curse is turned into a blessing upon them. The dubious hazards of their lives in their appointed sorrows, drive them more frequently, and the more fervently to commit themselves into the hand of their only savior. They are saved through childbearing.[6]

---

[2] Jocelyn M. Boryczka, *Suspect Citizens: Women, Virtue, and Vice in Backlash Politics* (Philadelphia, PA: Temple University Press, 2012), 49.
[3] Susan Hill Lindley, *"You have Stept out of your Place:" A History of Women and Religion in America* (Louisville, KY: Westminster John Knox Press, 1996), 16.
[4] Ulrich, 107.
[5] Cotton Mather, *Ornaments for the Daughters of Zion* (Boston, MA: Kneeland and Green, 1741), 54.
[6] Cotton Mather, *Tabitha Rediviva: An Essay to Describe and Commend the Good Works of a Virtuous Woman; Who Therein Approves Her Self a Real disciple of an Holy Savior. With Some Justice Done to the Memory of That Religious and Honorable Gentlewoman, Mrs. Elizabeth Hutchinson. Who Expired, 3 d. 12 m. 1712, 13.* (Boston, MA: J. Allen, 1713), 22; cited in Boryczka, 50.

Mather added that Eve was "the first believer of our Savior" and the "Mother of all that live unto God." She was also the "instrument of bringing him (Adam) to believe in the great Redeemer."[7] Moreover, women could give birth to children who embodied virtue, goodness, and the foundation of a Puritan Zion. For Mather, women were composed of vice but had the potential for virtue. They were daughters of both Eve and their new Zion.[8]

Puritans believed in the practical value of marriage. As Reverend Samuel Dexter (1700–1755) wrote in his diary on November 23, 1723, being a "woman of merit—a woman of good temper wand [sic] of prudent conduct and conversation"[9] was of great importance. Marriage was a choice made by the man and woman.[10] Puritan church records and personal letters demonstrate that the couple often fell deeply in love, such that it became almost sinful. Ministers often reminded their congregants that their greatest love was due to God, not their spouse.[11]

Puritan marriage was meant to symbolize Christ's relationship with the church. The union was loving, but the woman was to be obedient to her husband who symbolized Christ in the marriage. She should seek to serve and never anger him.[12] Puritan marriages were also expected to be sexual. One of the reasons God ordained marriage was to find sexual release.[13] The metaphorical example of Christ's relationship to his church and the couple's conjugal love were merged into a mystical relationship.[14] Language depicting this relationship was often highly sexualized. When discussing copulation, Cotton Mather wrote in 1722, "It will not be long before the consummation of the marriage, thy eternal cohabitation with thy

---

[7] Cotton Mather, *Tabitha Rediviva*, cited in Boryczka, 50.
[8] Boryczka, 49.
[9] *New England Historical and Genealogical Register*, XIV, 40.
[10] Edmund Morgan, *The Puritan Family: Religion and Domestic Relations in Seventeenth-Century New England* (New York, NY: Harper Perennial, 1966), 59.
[11] Diana Feige and Franz Feige. "Love, Marriage, and Family in Puritan Society," *Dialogue and Alliance* 9, no. 1 (Spring/Summer 1995): 101.
[12] Barbara J. MacHaffie, *Her Story: Women in the Christian Tradition*, 2nd ed. (Minneapolis, MN: Fortress Press, 2006), 130.
[13] Feige and Feige, 102.
[14] Belden C. Lane, "Two Schools of Desire: Nature and Marriage in Seventeenth-Century Puritanism," *Church History* 69, no. 2 (June 2000): 374.

savior."[15] While making physical love to her husband, the wife was also making love spiritually to Christ her Lord. The husband, therefore, represented Christ.

The family unit or "Little Commonwealth" was the model for the Puritan church and state.[16] The church consisted of families, not individuals, and the state was comprised of churches working together to create Zion. Edmund Morgan noted that the state existed in embryonic form when God gave Adam authority over Eve and his family. After the Fall, God arranged for the establishment of churches and states.[17] According to Mather, "Well-ordered societies naturally produce a good order in other societies. When families are under an ill discipline, all other societies being therefore ill disciplined, will feel that error in the first concoction."[18]

Within the Puritan family, the husband ruled over the wife, children, and servants.[19] The husband stood before the wife in God's stead. The wife, therefore, must revere her husband and submit to his instructions.[20] The more obedient the wife, the less visible she was in the community. Her spirituality was practiced in the home. If she displeased or disobeyed him, it was not uncommon for the husband to corporally punish his wife. Cotton Mather insisted, "It is the highest ignominy, not of the wife, but of the man for a man to beat his wife. But if you have a husband that will do so, bear it patiently; and know that you will have rewards hereafter for it, as well as praises here."[21] For Mather, the bruises endured at the hand of her husband glorified the wife on earth and in heaven.

The most important roles a Puritan woman played were that of wife and mother. To fill the new world with godly souls and

---

[15] Cotton Mather, *Bethiah: The Glory Which Adorns the Daughters of God, and the Piety, Wherewith Zion Wishes to See His daughters Glorious* (Boston, MA: Printed by Franklin for Gerrish, 1722), 31.

[16] Anthony Michael Petro, "Religion, Gender, and Sexuality," in *The Columbia Guide to Religion in American History*, eds. Paul Harvey, Edward J. Blum, and Randall Stephens (New York, NY: Columbia University Press, 2012), 193.

[17] Morgan, 133–35.

[18] Cotton Mather, *A Family Well-Ordered* (Boston: 1699), 3.

[19] Braude, 7.

[20] Morgan, 45.

[21] Cotton Mather, *Ornaments for the Daughters of Zion* (Boston, MA: Kneeland and Green, 1741), 98.

overcome the high numbers of children who did not live to adulthood, women spent many years of their lives pregnant or nursing.[22] Before modern medicine, childbirth was exceptionally dangerous. Because of God's curse on Eve, Mather believed God intended birth to be painful.[23] He also held that there were more godly women than men because of the fear of death in childbirth.[24] Yet, the more children she bore the more blessed she was by God and praised in the community. Judith Coffin (1625–1705) died at eighty years of age and her epitaph noted that she was a "fruitful vine" after living to see 177 of her children and grandchildren to the third generation.[25]

Puritan men honored women as "good wives." A good wife never challenged her husband, sacrificed for her family, demonstrated personal piety and modesty, and raised her children in line with the Puritan belief system. While remaining subordinate to her husband, the good wife was to protect her home from sin and dedicate her life to the wellbeing of her family.[26]

A good wife was domestic-focused and demonstrated her virtue in the home.[27] Puritan men limited opportunities for women to have social lives because it made them more fit for wifely submission.[28] Women were also not permitted to attend college as it did nothing to help her develop further skills for the home and made her less malleable to her husband.[29] Most women, however, were taught to read the Bible to their children. They were bound to their husbands' home and upon marriage ownership of their goods was transferred to their husbands. Puritan men appreciated their good wives, but the wife was utterly dependent upon her husband and the home he made for her. Spiritual equality tempered subordination. If the marriage became intolerable, the woman did have the right to

---

[22] Ulrich, 144.
[23] Cotton Mather, *Elizabeth in Her Holy Retirement* (Boston, MA: 1710), 2.
[24] Braude, 8.
[25] Joshua Coffin, *A Sketch of the History of Newbury, Newburyport, and West Newbury* (Boston, MA: 1845; N. H. Hampton: Peter Randall, 1977), 402.
[26] Boryczka, 53.
[27] Lindley, 25.
[28] Blum and Stephens, 193.
[29] Morgan, 42–43.

divorce. Puritans viewed marriage as a civil contract, not a sacrament, and the contract could be broken.[30]

Most Protestant churches viewed wives as extensions of their husbands. A man who spoke in church presumably spoke for his wife as well.[31] A Puritan woman, however, could become a full covenant member of her town's Congregational Church. If she left the church, she would receive her own dismissal letter. The Boston minister, John Cotton (1585–1652), held that women should not question ministers, but should provide a verbal account of their own conversion experience to the church. He also permitted women to sing and pray during worship.[32] Despite the limitations imposed on them, women outnumbered men in Puritan churches by the mid-seventeenth-century. Susan Lindley Hill agrees with Cotton Mather that it was because women depended more on God's comfort.[33]

Women were to work and spend their time on matters related to the home. It was believed that if she attempted to take on roles that were meant for the realm of men, bad things could happen. The governor of Massachusetts Bay Colony, John Winthrop (1642–1644; 1646–1649) believed Ann Hopkins (1615–1698), the wife of the governor of Connecticut Edward Hopkins (1600–1657), went mad because she dedicated too much time reading and writing. He noted that it was:

> A sad infirmity, the loss of her understanding and reason suffered by Anne Hopkins, the wife of the governor of Connecticut, came about by occasion of her giving herself wholly to reading and writing, and had written many books. Her husband, being very loving and tender of her, was loath to grieve her; but he saw his error, when it was too late. For if she had attended her household affairs, and such things as belong to women, and not gone out

---

[30] Ulrich, 110.
[31] MacHaffie, 127.
[32] John Cotton, *Singing of Psalms a Gospel Ordinance, 1650*, cited in Rosemary Radford Ruether and Rosemary Skinner Keller, eds, *Women and Religion in America, Vol. 2. The Colonial and Revolutionary Periods* (San Francisco, CA: Harper and Row, 1983), 191.
[33] Lindley, 23; Cotton Mather, *Tabitha Rediviva*, cited in Boryczka, 50.

of her way and calling to meddle in such things as are proper for men, whose minds are stronger, etc., she had kept her wits, and might have improved them usefully and honorably in the place God had set her.[34]

Writing almost a generation later, Lucy Hutchinson (1620–1681) agreed. In her *On the Principles of the Christian Religion, Addressed to Her Daughter* (ca. 1673), she deprecated women's intellectual abilities. "As our sex, through ignorance and weakness of judgment (which in the most knowing women is inferior to the masculine understanding of men), are apt to entertain fancies, and [be] pertinacious in them so we ought to watch ourselves and [...] embrace nothing rashly; but as our own imbecility is made known to us, to take heed of presumption in ourselves."[35] The irony in Hutchinson's belief is that her writings prove that Puritan-educated women did have the ability to write at a high level.

In 1630, Winthrop described the Massachusetts Bay Colony as becoming the "City Upon a Hill." England and the rest of the world would look upon this "City Upon a Hill" as a pure Christian commonwealth. The entire Puritan community, male and female, had prescribed roles to play if such a godly community was to take root. Women could help to create the City Upon a Hill by exhibiting traditional female virtues. They were to be pious, sacrificial, humble, modest, and obedient. Only then would they glorify God and realize Winthrop's vision.[36]

Women were also capable of destroying that vision. They had to be aware of their inherent nature and weaknesses derived from Eve. Self-control and honoring authority were key. Women who did not accept their place within the social order were a threat.[37] Widows who did not remarry and single women who managed to retain their property were particularly dangerous.[38]

---

[34] John Winthrop, *Journal* (13 April 1645), in Perry Miller and Thomas H. Johnson, eds., *The Puritans*, 2 vols. (1938; rev. ed. New York, NY: Harper & Row, 1963), 1:140.
[35] Lucy Hutchinson, *On the Principles of the Christian Religion*, ed. Julius Hutchinson (London: Longman, 1817), 5–6.
[36] Boryczka, 57.
[37] Carol Karlsen, *The Devil in the Shape of a Woman: Witchcraft in Colonial New England* (New York: W. W. Norton, 1998), 20.
[38] Boryczka, 56.

Anne Hutchinson (1591–1643) was one such woman. A devoted follower of John Cotton, she and her family followed him from England to Boston in 1634. Hutchinson was not shy about sharing her theological beliefs and, from 1636 to 1638, began to teach women in her home and comment on Cotton's sermons. Governor Winthrop warned her against holding such meetings.[39] She believed that aside from Cotton, Puritan ministers were preaching a doctrine of works rather than grace.[40] Her teachings stressed that the individual realized election by sensing the Holy Spirit's free gift of salvation.[41] For her beliefs, she was labeled an antinomian. Winthrop accused her of heterodoxy. Her accusations aimed at the Puritan ministers were seditious and endangered the entire community.[42] She was tried and banished from the colony in 1637 and tried by the church and excommunicated from the congregation in 1638. Several of her female defenders were whipped and excommunicated. Seeking religious toleration, Hutchinson and seven of her children moved to Rhode Island and from there to Long Island Sound. Other than her nine-year-old daughter Susanna, who was taken captive, they were massacred by the Siwanoy tribe in August 1643. When word reached the Puritan authorities of the massacre, they believed it was God's justice. Reverend Thomas Weld (1595–1661) held that:

> The Lord heard our groans to heaven, and freed us from our great and sore affliction […] I never heard that the Indians in those parts did ever before this commit the like outrage upon any one family or families; and therefore, God's hand is the more apparently seen herein, to pick out this woeful woman.[43]

---

[39] James A. Morone, *Hellfire Nation: The Politics of Sin in American History* (New Haven, NY: Yale University Press, 2003), 62.
[40] Carl J. Schneider and Dorothy Schneider, *In Their Own Right: This History of American Clergywomen* (New York, NY: The Crossroad Publishing Company, 1997), 4.
[41] Francis Bremer, *Anne Hutchinson: Troubler of the Puritan Zion* (Huntington, NY: Robert E. Krieger Publishing Company, 1981), 4.
[42] Schneider and Schneider, 4.
[43] John Denison, "The Tragedy of Anne Hutchinson," *Journal of American History* 5, no. 3 (1913): 12.

Pastor of the church at Concord, Peter Bulkley (1583–1659) struck a similar note. "Let her damned heresies, and the just vengeance of God, by which she perished, terrify all her seduced followers from having any more to do with her leaven."[44]

To Puritan leaders, Anne Hutchinson was the worst kind of woman: highly intelligent, articulate, not pious in a traditional sense, and disdainful of her role in Puritan society.[45] Hutchinson was fortunate to escape formal witchcraft charges, though some of her detractors believed that she had to have been a witch.

Women's sexuality, especially that of single women, also threatened the "City Upon a Hill." Cotton Mather warned women who wore clothes that he considered immodest, "You will have the wisdom to abandon such apparel, as you may render your virtue questionable. But you are to be well-advised unto this further wisdom; that your apparel not be a thing of more account than your virtue."[46]

Women who did not hold to the community standards faced the dunking stool or the stocks. A scold had a cage placed over her mouth so she could not speak.[47] In 1631, Massachusetts Bay Colony made adultery—a man having sex with a married woman—a capital offense for both partners. The New Haven, Plymouth, and Connecticut colonies soon followed suit.[48] Based on Leviticus 20, the 1648 Laws and Liberties of the Massachusetts Bay Colony allowed the death penalty for adultery.[49] Sex between a man and an unmarried woman was fornication.[50] Women were more likely than men to be punished, often by whipping, branding, or being forced to wear a badge that symbolized their crime.[51] Because of the fear of

---

[44] Eve LaPlante, *American Jezebel, the Uncommon Life of Anne Hutchinson, the Woman who Defied the Puritans* (San Francisco, CA: Harper Collins, 2004), 243.
[45] Lindley, 16.
[46] Cotton Mather, *Tabitha Rediviva*, cited in Boryczka, 52.
[47] Joanne Carlson Brown and Carole R. Bohn, eds. *Christianity, Patriarchy, and Abuse: A Feminist Critique* (Cleveland, OH: Pilgrim Press, 1989), 35.
[48] Meghan Norton, "The Adulterous Wife: A Cross-Historical and Interdisciplinary Approach," *Buffalo Women's Law Journal* 16, art. 5 (2007): 3–4.
[49] Ulrich, 94.
[50] Norton, 4.
[51] Ibid., 4–5.

public embarrassment, most husbands chose to punish unfaithful wives at home.

Puritans brought a fear of witchcraft from England to the New World. The sociological changes of living in a harsh environment, religious fervor, and the importance of female subjection led to projections of witchcraft on women when unexpected adversity struck.[52] If a man were impotent, a witch was likely to blame.[53]

Eve was vulnerable but not evil.[54] When a woman succumbed to Satan and became a witch, she employed her powers of seduction to ruin men and the community.[55] For these reasons and others, three-quarters of the 185 people accused of witchcraft in seventeenth-century New England were women.[56]

New England women that were accused of witchcraft were often socially and economically independent. In 1666, Katherine Harris of Wethersfield, Connecticut, inherited substantial property and wealth when her husband died. She had no intention of remarrying. She was tormented by her neighbors who vandalized her property. When Harris brought charges against the neighbors, rather than receiving satisfaction, she was accused of witchcraft. The accusations ended when she deeded her property to her son-in-law. Ann Braude determined that Harris defied the Puritan hierarchy. "Do not fight with your neighbors, do not assert your property rights, do not remain outside a household with a male head. If you are angry with your treatment do not say so. Be obedient to civil and religious authorities and then you will not be accused of witchcraft."[57]

Not all independent women were wealthy.[58] Many were poor widows or "the destitute"—those who lived outside the community because they were often unkempt, beggars, and had mental issues; they were easier marks for witchcraft accusations. Other women were a part of perceived heretical movements. In 1656,

---

[52] Frances Hill, *A Delusion of Satan: The Full Story of the Salem Witch Trials* (New York, NY: Doubleday, 1995), 31.
[53] Braude, 9.
[54] Morone, 95.
[55] MacHaffie, 126.
[56] Braude, 10.
[57] Ibid., 12–13.
[58] Hill, 32.

authorities stripped and whipped a Quaker girl to see if she bore marks of witchcraft.[59] Any woman who challenged the New England establishment was in danger of witchcraft charges. Between 1647 and 1691, at least 123 people were accused of witchcraft and sixteen were executed. These numbers are nothing compared to what occurred in Salem in 1692.[60]

Salem Village was a small Puritan community located nineteen miles north of Boston. It had recently recovered from a smallpox outbreak and lived in fear of a Native American attack. These concerns kept the citizens on edge. In the witch trials, the first accusations came from girls accusing women whom they knew well of witchcraft. They claimed that older women[61] had abused them with spirits that attempted to have them sign the devil's book and join them in a compact with Satan.

The Salem judges believed in spectral evidence, so they accepted stories from the girls about their dreams or visions. When in the presence of an accused witch, the girls often fainted or fell to the floor, screaming that they were being tortured. By the time the trials ended in May 1693, the authorities had executed fourteen women, one young girl, and five men. At least five other women died in jail while awaiting trial.

Not only were the older women accused of tormenting the young girls, but also some of the women were accused of sexually preying on men while they slept. One of the judges, Cotton Mather, blamed women's lust. He recounted Reverend John Louder's testimony against a woman of independent means, Bridget Bishop (ca. 1632–1692). She appeared in his bed "grievously oppressing him; in which miserable condition she held him, unable to help himself, till near Day."[62] In Susan Martin's (1621–1692) trial, Mather noted that Bernard Peach explained that she had come through his bedroom window and "took hold of this Deponent's Feet, and drawing his Body up into a Heap, she lay upon him near Two Hours."[63]

---

[59] Schneider and Schneider, 5.
[60] Morone, 83.
[61] Ibid., 32.
[62] Cotton Mather, *1692 On Witchcraft: Being the Wonders of the Invisible World*. Reprint, (New York, NY: Bell, 1974), 110.
[63] Ibid., 110.

There are many explanations for the panic in Salem, including jealousy and attention-seeking among the accusers, religious anxiety, and property disputes. The Puritan ministers who sat in judgment, however, believed that witchcraft could destroy their community. Their own misogyny and sexual anxieties convinced them that women were susceptible to entrapment by the devil. Therefore, their guilt was not only believable but also probable. The executions at Salem were the last in North America. The last known execution for witchcraft in Europe was in Poland in 1793.[64]

By the close of the seventeenth century, New England Puritanism had lost much of its religious fervor. Men had more options outside the church in the realm of work and politics. Making a profit required men to be aggressive and committed to monetary pursuits. Women, dedicated to their church, provided their children with religious education at home.[65] Women continued to be viewed as frail and emotional, but they were also considered more intuitive and nurturing and, thus, more religious and moral than men.[66]

Women in Seventeenth-Century England

The seventeenth century saw the English Civil War and the execution of Charles I (1625–1649), the Commonwealth Interregnum (1649–1660), and a restoration of the monarchy under Charles II (1660–1685). These events had no immediate effect on women. In literature, however, Eve was still receiving attention.

Baptists

The English Baptist movement was born in 1609 in Amsterdam. Women deacons were accepted. In *Paralleles, Censures, Observations*, the movement's first pastor John Smyth (1570–1612) wrote, "the

---

[64] Elizabeth Clark and Herbert Richardson, eds., *Women and Religion: The Original Sourcebook of Women in Christian Thought* (San Francisco, CA: HarperCollins, 1977), 143.

[65] Barbara Leslie Epstein, *The Politics of Domesticity: Women, Evangelism and Temperance in Nineteenth-Century America* (Middletown, CT: Wesleyan University Press, 1981), 27–28.

[66] MacHaffie, 131.

church has the power to elect, approve, and ordain her elders, also: to elect, approve her own deacons both men and women."[67]

Under Thomas Helwys (1575–1616), several of these first Baptists returned to London in 1612 where they established England's first Baptist church. Women could serve as deacons, visit the sick, and minister to people who needed consolation, especially other women.[68] There is no known evidence that any early Baptist women were pastors. Anne Hempstall, Mary Bilbrow, Joane Bauford, Susan May, Elizabeth Bancroft, and Arabella Thomas were preachers because "there was a deficiency of good men, wherefore it was but fit that virtuous women should supply their places."[69]

Quakers

Of all the seventeenth-century Christian sects in England and America, none were more open to women's leadership than the Society of Friends, also known as Quakers. Begun by George Fox (1624–1691) they believed in the scriptures, but also in divine revelation. When moved by the Holy Spirit, their bodies would "quake." Anyone touched by the "inner light" was to preach.[70] One of the founding Quakers, Margaret Fell (1642–1702), held that, "God hath said that his Daughters should prophesy as well as his sons. And where he hath poured forth his Spirit upon them, they must prophesy, though blind priests say to the contrary, and will not permit holy women to speak."[71] Female preachers in Britain included Elizabeth Hooten (1600–1646) and Barbara Blaugdone (1609–1704). Their counterparts in the American colonies were

---

[67] William T. Whitley, ed. *The Works of John Smyth* (Cambridge: University Press, 1915), 2:509.

[68] Edward Been Underhill, ed. *The Records of a Church Meeting in Broadmead, Bristol, 1640–1687* (London: J. Haddon, 1847), 398.

[69] *A Discoverie of Six Women Preachers in Middlesex, Kent, Cambridgeshire and Salisbury* (n.p., 1641), 1, cited in Pamela Durso, "She-Preachers, Bossy Women, and Children of the Devil: Women Ministers in the Baptist Tradition, 1609–2012," *Review & Expositor* 110, no. 1 (Winter 2013): 33–47.

[70] Marilyn J. Westerkamp, *Women and Religion in Early America, 1650–1850: The Puritan and Evangelical Traditions* (London and New York: Routledge, 1999), 80.

[71] Margaret Fell, *Women's Speaking Justified, Proved and Allowed of by the Scriptures* (London: 1667), 12.

Jenn Fenn Hoskens (1694–1764), Susanna Hudson (1720–1781), and Elizabeth Sampson (1713–1755).

The Friends were by most accounts an egalitarian society. The Holy Spirit was needed to understand scripture; tithes and the established church were unnecessary and Christians should be pacifists. Consequently, they faced persecution and imprisonment on both sides of the Atlantic. Quakers were expelled from the Massachusetts Bay Colony. Four Quakers, including Mary Dyer (1611–1660), a follower of Anne Hutchinson, were executed in Boston for preaching Quaker beliefs (1660). Rumors circulated that Dyer had given birth to a "monstrous baby" who died soon after birth. Cotton Mather and John Winthrop believed that the death was God's judgment.[72]

John Milton (1608–1674)

John Milton was a British Puritan and poet. His epic poem *Paradise Lost* (1667) is considered one of the greatest works of literature in the Western world. His depiction of Eve proved so popular that many people did not realize that was not drawn from Genesis.

Milton was influenced by Augustine and the second creation account. In *Paradise Lost*, Adam was the one blessed with reason and Eve was not.

> For well I understand in the prime end
> Of Nature her th' inferiour, in the mind
> And inward Faculties, which most excell,
> In outward also her resembling less
> His Image who made both, and less expressing
> The character of that Dominion giv'n
> O're other Creatures;[73]

For Adam, Eve was more than just an object of physical desire but, rather, a mate that complemented and completed him.[74] "Part

---

[72] Winthrop, 254.
[73] John Milton, *Paradise Lost*, 10 Books (Abingdon, Oxfordshire: Routledge, 2006), 8:540–45.
[74] J. A. Phillips, *The History of an Idea: Eve* (New York, NY: Harper and Row, 1984), 33.

of my Soul I seek thee, and the claim of my other half."[75] Before the Fall, Adam told the angel Raphael that he lost control of his reason when Eve was near.[76] He realized she was mentally less than him, but she was beautiful. Raphael warned Adam that a beautiful woman's seductions could lead him astray.

Milton presented Eve as childish, irresponsible, and vulnerable to flattery. She was therefore easier prey for the serpent's machinations. After Eve ate, she shared the fruit with her husband. Unlike earlier interpretations that Eve tempted Adam, Milton depicted Adam as preferring death to life without her.[77]

> Rather how hast thou yeelded to transgress
> The strict forbiddance, how to violate
> The sacred Fruit forbidd'n! som cursed fraud
> Of Enemie hath beguil'd thee, yet unknown,
> And mee with thee hath ruind, for with thee
> Certain my resolution is to Die;
> How can I live without thee, how forgoe
> Thy sweet Converse and Love so dearly joyn'd,
> To live again in these wilde Woods forlorn?
> Should God create another *Eve*, and I
> Another Rib afford, yet loss of thee
> Would never from my heart; no no, I feel
> The Link of Nature draw me: Flesh of Flesh,
> Bone of my Bone thou art, and from thy State
> Mine never shall be parted, bliss or woe.[78]

Adam, however, still blamed Eve for the Fall. Christ informed him that he was superior, and he should not have followed her lead.

> Was shee thy God, that her thou didst obey
> Before his voice, or was shee made thy guide,
> Superior, or but equal, that to her

---

[75] Milton, *Paradise Lost*, 4:487.
[76] Ibid., 4:638–40.
[77] Nehama Aschkenasy, *Eve's Journey: Feminine Image in Hebraic Literary Tradition* (Philadelphia, PA: University of Pennsylvania Press, 1986), 39.
[78] Milton, *Paradise Lost*, 9:902–916.

> Thou did'st resigne thy Manhood, and the Place
> Wherein God set thee above her made of thee,
> And for thee, whose perfection farr excell'd
> Hers in all real dignitie: Adornd
> She was indeed, and lovely to attract
> Thy Love, not thy Subjection, and her Gifts
> Were such as under Government well seem'd,
> Unseemly to beare rule, which was thy part
> And person, hadst thou known thy self aright.[79]

Adam's love, his physical desire for Eve, led him to "resign his manhood." In *Paradise Regained* (1671), Milton denounced women as deceivers and deceived.[80] Women had ruined Solomon[81] and Adam, but this would not happen to a virtuous man. Belial tells Satan to use women to seduce Christ, but Satan had to find other weapons against him.[82]

Milton's *Paradise Lost* was one of the most popular books among the Puritans. It had a lasting impact on how Eve and marriage were understood. Adam could not live without her. Romantic love, companionship, and conversation began to replace the belief that procreation was the main purpose of marriage.[83] This was a definite improvement. Milton, however, still believed women were inferior to men. He believed that a husband could leave an unsatisfactory wife. Elizabeth Clark notes that at times Milton seems progressive, but then he reverts to the patriarchal tradition.[84] In many ways, Milton was a typical seventeenth-century Protestant. He sang the praises of sex and marriage while defending patriarchy.[85]

---

[79] Ibid., *Paradise Lost*, 10:145–156.
[80] John Milton, *Paradise Regained* (CreateSpace Independent Publishing Platform, 2012), 4:150–171.
[81] Ibid., 2:170.
[82] Milton, *Paradise Lost*, 2:153–225.
[83] Clark and Richardson, 153.
[84] Ibid., 176.
[85] Katharine M. Rogers, *The Troublesome Helpmate: A History of Misogyny in Literature* (Seattle, WA: University of Washington Press, 1966), 159.

John Wesley (1703–1791)

John Wesley was an Anglican cleric, theologian, and a founder of Methodism. After Wesley died in 1791, the Methodist societies left the Church of England and became the Methodist denomination. Because of its stress on piety, missions, and revivalism, Methodism quickly took root in Britain and was particularly strong in North America. Its emphasis on free will embodied the American spirit and belief that with enough hard work people could rise above their current station.

Wesley's mother Susanna (1669–1742) often filled in for her husband Samuel (1662–1735), a dissenting pastor, and led Sunday evening prayers for more than 200 people. He saw that his mother's strong spiritual gifts would benefit the church. Wesley, therefore, allowed women to exercise those spiritual gifts in church, give personal testimonies, and discuss religious literature. He also appointed women as class leaders.[86] Sarah Mallet (1764–1846) and Mary Fletcher (1739–1815),[87] both Englishwomen, received conditional permission to preach.[88] He explained in his *Commentary of 1 Corinthians*.

> *Let your women be silent in the churches*—Unless they are under an extraordinary impulse of the Spirit. For, in other cases, it is not permitted them to speak—By way of teaching in public assemblies. But to be in subjection—To the man whose proper office it is to lead and to instruct the congregation.[89]

Although Wesley gave women a voice, after his death in 1791 the Methodists wanted to be accepted by the established denominations. They, therefore, adopted a more formal view of ministerial work in 1803. Pastoral and leadership roles were reserved for men.[90]

---

[86] MacHaffie, 136.
[87] Ibid., 136.
[88] Westerkamp, 115.
[89] John Wesley, "1 Corinthians 14," *John Wesley's Bible Notes and Commentary*, Bible Explore, last accessed 1 June 2021, http://www.godrules.net/library/wesley/wesley1cor14.htm.
[90] MacHaffie, 136.

First Great Awakening

The First Great Awakening was an intense religious revival in colonial America from the 1720s to ca. 1740s. In emotional sermons, preachers called people to repentance and rebirth. The revival involved Calvinists, the Dutch Reformed, Congregationalists, Presbyterians, Baptists, and some Anglicans.

Jonathan Edwards (1703–1758)

Often recognized as America's first great theologian, Jonathan Edwards was a Puritan pastor who promoted spiritual revitalization and took a lead role in the development of the "New Light" understanding of personal conversion and commitment to Jesus Christ. In this way, he shaped the evangelical Revival in Britain and America.

Edwards realized that women outnumbered men in the church. He attributed this to the religious enthusiasm of the Great Awakening that spoke to women and encouraged their piety.[91] Conversions among women were based often upon guilt, gratitude, and joy rather than on doctrinal reflection.[92]

Edwards maintained that Adam and Eve represent the entire human race. He did not believe that God recognized Adam as the leader of mankind at creation. Rather, Adam was incomplete because he was without a companion. Eve was meant to complete Adam and they were to rule together as a unit. "God in blessing, evidently speaks to them as the head of mankind."[93] Both men and women, therefore, are in the image of God. Edwards disagreed with the way that Calvin, Mather, and Milton interpreted Eve's role in the Fall. Edwards did not view her with suspicion.[94] Rather, Eve desired spiritual knowledge. She was not defying Adam's leadership or being lustful. Edwards held that Eve's desire for spiritual knowledge to be like God was admirable though misguided and defiant. Eve tempted Adam to join her in gaining spiritual knowledge, but she

---

[91] Anthony Michael Petro, *The Columbia Guide to Religion in American History* (New York: Columbia University Press, 2012), 194.
[92] Lindley, 43.
[93] Jonathan Edwards, "Genesis," *The Works of Jonathan Edwards* (Edinburgh: Banner of Truth Trust, 1995), 2:409–10.
[94] Zachary Hutchins, "Edwards and Eve: Finding Feminist Strains in the Great Awakening's Patriarch," *American Literature* 43, no. 3 (2008): 679.

did not force him into sin. Unlike Calvin and Mather, Edwards did not view Eve as responsible for the Fall. Adam, alone, was responsible for the original sin.[95]

Unlike many of his Catholic and Protestant predecessors, Edwards did not interpret Adam's naming of Eve as a sign of domination. Rather, he looked for ways to put the event in the best light. She was honored in that a woman would be the one to give birth to Christ. He also called Eve "mother of the living," not by "the universality of her maternity, but the quality of those that she was to be the mother of."[96] She also brought both physical and spiritual life—a distinction she shared with Mary and other women. In this manner, she and women had godlike qualities.[97] Edwards made it clear that women and mothers shared Eve's best attributes and therefore deserved honor.

Edwards reinterpreted the "American Jezebel." He compared Anne Hutchinson to a medieval mystic attempting to explain her spiritual experiences to her followers—just as he attempted to make his religious vision a reality so others might follow God. He attributed her occasional inability to speak and her fainting not as God's rebuke, but to illness.[98] Though she died from wounds inflicted by a Native American attack, Edwards explained her spiritual death as a mystic's eagerness to die and join the pure realm of spirit. "She wanted to be where strong grace might have more liberty, and be without the clog of a weak body."[99]

Edwards' interpretation of Eve helped remove the responsibility of women for the Fall. By naming Adam the progenitor of original sin, and by praising women's abilities to bring forth life, he gave women a sense of calling and hope. Following Calvin's interpretation of 1 Timothy 2:13, Edwards wrote, "The plain light of nature had taught all nations the superiority of man to woman, and

---

[95] Hutchins, 675–679; Edwards, *Works*, I: ch. 4, sec. 2.
[96] Edwards, "Genesis," *Works*, 2:332–33.
[97] Hutchins, 674.
[98] Sandra Gustafson, "Jonathan Edwards and the Reconstruction of 'Feminine' Speech," *American Literary History* 6, no. 2 (September 1994): 194–199.
[99] Jonathan Edwards, *A Faithful Narrative*, in C.C. Goen, ed., *The Great Awakening* (New Haven, CT: Yale University Press, 1972), 4:194.

his right of rule over her."[100] Women were not blamed for original sin, but they still were to be under the dominion of men.

Baptists in America

Baptists were present in colonial America as early as 1639, but the practice of their faith was often prohibited. Out of a fear of being dominated by larger churches, Baptist congregations did not create a formal organization until 1707, with the establishment of the Philadelphia Baptist Association. In 1746, there was a vigorous debate over whether or not women should opine on church business. After debating half a day, it was determined that women could "give a mute voice, by standing or lifting up of the hands." At the same time, women could offer verbal testimonies of their conversion. Other than this, women were not to risk "open[ing] the floodgate of speech."[101] The pastor of First Baptist Philadelphia, Morgan Edwards (1722–1795), however, noted that many Baptist churches had ordained deaconesses.[102] Some Baptist churches did not oppose this practice.

Most Particular or "Regular Baptists"[103] only permitted men to preach or perform the ordinances. The Separate Baptists[104] permitted women to participate in worship and church business meetings.[105] Separate Baptist churches in Virginia, the Carolinas, and Georgia often allowed women to serve as deaconesses and eldresses.[106] Martha Stearns Marshall (1726–1754), wife of prominent Separate Baptist minister Daniel Marshall (1706–1784), often preached in worship services led by her husband.[107] Robert Semple believed that Daniel Marshall's successful ministry was a result of Martha's "unwearied, and zealous co-operation." She was a woman "of good sense, singular piety, and surprising elocution," who on "countless

---

[100] Edwards, "1 and 2 Corinthians," *Works*, 2:50–51.
[101] A.D. Gillette, ed., *The Minutes of the Philadelphia Baptist Association, 1707–1807* (Philadelphia, PA: American Baptist Publication Society, 1844), 51.
[102] H. L. McBeth, *Women in Baptist Life* (Nashville, TN: Broadman Press, 1979), 39.
[103] Calvinistic Baptist churches that rejected Great Awakening.
[104] Churches that accepted the Great Awakening.
[105] Lindley, 43.
[106] Morgan Edwards, "Materials Towards a History of Baptists in the Province of North Carolina," cited in the *North Carolina Historical Review* (July 1930): 384–391.
[107] Pamela Durso, "She-Preachers, Bossy Women, and Children of the Devil," 2.

instances melted a whole congregation into tears by her prayers and exhortations."[108]

Any progress that Baptist women had made in colonial America ended at the turn of the nineteenth century. As David Benedict noted:

> The Baptists very generally in this country in former times decidedly approved females taking part in social religious meetings [...] Another portion of them, who are found chiefly in cities and populous places, are as decidedly opposed to anything of the kind [...] This restraint on the freedom of the female, and the same may be said of the lay brotherhood, right or wrong, is evidently on the increase.[109]

Lay preaching and women's leadership in the churches were detrimental to the desire of Baptist leaders who sought acceptance by the more established Christian denominations who permitted neither. Lay preaching by women was not part of Christian worship.[110] To remedy this problem, denominational leaders barred women from preaching. It would take more than a century and a half for Baptists to revisit the issue.

Women Take a Small Step Forward

In seventeenth and eighteenth-century England, the civil war and fears of a re-imposition of Catholicism dominated political life. Puritan beliefs kept women in the home and out of public life. In the American colonies, *Paradise Lost* proved as popular as in England and, combined with the sermons of Jonathan Edwards, helped redefine the Puritan relationship between Adam and Eve. Methodist and Baptist women initially assumed more important roles in the church and society, but engrained views of gender impeded their progress. Of the Christian denomination, the Quakers had the most egalitarian belief system.

---

[108] Robert Semple, *History of the Rise and Progress of the Baptists in Virginia* (Richmond: privately printed, 1810), 374.
[109] David Benedict, *A General History of the Baptist Denomination of America* (New York, NY: Sheldon and Company Publishers, 1860), 940n.
[110] H. L. McBeth, *Women in Baptist Life* (Nashville, TN: Broadman Press, 1979), 40.

CHAPTER EIGHT

Women in Nineteenth-Century America

By 1800 the effects of the Great Awakening had long run their course. Men were now being characterized as more aggressive, indifferent to religion, and more interested in events taking place outside the home and church. They were being depicted as the more sexual gender and more driven by their sexual desires. Men's morality began to depend on women.[1] Women now had to do whatever was necessary to keep their men satisfied at home and away from worldly vices. Women dominated church attendance and as a result Christianity took on a softer, more feminine nature. In an attempt to capitalize on the female attendees, ministers began to depict Christ as gentle and self-sacrificing.[2] The feminization of the church, however, often led to conflicts with some ministers who felt their influence waning as the church became an emotional outlet for women.[3]

Around the time of the American Revolution, the ideal of "Republican Motherhood" idealized the domestic role of women. Like all good Christian mothers, they taught their children not only Christianity but also the virtues of being good citizens of the republic. The meshing of these elements is the foundation of American Christian Patriotism.

---

[1] Randal Balmer, "American Fundamentalism," in *Fundamentalism and Gender*, ed. John Stratton Hawley (New York, NY: Oxford University Press, 1994), 53.
[2] Carl J. Schneider and Dorothy Schneider, *In Their Own Right: This History of American Clergywomen* (New York, NY: The Crossroad Publishing Company, 1997), 1–5.
[3] Randall Balmer, "American Fundamentalism," 51.

Following the American Revolution, men began to leave the farm for better-paying work in cities. Work outside the home was often perceived as the man's sphere. Most women remained in her traditional sphere of the home.

William McLoughlin held that men felt guilty for working outside the home and being away from their families for several hours a day. This led them to the belief they were neglecting their role as *paterfamilias*.[4] Because their wives now took on more home responsibility and leadership, husbands who felt guilty for their neglect in the home showered verbal adoration on their wives. A mother's love replaced the father's discipline as the ruling family principle. As described by Barbara Welter, these changes led to the development of what she called the "Cult of True Domesticity" or the "Cult of True Womanhood" in the mid-nineteenth century.[5]

Several significant events took place in the nineteenth century that had a direct effect on Christian women. The Second Great Awakening left a distinct mark on how Christian women were portrayed and what they could do. It led to the growth of small sects, such as Methodists and Baptists, into large denominations. Women also began to take larger roles in Mission Societies and push for social causes such as prohibition and suffrage. The great revivalist Charles Finney (1792–1875) invited women to participate in his city-wide revivals. The Catholic Church made several encyclicals that still affect the lives of Catholic women. At the end of the century, the revivalist Dwight Laymen Moody (1837–1899) became a household name and he did not fail to recognize and extol the virtues of the overwhelming number of females in his meetings. The Holiness Movement also had its origins in the nineteenth century, and its proponents opened up new avenues for women.

The Second Great Awakening

The nineteenth-century Second Great Awakening is difficult to categorize. It can be viewed as one large century-long awakening

---

[4] William G. McLoughlin, *Revivals, Awakenings, and Reform* (Chicago, IL: University of Chicago Press, 1978), 120–1.
[5] Barbara Welter, "The Cult of True Womanhood, 1820–1860," *American Quarterly* 18, no. 2 (Summer, 1966): 151–174.

or three different phases of the same awakening. As one phase often triggered or continued into the next, one general but long awakening is a more appropriate view and this chapter follows that assessment.

The Second Great Awakening took place in three phases. The first phase took place on the frontiers of Kentucky and Tennessee (ca. 1795–1810). The second phase (ca. 1810–1825) occurred in congregational churches, colleges, and universities. The third phase (ca. 1825–1835) was dominated by Charles Finney (1792–1875). The First Great Awakening was based on Calvinistic soteriology and order, the Second was Arminian and more emotional. A person was saved upon inviting Christ into his or her heart.

During the frontier revivals of the first phase, Arminianism dominated the meetings. It freed women and uneducated men from the institutional constraints placed on them by the educated Calvinist ministers. "Heart religion" was viewed as more important than theological "head religion," and the Holy Spirit allowed all people equal access to God. A trained minister was not necessary to provoke a religious experience, and in many ways the frontier aspects of the Second Great Awakening were anticlerical. Arminianism spawned a realignment of religious authority based on emotion, sentimentality, and religious liberty and away from the cold, systematic theology espoused by the Calvinistic ministers.[6] The acceptance of free will replaced predestination and meshed well with American individualism.[7] Claudia Stokes notes that the move away from Calvinistic hierarchy was replaced by populism and democratic inclusiveness. The status of wives and mothers rose, and ministers lost some of their standing as arbiters of morality. The interweaving of religion, women, and politics was the first major step in ending men's control of the pulpit.[8]

The largest revival of the first phase took place in Cane Ridge, Kentucky in 1801. An estimated twenty-five thousand people attended. These meetings were filled with religious anxiety, emotion, and a desire for instantaneous salvation. Women helped to

---

[6] Claudia Stokes, *The Altar at Home: Sentimental Literature and Nineteenth-Century American Religion* (Philadelphia, PA: University of Pennsylvania Press, 2014), 24.
[7] Randall Balmer, "American Fundamentalism," 52.
[8] Stokes, 21–29.

set the mood for the revival. Those who expressed emotion during the services were often perceived as the first to have felt the Holy Spirit's presence. Pastors often stoked emotion by telling a story of a praying or grieving mother.[9] Women were often permitted to pray aloud, give testimony of their conversion, and preach.

The people who attended these services were generally seated with others of their race and gender.[10] Most ministers made sure that women did not step too far out of gender norms and were quick to silence anyone whom they considered unruly.[11] Though women could sometimes preach, they held no leadership roles. Male ministers performed the ordinances.

The college and congregational church phase was led by educated, Calvinistic theologians and was more akin to the First Great Awakening. Other than their attendance, women rarely participated. It was led by men such as President Timothy Dwight of Yale University (1752–1817), Lane Seminary president Lyman Beecher (1775–1863), theologian Nathaniel Taylor (1786–1858), and Asahel Nettleton (1783–1844). The main concern of these men and other New England ministers was in making Calvinism more appealing.[12] A strong advocate for women's rights, Lyman Beecher, nonetheless, believed it was unfeminine for women to preach.[13] In a discourse delivered at the First Presbyterian Church in Newburyport, Massachusetts, in 1837, Rev. Jonathan F. Sears asked why women would want to go beyond the strictures given by the Apostle Paul. "They are designed, not to degrade, but to elevate, her character, —not to cramp, but to afford salutary freedom [...] Let woman throw off her feminine character, and her power to benefit society is lost."[14] President of the College of New Jersey, Ashbel Green (1762–1848) believed that allowing women to preach was unbiblical.

---

[9] Ibid., 43–45.
[10] Lindley, 61.
[11] Carl J. Schneider and Dorothy Schneider, 32.
[12] McLoughlin, *Revivals, Awakenings, and Reform*, 109–122.
[13] Keith J. Hardman, *Charles Grandison Finney, 1792–1875: Revivalist and Reformer* (Syracuse, NY: Syracuse University Press, 1987), 185.
[14] Jonathan F. Stearns, *A Discourse of Female Influence, and the True Christian Mode of Its Exercise* (Newburyport, MA: John Tilton, 1837), 17–18.

It was therefore, not to be expected, that he who formed them with this natural and retiring modesty, and under a qualified subjection to man, would ever require, or even permit them, to do anything in violation of his own order; and least of all that he would permit this, in his own immediate service. Hence, I apprehend it is, that we find in the New Testament such texts as the following—1 Timothy 2:11–14 [...][15]

Charles Finney

Charles Finney was a significant revivalist of the Second Great Awakening. His revivals (1825–1835) occurred primarily in New York State, where they were attended by thousands. He applied "New Measures" to his meetings. One was the "anxious bench," to which people struggling with a religious decision could come forward. He called out sinners by name—along with their sins. Finney's revivals were Arminian and he held a postmillennial eschatology.

Finney was different from many of the other revival ministers of his age. He encouraged men and women of all races to come to the anxious bench for prayer.[16] To the chagrin of many of his fellow ministers, Finney encouraged women to preach, pray, and testify. He continued to support the ones who became abolitionists, reformers, and suffragists.[17] He offered women leadership roles in his revivals. He believed that the Holy Spirit could enter anyone at any time. Later, he served as president of Oberlin, which was the first college in America to admit women. Finney, however, never pressed for women's ordination and appeared to believe that women should remain in the home. Nevertheless, he did much to advance women's roles within the church.[18]

---

[15] Cited in Rosemary Radford Ruether and Rosemary Skinner Keller, eds. *Women and Religion in America* (San Francisco, CA: Harper and Row, 1981–1986), 2:161.
[16] Dickson D. Bruce, Jr, *And They All Sang Hallelujah: Plain-Folk Camp Meeting Religion, 1800–1845* (Knoxville, TN: University of Tennessee Press, 1974), 61–94.
[17] Edward Blum, "Paul has been Forgotten: Women, Gender, and Revivalism in the Gilded Age," *The Journal of the Gilded Age and Progressive Era* 3, no. 3 (July 2004): 252.
[18] Barbara MacHaffie, *Her Story: Women in the Christian Tradition*, 2nd ed. (Minneapolis, MN: Fortress Press, 2006), 197.

Free Market

The Constitution's First Amendment Establishment Clause placed all religions on an equal playing field from the perspective of the federal government. In 1833, Massachusetts was the last state to end its support of a church or denomination. No longer could the Puritan Church that had long dominated New England rely on the government to ensure its ministers were paid and the pews full. Religion was a free market in which those who worked the hardest would benefit the most. Few denominations worked harder at adding souls to their congregations than the Methodists and Baptists. These denominations also benefited the most from the Second Great Awakening. Both denominations' numbers grew and as many as two-thirds of these new members were women.[19]

As Methodists and Baptists became more organized and desired greater acceptance in norms of American society, women began to lose some of the roles they had sometimes taken within their churches.[20] Separate gender spheres were imposed; there was a male hierarchy and women were forbidden from church leadership roles. These denominations maintained that women were equal to men in God's eyes, but that women must not serve as ministers and should stay home.[21] Even though John Wesley permitted women to preach upon occasion, the Methodist Church forbade female preaching in 1800.[22] Women were limited to watching over children, teaching Sunday School, and leading mission groups.

Led by Barton Stone (1772–1844) and Alexander Campbell (1788–1866), the Disciples of Christ was a direct result of the frontier revivals of the Second Great Awakening. Initially, Stone and Campbell allowed women to preach in revivals, but both changed

---

[19] MacHaffie, 95.

[20] There were dozens of Baptist groups at this time. The Triennial Convention was formed in 1814. Baptists in the South left the Triennial Convention in 1845 over the slavery issue and formed the Southern Baptist Convention (SBC). While more concerned with preserving slavery, the SBC held that women should not serve as official and should remain in the home.

[21] Carl J. Schneider and Dorothy Schneider, 37.

[22] Ibid., 25.

their opinions and forbade women any ministerial role other than deaconess, with the ability to minister only to women.[23]

Smaller groups such as the Wesleyan Methodist Church, Free Methodists, and Free Will Baptists had women preachers, primarily as circuit evangelists because so few men were available. These evangelists, however, frequently had to justify their work to male pastors of churches. By the 1850s, however, even these groups stepped back as they feared that people would confuse women's preaching with a belief in women's political causes. [24]

Missionary Societies

As a result of the Second Great Awakening, many women wanted to spread the gospel. Women had become Sunday School teachers and led women's prayer meetings. These meetings gave birth to women's missionary societies. Women often tithed and raised money for missionary societies they organized, served, and led. Many of these mission societies were autonomous, while others gave the money to their denomination's mission board. Many of these boards merged with their denomination but women still retained some authority.[25]

Missionary work was considered appropriate for married women. Initially, single women often found it difficult to be appointed as foreign missionaries. The American Board of Commissioners for Foreign Missions appointed 138 single women missionaries in 1860, but only thirty went overseas.[26] Most female missionaries were married and tasked with the same responsibilities they had at home. They had few, if any, ministerial responsibilities.[27]

Single women found it easier to serve in foreign missions after the Civil War. In 1873, Charlotte "Lottie" Digges Moon (1840–1912) became one of the first single women to serve on the foreign mission field. The Southern Baptist Convention's (SBC) Foreign Mission

---

[23] For more information see Bill Grasham, "The Role of Women in the American Restoration Movement," *Restoration Quarterly* 41, no. 4 (1999): 211–240.
[24] MacHaffie, 197.
[25] Lindley, 302–3. Examples include the Presbyterian, Lutheran, Methodist, and Mennonite Mission Boards.
[26] MacHaffie, 173.
[27] Ibid., 172.

Board appointed her as a missionary to China. Moon served first at a boy's school and later evangelized in the interior regions of P'ingtu and Hwangshien. Concerned that people were starving, she began to share her rations with everyone she believed in need. Eventually, her weight dropped to fifty pounds and she died of starvation. Moon was followed into missionary service by thousands of single Southern Baptist women.[28] The annual SBC foreign missions offering is named for her.[29] By 1900, there were forty ministerial societies in America led by women, and two-thirds of all foreign missionaries were women.

The money these societies raised gave women significant authority in Protestant churches.[30] Some men, however, were uncomfortable with women's leadership. Men complained that women were so consumed with financially supporting their own societies that they were damaging other ministries. Lindley notes that men often resented seeing that women could be more efficient than they were. Women also complained about decisions made by the men on mission boards. In many denominations, women were doing most of the fundraising but excluded from decisions on how the board spent those funds and who was sent to the field.[31] Women who complained were often reprimanded.

Social Movements

The development of women's missionary societies led to the formation of other reformist groups that were led by women.[32] By the middle of the nineteenth century, these new societies were consistent with the Cult of True Womanhood as it expanded from the home to the community. According to the Cult of True Womanhood, it was impossible to raise children to be good citizens if they

---

[28] Though not as famous as her older sister Lottie, Edmonia Moon (1851–1908) was the first single female missionary. She was appointed to China in 1872.
[29] Pamela R. Durso and Keith E. Durso, *The Story of Baptists in the United States* (Brentwood, TN: Baptist History and Heritage Society, 2006), 128–29.
[30] MacHaffie, 175.
[31] Lindley, 71.
[32] Anthony Michael Petro, "Religion, Gender, and Sexuality," in *The Columbia Guide to Religion in American History*, eds. Paul Harvey and Edward J. Blum, and Randall Stephens (New York, NY: Columbia University Press, 2012), 196.

lived in slums, worked in factories, and had alcoholic fathers.[33] The women in these reform groups believed that they had to protect the moral behavior of their husbands and sons.[34] The formation of societies such as the Women's Christian Temperance Union (WCTU), provided women a sense of belonging and a cause to believe in.[35]

Women's abolitionist societies were very active in the first half of the nineteenth century. The members of these societies were disturbed by the exploitation of Black women and the forced separation of families. Women soon began to believe their plight was similar to those of female slaves. They, too, were not treated with biblical equality as noted in Galatians 3:28. The women's abolition societies, therefore, helped give rise to women's rights organizations. Sarah (1792–1873) and Angelina Grimke (1805–1879) were at the forefront of both issues. The Grimke sisters were raised as Quakers in a slaveholding family in Charleston, South Carolina. Sarah developed a revulsion to slavery after seeing enslaved people whipped. She and her sister were ardent abolitionists and advocates for women's suffrage.[36] In 1837, Sarah published a series of articles under the title "Equality of the Sexes." These letters drew widespread ire from both men and women. The Congregational Association of Massachusetts denounced the letter and the sisters.[37]

Many men were disturbed by the women's suffrage movement and a large number of women did not embrace the cause. Some men disagreed with their wives participating in these societies for pragmatic reasons. Many husbands felt their wives were spending too much time away from the home, neglecting household duties, and disregarding their husbands.[38] Other men had qualms about women running their own societies. Men had little problem with women supporting orphanages, handing out bibles, and supporting foreign missionaries, but when the issues turned more political, men were not shy in voicing their opposition.[39]

---

[33] Carl J. Schneider and Dorothy Schneider, 91.
[34] MacHaffie, 166–67.
[35] Harvey, Blum, and Stephens, 196.
[36] Mary Malone, *Women and Christianity: From the Reformation to the 21st Century* (Maryknoll, NY: Orbis Books, 2003), 3:208–15; MacHaffie, 168.
[37] Malone, 3:211.
[38] Carl J. Schneider and Dorothy Schneider, 45.
[39] Lindley, 90.

When speaking in favor of abolition, men frequently told women to stay in their place.[40] The same was true for women's suffrage. Few women annoyed men more than Elizabeth Cady Stanton (1815–1902). Stanton pushed for women's suffrage and organized the first women's rights convention at Seneca Falls, New York, in 1848.

Most southern, Protestant men were strongly against the Grimke sisters, Stanton, and women's rights. Several SBC periodicals stressed that any effort to raise women to equality with men went against God's plan. One Baptist pastor from Georgia castigated men whose wives had joined the movement. Stanton reported that the pastor "felt called upon to denounce all women suffragists from the pulpit, not only with severity but with discourtesy, and had been so misguided as to declare that the husbands of suffragists were all feeble-minded."[41] Disciples of Christ leader, E.W. Herndon (1836–1904) stated, "Voting women violated the scriptural principle of wives submitting to their husband." Moreover, "if the saloon cannot be destroyed except by woman's suffrage, we say let the saloon stay open."[42] Southern women were taught not to speak in church or the public arena. Susan Lindley notes that when they did speak out, they had St. Paul "tossed in their face."[43]

Catholic Women

During the American colonial era, women kept important Catholic practices alive in the home. These private rituals were important as the era was dominated by Protestantism and its corresponding fear, if not hatred, of Catholicism. Though women performed this important domestic service, Catholic beliefs concerning women had changed little since the Middle Ages. Women were still more weak-minded than men, prone to sins of vanity, and considered spiritually and morally inferior to men.[44] Women still had to choose between Eve and Mary.

---

[40] MacHaffie, 169.
[41] Elizabeth C. Stanton, et al., *History of Woman Suffrage*, 6 vols. (Rochester, NY: 1881–1922), 4:922.
[42] E W. Herndon, "Woman's Suffrage," *Christian Quarterly Review* 7, (October 1888), 608.
[43] Lindley, 104.
[44] MacHaffie, 237.

The Establishment Clause helped the Catholic Church as it allowed it to stand on equal ground with other previously favored Christian denominations. The Catholic Church grew from one of the smallest religious groups in colonial America to be larger than any Protestant denomination by 1850.[45] The Cult of True Womanhood was readily accepted by many Catholic women. However, it was more difficult to achieve as most Catholic women were poor immigrants and had to work outside the home. Those who were involved were of the middle class. Considered the women's sphere, charitable societies provided a place in which women found camaraderie that eventually led to leadership roles in secular society.[46]

True Womanhood eventually led Catholic women to join movements for women's suffrage and equal rights. Bishop Joseph Machebeuf (1812–1899) of Colorado believed that supporters of women's equality were "old maids" and disgruntled housewives.

> Are the leaders of those pretended woman's rights, I will not say in Colorado, but in the large cities of the East; I said, in my first lecture: "Some old maids, disappointed in love," but ladies, better informed, answer for: Battalions of old maids, disappointed in getting husbands of any sort; women separated from their husbands, or divorced by men of sacred obligations imposed by God himself; "what God has joined together let no man put asunder." (Matthew xix 6.) Women who, although married, are discontented and wish to improve their condition by holding the reins of the family government, for, it is remarked, that there never was a woman happy in her home, who wished for female suffrage.[47]

Feminism challenged Catholic teachings that dated from the Patristic era. Pope Leo XIII (1878–1903) saw feminism as a threat to male supremacy.

---

[45] Jay P. Dolan, *The American Catholic Experience: A History from Colonial Times to Present* (Garden City, NY: Doubleday, 1985), 160–61.
[46] Lindley, 198–200.
[47] Rt. Rev. J. P. Machebeuf, *Woman's Suffrage: A Letter* (Denver: Triune Steam Printing House, 1877), 6.

> Wherefore as the Apostle admonishes: "As Christ is the head of the Church, so is the husband the head of the wife;" and just as the Church is subject to Christ, who cherishes it with the most chaste and lasting love, so it is becoming that women should also be subject to their husbands, and by them in turn be loved with faithful and constant affection.[48]

In 1880 Leo XIII explained that divorce damaged womanhood. "The dignity of womanhood is lessened and brought low, and women run the risk of being deserted after having ministered to the pleasures of men." Divorced women not only broke the sacrament of marriage, but they also lost their purpose by not "pleasuring men." Men only broke a sacrament.[49] In 1891, he discussed women in the workforce. "Women, again, are not suited for certain occupations; a woman is by nature fitted for home work, and it is that which is best adapted at once to preserve her modesty and to promote the good bringing up of children and the well-being of the family."[50]

Leo XIII defined the Catholic position on the changing world. He insisted on traditional Catholic teachings that promoted male headship, that women should remain in the home, minister to children, and serve their husbands. Hundreds of years of Catholic dogma were under assault from the secular world and, rather than adapt to the new world, the church held to its traditional beliefs.

Pope Leo XIII insisted that the family remained the most important concern for women not called to a religious vocation, and condemned birth control and divorce. Women could volunteer in charitable organizations but not for women's suffrage. However, when women gained the right to vote, the church urged women to use it to support Catholic causes.[51]

The Holiness Movement

Methodist Phoebe Palmer (1807–1874) founded the Holiness movement. She emphasized Wesley's doctrine of Christian perfection

---

[48] Leo VIII, Encyclical Letter, *Quod Apostolici Munereris*, 28 December 1878.
[49] Leo VIII, Encyclical Letter, *Arcanum Divinae*, 10 February 1880.
[50] Leo VIII, Encyclical Letter, *Rerum Novarum*, 15 May 1891,
[51] Lindley, 360.

that taught a Christian can live a life free of sin.[52] She received entire sanctification in July 1837 and believed it demanded that she reach the lost. Influential Methodist ministers and laypeople alike attended her Tuesday Night Prayer Meetings. As many as three hundred people would attend.[53]

Some Methodists denounced Palmer's beliefs as "too extreme, too emotional, to fit into the new formalism of urban and suburban Methodist respectability."[54] She was also criticized for rejecting the Apostle Paul's strictures on women. While in England in 1859, she was attacked for preaching.[55] In response to these criticisms, she wrote *Promise of the Father* in 1859. In this work, she identified two impediments to women as Christian leaders. The first was poor exegesis. Palmer believed that the "Father Promised," in Joel 2:28 and in Acts 2:17–18, that the Holy Spirit will be given to both men and women and that with the Holy Spirit's confirmation all are expected to prophesy and preach.[56] As she believed that she was living in the last days, every person was required to present the gospel—this meant men and women. She believed many men either misunderstood this mandate or defied it.[57] The second was that many men held unchristian views about women. She warned male ministers that their attempts to deny women the use of their spiritual gifts delayed the growth of the church and God's return. It also placed women under tremendous spiritual stress.

> We believe hundreds of conscientious, sensitive Christian women have actually suffered more under the slowly crucifying process to which they have been subjugated by men who bear the Christian name than many a martyr

---

[52] Randall Balmer, *Protestantism in America* (New York, NY: Columbia University Press, 2005), 238.
[53] Patricia Bizzell, "Frances Willard, Phoebe Palmer, and the Ethos of the Methodist Woman Preacher," *Rhetoric Society Quarterly* 36, no. 4 (Autumn 2006): 386.
[54] Charles Edwin Jones, *Perfectionist Persuasion: The Holiness Movements and American Methodism, 1867–1936*, ed. Kenneth E. Rowe (Metuchen, N.J.: The Scarecrow Press, Inc., 1974), 5:17.
[55] MacHaffie, 199.
[56] Ibid.
[57] Lindley, 120.

has endured in passing through the flames. We are aware that we are using strong language: but we do not use it in bitterness, but with feelings of deep humiliation before God that the cause of truth demands the utterance of such sentiments.[58]

Palmer, though a revivalist, did not describe her ministry as that of preaching. She knew it would only detract from her ministry. Instead, she describes herself as following God's command.

Preach we do not; that is, not in a technical sense. We would do it, if called; but we have never felt it our duty to sermonize in any way by dividing and subdividing with metaphysical hair-splitting in theology. We have nothing more to do than Mary, when, by the command of the Head of the Church, she proclaimed a risen Jesus to her brethren.[59]

Palmer's beliefs came through her interpretation of theology, which was based on prophetic tradition. The Holy Spirit, not men, authorized prophecy. She never even discussed female ordination or that women should be able to serve in ecclesiastical positions. Many Holiness churches followed the spirit of Palmer's teachings. Holiness churches such as those associated with the Church of the Nazarene, the Church of God (Anderson), and the Pilgrim Holiness Church had a high percentage of female ministers.[60] Palmer had also tremendous influence on Catherine Booth (1829–1890), co-founder of the Salvation Army, and its support for female ministers.

Palmer did not actively support women's rights.[61] She reminded women that there had to be a balance between taking care of the

---

[58] Phoebe Palmer, "Tongue of Fire on the Daughters of the Lord" in Thomas C. Oden, *Phoebe Palmer: Selected Writings* (New York, NY: Paulist Press, 1988), 38. This book is a shortened version of *Promise of the Father*.
[59] Harold E. Raser, *Phoebe Palmer: Her Life and Thought* (Lewiston, ME: The Edwin Mellen Press, 1987), 77.
[60] MacHaffie, 199.
[61] Lindley, 122.

home and sharing the gospel.[62] Anne C. Loveland maintains that her emphasis on the home kept her from promoting women's issues.[63]

Dwight Lyman Moody (1837–1899)

Dwight Lyman Moody was the greatest evangelist of the second half of the nineteenth century. Along with his song leader, Ira Sankey (1840–1908), he held revivals that drew thousands in England, Europe, and America. Moody made his headquarters in Chicago and in doing so made it a major center of the evangelical movement. He was also prominent in Keswickianism. Keswickianism taught that after the initial conversion, the person should seek a second blessing by the Holy Spirit. At that point, the person would become entirely sanctified and live a less sinful or even sinless life.[64]

Moody believed that women should remain in the home and attend to their families. His sermons were laced with sentimentalism that praised devout mothers for bringing fathers and sons to Christ.[65] He also was contemptuous of women who were involved with things beyond their homes. He saw them as little better than fallen women.[66] He also ensured that men and women sat in separate sections at his revivals. These beliefs and actions helped ensure male, conservative support.

Moody, however, was inconsistent in matters of gender. He accepted women into the Moody Bible Institute and invited Frances Willard (1837–1839), a preacher and temperance advocate, Sarah Smiley (d. 1917) and Mary Johnson (1824–1928), temperance leaders, to speak to women at his revivals. Willard noticed that she was speaking not just to women but advertisements listed her as a preacher and not relegated to women's groups. Not wanting to hurt

---

[62] Anne C. Loveland, "Domesticity and Religion in the Antebellum Period: The Career of Phoebe Palmer," *The Historian* 39, no. 3 (May 1977): 465.
[63] Ibid., 470.
[64] Peter Althouse, "Wesleyan and Reformed Impulses in the Kewsick and Pentecostal Movements," *The Pneuma Review*, last modified 20 June 2014, http://pneumareview.com/peter-althouse-wesleyan-and-reformed-impulses-in-the-keswick-and-pentecostal-movements/.
[65] Dwight L. Moody, *New Sermons, Addresses and Prayers* (Chicago, IL: H.S. Goodspeed, 1877), 3.
[66] "Progress of the Revival," *Boston Daily Globe*, January 5, 1877, 8.

the revival, Willard asked Moody about it. She recalled, "Mr. Moody [...] placed my name upon his program" to "literally preach" to men and women. "Brother Moody [...] perhaps you will hinder the work among these conservatives." Moody "laughed in his cheery way, and declared that 'it was just what they needed.'"[67] In response to her opponents, Willard published *Woman in the Pulpit* in 1888 in which she used careful exegesis to argue that women could serve in the ministry.

According to Edward Bloom, "Moody's rhetoric circumscribed women's roles and thereby maintained Protestant unity, but the actual revivals offered women an opportunity and space to undermine such barriers and assert their own understanding of the relationship between religion and social reform."[68] One reporter noted, we trust that these examples will not be lost sight of [...] The church everywhere needs the work of its women. Humanity needs it. No "sphere" should limit their work, moreover: In the home, in society, among all classes there is service that they are the best fitted to perform. May not a revival of woman's best work, and of man's grateful recognition of that work, follow these recent exhibitions of it?[69]

Not everyone welcomed the presence of women in Moody's revivals. A very popular speaker, Sarah Smiley, had been asked to address a Presbyterian congregation in New York. The Brooklyn Presbytery was outraged, and she was publicly rebuked.[70] In a letter to the *Boston Journal Daily*, a reader asked:

> "Where are the Ministers?" One writer grumbled that Willard had overstepped female boundaries: I saw, under

---

[67] Frances E. Willard, *Glimpses of Fifty Years: The Autobiography of an American Woman* (Chicago, IL: Woman's Temperance Publication Association/H. J. Smith & Co., 1889), 356–58.

[68] Edward Blum, "Paul Has Been Forgotten," 250.

[69] "Spheres and Work," Woman's Christian Temperance Union National Headquarters Historical Files, Joint Ohio Historical Society-Michigan Historical Collections—W.C.T.U. microfilm edition, reel 30, "A book of Miscellaneous Articles on Temperance, Lectures, etc., Compiled by Mrs. J.F. Willard." Subsequent entries from this reel will be noted as *FEW Scrapbook*.

[70] "Rev. Sarah Smiley and the Brooklyn Presbyterians," *New York Times*, January 28, 1874, 2; "Woman Preaching Before the Brooklyn Presbytery," *New York Times*, April 15, 1874, 5.

head of "Tabernacle Services;" in large letters? Sermon by Miss Frances Willard. The other day the horse-cars were placarded with the announcement that the same lady was going to "Preach" on Sunday. Revolted by these advertisements, this onlooker remarked, "I thought that the conventions of ministers had decided, more than once, that women could not and should not preach." Willard's actions, moreover, had ramifications beyond Moody's revivals. Fearing that other women might follow Willard's lead, this Protestant wondered, "What will become of the world if they disobey?"[71]

These rebukes did not deter Smiley or Willard from preaching and speaking. Moody, however, was disturbed by several of the messages the women delivered about scripture. Smiley taught that the only way to get at the truth of the Bible was to interpret it allegorically.[72] Willard believed that male biblical translators deliberately ignored women. For that reason, she later endorsed Elizabeth Cady Stanton's two-volume (1895–1898) *Woman's Bible*.[73] In 1877, Moody removed Willard from his revival team because she spent more time speaking at temperance events. The break was acrimonious and their feud was followed in the newspapers for several years.[74]

Some male theologians had no use for Stanton's *Woman's Bible*. They denounced its use of biblical criticism, the questioning of supernatural events, and its stress on scripture that emphasized women as leaders. The *Woman's Bible* was more a commentary on scripture than a new version or translation. Stanton responded to the criticism with her usual bluntness. "I do not believe that any man ever saw or talked with God, I do not believe that God inspired the Mosaic code, or told the historians what they say he did about woman, for all the religions on the face of the earth degrade her,

---

[71] Willard, *Glimpses of Fifty Years*, 356–58; "The Women's Meeting: Park Street Church Crowded," *FEW Scrapbook*.
[72] Sarah F. Smiley, *The Fulness of Blessing- or, the Gospel of Christ, as Illustrated from the Book of Joshua* (London: Hodder and Stoughton, 1876), 11–12.
[73] Kathi Kern, *Mrs. Stanton's Bible* (Ithaca, 2001).
[74] Edward Blum, "Paul Has Been Forgotten," 268.

and so long as woman accepts the position that they assign her, her emancipation is impossible."[75]

A Step Forward

At the beginning of the nineteenth century, many men were more interested in their jobs than in the church. Pastors realized that women outnumbered men at church services and therefore catered to them in their sermons. The advocates of the Cult of True Womanhood instilled the love of Christ with a sense of civic responsibility. Completely against the norms of previous centuries, women were assuming the role of the arbiters of Christianity, morality, and patriotism.

The Second Great Awakening had a significant effect on Christian women. In the frontier phase, the Arminian soteriology in the revivals freed women from the fatalistic grip of Calvinist predestination. Moody's revivals gave women ministerial roles and often featured them as speakers or preachers. Baptist, Methodist, and Disciples of Christ ministers and leaders exhorted from the pulpit and periodicals the traditional role of women. The Holiness Movement was the obvious exception.

Many of the women who participated in the Second Great Awakening determined that they could do more to hasten Christ's return. Among Baptists, Methodists, and the Disciples of Christ, women began to form prayer groups that eventually gave rise to mission societies. These missionary societies served as an entrée into social reform. Women became involved with issues such as temperance, better housing for the working classes, and women's suffrage. Catholic women also participated in these societies but in much smaller numbers. At the same time, the Catholic church continued to teach the subordination of women and denounced feminism.

By mid-century, Protestant men began to notice the prominence of women in revivals and complained that the church had been feminized. Many men did not care that women led mission societies but they did not want women to take political positions. They sought

---

[75] Elizabeth Cady Stanton, *The Woman's Bible*, Internet Archive, last modified 18 March 2018, https://archive.org/details/WomansBibleElizabethCadyStanton/page/n15/mode/2up.

to reclaim their patriarchal roles and end their wives' participation in women-led political societies. The damage, however, was done. Whereas in previous centuries women had taken one step forward and men pushed them back two, due to many men's waning interest in religion in the first half of the century, women were able to take two steps forward and men could push them back only one.

CHAPTER NINE

Women in the Twentieth and Twenty-First Centuries

Though white, Protestant, middle-class women took steps forward in the United States in the nineteenth century, they had a long way to go to reach legal, political, economic, and social equality with men. Within many fundamentalist and evangelical denominations, the church was no exception. They were expected to remain in the home, and obey their husbands. Catholic women fared little better. Educated women could find jobs as nurses, secretaries, and schoolteachers, but more prominent vocations were reserved for men. Moreover, women were not guaranteed the nationwide right to vote until 1920 and, thus, the ability to exercise their rights as full American citizens. Women, however, pressed the momentum they garnered in the nineteenth century and continued to organize for causes such as temperance, improvement of housing, regulation of child labor, and extension of suffrage. They also sought greater positions within their various churches. Following two world wars that created more employment opportunities for women, the reality of women working outside the home entered mainstream America.

Catholicism

The 1917 Code of Canon Law reaffirmed the Church's traditional understanding of marriage.[1] This dogma was upheld by popes who

---

[1] Ellen M. Leonard, "Separation of the Sexes: The Development of Gender Roles in Modern Catholicism," in *Equal at Creation*, eds. Joseph Martos and Pierre Hégy (Toronto: University of Toronto Press, 1998), 122–23.

feared modern challenges to church teachings and authority. The Church, however, also began to realize that for families to survive, more women would need to work outside the home. For much of the century, the church attempted to dictate which jobs women could safely hold.

At the beginning of the century, canon law recognized women's value within congregations and religious orders but accorded them no status within ecclesiastical orders or in making political decisions. The church would face many attempts from a changing world to undermine these time-honored practices. Whether Catholics followed the decrees or not, popes wrote many encyclicals and Councils announced papal policy.

Pope Benedict XV (1914–1922) supported guaranteeing American women the right to vote. Mary Daly, however, noted that this was a political calculation. Because he did nothing else to improve the status of women, he assumed that Catholic women would support Catholic candidates for political office.[2]

Pius XI's (1922–1939) 1929 encyclical, *Divini Illius Magistri*, denounced co-education. He also linked co-education with unnatural relationships between the genders. "Besides there is not in nature itself, which fashions the two quite different organisms, in temperament, in abilities, anything to suggest that there can be or ought to be promiscuity, and much less equality, in the training of the two sexes."[3]

In 1930, Pius XI penned *Casti Connubii*. The encyclical recognized the dignity of both sexes, their equality in soul, and the rights of married women, but insisted that for unity, balance, and order within the home, the man had to lead. Susan Lindley believed he was anticipating complementarianism when he wrote, "For if man is the head, the woman is the heart, and as he occupies the chief place of ruling, so she may and ought to claim for herself the chief place in love."[4] Any attempt for women to gain social, economic,

---

[2] Mary Daly, *The Church and the Second Sex: With a New Feminist PostChristian Introduction by the Author* (New York, NY: Harper and Row, 1975), 109.
[3] Pius XI, Encyclical Letter, *Divini Illius Magistri*, 31 December 1929.
[4] Pope Pius XI, *Casti Connubii*, 30 December 1930, Papal Archive, last accessed 1 July 2021, https://www.vatican.va/content/pius-xi/en/encyclicals/documents/hf_p-xi_enc_19301231_casti-connubii.html.

or psychological equality was "debasing and unnatural."[5] She was to be a domestic missionary to her children.[6] The letter also proffered the Church's traditional opposition to any use of artificial birth control.[7]

Following in Pius XI's footsteps, Pius XII (1939–1958) praised motherhood and the mother's importance in the home. Women without children, he opined, should practice "spiritual motherhood." Pius pitied any woman that was not in a religious order or not married. "In the impossibility of marriage, she discerns her own vocation and, sad at heart though resigned, she too [like those in religious orders] devotes herself entirely to the highest and most varied forms of beneficence."[8]

Mary Daly noted that Pope John XXIII (1958–1963) could not have been more different from Pius XII, in "temperament and stamp of mind."[9] He was willing to reexamine the place of women[10] in the home, society, and the church in his 1963 encyclical, *Pacem in Terris*. This encyclical broke with centuries of church teaching and tradition.

> Human beings have the right to choose freely the state of life they prefer, and therefore the right to set up a family, with equal rights and duties for man and woman, and also the right to follow to the priesthood or the religious life [...] Since women are becoming ever more conscious of their human dignity, they will not tolerate being as mere material instruments, but demand rights befitting a person both in domestic and public life.

Recognizing that times had changed and the church would have to change with it to remain relevant, John XXIII realized that women would no longer stand for being treated with less dignity

---

[5] Ibid.
[6] Martos and Hégy, 124.
[7] Susan Hill Lindley, *"You have Stept out of your Place:" A History of Women and Religion in America* (Louisville, KY: Westminster John Knox Press, 1996), 360.
[8] Pius XII, cited in *The Woman in the Modern World, papal teachings selected and arranged by the Benedictine Monks and Solesmes* (Boston, MA: St. Paul Editions, 1959), 31.
[9] Daly, 118.
[10] Pope John XXIII, Encyclical Letter, *Pacem in Terris*, 11 April 1963.

than men. His statement affirming his belief that women had the right to enter the priesthood was not only revolutionary but gave hope to many women who felt called to this vocation. John XXIII, however, also believed women had traditional roles. "Women have the right to working conditions in accordance with their requirements and their duties as wives and mothers."[11]

Though John XXIII did not live to see the conclusion of Vatican II (1962–1965), his desire to elevate the status of women was included in the Council's final official document, *Gaudium et Spes*.

> With respect to the fundamental rights of the person, every type of discrimination, whether social or cultural, whether based on sex, race, color, social condition, language or religion, is to be overcome and eradicated as contrary to God's intent. For in truth it must still be regretted that fundamental personal rights are still not being universally honored. Such is the case of a woman who is denied the right to choose a husband freely, to embrace a state of life or to acquire an education or cultural benefits equal to those recognized for men.[12]

Gaudium et Spes was a significant step forward for Catholic women. Much like *Pacem in Terris*, it argued that women should have rights equal to men but not aspire to be men. "Women now work in almost all spheres. It is fitting that they are able to assume their proper role in accordance with their own nature."[13] Women should also remember their roles as wives and mothers:

> Such is especially the case with respect to mothers of families, but due consideration must be given to every person's sex and age [...] The children, especially the younger among them, need the care of their mother at home. This domestic role of hers must be safely preserved, though

---

[11] Ibid.
[12] *Gaudium et Spes*, Papal Archive, 7 December 1965, last accessed 1 July 2021, https://www.vatican.va/archive/hist_councils/ii_vatican_council/documents/vat-ii_cons_19651207_gaudium-et-spes_en.html.
[13] *Gaudium et Spes*, in Walter M. Abbott, ed., *The Documents of Vatican II* (New York, NY: America Press), 267.

the legitimate social progress of woman should not be underrated on that account.[14]

Vatican II also released the "Declaration on Christian Education." This document reiterated that women deserved the same rights as men in education, vocation, and society, but women should do things only proper for women. People have "inalienable rights" but only in line with one's "native talents," "cultural background," and "ancestral heritage," and special attention must be given to "the social role which divine Providence allots to each sex in family life and in society."[15] The Council was clear: women could obtain an education, work outside the home, and participate in society as long as it was done within the spheres of traditional womanhood. If a family had to decide which parent would work outside the home and which would take care of the home and children, the Council was clear. John XXIII and Vatican II did much to change the status of women in the twentieth century.

Under Pope Paul VI (1963–1968), the Vatican issued several statements concerning the ordination of women. Though Pope John XXIII and Vatican II were somewhat receptive to a discussion, these declarations were not. The strongest was issued by the Sacred Congregation for the Doctrine of the Faith with the approval of Pope Paul VI on October 15, 1976, the *Inter Insigniores*, "On the Question of the Admission of Women to the Ministerial Priesthood." The document declared its opposition to the ordination of women because Christ did not have women among the twelve Apostles. When the priest consecrated the bread and the wine at the eucharist, the priest took the part of Christ. The priest, therefore, is an icon of the male Christ. In addition, Christ was described in scripture as the bridegroom who, again, by definition is male.[16]

From the beginning of Pope John Paul II's (1978–2005) pontificate, he affirmed that both male and female have worth, value, equality,

---

[14] Ibid., 257
[15] *Declaration on Christian Education*, in Walter M. Abbott, ed., *The Documents of Vatican II* (New York, NY: America Press), 639, 647.
[16] *Declaration on the Question of Admission of Women to the Ministerial Priesthood*, Papal Archive, 15 October 1976, last accessed 1 July 2021, https://www.vatican.va/roman_curia/congregations/cfaith/documents/rc_con_cfaith_doc_19761015_inter-insigniores_en.html.

and are in the image of God. "Perhaps, therefore, the analogy of sleep indicates here [...] a specific return to non-being [...] in order that the solitary 'man' may be God's creative initiative reemerging from that moment in his double unity as male and female."[17] Allen notes that "one can conclude that man (*adam*) falls into a 'torpor' in order to wake up as 'male' (*is*) and 'female' (*issa*)."[18] Allen noted that this did not suggest a hermaphrodite unity but rather different ways of being male and female. John Paul II further states, "The unity about which Genesis 2:24 speaks ('and the two will be one flesh') is without a doubt the unity that is expressed and realized in the conjugal act. The biblical formulation, so extremely concise and simple, indicates sex, that is, masculinity and femininity, as those characteristics of man—male and female—that allows them, when they become one flesh, to place their whole humanity at the same time under the blessing of fruitfulness."[19] Using sexual reproduction as his premise, John Paul II saw the male and female roles as differentiated, complementary, and a reflection of Triune unity.[20]

While determining that men and women were equal in many respects, John Paul II's emphasis on different and complementary roles of the sexes was the center of *On the Dignity of Women* (1988). When discussing Genesis 3:16 he noted that before the Fall, the man and woman were in complete unity. After the Fall, the consequences of sin led to a lack of equality. Man's domination of woman placed her at a disadvantage and damaged the mutual relationship derived from creation.[21] John Paul II, however, saw Ephesians 5:22–23 not as a wife's submission to her husband, but rather as mutual submission. He maintained that as the husband is the head of the wife, Christ is the head of the Church; the husband must be willing to give himself up for her, even if it meant

---

[17] Pope John Paul II, *Man and Woman, He Created Them: A Theology of the Body*, translated, introduced, and indexed by Michael M. Waldstein (Boston, MA: Pauline Books and Media, 2006), 159.
[18] Sister Prudence Allen, *The Concept of Woman: The Search for Communion of Persons, 1500–2015*, (Grand Rapids, MI: Eerdmans Publishing Company, 2016), 3:464.
[19] Pope John Paul II, *Man and Woman*, 167.
[20] Agneta Sutton, "The Complementarity and Symbolism of the Two Sexes: Karl Barth, Hans Urs von Balthasar, and John Paul II," *New Blackfriars* 87, no 1010 (July 2006): 418, 421.
[21] Pope John Paul II, *On the Dignity of Women*, Section 7, 15 August 1988.

his life. The relationship between Christ and the Church required the Church's submission to Christ. "In the relationship between husband and wife the 'subjection' is not one-sided but mutual."[22] Moreover, he compared the traditional subjection of wives to that of slaves and masters:

> The awareness that in marriage there is mutual "subjection of the spouses out of reverence for Christ," and not just that of the wife to the husband, must gradually establish itself in hearts, consciences, behavior and customs. This is a call which from that time onwards, does not cease to challenge succeeding generations; it is a call which people have to accept ever anew. Saint Paul not only wrote: "In Christ Jesus [...] there is no more man or woman," but he also wrote: "There is no more slave or freeman." Yet how many generations were needed for such a principle to be realized in the history of humanity through the abolition of slavery! And what is one to say of the many forms of slavery to which individuals and peoples are subjected, which have not yet disappeared from history? But *the challenge presented by the "ethos" of the Redemption* is clear and definitive.[23]

John Paul II did not agree with his two immediate predecessors. He held that women should follow the example of the Virgin Mary. Women, therefore, should find their dignity and unique humanness in either marriage or virginity, not in the workplace.[24]

Despite the strong movement within the Catholic Church to ordain women, John Paul II agreed with *Inter Insigniores* in every detail. In his 1994 Apostolic Letter, *Ordinatio Sacerdotalis*, he cited church tradition and *Inter Insigniores*, stating, "Wherefore, in order that all doubt may be removed regarding a matter of great importance, a matter which pertains to the Church's divine constitution itself, in virtue of my ministry of confirming the brethren (cf. Luke 22:32) I declare that

---

[22] Ibid., Section 24, 15 August 1988.
[23] Ibid., Section 24, 15 August 1988.
[24] Thomas Bokenkotter, *A Concise History of the Catholic Church* (New York: Doubleday, 2005), 467.

the Church has no authority whatsoever to confer priestly ordination on women and that this judgment is to be definitively held by all the Church's faithful."[25] On July 15, 1998, the Congregation for the Doctrine of the Faith issued a doctrinal commentary on *Ad tuendam fidem*. The commentary added that the reservation of the priesthood to men was "owed the full assent of the faith."[26]

Pope Benedict XVI (2005–2013) agreed with John Paul II's position. On May 29, 2008, the Vatican and the Congregation for the Doctrine of Faith proclaimed that any person who attempted to ordain a woman would be excommunicated.[27] In a February 9, 2010, interview with Peter Seewald, Benedict declared:

> The impossibility of women's ordination in the Catholic Church has been clearly decided by a *"non possumus"* of the supreme Magisterium. The Congregation for the Doctrine of the Faith laid this down under Paul VI in the 1976 document *Inter insigniores*, and John Paul II reinforced it in his 1994 apostolic letter *Ordinatio Sacerdotalis*. In this document, speaking in virtue of his office about the "divine constitution of the Church," he wrote "that the Church has no authority whatsoever to convey priestly ordination on women and that this judgment is to be definitively held by all the Church's faithful."[28]

---

[25] Pope John Paul II, *Ordinatio Sacerdotali*, 22 May 1994, New Advent, last accessed 1 July 2021, https://www.newadvent.org/library/docs_jp02os.htm.

[26] John Paul II, *Ad tuendam fidem*, Profession of Faith, 15 July 1998, Papal Archive, last accessed 1 July 2021, https://www.vatican.va/roman_curia/congregations/cfaith/documents/rc_con_cfaith_doc_1998_professio-fidei_en.html.

[27] "Vatican Decrees Excommunication for Participation in 'Ordination' of Women," *Catholic News Agency*, 29 May 2008, last accessed 1 July 201, https://www.catholicnewsagency.com/news/12780/vatican-decrees-excommunication-for-participation-in-ordination-of-women.

[28] "Pope Benedict XVI Light of the World: The Pope, The Church and Signs of the Times: A Conversation with Peter Seewald," *Women Priests*, last accessed 1 July 2021, https://www.womenpriests.org/benedict-xvi-light-of-the-world-the-pope-the-church-and-the-signs-of-the-times-a-conversation-with-peter-seewald/.

Concerning women working outside the home, John Paul II stressed that women could work outside the home only if necessary. In his June 29, 2009, encyclical, *Caritas in Veritate*, Benedict XVI contended that women and men should be treated the same as men in the workplace. He did not state that some jobs were for women and others for men as his predecessor had.[29]

Benedict XVI's corpus rarely spoke of wifely submission regarding Ephesians 5. Rather, he appeared to accept the teachings of John Paul II. The husband must be willing to give himself up for his wife as Christ gave himself up for the church.[30]

Pope Francis (2013–present) seems more receptive to women serving in some church roles previously reserved for men. Ordination to the priesthood, however, was not one of the roles. On November 2, 2016, he made his position clear. "[I]n Catholic ecclesiology there are two dimensions to think about […] The Petrine dimension, which is from the Apostle Peter, and the Apostolic College, which is the pastoral activity of the bishops, as well as the Marian dimension, which is the feminine dimension of the Church." The Holy Church was a woman and Christ her spouse. The priest who served the sacraments, therefore, must be male.[31]

In August of 2016, Pope Francis appointed a commission on women in the diaconate. When pressed on the commission's progress in May of 2019, he stated that the commission had completed its work but had not arrived at an agreement.[32]

Francis is much more receptive to women serving as catechists and in roles other than deacon or priest. On May 11, 2021, when discussing the need for lay involvement in evangelization in *Antiquum Ministerium*, Francis discussed the various ministerial roles of both

---

[29] Pope Benedict XVI, Encyclical Letter, *Caritas in Veritate*, 29 June 2009, Papal Archive, last accessed 1 July 2021, http://www.vatican.va/content/benedict-xvi/en/encyclicals/documents/hf_ben-xvi_enc_20090629_caritas-in-veritate.html.
[30] Pope Benedict XVI, *Weekly General Audience*, 14 January 2009, https://www.ncregister.com/news/ephesians-and-colossians.
[31] Hannah Brockhaus, "'No'—Pope Francis Refuses to Yield on Church's No Women Priests Stance," *Catholic Online*, 2 November 2016, https://www.catholic.org/news/hf/faith/story.php?id=71749.
[32] Jill Peterfeso, *Womanpriest: The Tradition and Transgression in the Comptemporary Catholic Church* (New York, NY: Fordham University Press, 2020), 170.

lay men and women who, guided by the Holy Spirit, played in the "building up of the church." Citing Vatican II, he stated:

> The Council Fathers repeatedly emphasized the great need for the lay faithful to be engaged directly, in the various ways their charism can be expressed, in the *"plantatio Ecclesiae"* and the development of the Christian community. Worthy of praise too is that army of catechists, both men and women, to whom missionary work among the nations is so indebted, who imbued with an apostolic spirit make an outstanding and absolutely necessary contribution to the spread of the faith and the Church by their great work.

As their work was the same as the presbyterate, these laypeople should be recognized as important but not at a priestly level. Francis made it possible for women to read from the Bible during Mass, act as altar servants, and distribute communion, but they remained barred from becoming deacons or priests.[33] *Antiquum Ministerium* was viewed by many as a significant step in allowing women to be equal collaborators in the church's ministry and a potential opening for women's ordination to ecclesiastical offices. Francis named art historian Barbara Jatta head of Vatican Museums in 2017 and Francesca Di Giovanni as one of the two undersecretaries in the Vatican's Secretariat of State in January 2020. In that same year, he promoted six women to senior positions overseeing the Vatican's finances. When asked about these recent promotions he stated, "We must move forward without fear to include women in advisory positions, also in governance. The place of women in the church is not just as functionaries […] Women's advice is very important."[34]

---

[33] Supreme Pontiff Francis, Apostolic Letter, *Antiquum Ministerium*, 10 May 2021, Papal Archive, https://www.vatican.va/content/francesco/en/motu_proprio/documents/papa-francesco-motu-proprio-20210510_antiquum-ministerium.html.
[34] Kevin Billings, "Pope Francis Appoints Six Women to Council Overseeing Vatican City Finances," *International Business Times*, 6 August 2020, https://www.ibtimes.com/pope-francis-appoints-six-women-council-overseeing-vatican-city-finances-3023964#:~:text=Pope%20Francis%20previously%20appointed%20two%20women%20to%20top,to%20open%20positions%20helping%20oversee%20the%20Vatican%E2%80%99s%20finances.

Concerning women working outside the home, Francis broke new ground in his April 8, 2016, exhortation, *Amoris Laetitia*.

> Masculinity and femininity are not rigid categories. It is possible, for example, that a husband's way of being masculine can be flexibly adapted to the wife's work schedule [...Rigid definitions of masculinity and femininity] can hinder the development of an individual's abilities, to the point of leading him or her to think, for example, that it is not really masculine to cultivate art or dance, or not very feminine to exercise leadership.[35]

Francis followed John Paul II's lead in his Post-Synodal Apostolic Exhortation, *Amoris Laetitia*, of 2016. He held that Ephesians 5 taught mutual submission. "Love excludes every kind of subjection whereby the wife might become a servant or a slave of the husband [...] The community or unity which they should establish through marriage is constituted by a reciprocal donation of self, which is also a mutual subjection."[36] This submission should be freely chosen and carried out with faithfulness, respect, and care.

The Catholic Church has made some modifications in its views of women's role in society. For the majority of these years, women were expected to work in jobs more in tune with their feminine nature. This status remained in place well until the time of Francis I, who broke down these gendered workplace roles. The idea of wifely submission also changed under John Paul II and was continued by those who followed him. Submission as depicted in Ephesians 5 no longer meant the wife's unbending subjugation to her husband, but rather it was now a mutual submission based on the sacrificial love displayed by Christ's love for the church. The status of women being permitted to attain the office of deacon remained the same. Though Francis I made overtures that he might consider women to the diaconate, his position on women serving as priests remained

---

[35] Francis, Post-Synodal Apostolic Exhortation, *Amoris Laetitia*, Papal Archive, 8 April 2016, https://www.vatican.va/content/dam/francesco/pdf/apost_exhortations/documents/papa-francesco_esortazione-ap_20160319_amoris-laetitia_en.pdf.
[36] Ibid.

in line with hundreds of years of papal dogma and, thus, remained forbidden.

Unlike previous centuries, however, female Catholic theologians began to resist the church's patriarchalism and the tradition of male-only ordination. Among them are Mary Daly (1928–2010), Rosemary Radford Ruether (1936–2022), and Elisabeth Schüssler Fiorenza (b. 1938).

According to Mary Daly, traditional Christianity was irredeemably steeped in sexism. She expected feminism to lead to a new, more egalitarian Christianity. One of her main ideas was that God should be perceived as a verb whose actions could be felt in women.[37] Her *Church and Second Sex* (1968) stressed the equality of men and women, and held that the church needed to "be purified of antifeminist notions and practices."[38]

Rosemary Radford Ruether maintains that women must move beyond the sexist Bible to construct a meaningful theology.[39] In *Womanguides: Readings toward a Feminist Theology*, she wrote that women must look to the unorthodox communities that reflect "questionings of male domination in groups where women did enter into critical dialogue." From these groups, women can find a "new community, a new theology, a new canon."[40] Ruether believes that sexist theology and beliefs are perpetuated in Christianity because women are excluded from leadership within the academic community.[41] In her chapter "Feminist Theology and Spirituality," she noted the "sex bias of patriarchal theology [...] must be evaluated as a blasphemous ratification of sin in God's name [...] Feminist theology engages in a systematic reconstruction of all the symbols of human relation to God to delegitimize sexist bias and to manifest an authentic vision of redemption as liberation from sexism."[42]

---

[37] Barbara MacHaffie, *Her Story: Women in the Christian Tradition*, 2nd ed. (Minneapolis, MN: Fortress Press, 2006), 326.
[38] Daly, 9.
[39] MacHaffie, 326.
[40] Rosemary Radford Ruether, *Womanguides: Readings toward a Feminist Theology* (Boston, MA: Beacon, 1985), x–xi.
[41] Rosemary Radford Ruether, "The Feminist Critique in Religious Studies" *Soundings: An Interdisciplinary Journal* 64, no. 4 (1981): 388–402.
[42] Rosemary Radford Ruether, "Feminist Theology and Spirituality," cited in Judith L. Weidman, ed., *Christian Feminism* (San Francisco,CA: Harper & Row, 1984), 9, 11–12.

Elisabeth Schüssler Fiorenza (b. 1938) believes that Christianity has the opportunity to become less sexist by correcting its traditions not found in scripture.[43] In *In Memory of Her: A Feminist Theological Reconstruction of Christian Origins* (1983), she stressed Paul's ideas of equality as recorded in Galatians 3:28 and the ministry of Thecla in the *Acts of Paul and Thecla*.[44] The book's title was taken from Jesus' words to the woman who anointed him. "Truly I say to you, wherever the gospel is preached in the whole world, what she has done will be told in memory of her" (Mark 14:9). Fiorenza then added that everyone knows the names of Peter and Judas, who denied and betrayed Jesus, but not the name of the woman who anointed Jesus.

Protestantism

Within Protestant Fundamentalism and Evangelicalism, men sought to buoy the churches' patriarchal status and replace the feminized church with a more masculine version of Christ and Christianity. Fundamentalism and conservative evangelicalism sought to keep women subservient in the home and in the church. In the second half of the century, conservative evangelical leaders protested, among other things, the feminist movement, the birth control pill, and the Equal Rights Amendment. These leaders defined biblical womanhood in a manner that echoed the Cult of True Womanhood. Mainline Protestant denominations proved more open to women serving in ministerial positions while many Pentecostal denominations disagreed. Protestant women, however, had gained a foothold in traditionally male spheres of life, and their slow advance within some Protestant denominations continued.

Fundamentalism

Fundamentalism was a movement of conservative individuals and churches, such as Baptists and Presbyterians, that came together in the late nineteenth century. Its purpose was to fight for a strict interpretation of anti-modern theologies.[45] Since 1910, fundamentalists

---

[43] MacHaffie, 326.
[44] Elisabeth Schüssler Fiorenza, *In Memory of Her: A Feminist Theological Reconstruction of Christian Origins*, 10th anniversary ed. (New York, NY: Crossroad, 1995).
[45] George M. Marsden, *Fundamentalism and American Culture* (New York, NY: Oxford University Press, 1980), 4–5.

have held to what is commonly known as the five "fundamentals" of the faith.

- Biblical inspiration and the infallibility of scripture
- Virgin birth of Jesus
- Belief in Christ's death and that it was a substitutionary atonement for sin
- Bodily resurrection of Jesus
- Historical reality of the miracles of Jesus[46]

Before the Civil War, proto-fundamentalists spoke of the dangers of allowing women to leave their traditional sphere. Founders of Princeton University's Association of Gentlemen, theologians Charles Hodge (1797–1878), Samuel Miller (1769–1850), and Archibald Alexander (1823–1886) defended the inerrancy of scripture and read it in a hierarchal manner. As Calvinists, they held that the subordination of women was defined by the created order. Hodge opposed anything that elevated women's place in society.[47] It was important to promote the "general good" by having a righteous order. He added, "We believe that the general good requires us to deprive the whole female sex of the right of self-government" because they are "incompetent to the proper discharge of the duties of citizenship." He maintained that anything else would lead to the assumption that they were wiser than Christ and his Apostles and "tear the Bible to pieces, or [...] extort, by violent exegesis, a meaning foreign to its obvious sense."[48] Hodge denounced anything that took women out of the home, even charitable work.[49] For Hodge, Alexander, and Miller, women were "a female appendage to the central drama of life."[50]

---

[46] Marsden, 117.
[47] Margaret Lamberts Bendroth, *Fundamentalism and Gender, 1875 to Present* (New York, NY: Yale University Press, 1993), 34.
[48] Charles Hodge, "The Bible Argument on Slavery," in *Cotton is King: Or, The Culture of Cotton and Its Relation to Agriculture, Manufactures and Commerce; and Also to the Free Colored People of the United States, and to Those who Hold that Slavery is in Itself Sinful* (Augusta, GA: 1860), 861, 863, 848. See also Bendroth, *Fundamentalism and Gender*, 35.
[49] Margaret Lamberts Bendroth, *Fundamentalism and Gender*, 36.
[50] Ronald W. Hogeland, "Charles Hodge, the Association of Gentlemen and Ornamental Womanhood: 1825–1855," *Journal of Presbyterian History* 53, no. 3 (1975): 251–52.

To add to their anxiety, many fundamentalists also held dispensational theology.[51] It taught that history is divided by God into ages, or dispensations, in which God has ordained certain principles in how the age would be administered and humanity was to administer it in that way. Dispensationalists vary in opinion of the number of ages from three to eight, with the most common system holding to seven. Order and obedience to the authority of the age are of paramount importance. The final dispensation was to be the restoration of Israel. Most dispensationalists were also premillennialists who held to a pretribulation rapture.[52] These teachings were spread by the 1909 *Scofield Reference Bible*, which listed the dispensations in the notes.

Dispensationalists traced the subordination of women to the Fall. They held that the consequences of Adam and Eve's sin in the Garden of Eden would remain until Christ's return.[53] Eve's sin demonstrated that women were naïve and unfit for leadership. Male leadership and female subordination were embedded in history and brought order to Christian life.[54] Dispensational theology, therefore, gave fundamentalists a rationale for the belief that women were inferior. At the time, women's groups were using scripturally laced pamphlets, tracts, and sermons to demand suffrage and other rights.[55] These women's groups often argued that biblical restrictions on women's leadership were cultural and temporary and that Christ's atoning death made all Christians equal. Fundamentalists believed dispensationalism trumped random scripture taken out of context in favor of an exegetical method that demonstrated how all scripture worked together, which proved the superiority of their system.[56] From the beginning of the movement, dispensationalists rejected the belief that women were morally superior to men. They also rejected the belief that men had no capacity for heart-felt religion and were naturally aggressive.[57] Fundamentalists viewed

---

[51] Dispensationalism was created by an Anglo-Irishman John Nelson Darby (1800–1882) of the Plymouth Brethren in the 1830s.
[52] Joseph Early, *A History of Christianity: An Introductory Survey* (Nashville: Broadman and Holman Publishers, 2015), 348.
[53] Margaret Lamberts Bendroth, *Fundamentalism and Gender*, 8.
[54] Ibid., 41.
[55] Ibid., 34.
[56] Ibid., 7.
[57] Ibid., 3; Randal Balmer, "American Fundamentalism," 51.

women as rivals to church power and, that by leaving the home, women were responsible for the moral breakdown of the family and America.[58] They were sinful and needed male oversight.[59] Fundamentalists, however, had to be careful in how they attempted to push women back into their traditional roles. Women comprised more than two-thirds of Protestant church membership, were becoming more socially liberated, and, if angered, might leave the church. As Margaret Lamberts Bendroth noted, women had to be won to the fundamentalist cause.[60]

One of the first ways fundamentalist men sought to tighten their traditional hold on the church was to rebrand Christianity. It needed to be more masculine. The American Christianity emerging in the twentieth century needed a Christ who was muscular and attuned to business. He was still empathetic but also very strict in matters concerning scripture, biblical doctrine, and the law.[61]

In the first half of the twentieth century, no one epitomized masculine Christianity and promoted traditional gender norms more than popular Presbyterian evangelist Billy Sunday (1862–1935). A former professional baseball player, Sunday often ran across the stage and pretended to slide into home plate. After beginning in the masculine dominion of the Young Men's Christian Association, he reminded his listeners that Christianity was the "robust red-blooded" faith of Jesus, the carpenter of Nazareth.[62] Sunday believed women should remain in the home.[63] He did allow suffragists who attended his meetings to march in together, but he also allowed the Ku Klux Klan to do the same in full robes.[64] For women, Sunday insisted, marriage and childrearing were their ultimate

---

[58] Lindley, 327.
[59] MacHaffie, 171.
[60] Margaret Lamberts Bendroth, "Fundamentalism and Femininity: Points of Encounter Between Religious Conservatives and Women, 1919–1935," *Church History* 61, no. 2 (June 1992): 226.
[61] Harvey, Blum, and Stephens, 198.
[62] Billy Sunday cited in Margaret Lamberts Bendroth, "Fundamentalism and Femininity," 228.
[63] Billy Sunday, cited in William McLoughlin, "Billy Sunday and the Working Girl of 1915," *Journal of Presbyterian History* (1962–1985) 54, no. 3 (Fall 1976): 376.
[64] Ibid., 377.

goals.⁶⁵ "All great women are satisfied with their common sphere in life and think it is enough to fill the lot God gave them in this world as wife and mother."⁶⁶

Sunday did not like the new woman of the twentieth century. He chastised women who smoked, wore rouge, and rode in cars, which he called "bedroom[s] on wheels." He despised dancing as nothing more than "a hugging match set to music." According to him, "three fourths of all the fallen women fell as a result of the dance."⁶⁷

Sunday believed that women who stayed in their place should be placed on a pedestal. He stated, "The virtue of womanhood is the rampart of our civilization and we must not let it be betrayed."⁶⁸ Unlike other fundamentalists, Sunday believed women were more moral than men. "It remains with womanhood today to lift our social life to a higher plane." Women, therefore, would lift society but only through patriarchy.

Bendroth offered several examples of fundamentalist attempts to masculinize its leaders. Baptist pastor William Bell Riley's (1861–1947) biographers described his love of outdoor sports and his rowdy male friends. Baptist pastor John Roach Straton (1875–1929) walked the streets of New York's red-light district without fear. As an article in the *Baptist Champion* stated, "the Bible is virile literature" and Christ himself "the most manly of men." "Christianity has no place for pusillanimity or churlishness." Baptist fundamentalists defended their leaders as "manly, full-blooded," and "vigorous," not a "soft, gushy and mushy group of men."⁶⁹ Between the world wars, the desire for a more masculine clergy began to manifest itself in Bible institutes. The Moody Bible Institute began to assign women to homemaking courses and men to those that prepared them for the ministry.⁷⁰ As late as 2017, Paige Patterson (b. 1942), the

---

⁶⁵ Billy Sunday, cited in William G. McLouhglin, "Billy Sunday and the Working Girl of 1915," *Journal of Presbyterian History* (1962–1985) 54, no. 3 (Fall 1976): 376.
⁶⁶ Billy Sunday, cited in William T. Ellis, *Billy Sunday: The Man and His Message* (Philadelphia, PA: Thomas Manufacturing Company, 1914), 227ff.
⁶⁷ Billy Sunday, cited in William G. McLoughlin, 376.
⁶⁸ Ibid., 384.
⁶⁹ Margaret Lamberts Bendroth, "Fundamentalism and Femininity," 229–30; A. William Lewis, "The Investment of Manhood," *Bible Champion* 34 (1929): 384; Kennedy, "Quit You Like Men, Be Strong," *Bible Champion* 30 (1924): 134 and "Notes and Comments," *Bible Champion*: 141.
⁷⁰ Lindley, 326.

former president of Southwestern Baptist Theological Seminary and architect of the Conservative Resurgence/Fundamentalist Takeover of the Southern Baptist Convention, ordered his vice-presidents to carry firearms on campus. He also proudly displayed his hunting trophies in his office.

Some fundamentalists viewed women as rivals both to men and evangelism. Women were a threat to pure doctrine and many pastors believed they could not be their partners in ministry.[71] William Bell Riley believed that pastors' wives could cause trouble for his ministry. He, therefore, warned potential ministers to "suppress your wife's ambition, and quiet her tongue."[72] Others believed that women interfered with evangelism and warned young ministers not to get married.[73]

Women's missionary organizations suffered the brunt of these assaults. There was a fear that women were aligning with male liberals and were attempting to take over conventions.[74] As evidence, inerrantists and dispensationalists complained about the lenient standards of those appointed to the mission field. Men who ran the denominational boards took power away from these missionary unions for fear, jealousy, and resentment of women in positions of power.[75]

Fundamentalists also condemned women whom they believed dressed in a suggestive manner. John Roach Straton (1875–1929) believed that in dressing provocatively, women "surrender to their lower passions, and drift into sin. The slavish following of foreign fashions in America has been an ally of vice for years."[76] Another minister noted that "many men are made to commit sin in their hearts by unclothed bodies of women who may be professed Christians and ignorant of the evil they are doing in causing a brother to

---

[71] Margaret Lamberts Bendroth, *Fundamentalism and Gender*, 32.
[72] William Belly Riley, "Managing Church Troubles," *King's Business* 26, (1935): 35.
[73] Michael S. Hamilton, "Women, Public Ministry, and American Fundamentalism, 1920–1950," *Religion and American Culture: A Journal of Interpretation* 3, no. 2 (Summer 1993): 174.
[74] Lindley, 326.
[75] Michael S. Hamilton, 185.
[76] John Roach Straton, "Moral Decay Through Subservience to Foreign Fashions in Women's Dress," unpublished sermon, Straton papers, American Baptist Historical Society.

stumble and become weak."⁷⁷ In *What is the Matter With the Church Today?*⁷⁸ A. R. Funderburk claimed, "Every man has a quantity of dynamite, or its equivalent, in him. The matches have, as a rule, been in the hands of the world's womanhood."⁷⁹

Baptist pastor John R. Rice (1895–1990) believed that women had no place in the pulpit or in church leadership. He claimed that the assertion that women were more moral and prone to religion than men was "a lie out of Hell." It is a "wicked, hellish, ungodly, satanic teaching that by nature men are not as good, that by nature women are […more] inclined toward God and morality."⁸⁰ In his book, *Bobbed Hair, Bossy Wives, and Women Preachers* (1941) he stated:

> [Bobbed hair] is the symbol of the wicked fashion of rebellious wives to their husbands' authority or of wicked daughters who rebel against their fathers […] Do not confuse the subject of bobbed hair with the general subject of woman's dress and use of cosmetics. The question of whether a Christian woman bobs her hair is of infinitely more importance than whether she paints her face or her lips or her fingernails […] Men wear short hair as a sign that they assume their responsibilities as made in the image of God and as rulers over their households. Women are to wear long hair to symbolize their submission to husband and father, taking their place with meekness as women surrendered to the will of God and subject to the authority God places over them.⁸¹

During the 1920s, fundamentalist men considered themselves the guardians of pure doctrine. As Bendroth notes, men presented themselves as psychologically superior to women and more capable of seeing through false doctrine.⁸² Presbyterian minister Clarence

---

⁷⁷ "More Concerning Women's Dress," *Moody Bible Institute Monthly* 31, (1930): 64.
⁷⁸ A. R. Funderburk, *What is the Matter with the Church Today?* (Author, NP: 1939).
⁷⁹ A. R. Funderburk, "The Word of God on Women's Dress," *Moody Bible Institute Monthly* 22, (1922): 759.
⁸⁰ John R. Rice, "Father, Mother, Home, and Heaven," *SL*, 9 (August 1946): 4.
⁸¹ John R. Rice, *Bobbed Hair, Bossy Wives, and Women Preachers: Significant Questions for Honest Christian Women Settled by the Word of God* (Wheaton, IL: Sword of the Lord Publishers, 1941), 15, 66, 71.
⁸² Margaret Lamberts Bendroth, *Fundamentalism and Gender*, 9.

Macartney (1879–1957) feared that women would fall into Mary Baker Eddy's (1821–1910) Church of Christ, Scientist. "When the apostle speaks of false teachers leading off 'silly women,' he stated, 'he has a very modern sound from Eve down to Mrs. Eddy, women have played a sad part in the spread of anti-Christian doctrines, and that under the guise of Christian teachings.'"[83] Euclid Phillips chimed in that "the adversary is clever enough in his dealings with men to inject in their theology many dangerous errors, but God made his masterpiece through a woman's brain."[84]

Fundamentalists often found themselves in a quandary. Women outnumbered men in the pews, held sway within families, were guaranteed the right to vote in 1920, and often controlled the budgets of mission societies. J. C. Massee (1871–1965) claimed, "Since woman is the determining factor in social life woman must of necessity be religious or destroy the very society she creates."[85] Clarence Macartney held that, "Woman is always greater or worse than man. She lifts him to the higher places, or brings him down to the depths, and has the power and has in herself to rise to higher places than man, or to sink into depths more abysmal."[86] Women could either damn or save the church.[87]

Fundamentalists could not afford to ignore women. Some pastors, therefore, began to flatter them. In 1989, Bailey Smith (1939–2019) appeared on *Larry King Live* to assert that "the highest form of God's creation is womankind."[88] Evangelicals also praised praying mothers. A prime example is in the chorus of the song "Praying Mothers" by Tammy Deville.

---

[83] Clarence M. Macartney, "Shall We Ordain Women as Ministers and Elders?" *Presbyterian* 7, (November 1929): 7.
[84] Euclid Philips, "Woman's Place in the Church," *Presbyterian* 16, (September 1930): 10.
[85] J. C. Massee, "Women Attend a Special Meeting," 30 January 1931, a reprinted excerpt from a standard sermon on "The Old Fashioned vs. the New Woman," Massee papers, American Baptist Historical Society.
[86] Clarence Macartney, *The Way of a Man With a Maid* (Nashville, TN: Publisher, 1931), 62.
[87] Margaret Lamberts Bendroth, "Fundamentalism and Femininity," 226.
[88] Bailey Smith, on *Larry King Live*, 21 March 1989.

> Praying mother, Christian homes,
> Keeping families together where they belong,
> Teaching trust, respect, faith and love,
> Reverence to our God above. With love godly mothers,
> We sing this song.[89]

Fundamentalist men also praised homemakers. An article in the *Way of Truth* reminded women that they were not wasting their time by dedicating themselves to the home and family.

> What a grave and sacred responsibility this is. To provide food, clothing, and shelter, may be the easiest part for many couples. To be a true *mother* goes far beyond supplying these temporal needs. The love, the nurturing, the careful guiding, the moral example, the moral teaching, the training, is the most important of all.[90]

This sentimentalism was apparent in most fundamentalist churches. Fundamentalist pastors praised women. The practice of praising mothers made every day Mother's Day.[91]

Between 1890 and 1920, fundamentalism was strong in both the Northern and Southern Baptist Conventions and in Northern Presbyterian Churches. Fundamentalism gained momentum until the 1925 Scopes Trial that led to its reputation as anti-intellectual. It did, however, return as a political force in the Southern Baptist Convention in the late 1970s and early 1980s and continues to dominate the denomination.

Evangelicalism

Evangelicalism is a Protestant theological movement, not a denomination. According to David Bebbington, evangelicals are those who emphasize the Bible, the cross, conversion, and activism.[92] Among

---

[89] Tammy Deville, "Praying Mothers," *The Way of Truth* 47, (May 1989): 2.
[90] "Mother," *The Way of Truth* 47, (May 1989): [ii], 1.
[91] Patrick Pasture, Jan Art and Thomas Buerman, *Gender and Christianity in Modern Europe: Beyond the Feminization Thesis* (Leuven, Belgium: Leuven University Press, 2012), 9.
[92] For more information see David Bebbington, *Evangelicalism in Modern Britain: A History from the 1730s to the 1980s* (New York, NY: Routledge, 1989).

its first influences were Pietism, Puritanism, Presbyterianism, and Moravianism, particularly Nicolaus Zinzendorf (1700–1760) and his Herrnhut community.[93] John Wesley's preaching and Arminian soteriology, and George Whitefield's revivals in the First Great Awakening, led to its early growth. The emphasis on instantaneous conversion in the Second Great Awakening furthered evangelicalism's expansion and popularity in the nineteenth-century United States. Evangelicals can be found in virtually any Protestant denomination, but especially in the Southern Baptist Convention, Assemblies of God, the Free Methodist Church, the Wesleyan Church, Reformed Churches, the Lutheran Church-Missouri Synod,[94] and many non-denominational churches. The Southern Baptist Convention is the largest evangelical denomination. It is also the most outspoken concerning women.

There are three groups (Revivalist, Progressive, and Conservative/Confessional) and several subgroups of American evangelicals.[95] The revivalists are not rigid in their beliefs, trust in instantaneous conversions, and maintain that Conservative/Confessionals are more interested in intellect and attempt to suppress religious enthusiasm.[96] The progressive evangelicals are not as theologically conservative as others and can be quite open-minded in their attitudes to women.

The largest group, the Conservatives/Confessional evangelicals, hold tightly to the Reformation's doctrinal formulas, biblical

---

[93] Brian Stiller, *Evangelicals Around the World: A Global Handbook for the 21st Century* (Nashville, TN: Thomas Nelson, 2015), 28, 90.

[94] The Wesleyan Churches are evangelical but they are a mainline denomination and their beliefs concerning women are more in line with them than the evangelicals. Though they are evangelical denominations, the Assemblies of God are discussed in the Pentecostal section and the The Lutheran Church-Missouri Synod is examined in the section with the other Lutheran churches who are mainline denominations.

[95] Most American evangelicals are white. In 2020, the largest number of evangelical Christians lived in Africa, with forty-two percent of the continent's population identifying as evangelical. If this trend continues, more than half of the world's evangelical population will be African by 2050. In the United States, evangelicals make up approximately twenty-five percent of the population. In 2020, there were 386 million evangelicals worldwide.

[96] Roger E. Olson, *The Westminster Handbook to Evangelical Theology* (Louisville, KY: Westminster John Knox Press, 2004), 241–42.

inerrancy, and order within the church and society. Many prominent conservative evangelicals are also fundamentalists. By the late 1970s, involvement in conservative politics became a hallmark of this group. They are active in traditional and social media and have large followings. Moreover, they are also the most outspoken proponents of traditional roles for women in the home, church, and society. Susanne Scholz believes that Conservative evangelicals articulate their message so well that many Christians believe their position is the official "Christian position on gender, family, and sexuality."[97]

Betty Friedan's (1921–2006) book *The Feminine Mystique* (1963) presented compelling evidence to challenge the belief that women were satisfied with being wives and mothers. She helped create many feminist organizations and became a leading advocate of the ratification of the Equal Rights Amendment (ERA). The *Feminine Mystique* was a catalyst for what became known as second-wave feminism.[98] In addition, "the Civil Rights Act of 1964, which prohibited discrimination on the grounds of sex as well as race, followed closely on the heels of a Presidential Commission that found that women were second-class citizens in almost every area of American life."[99] White women were earning 79 cents for each dollar earned by men; Black, Latina, and Indigenous women earned even less. Women did not advance professionally as quickly as men did. Women had more freedom from pregnancy with the birth control pill in 1960, and, with the 1972 *Roe v. Wade* decision, women could legally terminate an unplanned pregnancy. Even some evangelical women wearied of sexist sermons, songs, and liturgy. They complained that instead of helping them overcome the gender-based laws and unspoken rules that kept women in a subservient role to men, the church and its institutions perpetuated it.[100] Rather than be silent, they demanded change. Conservative evangelicals were quick to respond.

---

[97] Susanne Scholz, *The Bible as Political Artifact: On the Feminist Study of the Hebrew Bible* (Minneapolis, MN: 1517 Media, Fortress Press, 2017), 147.
[98] Becky Thompson, "Multiracial Feminism: Recasting the Chronology of Second Wave Feminism," *Feminist Studies* 28, no. 2 (Summer 2002): 338.
[99] MacHaffie, 280.
[100] Paul Harvey and Philip Goff, *The Columbia Documentary History of Religion in America Since 1945* (New York, NY: Columbia University Press, 2005), 200.

During the 1970s, conservative evangelicals joined forces with fundamentalists to speak out against abortion, the Equal Rights Amendment, feminism, gay rights, the elimination of prayer in public schools, and a host of other issues.[101] In 1979 many of these evangelicals came together as the Religious Right. Though Catholic, Mormon, and Jewish people joined, the Religious Right coalition was composed primarily of evangelical denominations. Conservative evangelical women were among the first to organize against feminism and the ERA. Popular conservative evangelical pastors, evangelists, and authors took up the call to defeat the ERA, defend the traditional role of women, and overturn *Roe v. Wade*. Founder of the Moral Majority Jerry Falwell (1933–2007) was the most powerful member of this group.

In 1973, Marabel Morgan (b. 1937) wrote *The Total Woman* to empower conservative evangelical women. She maintained that God placed separate roles and spheres of influence in both men and women. She reminded women, whose primary sphere was the home, that they controlled the family. Wives could influence their husbands and children to live righteous lives. To accomplish this, Morgan believed the wife must submit to the husband in all matters of leadership. "God always planned for woman to be under her husband's rule."[102] To ensure the husband is happy and satisfied, the wife must cater to her husband's every need, especially sexually. In its first year of publication, *The Total Woman* sold more than 500,000 copies making it the most successful non-fiction book of 1974. Since its publication, it has sold more than ten million copies and remains in print.[103]

Elisabeth Elliot (1926–2015) was another popular conservative evangelical woman. The wife of missionary Jim Elliot (1927–1956), who was killed by Indigenous people in Ecuador, Elisabeth Elliot is best remembered for her 1973 book, *Let Me Be a Woman*. She believed that the differences in men and women were by God's design and, within marriage, there was a divine order.

---

[101] Lindley, 343.

[102] Marabel Morgan, *The Total Woman* (Old Tappen, NJ: Fleming H. Revel Company, 1973), 38.

[103] Randal Balmer, "American Fundamentalism," in *Fundamentalism and Gender*, in Stratton, 54.

> One thing that makes a marriage work is the acceptance of a divine order. Either there is an order or there is not, and if there is one which is violated disorder is the result—disorder on the deepest level of the personality. I believe there is an order, established in the creation of the world, and I believe that much of the confusion that characterizes our society is the result of the violation of God's design […] Men and women are equal, we may say, in having been created by God. Both male and female are created in His image. They bear the divine stamp. They are equally called to obedience and responsibility, but there are differences in their responsibilities.[104]

Elliot maintained that gender differences were "baked into creation."[105] God obviously intended women to be mothers.

> How can we bypass the matter in our search for understanding about the personality? There is a strange unreality in those who would do so, an unwillingness to deal with the most obvious facts of all […] Every normal woman is equipped to be a mother. Certainly not every woman in the world is destined to make use of the physical equipment but surely motherhood in a deeper sense, is the essence of womanhood […] It is a going down into death in order to give life, a great human analogy of a great spiritual principle.[106]

Elliot believed also that Eve wanted to be something more than God created her to be when she capitulated to the serpent's temptation. She wondered what the world might have been like if Eve had discussed the situation with Adam. Elliot concluded, "What sort of world might it have been if Eve refused the Serpent's offer

---

[104] Elisabeth Elliot, *Let Me Be a Woman* (Wheaton, IL: Tyndale, 1976), 121, 127.
[105] Sally K. Gallagher, "The Marginalization of Evangelical Feminism," *Sociology of Religion* 65, no. 3 (Autumn 2004): 225.
[106] Elisabeth Elliot, 61–62.

and had said to him instead, 'Let me not be like God. Let me be a woman.'"[107]

Elliot described the importance of a wife surrendering to and obeying her husband. In "The Essence of Femininity," she declared:

> Unlike Eve, whose response to God was calculating and self-serving, the Virgin Mary's answer holds no hesitation about risks or losses or the interruption of her own plans. It is an utter and unconditional self-giving: "I am the Lord's servant [...] May it be to me as you said" (Luke 1:38). This is what I understand to be the essence of femininity. *It means surrender.* Think of a bride. She surrenders her independence, her name, her destiny, her will, herself to the bridegroom in marriage [...] The gentle and quiet spirit of which Peter speaks, calling it "of great worth in God's sight" (1 Peter 3:4), is the true femininity, which found its epitome in Mary.[108]

Attorney and founder of the Eagle Forum, Phyllis Schlafly (1924–2016) feared that, "the ERA [would] protect bigamists, legalize prostitution, and defang rape laws [...] the social and political goals of the ERAers are radical, irrational, and unacceptable to Americans." She also coined the acronym STOP ERA (Stop Taking Our Privileges.)[109] Though she was Catholic, her message resonated with evangelical women.

Beverly LaHaye (b. 1929), wife of evangelist and member of the Moral Majority Tim LaHaye (1926–2016), used biblical inerrancy against feminism and the ERA. She rejected any scriptural interpretation that allowed women any greater roles in either family or society. She maintained that God made two different and unequal sexes. Because God created men to rule, the ERA went against this

---

[107] Ibid., 24–25.
[108] Elisabeth Elliot, "The Essence of Femininity: A Personal Perspective," *Council on Biblical Manhood and Womanhood*, 14 April 2005, https://bible.org/seriespage/25-essence-femininity-personal-perspective.
[109] Seth Dowland, "Family Values and the Formation of a Christian Right Agenda," *Church History* 78, (September 2009): 621.

biblical mandate.[110] Barbara Walters' interview with Betty Friedan in 1978 moved LaHaye to action against feminism and the ERA. LaHaye was disturbed that Frieden and the National Organization for Women claimed to be speaking for all women. She noted that Frieden's discussions concerning women's rights did not include any Christian women. LaHaye feared that her goal was "to dismantle the bedrock of American culture: the family."[111] LaHaye made the point many times that Frieden's interview was the impetus behind the formation of the Concerned Women for America (CWA) in 1979. LaHaye's movement was powerful and, by the close of 1980, she stated there were more than 600,000 members in the CWA.[112]

Not all evangelical women were against the ERA. Founded in 1975, the Evangelical Women's Caucus (EWC)[113] argued that the ERA was necessary because God desired the equality of men and women in all ways and this included politically. They believed that a flawed and shallow interpretation of Scripture was used to suppress and subjugate women and did not resonate with God's love shown to women throughout the entirety of scripture.

This led the EWC to embrace an interpretation of womanhood that was based on equality rather than submission and an embracement of the ERA, support for women's ordination, and the usage of gender-inclusive language in all aspects of life.[114]

There is no doubt that Billy Graham (1918–2018) had the greatest influence on evangelicalism in the twentieth century. Through his worldwide crusades and television specials, he spoke to and led millions of people around the world to accept Christ and be "born again." Though Graham's ministry centered on evangelism, he discussed his views on gender roles and male headship. In an

---

[110] Griffis Chelsea, "In the Beginning was the Word: Evangelical Christian Women, the Equal Rights Amendment, and Competing Definitions of Womanhood," *Journal of Women's Studies* 38, no. 2 (2017): 148.

[111] "Beverly LaHaye Marks Three Decades of Promotiong Traditional Values through CWA," *Christian Examiner*, 20 December 2009, https://www.christianexaminer.com/Articles/Articles%20Dec09/Art_Dec09_06.html.

[112] Chelsea Griffis, 166.

[113] In 1990 the EWC changed its name to Evangelical and Ecumenical Women's Caucus (EEWC).

[114] Chelsea Griffis, 148.

article entitled "Jesus and the Liberated Woman," published in the December 1970 edition of *Ladies Home Journal*, Graham stated:

> The biological assignment was basic and simple. Eve was to be the child-bearer, and Adam was to be the breadwinner. Of course, there were peripheral functions for each but these were the fundamental roles, and throughout history there has been very little deviation from the pattern. And when society has tried to merge the sexes into one, and has failed to recognize their basic and important differences, serious consequences have ensued. [...] In any group of two or more people there naturally emerges a leader. This does not necessarily mean that the leader is mentally or physically stronger than the others, but simply that the qualities of leadership are present. The Lord God decreed that man should be the titular head of the family. The New Testament writers saw this most clearly: "Therefore, as the church is subject unto Christ, so let the wives be to their own husbands in everything." Ephesians 5:2[115]

Editor of *Christianity Today*, Harold Lindsell (1913–1998), was an outspoken proponent of women's subordination. Lindsell based his belief on male headship and women's subordination in biblical inerrancy. As noted in *Battle for the Bible* (1976) he accepted the Bible's infallibility. Throughout his writings and in his editorials for *Christianity Today*, Lindsell argued that feminism and egalitarianism went against the clear reading of scripture. This subordination was based on Eve's sin, and women, by not obeying their husbands, perpetuated sin. In a 1970 editorial, he wrote, "in the beginning, Eve bit into forbidden fruit and fell into subjection to Adam. Her descendants face a lesser temptation-equality with man instead of with God—but they are biting no less eagerly into their forbidden fruit."[116] Women gained true liberation by marrying well

---

[115] Billy Graham, "Jesus and the Liberated Woman," *Ladies Home Journal* (December 1970): 42.

[116] Harold Lindsell, "Eve's Second Apple," *Christianity Today* 14, (August 1970): 29.

and devoting themselves to raising their children rather than seeking self-fulfillment in careers outside the home.[117]

Lindsell believed much more than feminism or the ERA was at stake in these arguments. Those who spoke in favor of biblical egalitarianism and feminism were endangering the reliability of the Bible.

> At stake here is not the matter of women's liberation. What is the issue for the evangelical is the fact that some of the most ardent advocates of egalitarianism in marriage over against hierarchy reach their conclusion by directly and deliberately denying that the Bible is the infallible rule of faith and practice. Once they do this, they have ceased to be evangelical: Scripture no longer is normative. And if it is not normative in this matter, why should it be normative for matters having to do with salvation.[118]

Lindsell's core issue was never about women's rights or employment; it was about hermeneutics and biblical inerrancy. His hermeneutic taught that the Bible supported the wife's subjection to the husband and, without it, the marriage would not be stable.[119] His rationale for the husband's headship appealed to and confirmed what many evangelical men already believed.

Husband of Beverly LaHaye and author of the *Left Behind* series, Tim LaHaye was a premillennial, dispensational fundamentalist. Like his wife, LaHaye promoted a strong patriarchal family and believed God created women to be naturally responsive to strong leadership. Men, therefore, set the standard for how the family should function. In *Understanding the Male Temperament* (1977), he explained:

> Man is the key to a happy family life because a woman by nature is a responding creature. Some temperaments, of course, respond more quickly than others, but all normal women are responders. That is one of the secondary

---

[117] Sally K. Gallagher, 223.
[118] Harold Lindsell, "Egalitarianism and Scriptural Infallibility," *Christianity Today* 20 (1976): 45–46.
[119] Sally K. Gallagher, 225.

meanings of the word submission in the Bible. God would not have commanded a woman to submit unless he had instilled in her a psychic mechanism which would find it comfortable to do so. The key to feminine response has only two parts—love and leadership. I have never met a wife who did not react positively to a husband who gave her love and leadership. Deep within a woman lies a responding capability that makes her vulnerable to that combination.[120]

Jerry Falwell's Moral Majority unified the Religious Right into an organization that sought to bring conservative Christianity and Republican politics into a single organization. It focused on overturning *Roe. v. Wade*, stopping the ERA's ratification, and preventing gay people from gaining equal protection. The Moral Majority was a decisive factor in the defeat of Jimmy Carter (b. 1924) and the election of Ronald Reagan (1911–2004) in the 1980 presidential election. The Moral Majority remained a political force until the mid-1980s.

Falwell's speaking points espoused that women were reneging on their responsibilities as mothers, homemakers, and wives to their husbands by seeking self-fulfillment in careers outside the home. He also claimed that the ERA threatened female privileges such as non-participation in the selective service. Furthermore, Falwell and his followers believed that ratifying the ERA would devalue women who chose to stay home and raise children.[121] Susan Lindley and most feminists maintained that the Religious Right opposed the ERA to protect patriarchy.[122]

In 1980, Falwell made one of his strongest statements against the ERA and women working outside the home.

> I believe that at the foundation of the women's liberation movement their [sic] is a minority core of women who

---

[120] Timothy LaHaye, *Understanding the Male Temperament* (Grand Rapids, MI: Fleming H. Revell, 1977), 178.
[121] Daniel K. Williams, "Jerry Falwell's Sunbelt Politics: The Regional Origins of the Moral Majority," *Journal of Policy History* 22, (2010): 139.
[122] Lindley, 346.

were once bored with life, whose real problems are spiritual problems. Many women have never accepted their God-given roles. They live in disobedience to God's laws and have promoted their godless philosophy throughout our society. God Almighty created men and women biologically different and with differing needs and roles. He made men and women to complement each other and to love each other. Not all the women involved in the feminist movement are radicals. Some are misinformed, and some are lonely women who liked being housewives and helpmeets and mothers, but whose husbands spend little time at home and who take no interest in their wives and children. Sometimes the full load of rearing a family becomes a great burden to a woman who is not supported by a man. Women who work should be respected and accorded dignity and equal rewards for equal work. But this is not what the present feminist movement and equal rights movement are all about.

The Equal Rights Amendment is a delusion. I believe that women deserve more than equal rights. And, in families and in nations where the Bible is believed, Christian women are honored above men. Only in places where the Bible is believed and practiced do women receive more than equal rights. Men and women have differing strengths. The Equal Rights Amendment can never do for women what needs to be done for them. Women need to know Jesus Christ as their Lord and Savior and be under His Lordship.[123]

Falwell held that the ERA went against the mandate that the husband is the head of the wife by making her equal with a man.[124] Furthermore, the wife was the weaker vessel and needed to be in the home for her own protection and good. He held that the ERA made women equal to men.[125]

---

[123] "Jerry Falwell on the Equal Rights Amendment," *Jackie Whiting*, last accessed 1 July 2021, http://jackiewhiting.net/women/power/falwell.htm.
[124] Ibid.
[125] Ibid.

James Dobson (b. 1936) founded the *Focus on the Family* media organization in 1977. He is a strong proponent of male leadership in the home and believes that men have God-given biological traits that make them fit to rule. One characteristic of this, he believes, is that men are larger and have deeper voices than women. In *What Men Need to Know, What Women Should Understand* (1991) Dobson declared, "Boys and girls typically look to their fathers; whose size and power and deeper voices bespeak leadership."[126] Men are to make major decisions, and God holds the man accountable for the decisions. "Authority in the home has been assigned to men. It will not be popular to restate the age-old Biblical concept that God holds *men* accountable for leadership in their families […] God apparently expects *man* to be the ultimate decision-maker in his family."[127]

Dobson blamed the lack of women choosing to be homemakers as their primary vocation on the ERA, feminism, and a desire to find satisfaction outside the home. Moreover, he recommended that no woman should work outside the home if she has children under the age of eighteen. In the May 1989 edition of *Focus on the Family*, he lamented the changes to traditional womanhood.[128]

> Female sex-role identity has become a major target for change by those who wish to revolutionize the relationship between men and women. The women's movement and the media have been remarkably successful in altering the way females "see" themselves at home and in society. In the process, every element of the traditional concept of femininity has been discredited and scorned, especially those responsibilities associated with homemaking and motherhood.
>
> Thus, in a short period of time, the term *housewife* has become a pathetic symbol of exploitation, oppression, and—pardon the insult—stupidity, at least as viewed from the perspective of radical feminists. We can make no

---

[126] James Dobson, *Straight Talk: What Men Need to Know, What Women Should Understand*, revised and expanded (Dallas, TX: Word, 1991), 94.
[127] Ibid., 92–93.
[128] James Dobson, "Is It Important for Mothers to Stay Home During the Teen Years?" *Focus on the Family*, last accessed 1 July 2021, http://family.custhelp.com./cgi-bin/family.cfg/php/enduser/std_adp.php?p_faqid=974.

greater mistake as a nation than to continue this pervasive disrespect shown to women who have devoted their lives to the welfare of their families.[129]

Focus on the Family grew through the 1990s and, though Dobson no longer leads it, it remains popular. In November 2004, *Slate* named Dobson America's most influential evangelical leader.[130] Through its daily radio broadcast, magazines, and social media presence, Dobson's *Focus on the Family* continues to indoctrinate many evangelicals about traditional gender roles, same-sex attraction, and other conservative issues. Many psychiatrists, psychologists, and social scientists, however, have accused Dobson of misrepresenting *Focus on the Family's* research to advance his religious and political agenda.[131]

John MacArthur (b. 1939) is a dispensational fundamentalist and advocate of complementarianism. He wrote *Divine Design: God's Complementary Roles for Men and Women* (1994). MacArthur maintains that since God created Adam before Eve and Adam named Eve, he had authority over her.[132] God made woman for man. Moreover, woman is fully in the image of God, but she is not the glory of God. Man holds that role. She is the glory of man. Eve was not Adam's slave, but she willingly submitted to him while he cared for her every need. Eve, however, disobeyed God and did not consult Adam about the serpent's temptation. Adam not only sinned by disobeying God but also by allowing Eve to usurp his God-given leadership role. MacArthur sees sinful inclinations in man and woman from this time forward. "Women have a sinful inclination to usurp man's authority, and men have a sinful inclination to put women under their feet."[133]

---

[129] "Dr. Dobson Answers Your Questions," *Focus on the Family*, (May 1989): 8.
[130] Michael Crowley, "James Dobson: The Religious Right's New Kingmaker," *Slate*, 12 November 12 2004, Internet Archive, https://web.archive.org/web/20041117015847/http:/slate.msn.com/id/2109621/.
[131] Wayne Besen, "Focus on the Fallacies of James Dobson," *Huffington Post*, 15 July 2008, https://www.huffpost.com/entry/focus-on-the-fallacies-of_b_111183.
[132] John Macarthur, *Divine Design: God's Complementary Roles for Men and Women* (Colorado Springs, CO: David Cook 1994), 23.
[133] Ibid., 27.

MacArthur compared the husband's relationship with his wife to Christ's relationship with the church.[134] Christ is the perfect protector, provider, and head of the church. Christ, therefore, is the perfect role model for the husband who must protect and provide for his wife. Wives were not to be co-protectors or co-providers as the church has no such role with Christ.[135] God ordained his authority in the headship of husbands over wives and parents over children.[136]

MacArthur maintained that God's word demonstrated that women should find their fulfillment in getting married, raising children, and keeping house. Women precipitated the Fall and were given pain in childbearing for it. They now have the duty to raise godly children.[137] Therefore, a woman who takes a job outside the home and puts her children in daycare ignores her husband's role as family provider and reneges on family duties.[138] Moreover, MacArthur believes that if a woman works outside the home, there is a greater likelihood that she will have an affair and compromise her family.[139]

He also held that women should not serve as ministers. Those that did so rejected biblical inerrancy, and he found the increased enrollment of women training for the ministry disturbing.[140] Holding to 1 Timothy 2:11–14, MacArthur defined women as learners during worship services.[141] Women may proclaim the word of God but not during worship.

In 2006, *Christianity Today* named MacArthur one of the most influential preachers,[142] and many Christians still view him as a

---

[134] Melissa Reid, "Unjust Signifying Practices: Submission and Subordination Among Christian Fundamentalists," *Journal of Feminist Studies in Religion* 29, no. 2 (2013): 159.
[135] John Macarthur, 62.
[136] Ibid., 41.
[137] Ibid., 183.
[138] Ibid., 91.
[139] Ibid., 93.
[140] Ibid., 139.
[141] Ibid., 163–170.
[142] "The Top 25 Most Influential Preachers," *Christianity Today*, 1 February 2006, Internet Archive, https://web.archive.org/web/20060201142833/http:/www.christianitytoday.com/anniversary/features/top25preachers.html.

primary spokesman for evangelicalism.[143] Through his radio and television show, "Grace to You," MacArthur spoke to millions of evangelicals each week. MacArthur has continued to promote his patriarchal view of scripture. In a 2019 sermon he proclaimed, "When women take over a culture, men become weak. When men become weak, they can be conquered, when all the men have been slaughtered, you [women] can sit there with all your jewelry and junk. You've been conquered, because you overpowered your protector."[144] A few weeks before this sermon, he told the evangelical teacher Beth Moore (b. 1957) to "go home."[145]

Conservative evangelicals in the later 1980s continued to fight feminism by forming organizations such as the Council on Biblical Manhood and Womanhood (CBMW). Created in 1987, the CBMW positioned itself as a defender of gender orthodoxy against feminism and cultural relativism.[146] Its manifesto, the Danvers Statement (1987) promoted complementarianism. This statement outlined the evangelical theology of each gender as having specific roles. "Both Adam and Eve were created in God's image, equal before God as persons and distinct in their manhood and womanhood […] Distinctions in masculine and feminine roles are ordained by God as part of the created order, and should find an echo in every human heart." It entails a "loving, humble leadership of redeemed husbands, and the intelligent, willing support of that leadership by redeemed wives."[147] These roles complement each other and are not interchangeable. As noted by Emily Allison, "Men are to lead; women are to follow. Men are to initiate; women are to accept.

---

[143] "'God's Warriors:' Fighters for Faith," *Larry King Live 20 August 2007*, CNN Transcripts, last accessed 1 July 2021, https://transcripts.cnn.com/show/lkl/date/2007-08-20/segment/01.

[144] "John MacArthur: 'If Women Are in Charge, We're in Trouble,'" *Relevant*, 13 November 2019, https://relevantmagazine.com/culture/john-macarthur-if-women-are-in-charge-were-in-trouble/.

[145] Bob Smietana, "Accusing SBC of 'Caving,' John MacArthur Says of Beth Moore: 'Go Home,'" *Religion News*, 19 October 2019, https://relevantmagazine.com/culture/john-macarthur-if-women-are-in-charge-were-in-trouble/.

[146] Sally K. Gallagher, 227.

[147] "The Danvers Statement," *The Council on Biblical Manhood and Womanhood*, last accessed 1 July 2021, https://cbmw.org/about/danvers-statement/.

Men are to be strong, decisive, and straightforward; women are to be soft, compliant, and strategic."[148]

Wayne Grudem (b. 1948) and John Piper wrote the Danvers Statement. Grudem maintains that husbands are the decision-makers in the family, but should consult their wives.[149] According to these authors, egalitarianism is a threat because it eradicates "gender-based differences between status, prominence, or authority of one person and another. On the other side stands the teaching of the Bible that God affirms both the honor of all human beings and the God-ordained differences among them, including differences in men's and women's roles in marriage."[150] Grudem stated that, if a woman takes a leadership role in church, the church runs the risk of "the withdrawal of God's hand of protection and blessing."[151]

In *Making of Biblical Manhood and Womanhood*,[152] Beth Allison Barr tells how Grudem believed that a female pastor, imprisoned for trying to murder the husband of her lover, came to this fate because she was preaching. When asked whether her fate had to do with her preaching, Grudem noted, "In this case it seems to me that there's an air of disobedience to the command of scripture regarding male leadership and teaching in the church."[153] Grudem maintains that specific gender roles would never allow him to vote for a woman as president of the United States.[154]

---

[148] Emily Joy Allison, *#Church Too: How Purity Culture Upholds Abuse and How to Find Healing* (Minneapolis, MN: 1517 Media, Broadleaf Books, 2021), 147.

[149] John P. Bartkowski, "Debating Patriarchy: Discursive Disputes over Spousal Authority among Evangelical Family Commentators," *Journal for the Scientific Study of Religion* 36, no. 3. (September 1997): 397.

[150] Vern S. Poythress and Wayne A. Grudem, *The Gender-Neutral Bible Controversy: Muting the Masculinity of God's Words* (Nashville, TN: B&H, 2000), 141–42.

[151] "Women Pastors: Not the 'Path to Blessing,'" *Belief Net*, last accessed 1 July 2021, https://www.beliefnet.com/faiths/christianity/2006/10/women-pastors-not-the-path-to-blessing.aspx.

[152] Beth Allison Barr, *The Making of Biblical Womanhood: How the Subjugation of Women Became the Gospel Truth* (Grand Rapids, MI: Brazos Press, 2021), 178.

[153] "Women Pastors: Not the 'Path to Blessing,'" *Belief Net*, last accessed 1 July 2021, https://www.beliefnet.com/faiths/christianity/2006/10/women-pastors-not-the-path-to-blessing.aspx.

[154] Beth Allison Barr, "No Room in Wayne Grudem's World for a Female President," *Patheos*, 31 July 2016, https://www.patheos.com/blogs/anxiousbench/2016/07/wayne-grudem-donald-trump-and-the-female-elephant-in-the-room/.

John Piper (b. 1946) is perhaps the most influential evangelical in the twenty-first century. Through his hugely popular books and his *Desiring God* webpage, he promotes his view of mature manhood and womanhood.

> At the heart of mature manhood is a sense of benevolent responsibility to lead, provide for, and protect women in ways appropriate to a man's differing relationships [...] At the heart of mature womanhood is a freeing disposition to affirm, receive, and nurture strength and leadership from worthy men in ways appropriate to a woman's differing relationships.[155]

Piper does not believe that women should teach seminary courses to men preparing for the pastorate.[156] Women are discouraged from working outside of the home "because mothering and homemaking are huge and glorious jobs."[157] "A (female) drill sergeant might epitomize directive influence over the privates in the platoon. And it would be hard for me to see how a woman could be a drill sergeant—hut two, right face, left face, keep your mouth shut, private—over men without violating their sense of manhood and her sense of womanhood."[158] Women should not serve as police officers because it would offend the sense of manhood of the men they arrested. Piper maintains that the "egalitarian myth"—that

---

[155] Aimee Byrd, "John Piper's Advice for Women in the Workforce," *Aimee Byrd*, 14 June 2020, https://aimeebyrd.com/2020/06/14/john-pipers-advice-for-women-in-the-workforce/#:~:text=Piper%20lays%20out%20his%20definitions%3A%20At%20the%20heart,husband%20will%2C%20but%20he%20will%20be%20a%20man.

[156] John Piper, "Is There a Place for Female Professors at Seminary?" *Desiring God*, 22 January 2018, https://www.desiringgod.org/interviews/is-there-a-place-for-female-professors-at-seminary.

[157] John Piper, "Is It Okay for Mothers to Work Full-Time Outside of the Home?" *Desiring God*, 22 June 2010, https://www.desiringgod.org/interviews/is-it-okay-for-mothers-to-work-full-time-outside-of-the-home.

[158] Aimee Byrd, "John Piper's Advice for Women in the Workforce," *Aimee Byrd*, 14 June 2020, https://aimeebyrd.com/2020/06/14/john-pipers-advice-for-women-in-the-workforce/#:~:text=Piper%20lays%20out%20his%20definitions%3A%20At%20the%20heart,husband%20will%2C%20but%20he%20will%20be%20a%20man.

men and women are defined by their "competencies" rather than gender role—is partly to blame for the #MeToo revolt against sexual abuse by powerful men. Even fictional female superheroes such as Wonder Woman, Catwoman, and Superwoman are nothing more than Hollywood's attempt to subvert the importance that men are to protect women.[159]

Among the Danvers signees are prominent women such as Beverly LaHaye, Joyce Rogers (1931–2005), wife of prominent Southern Baptist Pastor Adrian Rogers (1931–2005), and, notably, Dorothy Patterson (b. 1943), wife of Paige Patterson. As noted by Elizabeth Flowers, "Dorothy reigned throughout the 1990s as the 'matriarch of complementarianism.'"[160] An unlikely role model for complementarian women, she is a highly educated woman with three theological degrees—two of which are doctorates. She always, however, introduced herself as a wife, mother, and homemaker.[161] Patterson put her theological acumen to work in "The High Calling of Wife and Mother in Biblical Perspective" in *Recovering Biblical Manhood and Womanhood* (1991). "Too many women rush headlong into a career outside the home, determined to waste no time or effort on housework or baby-sitting but rather seeking to achieve position and means by directing all talents and energies toward non-home professional pursuits."[162] God gave man the responsibility for taking care of his family. If the woman takes on that role, it can be a "debilitating blow to the man personally and to the marriage."[163] Ignoring gender differentiations is the root of many marital problems.

> The efforts of contemporary society to eradicate the differences between the sexes have spawned an increase in strident lesbianism and open homosexuality, a quantum

---

[159] Bob Allen, "John Piper Blames Abuse of Women on 'Egalitarian Myth,'" *Baptist News Global*, 20 March 2018, https://baptistnews.com/article/john-piper-blames-abuse-of-women-on-egalitarian-myth/#.YMYyYfKSlzo.

[160] Elizabeth H. Flowers, *Into the Pulpit: Southern Baptist Women and Power since World War II* (Chapel Hill, NC: University of North Carolina Press, 2014), 130.

[161] Ibid., 130.

[162] Dorothy Patterson, "The High Calling of Wife and Mother in Biblical Perspective," in *Recovering Biblical Manhood and Womanhood: A Response to Evangelical Feminism*, eds. John Piper and Wayne Grudem (Nashville, TN: Crossway, 1991), 380.

[163] Ibid.

upward leap in divorces, an increase in rapes and sexual crimes of all sorts—and families smaller in size than ever before. We are part of a generation of women who have prostituted the creative purposes of God by prophesying "out of their own imagination" (Ezekiel 13:17), who have erected for themselves "male idols" to supplant the Creator's design (Ezekiel 16:17), and who have cast aside the greatest blessing of the Creator, i.e., the fruit of the womb (Ezekiel 16:20, 44–45).[164]

While her husband served as president of Southeastern Baptist Theological Seminary and Southwestern Baptist Theological Seminary, Patterson taught classes on homemaking for pastors' wives. These courses became a concentration in Homemaking—for females only—as part of their Bachelor of Arts in Humanities degree.

The Council on Biblical Manhood and Womanhood wields a tremendous amount of influence in evangelical circles, especially in the Southern Baptist Convention. Claiming biblical inerrancy as its rationale, SBC conservatives and fundamentalists began a struggle in 1979 to wrest control of the Convention from liberals and moderates who supported women in the ministry. With the Takeover nearly complete in 1984, the SBC passed a resolution encouraging women neither to take on pastoral roles nor seek ordination.[165] Approval of this resolution soon became a litmus test for all those who sought employment within the SBC. The SBC then endorsed complementarianism. In 2000, the SBC added Amendment 18 to its official statement of faith, the *Baptist Faith and Message* (BFM). The amendment conformed to the CBMW's statement and established complementarianism as the denomination's official position:

> The husband and wife are of equal worth before God, since both are created in God's image. The marriage relationship models the way God relates to His people. A husband is to love his wife as Christ loved the church.

---

[164] Ibid., 381.
[165] *Resolution on Ordination and the Role of Women in Ministry*, Southern Baptist Convention, 1 June 1984, last accessed 1 July 2021, https://www.sbc.net/resource-library/resolutions/resolution-on-ordination-and-the-role-of-women-in-ministry/.

He has the God-given responsibility to provide for, to protect, and to lead his family. A wife is to submit herself graciously to the servant leadership of her husband even as the church willingly submits to the headship of Christ. She, being in the image of God as is her husband and thus equal to him, has the God-given responsibility to respect her husband and to serve as his helper in managing the household and nurturing the next generation.[166]

All faculty members at SBC seminaries and many denominational employees who work in ministerial roles must sign the BFM. Those who were already employed by the SBC but refused to sign the document lost their positions. The CBMW is such a vital part of the SBC that its headquarters is on the Southern Baptist Theological Seminary (SBTS) campus in Louisville, Kentucky. Though the CBMW is composed of evangelicals from different denominations, Southern Baptists are its main proponents. SBC leaders such as Albert Mohler (b. 1959), president of SBTS, Denny Burk, professor of biblical studies at SBTS, Boyce College and president of CBMW, Russell Moore (b. 1971), former President of the SBC Ethics and Religious Liberty Commission (ERLC), and Owen Strachan, formerly of the SBC's Midwestern Baptist Theological Seminary and current Provost of Grace Bible Seminary, are defenders of strict complementarianism.[167]

Some evangelicals, such as Wayne Grudem,[168] Bruce Ware,[169] and Owen Strachan, are willing to reinterpret Trinitarian theology to make their point. The central issue concerns "eternal functional subordination," or EFS. This theory maintains that there is a

---

[166] *Baptist Faith and Message 2000*, Southern Baptist Convention, last accessed 1 July 2021, https://bfm.sbc.net/bfm2000/#xviii-the-family.

[167] In 2017 at the annual conference of the SBC ERLC annual conference, the Council on Biblical Manhood and Womanhood authored the Nashville Statement. Signed by one hundred and fifty, mostly SBC leaders, this document promotes a heterosexual only definition of marriage, condemns same-sex attraction, transgender identity, fornication, adultery, polygamy, and fornication.

[168] Wayne Grudem, *Systematic Theology: An Introduction to Biblical Doctrine* (Grand Rapids, MI: Zondervan: 1994), 251, 251. There are several examples throughout the text.

[169] Bruce A. Ware and John Starke, *One God in Three Persons: Unity of Essence, Distinction of Persons, Implications for Life* (Wheaton, IL: Crossway, 2015), 237–248.

relationship of authority and submission between the Father and the Son. The Son is of the same essence as the Father and therefore not ontologically subordinate, but rather the Son is functionally subordinate to the Father. This concept contradicts normative Christian theology that dates back to the fourth century. Known as Nicene theology, it teaches that the Father and Son are equal in all respects. By making the Father and Son relationship hierarchal, these scholars and some complementarians have distorted the relationship to justify the submission of wives to husbands. Strachan made this point clear in *The Grand Design: Male and Female He Made Them* (2016). "Husbands are called to exercise leadership over their wives patterned after Trinitarian order (God the Father's authority over the Son): God –> Christ –> Husband –> Wife (1 Corinthians 11:3)."[170] Despite its unorthodox implications, EFS remains popular in many evangelical circles.

Many people believe complementarianism contributes to sexual violence by emphasizing male headship and female submission. As Emily Joy Ellison notes, a submissive wife must always do what her husband requests, including in the bedroom. Sexual predators such as Harvey Weinstein (1952) are not just in Hollywood. They are also in church pews and in the pulpit.[171] Bob Smietana quoted Albert Mohler as stating that complementarianism could lead to abuse.

> "Some men have cited complementarian doctrine as an excuse for lording over their wives rather than leading and serving," he said, "and even taking advantage to the point of abuse and denying that abuse is abuse." … "We need to recognize that we have sinned against women when we have allowed complementarianism to be presented in a way that implies male superiority and leads in sinfulness to male tyranny and terror and sin," Mohler declared.[172]

---

[170] Owen Strachan and Gavin Peacock, *The Grand Design: Male and Female He Made Them* (Ross-Shire, Scotland: Christian Focus, 2016), 91.

[171] Emily Joy Allison, 149–150.

[172] Albert Mohler, quoted in Bob Smietana, "How Complementarianism Fueled a Culture of Abuse in the Church of Jennifer Lyell," *Church and Ministries*, 20 October 2019.

Russell Moore agrees. "What we are seeing now is a sifting of hyper-complementarianism and a biblical complementarianism," he added, noting that the "hyper" variety emphasizes the distinctions between men and women in such a way that magnifies those distinctions "beyond the commonness and the sameness that we have."[173] For Mohler and Moore, complementarianism is not the problem; the men who take advantage of it are.

Paige Patterson takes complementarianism to its logical conclusions. In a sermon, he described telling an abused woman to return to her husband. The woman returned to the church the next week with a black eye. Patterson stated that he was happy because the husband was at church with her that day.[174] Rachael Denhollander (b. 1984) claims that complementarian culture is the problem. It defends male leaders but views women leaders and survivors of abuse as expendable.[175]

No denomination has been accused of sexual violence against women more in recent years than the Southern Baptist Convention. In 2019, the *Houston Chronicle* and the *San Antonio Express* published a six-part series that listed 380 Southern Baptist Church leaders convicted of sexually abusing more than 700 victims.[176] Trustees fired Paige Patterson as president of Southwestern Baptist Theological Seminary in 2018 for covering up a female student's sexual assault allegation. While president of Southeastern Baptist Theological Seminary in 2003, Patterson also allegedly concealed a rape allegation made by a female seminary student against a male seminary student.

Complementarian evangelical males may have the loudest voice in the room, but they are not alone. Egalitarian organizations such as Christians for Biblical Equality (CBE) are making their positions

---

[173] Russell Moore, quoted in Brandon Showalter, "Will Complementarianism Survive #MeToo? Russell Moore Explains," *Church and Ministries*, 7 August 2018.

[174] Paige Patterson, *Advice to Victims of Domestic Violence*, Internet Archive, last accessed 1 July 2021, https://archive.org/details/PaigePattersonsbcAdviceToVictimsOfDomesticViolence.

[175] Bob Smietana, "How Complementarianism Fueled a Culture of Abuse in the Church of Jennifer Lyell," *Church and Ministries*, 20 October 2019.

[176] Robert Downen, Lisa Olsen and John Tedesco, "20 Years, 700 Victims: Southern Baptist Sexual Abuse Spreads as Leaders Resist Reforms," *Houston Chronicle*, last accessed 1 July 2021, https://www.houstonchronicle.com/news/investigations/article/Southern-Baptist-sexual-abuse-spreads-as-leaders-13588038.php.

known. Established in 1988, shortly after the creation of the Council on Biblical Manhood and Womanhood, the CBE "exists to promote biblical justice and community by educating Christians that the Bible calls women and men to share authority equally in service and leadership in the home, church, and world."[177] CBE has members from more than one hundred denominations and sixty-five countries. Several female egalitarian scholars have their roots in evangelicalism. These include Dr. Nancy Hardesty,[178] at Clemson University, Dr. Molly Marshall, president of Central Baptist Theological Seminary,[179] Dr. Susan Shaw,[180] at Oregon State University, and Dr. Beth Allison Barr,[181] at Baylor University. There are also a host of male egalitarian scholars active in today's colleges and universities.[182]

Mainline Denominations

The largest of the mainline denominations are the United Methodist Church (USA), the Evangelical Lutheran Church in America, the Episcopal Church, the Presbyterian Church (USA), and the American Baptist Churches (USA). Within mainline denominations, women have more options to serve in the ministry. Most also hold to the belief that men and women are equal in all aspects of life, and that there is no shame for a woman to work outside the home. Mainline denominations disagree with evangelical denominations such as the Missouri Lutheran Synod and the Southern Baptist Convention who hold antithetical positions concerning women. Women within these denominations, however, still had to

---

[177] *CBE's Mission and Values*, Christians for Biblical Equality, last accessed 1 July 2021, https://www.cbeinternational.org/content/cbes-mission.

[178] Hardesty is best known for *All We're Meant to Be: Biblical Feminism for Today* (1974), which introduced many conservative Protestants to Christian feminism.

[179] A graduate and faculty member of the Southern Baptist Theological Seminary, she was compelled to resign from her position in 1994 when new president, Dr. Albert Mohler, threatened to put the first and only female theology professor on trial for heresy. She was accused of teaching outside the school's guiding document, "The Abstract of Principles," but no specifics were cited.

[180] Shaw is the author of *God Speaks to Us, Too: Southern Baptist Women on Church, Home, and Society* and frequent contributor to *Baptist News Global*.

[181] Barr is author of the recently released *Making of Biblical Womanhood*.

[182] Marg Mowczko, "Prominent Biblical Scholars on Women in Ministry," *Marg Mowczko*, 30 June 2015, https://margmowczko.com/prominent-biblical-scholars-on-women-in-ministry/.

overcome many obstacles to serve as full members of their respective clergies. Following the Civil War, women began to move forward within mainline denominations and other non-evangelical denominations. Women deacons began to appear in several of these denominations. They served as nurses, social workers, and missionaries. Many women perceived their lack of ordination as a means to dispel any hope they might have to join men in traditionally male roles.[183] Female ordination was present but rare in most of these denominations until the 1920s.

The Methodist Church

The Methodist Church has a long history of women in ministerial roles. The Methodist Church did not ordain female ministers until the turn of the twentieth century. The Methodist General Council (MGC) approved the appointment of female deaconesses in the local church in 1888.[184] In 1896, the MGC seated and elected four women as delegates. The MGC recognized women as lay people in the church in 1906.[185] In 1920, the Methodist Church granted local preaching licenses to women. In 1924, an advisory committee permitted the ordination of women as local preachers that allowed them to preach, conduct worship, perform ordinances, and officiate weddings. They were not, however, allowed to be seated members of the General Conference. The Conference did not seat them because all ministers present receive a position in a local church. The leaders of the General Conference did not want to force a female minister on a congregation.[186] The General Conference changed its position in 1956 by allowing women to attend the Conference and seek placement within a local church.[187]

The United Methodist Church (UMC) was born in 1968 with the merger of the Evangelical United Brethren church and the Methodist church. The United Brethren Church had ordained women to the

---

[183] MacHaffie, 206.
[184] Ruth A. Tucker and Walter Liefeld, *Daughters of the Church: Women and Ministry from the New Testament Times to the Present* (Grand Rapids, MI: Zondervan, 1987), 282.
[185] Tucker and Liefeld, 386.
[186] MacHaffie, 275.
[187] Lindley, 312.

ministry since 1847 and granted women conference membership in 1889. The UMC elected its first female bishop, Marjorie Swank Matthews (1916–1986), on July 17, 1980. The UMC ordains more women to the ministry than any other denomination. In 2016, the UMC had more than 12,300 female ministers.[188]

The Lutheran Churches

The Lutheran Church appointed women deacons as early as 1830. The overwhelming majority of women deacons were in Europe. In the United States, there were only five hundred deaconesses by 1940. Ordination to the pastorate was a different situation. The Lutheran Church forbade women to serve as pastors because God created Adam before Eve, and, also, many Lutheran leaders deemed women inappropriate to serve in this office. Many American women viewed serving in the diaconate as demeaning in comparison to ministerial opportunities open to men. The first ordinations to the pastorate were in Norway in 1938 and in the Church of Sweden in 1958.[189] In 1969, the door began to open for women's ordination. At the 1969 pan Lutheran Council in the USA, the representatives (American Lutheran Church [ALC], Lutheran Church America [LCA], and Lutheran Church-Missouri Synod [LCMS]) produced a report on women's ordination. According to the report:

1. There is not conclusive biblical or theological evidence for or against women's ordination.
2. Sociological, psychological, and ecumenical issues are not conclusive.
3. Lutheran churches may differ.
4. Lutheran churches should make their decisions in consultation with other Lutheran churches.
5. The bigger issue is the office of ministry and the ministry of the whole people of God.[190]

---

[188] "Clergywomen," *General Board of Higher Education and Ministry*, United Methodist Church, last accessed 1 July 2021, https://www.gbhem.org/clergy/clergywomen/.
[189] Lindley, 314.
[190] Raymond Tiemeyer, *The Ordination of Women* (Minneapolis, MN: Augsburg, 1970), 54–55.

After this Council, the LCA and the ALC began to ordain women in 1970 and the Association of Evangelical Lutheran Churches (AELC) in 1976.[191] In 1988, the LCA, ALC, and ECLC merged to become the Evangelical Lutheran Church of America (ELCA). In 2017, the ELCA reported 1,228 Ministers of Word and 16,232 Ministers of Word and Sacrament with approximately twenty-seven percent composed of women.[192]

The evangelical LCMS did not follow suit and, as of May 2021, does not ordain women. Women cannot vote in local congregations, serve as delegates to District and Synod Conventions, or hold elected positions. The 1969 LCMS Synod defended this position. "Those statements of Scripture which direct women to keep silent in the church and which prohibit them to teach and to exercise authority over men, we understand to mean that women ought not to hold the pastoral office."[193]

In 1972, the Commission on Theology and Church Relations urged the 1973 Synod members to recognize the right of each congregation to determine whether it would allow women the right to vote.[194] The LCMS did not and has not expanded women's roles.

The Episcopal Church

Formed in 1785, the Episcopal Church is a member of the worldwide Anglican communion and is largely composed of Americans. In 1872, the General Convention formed the Women's Auxiliary to the Board of Missions to recruit missionaries and raise funds.[195] The Women's Auxiliary, however, could not elect delegates to serve on the National Council until 1935. As women could not vote in the General Convention, the Women's Auxiliary would nominate four women and the General Convention would elect them to the

---

[191] Tucker and Liefeld, 385.
[192] "ELCA Facts," *Evangelical Lutheran Church in America*, Internet Archive, last accessed 1 July 2021, https://web.archive.org/web/20180920084229/https://www.elca.org/News-and-Events/ELCA-Facts.
[193] Lutheran Church-Missouri Synod, *Convention Proceedings* 1969, Resolution 2, 17.
[194] Lutheran Church-Missouri Synod, *Convention Workbook* 1973, Appendix A, 37–38.
[195] Ibid., 95.

Council.¹⁹⁶ Women finally gained the right to vote in the House of Deputies in 1970.¹⁹⁷

Though unofficial, some Episcopal churches had set apart women as deacons as early as 1857 but without official General Convention recognition. The Episcopal Church officially recognized the order of deaconesses in 1889. The church, however, stipulated that a deaconess was not a deacon and, thus, not ordained. This restriction remained until 1970 when the General Convention passed a canon stating that there was no distinction between a male deacon and a female deaconess, which allowed women to seek diaconal ordination.¹⁹⁸

Ordination to the diaconate was often the first step to ordination to the priesthood. Many Episcopal priests rightly feared that women deacons would attempt to enter the priesthood. Their fears were justified in the early 1970s when women began to seek ordination, but the General Convention refused. In 1974, deaconesses appealed to the Church of the Advocate in Philadelphia. Presided over by a bishop friendly to their cause, eleven women received ordination to the priesthood and became known as the "Philadelphia Eleven." In 1975, four more women were ordained to the priesthood in the Washington D.C. diocese. These unapproved ordinations forced a discussion in the 1976 General Convention. After several heated debates, the Convention found in favor of women's ordination and changed its canon law accordingly.¹⁹⁹ Though canon law had changed, it was not binding and three dioceses refused to follow it. When the conservative members left the three dioceses that failed to affirm female ordination, these dioceses then affirmed women's ordination to the priesthood. Following this action, the fifteen ordained women became Episcopal priests in 1977. The final step for women, ordination as bishop, came in Boston in 1989 when Reverend Barbara Harris (1930–2020) became the first female Episcopalian bishop.²⁰⁰

---

[196] Ibid., 127.
[197] "Women Delegates: Post 1946," *Archives of the Episcopal Church*, last accessed 1 July 2021, https://www.episcopalarchives.org/house-of-deputies/women/delegates2.
[198] Pamela W. Darling, *New Wine: The Story of Women Transforming Leadership and Power in the Episcopal Church* (Cambridge: Cowley, 1994), 107–13.
[199] Tucker and Liefeld, 380.
[200] RIP: The Rt. Rev. Barbara C. Harris, Anglican Communion's first female bishop, dies at 89—Episcopal News Service, last accessed 1 May 2021.

Presbyterian Church USA

At the turn of the twentieth century, the Presbyterian Church in the United States (PCUSA) was the largest Presbyterian group and staunchly against women in the ministry.[201] Women could not speak, offer resolutions, or make reports at the General Assembly. Organized in 1912, the "Women of the Church" could not even read its own report to the General Assembly until 1925. After a female read the 1925 report, male clerics immediately protested. Rather than disrupt the Assembly, the women complied. In 1927, the Assembly determined that women could read their own report.[202]

The denomination did, however, allow women to have their own mission boards but with very little autonomy. In 1923, while reorganizing their boards, the Presbyterian church eliminated the Board of Home Missions and the Woman's Board of Foreign Missions. Janet Wilson James observed that within two years the Foreign Mission's Boards' morale and revenue had dropped.[203] At the same 1923 General Assembly that terminated the Women's Mission Boards, the Assembly voted to allow the ordination of women as deacons but not as ruling or teaching elders. Unlike the elders, deacons could neither preach nor administer the sacraments. Susan Hill Lindley noted that the Assembly opened the office of deacon to women to appease them after eliminating their mission boards.[204] The United Presbyterian Church of North America (UPCNA) took this action earlier in 1906 and with similar stipulations.

After two years of study, the PCUSA General Council brought three overtures to the General Assembly in 1929. Overture A, seeking full equal rights to women, failed. Overture B, allowing women's ordination as ruling elders, passed. Overture C, which sought to license women as evangelists, also failed.[205] These Overtures

---

[201] The Cumberland Presbyterian Church was the exception as they had ordained women since 1889.
[202] Tucker and Liefeld, 380–381.
[203] Janet Wilson James, "Women in American Religious History: An Overview," in *Women in American Religion*, Janet Wilson James, ed., (Philadelphia, PA: University of Pennsylvania Press, 1980), 23–24.
[204] Lindley, 312.
[205] Ibid.

were circulated before the Assembly and vigorously debated in denominational journals and on the Assembly floor.

Nothing changed between 1929 and 1955. The General Assembly, however, continued to receive overtures from several local presbyteries to allow the ordination of women. At the 1956 General Assembly, the assembly entertained an overture to ordain female ministers, and it passed by a wide margin. Nonetheless, many men continued to oppose women in the ministry. In 1958, the UPCNA merged with the PCUSA and became the United Presbyterian Church in the U.S.A. (UPCUSA) and thus, also ordained women.[206] The Southern Presbyterians began to ordain women as deacons, ruling elders, and teaching elders in 1964.[207] In the 1978 General Assembly, the PCUSA elected Sara B. Mosley (1918–2013) its first female moderator. Although most members of the PCUSA are female, as of 2019, women made up only twenty-eight percent of its ordained ministry.[208]

American Baptist Churches

Unlike their brethren to the South, the Northern Baptist Convention (now the American Baptist Churches USA, or ABCUSA) is much more progressive and has a long tradition of supporting women in church and denominational leadership. In the late nineteenth century, the NBC was already ordaining women to the ministry. Frances E. Townley (1849–1909) may have been the first.[209] She was ordained for pragmatic reasons. The deacons of the Fairfield Baptist Church in Fairfield, Nebraska, grew tired of trying to find ordained ministers. Townley endured much criticism for performing the ordinances.[210] The Northern Baptist Convention also had

---

[206] Ibid., 313.
[207] Ibid.
[208] "The Rise of Women in the Pulpit," *The Presbyterian Outlook*, 8 October 2019, https://pres-outlook.org/2019/10/the-rise-of-women-in-the-pulpit/.
[209] Frances E. Townley, *The Self-Told Story of Frances E. Townley* (Butler, IN: Higley Publisher, 1908), 276–81.
[210] Pamela Durso and Keith Durso, *The Story of Baptists in the United States* (Brentwood, TN: Baptist History and Heritage Society, 2006), 152–153.

no qualms about electing Helen Barrett Montgomery (1861–1934)[211] president of its annual convention in 1921, much to the chagrin of the Northern Baptist fundamentalists who would have seen this action as another sign of creeping modernism.

Though the ABCUSA has been open to women in ministry, few churches have female ministers. Many churches and congregations are uncomfortable calling a woman as their pastor. To remedy this problem, the ABCUSA adopted a statement on the status of women in 1965, asserting "there should be no differential treatment of men and women in the church, family, or society and that there should be equal opportunity for full participation in the work of our God." The ABCUSA hoped to work toward "full participation of women in the life and work of the church (including pastorates) in all countries."[212] By 2017, approximately thirteen percent of ABCUSA ministers were female.[213]

Pentecostalism

Initially, women in the Pentecostal or Holiness churches had a tremendous amount of freedom to exercise their spiritual gifts. Women played roles in the beginnings of churches, and some women were the actual persons who started them. The common belief was the Holy Spirit can use either a man or woman when testifying, prophesying, or preaching.[214] Some believed the end of time was upon them, as evidenced by the appearance of spiritual gifts described in Acts 2 and Joel 2:28–32. There was also a belief that the "eleventh hour laborers" that Jesus mentioned in his Laborers in the Vineyard parable were women.[215] Pauline distinctions and old rules did not

---

[211] Montgomery is believed to be the first female translator of the New Testament from Greek.

[212] "Status of Women," American Baptist Convention, 1965 *American Baptist Quarterly* 5 (June–September 1986): 321.

[213] Eileen Campbell Reed, "State of Clergywomen in the United States: A Statistical Update 2018," *Eileen Campbell Reed*, last accessed 1 July 2021, https://eileencampbellreed.org/wp-content/uploads/Downloads/State-of-Clergywomen-US-2018-web.pdf.

[214] Tucker and Liefeld, 360.

[215] Matthew 20:1–16.

apply when the return of Christ was imminent.²¹⁶ When it proved to be not the eleventh hour, many of the Pentecostal churches began to change their stance on women serving in the ministry. Moreover, the rise of fundamentalism led to less freedom for women in the Pentecostal churches. These churches desired acceptance by the larger denominations and eliminating women from leadership roles was the status quo.²¹⁷ Some denominations like the Pentecostal Church of God, however, continued to allow women to serve as pastors.

The Assemblies of God

The Assemblies of God identify as an evangelical denomination. In the first decade of the twentieth century, women and men in the Assemblies of God performed virtually the same ecclesiastical duties, but this situation would not last. In 1914, the organizing council of the Assemblies of God noted that Galatians 3:28 made men and women equal in the Spirit, but while on earth, 1 Timothy 2:12 took precedence. Women were still subject to men. Women would be ordained as evangelists and missionaries, but not as elders (pastors). An article in the *Evangel* explained the church's position.

> We know of no Movement where women of ability and filled with the Holy Ghost have been more highly honored or given much more freedom than among us. She has been given the right to be ordained, to preach, witness, give advice, act as an evangelist, missionary, etc. The only thing not thrown unscripturally upon her weak shoulder is that making of her a ruling elder.²¹⁸

---

[216] Edith Blumhofer, "Women in Pentecostalism," *Union Seminary Quarterly Review* 57, (2003): 104.
[217] MacHaffie, 278.
[218] Quoted in Charles H. Barfoot and Gerald T. Sheppard, "Prophetic vs. Priestly: The Changing Role of Women Clergy in Classical Pentecostal Churches," *Review of Religious Research* 22, (September 1980): 8.

The Assemblies of God began to license women as assistant pastors in 1920. In theory, when the pastor was away, he could leave his wife in charge. This remained the status quo until 1935 when, in a surprise decision at the Assemblies of God annual meeting, the denomination voted to grant women ordination as elders.[219] Though some women pastor churches in the twenty-first century, most ordained female ministers co-pastor with their husbands who serve as the primary pastor. In 2009, the Assemblies of God elected its first woman, Reverend Beth Grant, to its Executive Presbytery.[220] In 2018, Donna L. Barrett became the first woman elected to serve as the general secretary of the Assembly's General Council. In 2018, the Assemblies of God estimated that twenty-five percent of its ministers are female.[221]

The Church of God-Cleveland

The Church of God-Cleveland (COGC) authorized female deacons in 1908 but then determined not to ordain them. Women could preach and exercise their spiritual gifts but not serve in positions of authority. In 1913, the General Assembly excluded women from participation in church government and business and then denied them the right to perform marriages. In 1916, the COGC created a male Body of Elders, which cost women the right to vote in General Assemblies.[222] These dictums remained in place until late in the twentieth century. In 1990, the General Assembly decided that women could perform weddings, baptisms, and other pastoral functions. The General Assembly determined in 1992 that women could vote in the General Assembly. When brought before the Assembly

---

[219] Blumhofer, 112–114.
[220] Cecil M. Robeck, Jr., "Women in the Pentecostal Movement," *Fuller Studio*, last accessed 1 July 2021, https://fullerstudio.fuller.edu/women-in-the-pentecostal-movement/.
[221] Rev. Loralie Crabtree, "Women Ministers in the Assemblies of God," *Northpoint*, last accessed 1 July 2021, https://northpoint.edu/wp-content/uploads/2021/03/3.24.21-Rev.-Loralie-Crabtree-Presentation.pdf.
[222] Lindley, 335.

in 2010, the delegates determined, by a wide margin, that women could hold any ecclesiastical position other than bishop.[223]

The Foursquare Church

Founder of the International Church of the Foursquare Gospel, Aimee Semple McPherson (1890–1944) was the best-known Pentecostal preacher of her era. Coming from a Salvation Army background, she had no qualms about having women preach. She called herself an evangelist and believed in traditional gender roles. Any woman, married or single, could be ordained a pastor. Since she died in 1944, the number of ordained women, however, has dropped from sixty-seven to thirty-seven percent in 2018.[224] Since 1944, men have held all national offices. Moreover, no other woman has served as president of the International Church of the Foursquare Gospel.

Black Churches

Like most white denominations, most Black churches tend to have largely female congregations but a male clergy.[225] Though women may preach or prophesy, the leadership roles are reserved for men.[226] As noted by Rosemary Radford Ruether, Black churches are "suprapatriarchal."[227] She believes this is because only within the church can a Black man find a meaningful source of power. The ministry is also one of the primary ways for Black men to enter politics, as seen

---

[223] Cecil M. Robeck, Jr., "Women in the Pentecostal Movement," *Fuller Studio*, last accessed 1 July 2021, https://fullerstudio.fuller.edu/women-in-the-pentecostal-movement/; "Church of God: Women Can be Leaders, Not Bishops," *The Reporter*, 13 August 2010, https://reporter.lcms.org/2010/church-of-god-women-can-be-leaders-not-bishops/.
[224] Eileen Campbell Reed, "State of Clergywomen in the United States: A Statistical Update 2018," *Eileen Campbell Reed*, last accessed 1 July 2021, https://eileencampbellreed.org/wp-content/uploads/Downloads/State-of-Clergywomen-US-2018-web.pdf.
[225] TeResa Green, "A Gendered Spirit: Race, Class, and Sex in the African American Church," *Race, Gender, and Class in American Politics* 10, no. 1 (2003): 115.
[226] MacHaffie, 282.
[227] Rosemary Radford Ruether, "Crisis in Sex and Race: Black Theology vs. Feminist Theology," *Christianity and Crisis* 34, (15 April 1974): 69.

in the examples of Adam Clayton Powell Jr. (1908–1972), Andrew Young (b. 1932), Jesse Jackson (b. 1941),[228] and Raphael Warnock (b. 1969).

According to Susan Lindley, Black women agreed to leave leadership roles to Black men.[229] Black women did not want to contribute to the emasculation of Black men. Other scholars have posited that it may be that Black denominations seek acceptance from the larger American Christian populace that promotes patriarchy and relegates women to a subjected role.[230] TeResa Green notes that Black male ministers have no problem rejecting Paul's dictums that slaves obey their masters but do not take the same stance on Paul's statements on women.[231] Green states, "In their desire to make up for the barriers that pervaded American society, African American men tended to monopolize positions of religious leadership in most African American religious denominations. To bolster the Black male image, and in a display of solidarity to the race, many Black women willingly acquiesced to this monopolization."[232]

In her 2018 *State of the Clergywoman*, Eileen Campbell-Read concluded that the Methodist family of historic Black churches (e.g., Christian Methodist Episcopal [CME], African Methodist Episcopal [AME], and AME Zion) are the most open to female ministers.[233] The AME has by far the most female clergy; the clergy numbers 4413, with more than twenty-five percent of its pastors, 1189, being female. The CME church elected its first woman, Teresa E. Snorton (b. 1955), as bishop in 2010.[234] Black Baptist denominations (e.g, the National Baptist Convention of America, Inc., National Baptist

---

[228] Green, 117.
[229] Lindley, 177–78.
[230] F. E. Harris, Sr., *Ministry for Social Crisis: Theology and Praxis in the Black Church Tradition* (Macon, GA: Mercer University Press, 1993), 61.
[231] Green, 121.
[232] Ibid., 124.
[233] Eileen Campbell Reed, "State of Clergywomen in the United States: A Statistical Update 2018," *Eileen Campbell Reed*, last accessed 1 July 2021, https://eileencampbellreed.org/wp-content/uploads/Downloads/State-of-Clergywomen-US-2018-web.pdf.
[234] Greg Garrison, "First Female Bishop in Christian Methodist Episcoal Church Oversees Alabama," *Alabama*, last modified 5 March 2012, https://www.al.com/spotnews/2012/03/first_female_bishop_in_christi.html#:~:text=CME%20Bishop%20Teresa%20E.%20Snorton.%20BIRMINGHAM%2C%20Alabama%20--,

Convention, USA, Inc.) are the least open to female pastors. Though women account for up to seventy-five percent of Black Baptist denominational memberships, they constitute less than ten percent of church leadership and less than one percent of its pastors.[235]

Black Pentecostal churches are the most varied. The Church of God in Christ does not allow women to serve as bishops or elders, but women may preach. The First Baptized Holiness Church of God in the Americas and the Mount Calvary Holy Church of America, however, accept women in all ministerial positions.[236] Within many traditional Black denominations, women are still waiting to assume leadership roles.

Conclusion

In the twentieth century and the first decades of the twenty-first century, women made strides as deacons, pastors, and leaders in several denominations. Women served as faculty at Bible institutes, evangelical colleges and universities, and mainline denomination seminaries. While full equality was not yet achieved, gains for women leaders were undeniable. More women were going to seminary, becoming ordained, and affirmed in their calling to serve God. Organizations like Christians for Biblical Equality provided these women with biblical resources to support their gifting and calling. While remaining true to its traditions concerning women, the Catholic Church, under the pontificate of Francis I, tried to include women in more leadership roles. Ordination of women, however, is no closer to fruition than it was in the medieval era. The church continues to promote the concept of gendered spheres, but it no longer denigrates women as harshly as it has for centuries.

Within Protestant denominations, there have been changes in positions concerning women but also retrenchment. Many of the mainline denominations have determined that women may serve

---

has%20about%20850%2C000%20members%20in%203%2C500%20U.S.%20churches.

[235] Courtney Lyons, "Breaking Through the Extra-Thick Stained-Glass Ceiling: African American Baptist Women in Ministry" *Review and Expositor* 110, no. 1 (Winter 2013): 77–91.

[236] Green, 126.

in the ministry and promote egalitarianism within the church, home, society, and workforce. Most Pentecostal denominations, while remaining theologically conservative, have invited women to serve in ministry. Predominantly, Evangelicalism, does not conform to this set of beliefs. The Assemblies of God, are now open to women serving as ministers. The Lutheran Church-Missouri Synod remains firmly opposed to women in the ministry. The Southern Baptist Convention has adopted a more strident position. Not only are women forbidden to serve as ministers in their churches, but they also have promoted complementarianism that subjugates wives to their husbands.

As the twenty-first century progresses, men continue to attempt to control the debate over the nature, role, and purpose of women, but they have powerful egalitarian scholars countering their views. Within denominations that are egalitarian and open to female ministers, men serve as powerful allies to women in leveraging an egalitarian future for families, marriages, churches and organization.

Final Thoughts

Researching and writing this book has been laborious. Three years of research and two years of writing, even with a sabbatical/COVID-19 quarantine year, is a long time. My dining room has hundreds of books and journal articles covering every inch of available space. Still, it has proven to be a worthwhile labor. When I went into this project, I was searching for answers. To find these answers, I had to start at the beginning and see how Christian patriarchal teachings and beliefs concerning women evolved. With my work now complete, I have arrived at several conclusions.

Christianity has utilized a biased reading of the sacred biblical texts to privilege men as leaders in church, home, and in most vocations. From the Old Testament to the twenty-first century, men authored, translated, and edited most of Scripture and have largely controlled the Catholic and Protestant denominations. Though women have always been present in and contributed to Christianity over the last two thousand years, men's voices and opinions were more valued than those of women.

The Jesus of the gospels in no way subjugates women. Rather, he goes out of his way to minister to, care for, and heal women, many of whom were not even Jewish, throughout his ministry. The fact that women were the first to announce the good news of his resurrection highlights their importance to the kingdom of God. Moreover, Jesus' message speaks equality for all people.

The earliest letters attributed to Paul appear to promote an egalitarian church given the imminent return of Christ. When this did not happen, the later letters modify the treatment of women to make Christianity more palatable to the Romans who looked upon the Christians with suspicion. For a few years, women were equal to men. Church authorities used these later Pauline letters to subjugate women while interpreting earlier passages like Galatians 3:28 as an event that will happen in the world to come.

Women have preached and ministered throughout history, but when a denomination wanted to appear more similar to other established Christian organizations, the men in charge forced women to take a step back. Christianity followed the norms of patriarchal culture and state to gain acceptance and favor since Paul's time. Those who knew about this book have asked me if the men of these different eras were just following the strictures of their culture and times. If so, they suggested, perhaps I should not judge them harshly for echoing societal beliefs. My answer is that Christian men should have a responsibility to be better than societal norms. These men had Christ's teachings to rely upon, and he placed no limitations upon women. Jesus came to bring freedom and salvation to everyone, including women.

Christianity also uses women as scapegoats, starting with the first woman. Why is there sin in the world? It is because Eve was first in the Fall. Why do men fall into sexual sin? It is because Eve tempted Adam, and all women are, thus, temptresses. Why is sex bad? Because there was no sex in the Garden of Eden before the Fall. Eve tempted Adam to have sex before God determined the timing for sex was correct. Sex, therefore, is bad, and women are the cause of it and crave it. Even the angels desire them. Why can't men trust women? Because Eve deceived Adam. Why can't women be leaders? Because a woman led man into sin. Why did the plague destroy our crops? Because of witches. Why can't my wife and I have a baby? A woman placed a curse on us. Why is society so fragmented today? It is because women left the home to work and neglected their children. Why do husbands have affairs? It is because their wives are not taking care of their sexual needs. Why don't I have a satisfying marriage and all we do is fight? It is because God created the woman second, and she is not being subservient.

Over the centuries, Christianity has also depicted women as mentally inferior to men. They do not have the intelligence to leave the home, gain employment, or serve in leadership roles in society. This concept does not appear in the New Testament. Even in the Old Testament in which men used women as tools for their advancement, the stories rarely depict women as weak-minded.

Rather, Old Testament women often appear much more intelligent than their male counterparts. The belief that women are not mentally fit for anything beyond being a wife and mother has its roots in Plato and Aristotle rather than Genesis, Jesus, and Paul. Because many Church Fathers relied heavily on Plato and the most important theologian of the Middle Ages, Aquinas, relied on Aristotle, this belief found its way into Christian theology.

Women whom men depict as good (saints) or evil (witches) are two sides of the same coin. Throughout history, women who performed in a manner appropriate for their gender were deemed good or saints. The Virgin Mary obediently followed God's command and served as a mother. Augustine's mother, Monica, was a doting mother who was beaten by her husband but never left him. In Colonial America, Puritan wives who stayed in their place were called "good wives." In many evangelical denominations, a woman who stays at home, raises children, and cares for her husband is denoted a biblical woman. These women were recognized as good because they stayed within the roles prescribed to them by men. Evil women did the opposite. They did not conform to gender norms.

In the modern era, biblical inerrancy has attempted to keep women subjugated. The Pauline corpus makes several statements that appear to require women's silence and submission. The question, however, is what did the letters mean when they were written? Who was the intended audience? These letters were written in a time when women were subservient. Yet, women in the early church led at the highest level as apostles, prophets, teachers, deacons, and church planters. Like women, the church also emancipated slaves. Paul tells Philemon to receive his slave Onesimus as a brother; Onesimus becomes bishop of Ephesus. Even so, denominations such as the Southern Baptist Convention used the same arguments to condone slavery and segregation that they now use to promote complementarianism. It appears hypocritical to denounce one and not the other.

There are many Christian men and women who affirm complementarianism and believe it is the clearest depiction of biblical manhood and womanhood. Wives find strength, leadership, and affirmation for their chosen lives in this system. Husbands find comfort, affirmation, and a sense of biblical fidelity in wives who have chosen to graciously submit to their authority. This view works well for many Christian couples. They have faith in their biblical interpretation and live their lives in accordance to it. Many theologians who teach in universities and seminaries which advocate complementarianism see themselves as defenders of orthodoxy and believe their view is the only valid interpretation of biblical manhood and womanhood. As in previous centuries, they often belittle those, especially women, who do not agree with them. I see no end to this practice in the near future.

Control is another aspect that runs the gamut of Christianity. Perhaps out of fear, a lack of empathy for women, or that men are physically stronger than women, men have always sought to control women. Women cannot touch the sacraments without contaminating them. In order not to tempt monks, nuns should be cloistered. Women must wear conservative clothing. It is easier to control a woman who is forbidden to leave the house. Therefore, gender roles and spheres have played a large role in men's attempt to control women. Over the last thirty years, much of it has had to do with the fear of damaging a man's ego by proving women are equal in work, church and the home. Theologians such as John Piper teach that the man is the breadwinner, and the woman should remain at home taking care of children. Pastors and theologians taught this for hundreds of years, but rather than the belief that the world is too rough for a woman, the fear now is that if the woman makes more money than the man, it will hurt his ego. Piper believed that a man's manliness would be damaged if he had a woman as his drill sergeant. As gender roles and spheres developed over nearly two millennia, control over women boosts the self-confidence of weak men. As a man, I can affirm that we are fragile. My research, however, has taught me that this condition is neither inherent nor biblical, in much the same way that women are no less worthy than men in God's eyes and are capable of serving Him in whatever leadership position God gifts and calls them as has been the case throughout history.

BIBLIOGRAPHY

Primary Source Collections

Multi-Volume Works

The Ante-Nicene Fathers: Translations of the Writings of the Fathers Down to A.D. 325. Edited by Alexander Roberts and James Donaldson. 10 vols. 1885–1887. Reprint, Grand Rapids: Eerdmans Publishing Company, 1993.

A Select Library of Nicene and Post-Nicene Fathers of the Christian Church. Edited by Philip Schaff and Henry Wace. 28 vols. in 2 series. 1886–1889. Reprint, Grand Rapids: Eerdmans Publishing Company, 1992.

Aquinas, Thomas. *Summa Theologica.* Translated by the Fathers of the English Dominican Province. London: Bums Oats and Washbourne Ltd., 1981.

Aristotle, *Generation of Animals*, ed. G. P. Gould. Cambridge: Harvard University Press, 1979.

_____. *History of Animals, Books 7–10*, Edited and translated by D. M. Balme. Cambridge: Harvard University Press, 1991.

Calvin, John. *Calvin's Commentaries.* 22 vols. Grand Rapids: Baker, 1999.

_____. *1536 Institutes of Christian Religion, Calvini Opera Selecta*, edited by Peter

Barth and William Niesel. 5 vols. Munich: Christian Kaiser Verlag, 1974.

_____. *Calvini Opera*, edited by William Baum, Edward Cunitz, and Edward Reuss. Translated by David E. Holwerda. 59 vols. Brunswick: Schwestche, 1863–1900.

Migne, J.P, ed. *Complete Works, Patrologiae Cursus Completus*, series Graeca, vols. 47–63. Paris: J.P. Migne, 1858.

CTS *Calvin Translation Society*, 40 vols. (Edinburgh 1843–55).

Jurgens, William A. *The Faith of the Early Fathers*. 3 vols. Collegeville: Liturgical Press, 1970.

Luther, Martin. *Luther's Works*, 55 vols., edited by J. Pelikan and H.T. Lehmann, American Edition. Philadelphia: Concordia, St. Louis, Fortress Press and Muhlenberg Press, 1958ff.

Luther, Martin. *Luthers Werkes, Tischreden*. 6 vols. Weimar: Verlag Hermann Böhlaus Nachfolger, 1912–21.

MacHaffie, Barbara J. ed., *Readings in Her Story: Women in Christian Tradition*. Minneapolis: Fortress Press, 1992.

Philo. *The Works of Philo: Complete and Unabridged*. Translated by C. D. Yonge. Peabody: Hendrickson Publishers, 1993.

Plato. *The Collected Dialogues*, edited by Edith Hamilton and Huntington Cairns. Princeton: Princeton University Press, 1969.

Whitley, William T., ed. *The Works of John Smyth*. 2 vols. Cambridge: University Press, 1915.

Single Volume Works

A Discoverie of Six Women Preachers in Middlesex, Kent, Cambridgeshire and Salisbury. N.P., 1641.

Anderson, Roberta, and Dominic Aiden, eds., *Medieval Religion: A Sourebook*. New York: Routledge, 2007.

Bede, *Ecclesiastical History of the English People*, edited and translated by Bertram Colgrave and R. A. B. Mynors. Oxford, Oxford University Press, 1969.

Clark, Elizabeth and Herbert Richardson, eds. *Women and Religion: A Feminist Sourcebook of Women in Christian Thought*. San Francisco: HarperCollins, 1977.

Cotton, John. *Singing of Psalms a Gospel Ordinance*. N.P., 1650.

De Voragine, Jacobus. *The Golden Legend Book: Readings on the Saints*. Translated by William Granger Ryan. Princeton: Princeton University Press, 2012.

Dobson, James Dobson. *Straight Talk: What Men Need to Know, What Women Should Understand*, revised and expanded. Dallas: Word, 1991.

Edwards, Jonathan. *A Faithful Narrative*, in Goen, C. C., ed. *The Great Awakening*. 12 vols. New Haven: Yale University Press, 1972.

Elliot, Elisabeth. *Let Me Be a Woman*. Wheaton: Tyndale, 1976.

Erasmus, *The Collected Works of Erasmus*. Toronto: University of Toronto Press, 1974.

Erasmus, *Opus Epistolarum Erasmi Roterodami*, edited by P.S. Allen. Oxford, 1906–58.

Funderburk, A. R. *What is the Matter with the Church Today?* N.P., 1939.

Galen. *Selected Works*. Translated by P. N. Singer. Oxford: Oxford University Press, 1997.

Gaudium et Spes, in Walter M. Abbott, ed., *The Documents of Vatican II*. New York: America Press, 1966.

Gillette, A.D., ed. *The Minutes of the Philadelphia Baptist Association, 1707–1807*. Philadelphia: American Baptist Publication Society, 1844.

Gregory of Tours. *The History of the Franks*. Translated by Lewis Thorpe. Harmondsworth: Penguin Books, 1974.

Gregory the Great. *A Select Library of Nicene and Post-Nicene Fathers of the Christian Church*, Second Series. Vol. 12, *The Book of Pastoral Rule and Selected Epistles of Gregory the Great*. Translated by James Barmby. New York: The Christian Literature Company, 1895.

Grudem, Wayne. *Biblical Foundations for Manhood and Womanhood*. Wheaton: Crossway, 2002.

_____. *Countering the Claims of Evangelical Feminism*. Colorado Springs: Multnomah, 2006.

_____. *Systematic Theology: An Introduction to Biblical Doctrine*. Grand Rapids: Zondervan: 1994.

John Chrysostom. *A Theodore. Sources Chretiennes*. Translated by Jean Dumortier. Paris: Les Editions du Cerf, 1966.

Kramer, Henrich and James Sprenger. *Malleus Maleficarum*. Translated by Montague Summers. New York: Dover Publications, Inc., 1971.

LaHaye, Timothy, *Understanding the Male Temperament*. Grand Rapids: Fleming H. Revell, 1977.

Luther, Martin. *Table Talk*. Translated by William Hazlitt. London: HarperCollins Publishers, 1995.

Macarthur, John. *Divine Design: God's Complementary Roles for Men and Women*. Colorado Springs: David Cook 1994.

Machebeuf, Rt. Rev. J. P. *Woman's Suffrage: A Letter*. Denver: Triune Steam Printing House, 1877.

Mather, Cotton. *Bethiah: The Glory Which Adorns the Daughters of God, and the Piety, Wherewith Zion Wishes to See His Daughters Glorious*. Boston: Printed by Franklin for Gerrish, 1722.

_____. *A Family Well-Ordered*. Boston: 1699.

_____. *Elizabeth in Her Holy Retirement*. Boston, 1710.

_____. (1692) *On Witchcraft: Being the Wonders of the Invisible World*. Reprint, New York: Bell, 1974.

_____. *Ornaments for the Daughters of Zion*. Boston: Kneeland and Green, 1741.

Milton, John. *Paradise Lost*. Abingdon, Oxfordshire: Routledge, 2006.

_____. *Paradise Regained*, 4 bks. CreateSpace Independent Publishing Platform, 2012.

Moody, Dwight L. *New Sermons, Addresses and Prayers*. Chicago: H.S. Goodspeed, 1877.

Morgan, Marabel. *The Total Woman*. Old Tappen: Fleming H. Revel Company, 1973.

Morton, James, ed. and trans. *The Ancren Riwle*. London: Camden Society [LVII], 1853.

Palmer, Phoebe. "Tongue of Fire on the Daughters of the Lord" in Thomas C. Oden, *Phoebe Palmer: Selected Writings*. New York: Paulist Press, 1988.

Patterson, Dorothy. *The Sensuous Woman Reborn*. Dallas: Crescendo Publications, 1976.

Piper, John and Wayne Grudem. *Recovering Biblical Manhood and Womanhood: A Response to Evangelical Feminism*. Wheaton: Crossway Books, 2006.

Pius XI. cited in *The Woman in the Modern World, papal teachings selected and arranged by the Benedictine Monks and Solesmes*. Boston: St Paul Editions, 1959.

Plato. *Timaeus*. Translated by Benjamin Jowett. Lexington: CreativeSpace Independent Publishing Platform, 2014.

Pope John Paul II. *Mand and Woman, He Created Them: A Theology of the Body*, translated, introduced, and indexed by Michael M. Waldstein. Boston: Pauline Books and Media, 2006.

Rice, John. *Bobbed Hair, Bossy Wives, and Women Preachers: Significant Questions for Honest Christian Women Settled by the Word of God*. Wheaton: Sword of the Lord Publishers, 1941.

Schaeffer, Francis. *Genesis in Space and Time*. Downers Grove, IL: Inter-Varsity Press, 1972.

Smiley, Sarah F. *The Fulness of Blessing—or, the Gospel of Christ, as Illustrated from the Book of Joshua*. London: Hodder and Stoughton, 1876.

Smith, Henry. *The Works*, edited by T. Fuller. Edinburgh: James Nichol, 1866.

"Spheres and Work," Woman's Christian Temperance Union National Headquarters Historical Files, Joint Ohio Historical Society-Michigan Historical Collections—W.C.T.U. microfilm edition, reel 30, "A book of Miscellaneous Articles on Temperance, Lectures, etc., Compiled by Mrs. J.F. Willard."

Strachen, Owen and Gavin Peacock, *The Grand Design: Male and Female He Made Them*. Ross-Shire: Christian Focus, 2016.

Straton, John Roach. "Moral Decay Through Subservience to Foreign Fashions in Women's Dress," unpublished sermon, Straton papers, American Baptist Historical Society.

The Register of the Company of Pastors of Geneva in the Time of Calvin, edited by Philip E. Hughes. Grand Rapids: Eerdmans, 1966.

Ware, Bruce. *Big Truths for Young Hearts: Teaching and Learning the Greatness of God*. Wheaton: Crossway, 2009.

Ware, Bruce and John Starke, *One God in Three Persons: Unity of Essence, Distinction of Persons, Implications for Life*. Wheaton: Crossway, 2015.

Willard, Frances E. *Glimpses of Fifty Years: The Autobiography of an American Woman*. Chicago: Woman's Temperance Publication Association/ H. J. Smith & Co., 1889.

Winthrop, John. *The Journal of John Winthrop 1630–1649*, eds James Savage, Richard S. Dunn and Laetitia Yaendle. Cambridge: Belknap Press, 1996.

Secondary Sources

Allison, Emily Joy. *#Church Too: How Purity Culture Uphold Abuse and How to Find Healing*. Minneapolis: 1517 Media, Broadleaf Books, 2021.

Ammerman, Nancy. *Southern Baptists Observed: Multiple Perspectives on a Changing Denomination*. Knoxville: University of Tennessee Press, 1993.

Anderson, George and J. Francis Stafford & Joseph A. Burgess. *The One Mediator, The Saints, and Mary. Lutherans and Roman Catholic in Dialogue. VIII*. Minneapolis: Augsburg Fortress, 1992.

Arendt, H. *Love and Saint Augustine*. Chicago: University of Chicago Press, 1996.

Arnold, John H. *The Oxford Handbook of Medieval Christianity*. Oxford: Oxford University Press, 2014.

Aschkenasy, Nehama. *Eve's Journey: Feminine Image in Hebraic Literary Tradition*. Philadelphia: University of Pennsylvania Press, 1986.

Atkins, Anne. *Split Image: Male and Female after God's Likeness*. Grand Rapids: Eerdmans, 1987.

Ayers, Robert H. *Language, Logic, and Reason in the Church Fathers: A Study of Tertullian, Augustine, and Aquinas*. New York: Georg Olms Verlag, 1979.

Bach, Alice., ed. *Women in the Hebrew Bible: A Reader*. New York: Routledge, 1999.

Bakan, David. *And They Took Themselves Wives: The Emergence of Patriarchy in Western Civilization*. San Francisco: Harper and Row, 1979.

Balmer, Randall. *Protestantism in America*. New York: Columbia University Press, 2005.

Banner, William Augustus. *The Path of St. Augustine*. Lanham: Rowman & Littlefield, 1996.

Barber, Malcolm. *The Cathars: Dualist Heretics in Languedoc in the High Middle Ages*. New York: Longman, 2000.

Barnes, T.D. *Tertullian: A Historical and Literary Study*. Oxford: Clarendon Press, 1971.

Barr, Beth Allison. *The Making of Biblical Womanhood: How the Subjugation of Women Became the Gospel Truth*. Grand Rapids: Brazos Press, 2021.

Barstow, Anne Llewellyn. *Married Priests and the Reforming Papacy: The Eleventh Century Debates*. New York: The Edwin Mellen Press, 1982.

Bauckham, Richard. *Gospel Witness: Named Women in the Gospels*. Grand Rapids: Eerdmans, 2002.

Bauman, Richard. *Women and Politics in Ancient Rome*. New York: Routledge, 1992.

Bäumer, Regimius, and Leo Scheffczyk, eds., *Marienlexikon*. Regensburg: Institutum Marianum, 1994.

Baur, Chrysostomus. *John Chrysostom and His Time*. 2 vols. Translated by Sr. M. Gonzaga. Westminster: The Newman Press, 1959.

Beal, John P., Thomas A. Coriden, and Thomas J. Green, eds. *New Commentary on the Code of Canon Law: An Entirely New and Comprehensive Commentary by Canonists from North America and Europe, With a Revised English Translation of the Code*. New York: Paulist Press, 2000.

Bebbington, David. *Evangelicalism in Modern Britain: A History from the 1730s to the 1980s*. New York: Routledge, 1989.

Bendroth, Margaret Lamberts. *Fundamentalism and Gender, 1875 to Present*. New York: Yale University Press, 1993.

Bengtson, Gloria E., Ed. *Lutheran Woman in Ordained Ministry, 1970–1995, Reflections and Perspectives*. Minneapolis: Augsburg Press, 1995.

Benedict, David. *A General History of the Baptist Denomination of America.* New York: Sheldon and Company Publishers, 1860.

Bennett, Judith M. and Ruth Mazo Karras, eds. *The Oxford Handbook of Women & Gender in Medieval Europe.* Oxford: Oxford University Press, 2013.

Bettella, Patrizia. *The Ugly Women: Transgressive Aesthetic Models in Italian Poetry from the Middle Ages to the Baroque.* Toronto: University of Toronto Press, 2005.

Bilezikian, Gilbert. *Beyond Sex Roles: What the Bible Says about a Woman's Place in Church and Family*, 3rd ed. Grand Rapids: Baker Books, 2006.

Bitel, Lisa M. and Felice Lifshitz, eds. *Gender and Christianity in Medieval Europe: New Perspectives.* Philadelphia: University of Pennsylvania Press, 2008.

Blamires, Alcuin., ed. *Woman Defamed and Defended: An Anthology of Medieval Texts.* Oxford: Oxford University Press, 1992.

Blankenhorn, David, Don Browning, and Mary Stewart Van Leeuwen, eds. *Does Christianity Teach Male Headship: The Equal-Regard Marriage and Its Critics.* Grand Rapids: Eerdmans Publishing, 2004.

Bokenkotter, Thomas. *A Concise History of the Catholic Church.* New York: Doubleday, 2005.

Børresen, Kari Elisabeth. *Subordination et Equivalence. Nature et rôle de la femme d'aprés Augustin et Thomas d'Aquin.* Paris: Maison Mame, 1963.

_____. Børresen, Kari Elisabeth, ed. *The Image of God: Gender Models in Judaeo-Christian Tradition.* Minneapolis: Fortress Press, 1995.

_____. "Women's Studies of the Christian Tradition: New Perspectives." In *Religion and Gender*, edited by U. King. Oxford: Blackwell, 1995.

Boryczka, Jocelyn M. *Suspect Citizens: Women, Virtue, and Vice in Backlash Politics.* Philadelphia: Temple University Press, 2012.

Botte, Dorn Bernard. *La Tradition Apostolique de Saint Hippolyte.* Miinster, Westfalen: Aschendorff, 1963.

Braude, Ann. *Sisters and Saints: Women and American Religion.* Oxford: Oxford University Press, 2008.

Brecht, Martin. *His Road to Reformation*, 1483–1521. Translated by James Schaaf. Philadelphia: Fortress Press, 1985.

Bremer, Francis. *Anne Hutchinson: Troubler of the Puritan Zion.* Huntington: Robert E. Krieger Publishing Company, 1981.

Brett, Edward Tracy. *Humbert of Romans: His Life and Views of Thirteenth-Century Society.* Toronto: Pontifical Institute for Medieval Studies, 1984.

Brooke, Christopher. *A General History of Europe: Europe in the Central Middle Ages, 962–1154.* Essex: Longman Group Limited, 1975.

Brown, Joanne Carlson and Carlole R. Bohn, eds. *Christianity, Patriarchy, and Abuse: A Feminist Critique.* Cleveland: Pilgrim Press, 1989.

Brown, Peter. *Augustine of Hippo: A Biography.* London: Faber & Faber, 1967.

_____. *The Body and Society: Men, Women, and Sexual Renunciation in Early Christianity.* New York: Columbia University Press, 1988.

Bruce, Jr., Dickson D. *And They All Sang Hallelujah: Plain-Folk Camp Meeting Religion, 1800–1845.* Knoxville: University of Tennessee Press, 1974.

Bruce, F. F. *New Testament History.* New York.: Galilee-Doubleday, 1969.

Bullough, Vern L. and James A. Brundage., eds. *Handbook of Medieval Sexuality.* New York: Routledge, 2000.

Burge, Ryan P. *The Nones: Where They Came From, Who They Are, and Where They are Going.* Minneapolis: 1517 Media, Fortress Press, 2021.

Butler, R. D. *The New Prophecy and New Visions: Evidence of Montanism in The Passion of Perpetua and Felicitas.* Washington, D.C.: The Catholic University of America Press, 2006.

Caldwell, Lauren. *Roman Girlhood and the Fashioning of Femininity.* Cambridge University Press, 2014.

Campbell-Reed, Eileen. *Anatomy of a Schism: How Clergywomen's Narratives Reinterpret the Fracturing of the Southern Baptist Convention.* Knoxville: University of Tennessee Press, 2016.

Carmichael, Calum M. *Women, Law, and the Genesis Traditions.* Edinburgh: Edinburgh University Press, 1979.

Cary, Phillip. *Augustine's Invention of the Inner Self: The Legacy of a Christian Platonist.* Oxford: Oxford University Press, 2000.

Cherewatuk, Karen and Ulrike Wiethaus. *Dear Sister: Medieval Women and the Epistolary Genre.* Philadelphia: University of Pennsylvania Press, 1993.

Christ-Von Wedel, Christine. *Erasmus of Rotterdam: Advocate of a New Christianity.* Toronto: University of Toronto Press, 2013.

Clack, Beverly, ed. *Misogyny in the Western Philosophical Tradition: A Reader.* London: MacMillan Press, 1999.

Clark, Elizabeth A. *Jerome, Chrysostom, and Friends.* New York: The Edwin Mellen Press, 1979.

_____. *Women in the Early Church.* Collegeville: Liturgical Press, 1990.

Clark, Elizabeth and Herbert Richardson, eds. *Women and Religion: A Feminist Sourcebook of Christian Thought.* San Francisco: Harper Collins, 1977.

Coffin, Joshua. *A Sketch of the History of Newbury, Newburyport, and West Newbury*. Boston, 1845; N. H. Hampton: Peter Randall, 1977.

Collins, John L. *A Short Introduction to the Hebrew Bible*, 3rd ed. Minneapolis: Fortress Press, 2018.

Conser, Jr., Walter H. *Southern Crossroads: Perspectives on Religion and Culture*. Lexington: University of Kentucky Press, 2008.

Cooper, K. *The Virgin and the Bride: Idealized Womanhood in Late Antiquity*. Cambridge: Harvard University Press, 1996.

Cott, Nancy F. *The Bonds of Womanhood: "Woman's Sphere" in New England, 1780–1835*. New Haven: Yale University Press, 1977.

Crandall, Barbara. *Gender and Religion: The Dark Side of Scripture*, 2nd ed. New York: Continuum International Publishing Group, 2012.

Crawford, Patricia. *Women and Religion in England, 1500–1720*. New York: Routledge, 1993.

Crowther, Kathleen M. *Adam and Eve in the Protestant Reformation*. Cambridge: Cambridge University Press, 2010.

Culham, Phyllis. "Women in the Roman Republic." In *The Cambridge Companion to the Roman Republic*. Cambridge: Cambridge University Press, 2004.

D'Ambra, Eve. *Roman Woman*. New York: Cambridge University Press, 2007.

Daly, Mary. *The Church and the Second Sex: With a New Feminist PostChristian Introduction by the Author*. New York: Harper and Row, 1975.

Daniel-Hughes, C.D. "Dressing for the Resurrection: Modest Dress as Embodied Theology in Tertullian of Carthage." PhD Dissertation, Harvard Divinity School, September 2007.

Darling, Pamela W. *New Wine: The Story of Women Transforming Leadership and Power in the Episcopal Church*. Cambridge: Cowley, 1994.

Dauphinais, Michael, Barry David, and Matthew Levering, eds. *Aquinas the Augustinian*. Washington D.C.: Catholic University Press of America, 2007.

De Beauvoir, Simon. *The Second Sex*. Translated by H.M. Parshley. London: Vintage, 1997.

DeBerg, Betty A. *Ungodly Women: Gender and the First Wave of American Fundamentalism*. Macon: Mercer University Press, 2000.

DeConick, April D. *Holy Misogyny: Why the Sex and Gender Conflicts of the Early Church Still Matter*. New York: Bloomsbury, 2011.

Denzinger-Schoenmetzer, D. S. *Enchiridion Symbolorum*, Ed. XXXIV. Feiburg im Breisgau, Germany: Herder, 1967.

Degler, Carl. At Odds: *Women and the Family in America from the Revolution to the Present*. New York: Oxford University Press, 1980.

Dickson, D. Bruce, Jr, *And They All Sang Hallelujah: Plain-Folk Camp Meeting Religion, 1800–1845*. Knoxville: University of Tennessee Press, 1974.

Dix, Gregory, ed. *The Treatise on the Apostolic Tradition of St. Hippolytus of Rome, Bishop and Martyr*. 2nd ed. London: S.P.C.K., 1968.

Dolan, Jay P. *The American Catholic Experience: A History from Colonial Times to Present*. Garden City: Doubleday, 1985.

Douglas, Ann. *The Feminization of American Culture*. New York: Avon, 1977.

Douglass, Jane Dempsey. *Women, Freedom, and Calvin*. Philadelphia: Westminster Press, 1985.

Dowland, Seth. *Southern Masculinity: Perspectives of Manhood in the South since Reconstruction*. Athens: University of Georgia Press, 2009.

Duby, Georges, Michelle Perrot, and Christine Klapisch-Zuber, eds. *A History of Women: The Silences of the Middle Ages*. Cambridge: Belknap Press of Harvard University Press, 1992.

Dunning, Benjamin H. *Specters of Paul: Sexual Difference in Early Christian Thought*. Philadelphia: University of Pennsylvania Press, 2011.

Durso Pamela R. and Keith E. Durso. *The Story of Baptists in the United States*. Brentwood: Baptist History and Heritage Society, 2006.

Early, Joseph. *A History of Christianity: An Introductory Survey*. Nashville: Broadman and Holman Publishers, 2015.

Ehrman, Bart. *Forged: Writing in the Name of God—Why the Bible Authors are Not Who We Think They are*. New York: Harper Collins Publishers, 2011.

_____. *The New Testament: A Historical Introduction to the Early Christian Writings*, 6th ed. Oxford: Oxford University Press, 2016.

Eisen, Ute. *Women Officeholders in Early Christianity: Epigraphical and Literary Studies*. Collegeville: Liturgical Press, 2000.

Elwell, Walter A., ed. *Evangelical Dictionary of Theology*. Grand Rapids: Baker Academic, 2001.

Epstein, Barbara Leslie. *The Politics of Domesticity: Women, Evangelism, and Temperance in Nineteenth Century America*. Middletown: Wesleyan University Press, 1981.

Eslinger, Ellen. *Citizens of Zion: The Social Origins of Camp Meeting Revivalism*. Knoxville: University of Tennessee Press, 1999.

Fantham, Elaine, Helen Peet Foley, Natalie Boymel Kampen, Sarah B. Pomeroy, and H. Alan Shapiro. *Women in the Classical World*. New York: Oxford University Press, 1994.

Fell Margaret. *Women's Speaking Justified, Proved and Allowed of by the Scriptures*. London: N.P., 1667.
Fletcher, Jesse C. *The Southern Baptist Convention: A Sesquicentennial History*. Nashville: Broadman and Holman, 1994.
Flowers, Elizabeth H. *Into the Pulpit: Southern Baptist Women and Power Since World War II*. Chapel Hill. The University of North Carolina Press, 2003.
Ford, David Carlton. "Misogynist or advocate? St. John Chrysostom and his Views on Women." PHD Dissertation: Drew University, 1989.
_____. *Women and Men in the Early Church: The Vision of John Chrysostom*. South Canaan: St. Tikhon's Monastery Press, 2017.
Foster, Thomas A. *Women in Early America*. New York: NYU Press, 2015.
Fox, R. L. *Pagans and Christians*. New York: Harper, 1988.
Friedberg A., ed. *Corpus Juris Canonici*. Leipzig 1879–1881, reprint Graz, 1955.
Friend, Craig Thompson. *Southern Masculinity: Perspectives on Manhood in the South Since Reconstruction*. Athens: University of Georgia Press, 2009.
Frier, Bruce W. and Thomas A.J. McGinn, *A Casebook on Roman Family Law*. Oxford University Press: American Philological Association, 2004.
Gambero, L. *Mary and the Fathers of the Church: The Blessed Virgin Mary in Patristic Thought*. Translated by T. Buffer. San Francisco: Ignatius Press, 1999.
Gardner, Jane F. *Women in Roman Law and Society*. Bloomington: University of Indiana Press, 1986.
George, Charles H. and Katherine George. *The English Protestant and the Family*. Princeton: Princeton University Press, 1961.
Gilmore, David D. *Misogyny: The Male Malady*. Philadelphia: University of Pennsylvania Press, 2001.
Goff Stan. *The Misbegotten Man: Reflections on War, Sex, and Church*. London: Lutterworth Press, 2015.
Gregg, Joan Young. *Devils, Women, and Jews: Reflections of the Other in Medieval Sermons*. New York: State University Press, 1997.
Grundmann, Herbert. *Religious Movements in the Middle Ages*. Translated by Steven Rowan. Notre Dame: University of Notre Dame Press, 1995.
Gryson, Roger. *The Ministry of Women in the Early Church*. Translated by Jean Laporte and Mary Louise Hall, Collegeville, Minn.: The Liturgical Press, 1980.

Guy, John. *My Heart is My Own: The Life of Mary Queen of Scots*. London: Fourth Estate, 2004.

Hampson, Daphne. *Theology and Feminism: Signposts in Theology*. Oxford: Basil Blackwell, 1990.

Hanson, R. P. C. *Studies in Christian Antiquity*. Edinburgh: T & T Clark, Ltd., 1985.

Hardman, Keith J. *Charles Grandison Finney, 1792–1875: Revivalist and Reformer*. Syracuse: Syracuse University Press, 1987.

_____. *Seasons of Refreshing: Evangelism and Revivals in America*. Grand Rapids: Baker Book House, 1994.

Harris, Sr., F. E. *Ministry for Social Crisis: Theology and Praxis in the Black Church Tradition*. Macon: Mercer University Press, 1993.

Haskins, Susan. *Mary Magdalene: Myth and Metaphor*. San Francisco: HarperCollins, 1993.

Harvey, Paul and Edward J. Blum, and Randall Stephens, eds. *The Columbia Guide to Religion in American History*. New York: Columbia University Press, 2012.

Harvey, Paul and Philip Goff. *The Columbia Documentary History of Religion in America Since 1945*. New York: Columbia University Press, 2005.

Hawley, John Stratton, ed. *Fundamentalism and Gender*. New York: Oxford University Press, 1994.

Hayter, Mary. *The New Eve in Christ: The Use and Abuse of the Bible in the Debate about Women in the Church*. Grand Rapids: Eerdmans Publishing House, 1987.

Hein, David and Gardiner H. Shattuck, Jr., *The Episcopalians*. Westport: Praeger, 2004.

Hempton, David. *Methodism: Empire of the Spirit*. New Haven: Yale University Press, 2005.

Hill, Frances. *A Delusion of Satan: The Full Story of the Salem Witch Trials*. New York: Doubleday, 1995.

Hollenweger, Walter, J. *The Pentecostals*. London: SCM Press Ltd., 1972.

Holwerda, David E., ed. *Exploring the Heritage of John Calvin: Essays in Honor of John Bratt*. Grand Rapids: Baker Book House, 1976.

Hurley, James B. *Man and Woman in Theological Perspective*. Grand Rapids: Zondervan, 1981.

Hutchinson, Lucy Hutchinson. *Principles of the Christian Religion*, edited by Julius Hutchinson. London: Longman, 1817.

Jardine, Lisa. *Erasmus, Man of Letters*. Princeton: Princeton University Press, 1993.

Jones, Charles Edwin. *Perfectionist Persuasion: The Holiness Movements and American Methodism, 1867–1936*, edited by Kenneth E. Rowe. Vol. 5. Metuchen: The Scarecrow Press, Inc., 1974.

Jordan, Michael. *The Historical Mary: Revealing the Pagan Identity of the Virgin Mother*. Berkley: Seastone, 2004.

Juliussen-Stevenson, Heather. "Performing Christian female identity in Roman Alexandria." PhD Dissertation, University of Maryland, College Park, 2008.

Junster, Susan. Disorderly Women: *Sexual Politics and Evangelicalism in Revolutionary New England*. Ithaca: Cornell University Press, 1994.

Karlsen, Carol. *The Devil in the Shape of a Woman: Witchcraft in Colonial New England*. New York: W. W. Norton, 1998.

Keener, Craig S., *Paul, Women, & Wives: Marriage and Women's Ministry in the Letters of Paul*. Peabody: Hendrickson Publishers, 1992.

Kelly, J.N.D. *Golden Mouth: The Story of John Chrysostom, Ascetic, Preacher, Bishop*. Ithaca: Cornell University Press, 1995.

Kern, Kathi. *Mrs. Stanton's Bible*. Ithaca: Cornell University Press, 2001.

Klapisch-Zuber, Christine, ed. *A History of Women in the West: Silence of the Middle Ages*. Cambridge: Harvard University Press, 1992.

Knight, III., George W. *The New Testament Teaching on the Role Relationship of Men and Women*. Grand Rapids: Baker Books, 1977.

Kraemer, Ross Shepard and Mary Rose D'Angelo. *Women and Christian Origins*. Oxford: Oxford University Press, 1999.

Kvam, Kristen E., Linda S. Schearing, and Valerie H. Ziegler, eds. *Eve & Adam: Jewish, Christian, and Muslim Readings on Genesis and Gender*. Bloomington: University of Indiana Press, 1999.

LaPlante, Eve. *American Jezebel, the Uncommon Life of Anne Hutchinson, the Woman who Defied the Puritans*. San Francisco: Harper Collins, 2004.

LaPorte, J. *The Role of Women in Early Christianity*. New York: Edwin Mellen Press, 1982.

Latimer, Hugh. *Works*. Edited by G. E. Corrie. Cambridge: Cambridge University Press, 1844–45.

Lefkowitz, Mary R. and Maureen B. Fant. *Women's Life in Greece and Rome: A Sourcebook in Translation*, 3rd ed. Baltimore: Johns Hopkins Press, 2005.

Lerner, Gerda. *The Creation of Patriarchy*. Oxford: Oxford University Press, 1986.

Lindley, Susan Hill. *"You Have Stept Out of Your Place:" A History of Women and Religion in America*. Louisville: Westminster John Knox Press, 1996.

Loader, William. *Sexuality and the Jesus Tradition*. Grand Rapids: Eerdmans Publishing, 2005.

Roper, Lyndal. *Witch Craze*. New Haven: Yale University Press, 2004.

Kurant-Nunn, Susan C. and Merry E. Wiesner-Hanks. *Luther on Women*. Cambridge: Cambridge University Press, 2003.

Macartney, Clarence. *The Way of a Man With a Maid*. Nashville: N.P., 1931.

MacDonald, Dennis. *The Legend and the Apostle Paul: The Battle for Paul in Story and Canon*. Philadelphia: Westminster Press, 1983.

Machebeuf, Rt. Rev. J. P. *Woman's Suffrage: A Letter*. Denver: Triune Steam Printing House, 1877.

MacHaffie, Barbara J. *Her Story: Women in the Christian Tradition*, 2nd ed. Minneapolis: Fortress Press, 2006.

Madigan, Kevin and Carolyn Osiek, eds. *Ordained Women in the Early Church: A Documentary History*. Baltimore: Johns Hopkins University Press, 2005.

Malone, Mary T. *Women and Christianity*, Vol. 1, *The First Thousand Years*. Maryknoll: Orbis Books, 2000.

———. *Women and Christianity*, Vol. 2, *From 1000 to the Reformation*. Maryknoll: Orbis Books, 2001.

———. *Women and Christianity*, Vol. 3, *From the Reformation to the 21st Century*. Maryknoll: Orbis Books, 2003.

Marsden, George M. *Fundamentalism and American Culture*. Oxford: Oxford University Press, 2006.

———. *Jonathan Edwards: A Life*. New Haven: Yale University Press, 2003.

Martos, Joseph and Pierre Hégy, eds. *Equal at the Creation: Sexism, Society, and Christian Thought*. Toronto: University of Toronto Press, 1998.

Matthews, Alice. *Gender Roles and the People of God: Rethinking What We Were Taught About Men and Women in the Church*. Grand Rapids: Zondervan, 2017.

McBeth, H. L. *The Baptist Heritage: Four Centuries of Baptist Witness*. Nashville: Broadman and Holman, 1987.

———. *Women in Baptist Life*. Nashville: Broadman Press, 1979.

McDannell, Colleen. *The Christian Home in Victorian America, 1840–1900*. Bloomington: Indiana University Press, 1986.

McLoughlin, William G. *Revivals, Awakenings, and Reform*. Chicago: University of Chicago Press, 1978.

Methuen, Charlotte. *Gender and Christian Religion*. Woodbridge: Boydell Press, 1998.

Miller, Patricia Cox. *Women in Early Christianity: Translations from Greek Texts*. Washington: Catholic University of America, 2005.

Miller, Richard W. *Woman and the Shaping of Catholicism: Women Through the Ages*. Liguori: Liguori Publications, 2009.

Mitchell, Linda E., ed. *Women in Medieval Western European Culture*. New York: Garland Publications, 1999.

Moore, Rebecca. *Women in the Christian Tradition*. New York: New York University Press, 2015.

Moorman, J. *The Franciscan Order form its Origins to the Year 1517*. Oxford: Oxford University Press, 1968.

Morgan, Edmund S. *The Puritan Family: Religion and Domestic Relations in Seventeenth-Century New England*. New York: Harper Perennial, 1966.

Morone, James A. *Hellfire Nation: The Politics of Sin in American History*. New Haven: Yale University Press, 2003.

Munier, C. *Concilia Africae a.345–a.525*. Turnhout: Brepols, 1974.

Munro, Winsome. "Patriarchy and Charismatic Community in Paul." In *Women and Religious Paper for Working Groups on Women and Religion, 1972–73*, revised ed., edited by Judith Plaskow and Joan Arnold Romero. Missoula: Scholars Press, 1974.

Murray, Jacqueline and Konrad Eisenbichler, eds. *Desire and Discipline: Sex and Sexuality in the Premodern West*. Toronto: University of Toronto Press, 1996.

Newman, Barbara. *From Virile Woman to Woman Christ: Studies in Medieval Religion and Literature*. Philadelphia: University of Pennsylvania Press, 1995.

Nichols, John A. and Lillian Thomas Shank, eds. *Medieval Religious Women*. Vols I-UL. Kalamazoo: Cistercian Publications, 1984–95.

Norris, Pamela. *Eve: A Biography*. New York: New York University Press, 1999.

Oden, Thomas C. *John Wesley's Teaching: Pastoral Theology*. Vol. 3. Grand Rapids: Zondervan, 2012.

O'Donnell, James. *Augustine: A New Biography*. New York: Harper Collins, 2005.

O'Faolain, Julia, and Lauren Martines, eds. *Not in God's Image: Women in History from the Greeks to the Victorians*. New York: Harper and Row, 1973.

Olson, Roger. *The Westminster Handbook to Evangelical Theology*. Louisville: Westminster John Knox Press, 2004.

Ortwell, John H. *And Sarah Laughed: The Status of Women in the Old Testament*. Philadelphia: Westminster Press, 1977.

Osborn, E. *Tertullian: First Theologian of the West*. Cambridge: Cambridge University Press, 1997.

Otterbein, Adam J. *The Diaconate According to the Apostolic Tradition of Hippolytus and Derived Documents*. Washington, D.C.: Catholic University of America Press, 1945.

Oulton, J. E. L. *Alexandrian Christianity*. Philadelphia: Westminster, 1954.

Owst Gerald R. *Literature and Pulpit in Medieval England*. Cambridge: Cambridge University Press, 1933.

Ozment, Steven. *When Fathers Ruled: Family Life in Reformation Europe*. Cambridge: Harvard University Press, 1983.

Pagels, Elaine. *Adam, Eve, and the Serpent*. New York: Random House, 1988.

Parker, T. H. L. *Calvin: An Introduction to His Thought*. Louisville: Westminster John Knox Press, 1995.

Pasture, Patrick, Jan Art and Thomas Buerman. *Gender and Christianity in Modern Europe: Beyond the Feminization Thesis*. Leuven, Belgium: Leuven University Press, 2012.

Payer, Pierre J. *The Fall, Original Sin, and Concupiscence*. Toronto: University of Toronto Press, 1993.

Payne, Philip. *Man and Woman, One in Christ: An Exegetical and Theological Study of Paul's Letter*. Grand Rapids: Zondervan, 2009.

Peterfeso, Jill. *Womanpriest: The Tradition and Transgression in the Contemporary Catholic Church*. New York, NY: Fordham University Press, 2020.

Peters, Edward, ed. *Heresy and Authority in Medieval Europe: Documents in Translation*. Philadelphia: University of Pennsylvania Press, 1980.

Petri, Thomas. *Aquinas and the Theology of the Body: The Thomist Foundations of John Paul II's Anthropology*. Washington, D.C.: Catholic University of American Press, 2016.

Petroff, Elizabeth. *Body and Soul: Essays on Women and Mysticism*. New York: Oxford University Press, 1994.

Phillips, J.A. *The History of an Idea: Eve*. New York: Harper and Row, 1984.

Pierce, Ronald W. and Rebecca Merrill Groothuis. *Discovering Biblical Equality: Complementarity Without Hierarchy*. Downers Grove: IVP Academic, 2005.

Polidoulis Kapsalis, Maria-Fotini. 2001. "Image as authority in the writings of John Chrysostom." PHD Dissertation: University of St. Michael's College, 2001.

Poythress, Vern S. and Wayne A. Grudem. *The Gender-Neutral Bible Controversy: Muting the Masculinity of God's Words*. Nashville: Broadman and Holman, 2000.

Pomeroy, Sarah. *Goddesses, Whores, Wives, and Slaves: Women in Classical Antiquity*. New York: Schocken Books, 1995.

Porterfield, Amanda. *Female Piety in Puritan New England: The Emergence of Religious Humanism*. New York: Oxford University Press, 1992.

Power, Eileen. *Medieval Women*, edited by M.M. Postan. Cambridge: Cambridge University Press, 1975.

Putney, Clifford. *Muscular Christianity: Manhood and Sports in Protestant America, 1880–1920*. Cambridge: Harvard University Press, 2001.

Radford Ruether, Rosemary, and Rosemary Skinner Keller, eds. *Women and Religion in America*, Vol. 2, *The Colonial and Revolutionary Periods*. San Francisco: Harper and Row, 1983.

Rankin, D. I. *Tertullian and the Church*. Cambridge: Cambridge University Press, 1995.

Raser, Harold E. *Phoebe Palmer: Her Life and Thought*. Lewiston: The Edwin Mellen Press, 1987.

Richter, Daniel K. *Before the Revolution*. Cambridge: Harvard University Press, 2011.

Rogers, Katharine M. *The Troublesome Helpmate: A History of Misogyny in Literature*. Seattle: University of Washington Press, 1966.

Rubin, Miri and Walter Simmons, eds. *The Cambridge History of Christianity: Christianity in Western Europe c. 1100–1500*. New York: Cambridge University Press, 2009.

Ruether, Rosemary Radford and Rosemary Skinner Keller. *Woman and Religion in America: The Nineteenth Century*, Vol 1. San Francisco: Harper and Row, 1981.

_____. *Religion and Sexism: Images of Woman in the Jewish and Christian Traditions*. Eugene: Wipf and Stock Publishers, 1998.

_____. *Women and Redemption: A Theological History*. Minneapolis: Fortress Press, 1998.

Rummel, Erika, ed. *Erasmus on Women*. Toronto: University of Toronto Press, 1996.

Scarre, Geoffrey and John Callow. *Witchcraft and Magic in Sixteenth and Seventeenth-Century Europe*, 2nd ed. Basingstoke: Palgrave, 2001.

Schenk, Christine. *Crispina and Her Sisters: Women and Authority in Early Christianity*. Philadelphia: Fortress Press, 2017.

Schneider, Carl J. and Dorothy Schneider. *In Their Own Right: This History of American Clergywomen*. New York: The Crossroad Publishing Company, 1997.

Scholz, Susanne. *The Bible as Political Artifact: On the Feminist Study of the Hebrew Bible*. Minneapolis: 1517 Media, Fortress Press, 2017.

Seaver, Paul S. *Wallington's World: A Puritan Artisan in Seventeenth-Century London*. Stanford: Stanford University Press, 1985.

Semple, Robert. *History of the Rise and Progress of the Baptists in Virginia*. Richmond: privately printed, 1810.

Sherman-White, A. N. *Roman Citizenship*. Oxford: Oxford University Press, 1979.

Sider, R. D. *Ancient Rhetoric and the Art of Tertullian*. Oxford: Oxford University Press, 1971.

_____. *Christian and Pagan in the Roman Empire: The Witness of Tertullian*. Washington D.C.: The Catholic University of America Press, 2001.

Silver, Morris. Wives. *Single Women and "Bastards" in the Ancient Greek World: Law and Economics Perspectives*. Barnsley, UK: Oxbow Books, 2018.

Silverman, Kenneth, *The Life and Times of Cotton Mather*. New York: Harper and Row Publishers, 1984.

Soskice, Janet Martin. *After Eve: Women, Theology, and the Christian Tradition*. London: Collins Religious Division, 1990.

_____. *Feminism and Theology*. Oxford: Oxford University Press, 2003.

Southern, R. W. *Western Society and the Church in the Middle Ages*. London: Penguin Books, 1970.

Smiley, Sarah F. *The Fulness of Blessing- or, the Gospel of Christ, as Illustrated from the Book of Joshua*. London: Hodder and Stoughton, 1876.

Smith, Christian. *American Evangelicalism: Embattled and Thriving*. Chicago: The University of Chicago Press, 1998.

Spain, Rufus. *At Ease in Zion: Social History of Southern Baptists, 1865–1900*. Nashville: Vanderbilt University Press, 1961.

Stam, John. *Episcopacy in the Apostolic Tradition of Hippolytus*. Basel: Friedrich Reinhardt Komissionsverlag, 1969.

Stanton, Elizabeth C. *History of Woman Suffrage*, 6 vols. New York: Fowler and Wells, 1881.

Stearns, Jonathan F. *A Discourse of Female Influence, and the True Christian Mode of Its Exercise*. Newburyport: John Tilton, 1837.

Stenton, Doris Mary. *The English Woman in History*. London: George Allen and Unwin, 1957.

Stiller, Brian. *Evangelicals Around the World: A Global Handbook for the 21st Century*. Nashville: Thomas Nelson, 2015.

Stokes, Claudia. *The Altar at Home: Sentimental Literature and Nineteenth-Century American Religion*. Philadelphia: University of Pennsylvania Press, 2014.

Stricklin, David. *A Genealogy of Dissent: Southern Baptist Protest in the Twentieth Century*. Lexington: University of Kentucky Press, 1999.

Stump, Eleonore and Norman Kretzmann, eds. *The Cambridge Companion to Augustine*. Cambridge University Press, 2001.

Sweet, Leonard. *The Minister's Wife: Her Role in Nineteenth-Century American Evangelicalism*. Philadelphia: Temple University Press, 1983.

Swidler Arlene and Leonard Swidler eds. *Women Priests*. Mahwah: Paulist Press, 1977.

Thompson, Bard. *Humanists and Reformers: A History of the Renaissance and Reformation*. Grand Rapids: William B. Eerdmans Publishing Company, 1996.

Townsley, Frances E. *The Self-Told Story of Frances E. Townsley*. Butler: Higley Publisher, 1908.

Torjesen, Karen Jo. *When Women Were Priests: Women's Leadership in the Early Church & the Scandal of their Subordination in the Rise of Christianity*. San Francisco: HarperCollins, 1993.

Trible, Phyllis. *God and the Rhetoric of Sexuality*. Philadelphia: Fortress Press, 1978.

Tuana, Nancy. *The Less Noble Sex: Scientific, Religious, and Philosophical Conceptions of Woman's Nature*. Bloomington: University of Indiana Press, 1983.

Tucker, Ruth A. and Walter Liefeld. *Daughters of the Church: Women and Ministry from the New Testament Times to the Present*. Grand Rapids: Zondervan, 1987.

Ulrich, Laurel Thatcher. *Good Wives: Image and Reality in the Lives of Women in Northern New England, 1650–1750*. New York: Random House, 1980.

Underhill, Edward Been, ed. *The Records of a Church Meeting in Broadmead, Bristol, 1640–1687*. London: J. Haddon, 1847.

Van Vuuren, Nancy. *The Subversion of Women as Practiced by Churches, Witch-Hunters and Other Sexists*. Philadelphia: Westminster Press, 1973.

Venarde, Bruce L. *Women's Monasticism and Medieval Society*. Ithaca: Cornell University Press, 1997.

Wakefield, Walter and Austin P. Evans, trans. *Heresies of the High Middle Ages*. New York: Columbia University Press, 1991.

Weidman, Judith L. ed. *Christian Feminism*. San Francisco: Harper & Row, 1984.

Wendel, Francois. *Calvin: Origins and Developments in His Religious Thought*. Grand Rapids: Baker Books, 1997.

Wessinger, Catherine, ed. *Religious Institutions and Women's Leadership*. Columbia: University of South Carolina Press, 1996.

Wickham, Chris. *Medieval Europe: From the Breakup of the Western Roman Empire to the Reformation*. New Haven: Yale University Press, 2016.

Wiesner-Hanks, Merry E. *Women and Gender in Early Modern Europe*. Cambridge: Cambridge University Press, 2008.

Willard, Frances E. *Glimpses of Fifty Years: The Autobiography of an American Woman*. Chicago: Woman's Temperance Publication Association/ H. J. Smith & Co., 1889.

Westerkamp, Marilyn J. *Women and Religion in Early America, 1600–1850: The Puritan and Evangelical Tradition*. London: Routledge, 1999.

Witherington, Ben. *Women and the Genesis of Christianity*. Cambridge: Cambridge University Press, 1990.

Woodbridge, John D. James III, *Church History, Volume Two: From Pre-Reformation to the Present Day*. Grand Rapids: Zondervan Academic, 2013.

Yakiyama, Mariko. "Maximilla's Redressing the Ignorance of Eve through Sexual Renunciation: A Comparison of the Acts of Andrew and the Writings of Clement of Alexandria" PHD Dissertation: Claremont Graduate University, 2007.

Encyclopedias, Dictionaries, Series

Audi, Robert, ed. *The Cambridge Dictionary of Philosophy*. Cambridge: Cambridge University Press, 1995.

Butler, Trent C., ed., *Holman Bible Dictionary*. Nashville: Holman Bible Publishers, 1991.

Cantor, Norman F., ed. *The Encyclopedia of the Middle Ages*. New York: Penguin, 1999.

Cross, F.L. and E. A. Livingstone, eds., *The Oxford Dictionary of the Christian Church*, 3rd ed. Oxford: Oxford University Press, 2005.

Dyck, Cornelius J. and Dennis D. Martin, eds. *The Mennonite Encyclopedia*. Vol 5. Scottsdate: Herald Press, 1990.

Ferguson, Everett, ed. *The Encyclopedia of the Middle Ages*, 2nd ed. New York: Garland Publishing, 1998.
Fitzgerald, Allan D. *Augustine: Through the Ages*. Grand Rapids: Eerdmans Publishing, 1999.
Hawthorne, Gerald F., Ralph P. Martin, and Daniel G. Reid, eds. *Dictionary of Paul and His Letters*. Downers Grove: InterVarsity Press, 1993.
Lindley, Susan Hill and Eleanor J. Stebner, eds. *The Westminster Handbook to Women in American Religious History*. Louisville: Westminster/John Knox Press, 2008.
Speake, Jennifer and Thomas G. Bergin, eds. *Encyclopedia of the Renaissance and Reformation*, rev. ed. Aylesbury: Market House Books, Ltd., 2004.

Commentaries

Albright, W. F. and C. S. *Matthew*. The Anchor Yale Bible Commentary Series. New York: Doubleday, 1971.
Achtemeier, Paul J. *First Peter*. Hermeneia Commentary Series on the Bible, edited by Helmut Koester. Philadelphia: Fortress Press, 1996.
Barth, Markus. *Ephesians: Translation and Commentary on Chapters 4–6*. The Anchor Yale Bible Commentary Series. New York: Doubleday, 1974.
Beasley-Murray, George R. *John*. Word Biblical Commentary Series, edited by David Allen Hubbard, Glenn W. Barker, John D. Watts, and Ralph P. Martin. Waco: Word Book Publishers, 1987.
Boling, Robert G. *Judges*. The Anchor Yale Bible Commentary Series. New York: Doubleday, 1975.
Bovon, Francois. *Luke 1:1–9:50*. Hermeneia Commentary Series on the Bible, edited by Helmut Koester. Philadelphia: Fortress Press, 2002.
Brown, Raymond E. *The Gospel According to John* (i–xii). The Anchor Yale Bible Commentary Series. New York: Doubleday, 1966.
Brown, Raymond E. *The Gospel According to John* (xiii-xxi). The Anchor Yale Bible Commentary Series. New York: Doubleday, 1970.
Budd, Philip J. *Numbers*. Waco: Word Book Publishers, 1984.
Bush, Frederic W. *Ruth, Esther*. Dallas: Word Book Publishers, 1996.
Butler, Trent C. *Judges*. Nashville: Thomas Nelson, 2009.
Christensen, Duane L. *Deuteronomy* 21:10–34.12. Nashville: Thomas Nelson, 2002.
Conzelmann, Hans. *1 Corinthians*. Hermeneia Commentary Series on the Bible, edited by Helmut Koester. Philadelphia: Fortress Press, 1976.

DeVries, Simon J. *1 Kings*. Waco: Word Book Publishers, 1985.

Dibelius, Martin. *The Pastoral Epistles*. Hermeneia Commentary Series on the Bible, edited by Helmut Koester. Philadelphia: Fortress Press, 1972.

Durham, John I. *Exodus*. Waco: Word Book Publishers, 1987.

Evans, Craig A. *Mark 8:27–16:20*. Word Biblical Commentary Series, edited by David Allen Hubbard, Glenn W. Barker, John D. Watts, and Ralph P. Martin. Nashville: Thomas Nelson, 2000.

Fitzmeyer, Joseph A. *The Gospel According to Luke (x–xxiv)*. The Anchor Yale Bible Commentary Series. New Haven: Yale University Press, 1985.

Guelich, Robert A. *Mark: 1–8:26*. Word Biblical Commentary Series, edited by David Allen Hubbard, Glenn W. Barker, John D. Watts, and Ralph P. Martin. Dallas: Word Book Publishers, 1989.

Hagner, Donald A. *Matthew 1–13*. Word Biblical Commentary Series, edited by David Allen Hubbard, Glenn W. Barker, John D. Watts, and Ralph P. Martin. Dallas: Word Book Publishers, 1993.

_____. *Matthew 14–28*. Word Biblical Commentary Series, edited by David Allen Hubbard, Glenn W. Barker, John D. Watts, and Ralph P. Martin. Dallas: Word Book Publishers, 1995.

Hartley, John E. *Leviticus*. Nashville: Thomas Nelson, 1992.

Johnson, Luke Timothy. *The First and Second Letters to Timothy*. The Anchor Yale Bible Commentary Series. New York: Doubleday, 2001.

Klein, Ralph W. *1 Samuel*. Waco: Word Book Publishers, 1983.

Lea, Thomas D. and Hayne P. Griffith, Jr. *The New American Commentary: 1, 2 Timothy, Titus*. Nashville: Broadman Press, 1992.

Levine, Baruch A. *Numbers 1–20*. The Anchor Yale Bible Commentary Series. New York: Doubleday, 1993.

Lincoln, Andrew T. *Ephesians*. Word Biblical Commentary Series, edited by David Allen Hubbard, Glenn W. Barker, John D. Watts, and Ralph P. Martin. Waco: Word Book Publishers, 1990.

Longenecker, Richard N. *Galatians*. Word Biblical Commentary Series, edited by David Allen Hubbard, Glenn W. Barker, John D. Watts, and Ralph P. Martin. Dallas: Word Book Publishers, 1990.

Luz, Ulrich. *Matthew 8–20*. Hermeneia Commentary Series on the Bible, edited by Helmut Koester. Philadelphia: Fortress Press, 2001.

_____. *Matthew 21–28*. Hermeneia Commentary Series on the Bible, edited by Helmut Koester. Philadelphia: Fortress Press, 2005.

Mann, C.S. *Mark*. The Anchor Yale Bible Commentary Series. New York: Doubleday, 1986.

Martyn, J. Louis. *Galatians*. The Anchor Yale Bible Commentary Series. New York: Doubleday, 1997.

McCarter, P. Kyle. *II Samuel*. The Anchor Yale Bible Commentary Series. New York: Doubleday, 1984.

Murphy, Roland E. *Proverbs*. Word Bible Commentary. Nashville: Thomas Nelson, 1998.

Michaels, J. Ramsey. *1 Peter*. Word Biblical Commentary Series, edited by David Allen Hubbard, Glenn W. Barker, John D. Watts, and Ralph P. Martin. Waco: Word Book Publishers, 1988.

Milgrom, Jacob. *Leviticus 1–16*. The Anchor Yale Bible Commentary Series. New York: Doubleday, 1991.

Milgrom, Jacob. *Leviticus 17–22*. The Anchor Yale Bible Commentary Series. New York: Doubleday, 2000.

Murphy, Roland E. *Ecclesiastes*. Dallas: Word Book Publishers, 1992.

Newsome, Carol A. and Sharon H. Ringe, eds. *Women's Bible Commentary With Apocrypha: Extended Edition*. Louisville: Westminster John Knox Press, 1992.

Noland, John. *Luke 9:21–18*. Word Biblical Commentary Series, edited by David Allen Hubbard, Glenn W. Barker, John D. Watts, and Ralph P. Martin. Dallas: Word Book Publishers, 1993.

O'Brien, Peter T. *Colossians, Philemon*. Word Biblical Commentary Series, edited by David Allen Hubbard, Glenn W. Barker, John D. Watts, and Ralph P. Martin. Waco: Word Book Publishers, 1982.

Oden, Thomas C., ed. *Ancient Christian Commentary on Scripture: Colossians, 1–2 Thessalonians, 1–2 Timothy, Titus, Philemon*. Downers Grove: Intervarsity Press, 2000.

_____. *Ancient Christian Commentary on Scripture: Galatians, Ephesians, Philippians*. Downers Grove: Intervarsity Press, 1999.

_____. *Ancient Christian Commentary on Scripture: 1–2 Corinthians*. Downers Grove: Intervarsity Press, 1999.

_____. *Ancient Christian Commentary on Scripture: Genesis 1–11*. Downers Grove: Intervarsity Press, 2001.

Orr, Walter F. and James Arthur Walther. *1 Corinthians*. The Anchor Yale Bible Commentary Series. New York: Doubleday, 1976.

Propp, William H. *Exodus 19–40*. The Anchor Yale Bible Commentary Series. New York: Doubleday, 2006.

Speiser, E. A. *Genesis*. The Anchor Yale Bible Commentary Series. New York: Doubleday, 1987.

Quinn, Jerome D. *The Letter to Titus.* The Anchor Yale Bible Commentary Series. New York: Doubleday, 1990.

Wenham, Gordon J. *Genesis 1–15.* Word Biblical Commentary Series. Grand Rapids: Zondervan, 1987.

Wenham, Gordon J. *Genesis 1–15.* Word Biblical Commentary Series. Dallas: Word Book Publishers, 1994.

Papal Encyclicals

Leo XIII. Encyclical Letter, *Quod Apostolici Munereris*, 28 December 1878.

Leo XIII. Encyclical Letter, *Arcanum Divinae*, 10 February 1880.

Leo XIII. Encyclical Letter, *Rerum Novarum*, 15 May 1891.

Pope Pius XI. *Casti Connubii,* 30 December 1930, Papal Archive, last accessed 1 July 2021, https://www.vatican.va/content/pius-xi/en/encyclicals/documents/hf_pxi_enc_19301231_casti-connubii.html.

Pope John XXIII. Encyclical Letter, *Pacem in Terris*, 11 April 1963.

Pope John Paul II. *On the Dignity of Women*, Section 7, 15 August 1988.

Pope John Paul II. *Ordinatio Sacerdotali,* 22 May 1994, New Advent, last accessed 1 July 2021, https://www.newadvent.org/library/docs_jp02os.htm.

John Paul II, *Ad tuendam fidem.* 15 July 1998, Papal Archive, last accessed 1 July 2021, https://www.vatican.va/roman_curia/congregations/cfaith/documents/rc_con_cfaith_doc_1998_professio-fidei_en.html.

Pope Benedict XVI, Encyclical Letter, *Caritas in Veritate,* 29 June 2009, Papal Archive, last accessed 1 July 2021, http://www.vatican.va/content/benedict-xvi/en/encyclicals/documents/hf_ben-xvi_enc_20090629_caritas-in-veritate.html.

Journal Articles

Allen, Christine Garside. "Plato on Women." *Feminist Studies*, no. 2/3 (1975): 131–138.

Anders, Sarah Frances. "The Role of Women in American Religion." *Southwestern Journal of Theology* 18, (1976): 51–61.

Anderson, Gary. "Celibacy or Consummation in the Garden? Reflections of Early Jewish and Christian Interpretations of the Garden of Eden." *The Harvard Theological Review* 82, no. 2 (April 1989): 121–148.

Barfoot, Charles H. and Gerald T. Sheppard, "Prophetic Vs. Priestly: The Changing Role of Women Clergy in Classical Pentecostal Churches." *Review of Religious Research* 22, (September 1980): 8.

Barr, Jane. "The Vulgate Genesis and Jerome's Attitudes to Women." in *Studia, Patristica* XVIII (Pergamon Press, Oxford and New York, 1982), and in OTWSA no. 20/21 (Pretoria 1982): 1–20.

Bartkowski, John P. "Debating Patriarchy: Discursive Disputes over Spousal Authority among Evangelical Family Commentators." *Journal for the Scientific Study of Religion* 36, no. 3 (September 1997): 393–410.

_____. and Lynn M Hempel. "Sex and Gender Traditionalism Among Conservative Protestants: Does the Difference Make a Difference?" *Journal for the Scientific Study of Religion* 48, no. 4 (December 2009): 806–816.

Beagon, Philip M. "The Cappadocian Fathers, Women and Ecclesiastical Politics." *Vigiliae Christianae* 49, no. 2 (May 1995): 165–179.

Bendroth, Margaret Lamberts. "Fundamentalism and Femininity: Points of Encounter Between Religious Conservatives and Women, 1919–1935." *Church History* 61, no. 2 (June 1992): 221–233.

Bizzell, Patricia. "Frances Willard, Phoebe Palmer, and the Ethos of the Methodist Woman Preacher." *Rhetoric Society Quarterly* 36, no. 4 (Autumn 2006): 377–398.

Blum, Edward. "Paul has been Forgotten: Women, Gender, and Revivalism in the Gilded Age." *The Journal of the Gilded Age and Progressive Era* 3, no. 3 (July 2004): 247–270.

Blumhofer, Edith. "Women in Pentecostalism." *Union Seminary Quarterly Review* 57, (2003): 101–122.

Bonaiuti, Ernesto and Giorgio La Piana. "The Genesis of St. Augustine's Idea of Original Sin." *The Harvard Theological Review* 10, no. 2 (April 1917): 159–175.

Breyfogle, Caroline M. "The Social Status of Woman in the Old Testament." *The Biblical World* 35, no. 2 (February 1910): 106–116.

Brooten, Bernadette J. "Jewish Women's History in the Roman Period: A Task for Christian Theology." *The Harvard Theological Review* 79, no. 1/3 (Jan.-Jul. 1986): 22–30.

Bullough, Vern L. "Sex Education in Medieval Christianity." *The Journal of Sex Research* 13, no. 3 (August 1977): 185–196.

Calhoun, David B. "John Knox (1514–1572) "After Five Hundred Years." *Presbyterian* 40, no. 1–2 (Fall 2014): 1–13.

Carlson, Eric Josef. "Clerical Marriage and the English Reformation." *Journal of British Studies*. 31, no. 1 (January 1992): 1–31.

Castelli, Elizabeth. "Virginity and Its Meaning for Woman's Sexuality in Early Christianity." *Journal of Feminist Studies in Religion* 2, no. 1 (Spring 1986): 61–88.

Chaves, Mark and James Cavendish. "Recent Changes in Women's Ordination Conflicts: The Effect of a Social Movement on Intraorganizational Controversy." *Journal for the Scientific Study of Religion* 36, no. 4 (December 1997): 574–584.

Church, F. Forrester. "Sex and Salvation in Tertullian." *The Harvard Theological Review* 68, no. 2 (April 1975): 83–101.

Clark, Elizabeth. "Ideology, History, and the Construction of "Woman" in Late Ancient Christianity." *Journal of Early Christian Studies* 2, (1994): 155–184.

_____. "John Chrysostom and the Subintroductae." *Church History* 46, (1977): 171–185.

_____. "Women, Gender, and the Study of Church History." *Church History* 70, no. 3 (September 2001): 395–426.

Classen, Albrecht and Tanya Amber Settle. "Women in Martin Luther's Life and Theology." *German Studies Review* 14, no. 2 (May 1991): 231–260.

Como, David R. "Women, Prophesy, and Authority in Early Stuart Puritanism." *Huntington Library Quarterly* 61, no. 2 (1998): 203–222.

Cott, Nancy F. "Young Women in the Second Great Awakening." *Feminist Studies* 3, no. 1 and 2 (Autumn 1975): 15–29.

Cowing, Cedric B. "Sex and Preaching in the Great Awakening." *American Quarterly* 20, no. 3 (Autumn 1968): 624–644.

Davies, J. G. "Deacons, Deaconesses and the Minor Orders in the Patristic Period." *Journal of Ecclesiastical History* 14, no. 1 (April 1963): 11–15.

Denison, John and John Denison Champlin. "The Tragedy of Anne Hutchinson." *Journal of American History* 5, (1913): 1–11.

Desjardins, Michel. "Why Women Should Cover Their Heads and Veil Their Faces: Clement of Alexandria's Understanding of The Body and His Rhetorical Strategies in the *Paedagogus*." *Scriptura*, no. 90 (2005): 700–708.

Dodds, E.R. "Augustine's Confessions: A Study of Spiritual Maladjustment." *The Hibbert Journal* 26, (1927): 459–473.

Dossey, Leslie. "Wife Beating and Manliness in Late Antiquity." *Past and Present*, no. 199 (May 2008): 3–40.

Dowland, Seth. "Family Values and the Formation of a Christian Right Agenda." *Church History* 78, (September 2009): 606–631.

Dray, Stephen. "Women in Church History: An Examination of pre-Reformation Convictions and Practice." *Evangel* 21, no. 1 (Spring 2003): 22–25.

Dunn, Geoffrey D. "Rhetoric and Tertullian's 'De virginibus velandis.'" *Vigiliae Christianae* 59, no. 1 (February 2005): 1–30.

———. "Tertullian and Rebekah: A Re-Reading of an 'Anti-Jewish' Argument in Early Christian Literature." *Vigiliae Christianae*, (1998): 119–145.

Durso, Pamela R. "She-Preachers, Bossy Women, and Children of the Devil: Women Ministers in the Baptist Tradition, 1609–1612." *Review and Expositor* 110, (Winter 2013): 33–47.

Edwards, Morgan. "Materials Towards a History of Baptists in the Province of North Carolina," cited in the *North Carolina Historical Review*, (July 1930): 384–391.

Elshtain, Jean Bethke. "Christianity and Patriarchy: The Odd Alliance." *Modern Theology* 9, no. 2 (April 1993): 109–122.

Eriksen, Annelin. "Sarah's Sinfuflness Egalitarianism, Denied Difference, and Gender in Pentecostal Christianity." *Current Anthropology* 55, no. 10 (December 2014): 262–270.

Everton, Sean F. "The Promise Keepers: Religious Revival or Third Wave of the Religious Right?" *Review of Religious Research* 43, no. 1 (September 2001): 51–69.

Farley, Margaret A. "Sources of Sexual Inequality in the History of Christian Thought." *Journal of Religion* 2, (1976): 152–176.

Feige, Diana and Franz Feige. "Love, Marriage, and Family in Puritan Society." *Dialogue and Alliance* 9, no. 1 (Spring/Summer 1995): 96–114.

Felch, Susan M. "The Rhetoric of Biblical Authority: John Knox and the Question of Women." *The Sixteenth Century Journal* 26, no. 4 (Winter 1995): 805–822.

Femenias, Maria Luisa. "Women and Natural Hierarchy in Aristotle." *Hypatia* 9, no. 1 (Winter 1994): 164–172.

Ferry, Anne. "Milton's Creation of Eve." *Studies in English Literature, 1500–1900* 28, no. 1 (Winter 1988): 113–132.

Fessenden, Tracy. "The Convent, the Brothel, and Protestant Woman's Sphere." *Signs* 25, no. 2 (Winter 2000): 451–478.

Finlay, B. "Was Tertullian a Misogynist? A Reconsideration." *The Journal of the Historical Society* 3, no. 3–4 (June 2003): 503–525.

Fletcher, Anthony. "The Future of Patriarchy in England 1560–1660." *Transactions of the Royal Historical Society* 4, (1994): 61–81.

Frohnhofen, Herbert. "Women Deacons in the Early Church." *Theology Digest* 34, no. 2 (Summer 1987): 149–153.

Gallagher, Sally K. "The Marginalization of Evangelical Feminism." *Sociology of Religion* 65, no. 3 (Autumn 2004): 215–237.

Graham, Billy. "Jesus and the Liberated Woman." *Ladies Home Journal* (December 1970): 40–44, 114.

Grasham, Bill. "The Role of Women in the American Restoration Movement." *Restoration Quarterly* 4, no. 4 (1999): 211–240.

Greaves, Richard L. "The Role of Women in Early English Nonconformity." *Church History* 52, no. 3 (1983): 299–311.

Green, TeResa. "A Gendered Spirit: Race, Class, and Sex in the African American Church." *Race, Gender, and Class in American Politics* 10, no. 1 (2003): 115–128.

Greenspahn, Frederick E. "A Typology of Biblical Women." *Judaism* 32, (1983): 43–50.

Gustafson, Sandra. "Jonathan Edwards and the Reconstruction of 'Feminine' Speech." *American Literary History* 6, no. 2 (September 1994): 185–212.

Hamilton, Michael S. "Women, Public Ministry, and American Fundamentalism, 1920–1950." *Religion and American Culture: A Journal of Interpretation* 3, no. 2 (Summer 1993): 171–196.

Harrison, N.V. "Women, Human Identity, and the Image of God: Antiochene Interpretations." *Journal of Early Christian Studies* 9, no. 2 (Summer, 2001): 205–224.

Hellig, Jocelyn. "Lilith as a Focus of Judaism's Gender Construction." *Dialogue & Alliance* 12, no. 1 (Spring-Summer 1998): 35–49.

Hendrix, Scott. "Masculinity and Patriarchy in Reformation Germany." *Journal of the History of Ideas* 56, no. 2 (April 1995): 177–193.

Herndon, E. W. "Woman's Suffrage." *Christian Quarterly Review* 7, (October 1888): 608.

Hieatt, A. Kent. "Eve as Reason in a Tradition of Allegorical Interpretation of the Fall." *Journal of the Warburg and Courtland Institutes* 43, (1980): 221–226.

Higgins, Jean M. "The Myth of Eve: The Temptress." *Journal of the American Academy of Religion* 44, (December 1976): 639–647.

Hogeland, Ronald W. "Charles Hodge, the Association of Gentlemen and Ornamental Womanhood: 1825–1855." *Journal of Presbyterian History* 53, no. 3 (1975): 251–52.

Horowitz, Maryanne Cline. "Aristotle and Women." *Journal of the History of Biology* 9, no. 2. (Autumn 1976): 183–213.

———. "The Image of God: Is Woman Included?" *The Harvard Theological Review* 72, no. 3–4 (July–October 1979): 175–206.

Hunter, David G. "The Paradise of Patriarchy: Ambrosiaster on Woman as (Not) God's Image." *The Journal of Theological Studies* 43, no. 2 (October 1992): 447–449.

Hutchins, Zachary. "Edwards and Eve: Finding Feminist Strains in the Great Awakening's Patriarch." *American Literature* 43, no. 3 (2008): 671–686.

Hutson, Christopher R. "Saved Through Childbearing: The Jewish Context of 1 Timothy 2:15." *Novum Testamentum* 56, (2014): 392–410.

Hutton, Ronald. "Writing the History of Witchcraft: A Personal View." *The Pomegranate: The International Journal of Pagan Studies* 12, (2010): 239–262.

Karras, Valerie. "Male Domination of Women in the Writings of Saint John Chrysostom." *The Greek Orthodox Theological Review* 36, no. 2 (1991) 131–139.

Keane, Marie-Henry. "Woman in the Theological Anthropology of the Early Fathers." *Journal of Theology for Southern Africa* 62, (March 1988): 3–13.

Kerber, Linda. "The Republican Mother: Women and the Enlightenment—An American Perspective." *American Quarterly* 28, no. 2 (1976): 187–205.

Kinder, Donald. "Clement of Alexandria: Conflicting Views on Women." *The Second Century Journal: A Journal of Early Christian Studies* 7, no. 4 (Winter 1989–90): 219–220.

Lane, Belden C. "Two Schools of Desire: Nature and Marriage in Seventeenth-Century Puritanism." *Church History* 69, no. 2 (June 2000): 372–402.

Lindsell, Harold. "Egalitarianism and Scriptural Infallibility." *Christianity Today* 20 (1976).

———. "Eve's Second Apple." *Christianity Today* 14 (August 1970).

Lievestro, C. T. "Tertullian and the Sensus Argument." *The Journal of the History of Ideas* 17, no. 2 (April 1956): 264–268.

Loveland, Anne C. "Domesticity and Religion in the Antebellum Period: The Career of Phoebe Palmer." *The Historian* 39, no. 3 (May 1977): 455–471.

Mattox, Mickey L. "Luther on Eve, Women and the Church." *Lutheran Quarterly* 17, (2003): 456–474.

McBeth, Harry Leon. "The Changing Role of Women in Baptist History." *Southwestern Journal of Theology* 22, (Fall 1979): 84–96.

_____. "The Ordination of Women." *Review & Expositor* 78, no. 4 (Fall 1981): 515–530.

McChrystal, Deirdre Keenan. "Redeeming Eve." *English Literary Renaissance* 23, no. 3 (Autumn 1993): 490–508.

McCluskey, Colleen. "An Unequal Relationship between Equals: Thomas Aquinas on Marriage." *History of Philosophy Quarterly* 24, no. 1 (January 2007): 1–18.

McCoy, Katie. "Anchored against the Tide: Female Pastors in the SBC and Contemporary Drifts Toward Compromise." *Baptist Theology*, (January 2011): 1–9.

McLoughlin, William G. "Billy Sunday and the Working Girl of 1915." *Journal of Presbyterian History* (1962–1985) 54, no. 3 (Fall 1976): 376–384.

McNamara, J. A. "Sexual Equality and the Cult of Virginity in Early Christian Thought." *Feminist Studies* 3, (1976): 145–158.

Milhaven, John Giles. "Thomas Aquinas on Sexual Pleasure." *The Journal of Religious Ethics* 5, no. 2 (Fall 1977): 157–181.

Mouton, Ethan, "Reimagining Ancient Household Ethos? On the Implied Rhetorical Effect of Ephesians 5:21–23." *Neotestamentica* 48, no. 1 (2014): 163–185.

Nolan, Michael, "The Mysterious Affair at Macon: The Bishops and the Souls of Women." *New Blackfriars* 74, no. 876 (November 1993): 501–507.

Norton, Meghan. "The Adulterous Wife: A Cross-Historical and Interdisciplinary Approach," *Buffalo Women's Law Journal* 6, Article 5 (2007): 1–22.

Olugbade, Kola. "Women in Plato's Republic." *The Indian Journal of Political Science* 50, no. 4 (October–December 1989): 503–518.

O'Meara, John. "Saint Augustine's Understanding of the Creation and Fall." *The Maynooth Review* 10, (May 1984): 52–62.

O'Neal, William J. "The Status of Women in Ancient Athens." *International Social Sciences Review* 68, no. 3 (Summer 1993): 115–121.

Padia, Chandrakala. "Plato, Aristotle, Rousseau and Hegel on Women: A Critique." *The Indian Journal of Political Science* 55, no. 1 (January–March 1994): 27–36.

Patterson, Cynthia. "'Not Worth the Rearing:' The Causes of Infant Exposure in Ancient Greece." *Transactions of the American Philological Association* (1974–2014) 115, (1985): 103–123.

Patterson, Dorothy. "Why I Believe Southern Baptist Churches Should Not Ordain Women." *Baptist History and Heritage* 23, no. 3 (July 1988): 56–62.

Phipps, William E. "Adams Rib: Bone of Contention." *Theology Today* 45, no. 1 (1988): 263–273.

———. "The Menstrual Taboo in the Judeo-Christian Tradition." *Journal of Religion and Health* 19, no. 4 (Winter 1980): 298–303.

Poorthuis, M. "Who is to Blame: Adam or Eve? A possible Jewish source for Ambrose's 'De paradiso' 12, 56." *Vigiliae Christianae* 50, no. 2 (1996): 125–135.

Potter, Mary. "Gender Equality and Gender Hierarchy in Calvin's Theology." *Signs* 11, no. 4 (Summer 1986): 725–739.

Reese, Alan W. "Learning Virginity: Erasmus' Ideal of Christian Marriage." *Bibliotheque d"Humaninisme et Renaissance* 57, no. 3 (1995): 551–567.

Reid, Melissa. "Unjust Signifying Practices: Submission and Subordination Among Christian Fundamentalists." *Journal of Feminist Studies in Religion* 29, no. 2 (2013): 154–161.

Roy, J. "An Alternative Sexual Morality for Classical Athenians." *Greece & Rome* 44, no. 1 (April 1977): 11–22.

Ruether, Rosemary Radford. "Church and Family II: Church and Family in the Medieval and Reformation Periods." *New Blackfriars* 65, no. 764 (February 1984): 77–86.

———. "The Feminist Critique in Religious Studies." *Soundings: An Interdisciplinary Journal* 64, no. 4 (1981): 388–402.

———. "Crisis in Sex and Race: Black Theology vs. Feminist Theology." *Christianity and Crisis* 34, (15 April 1974): 67–73.

Russett, Cynthia. "All About Eve. What Men have Thought About Women Thinking." *The American Scholar* 74, no. 2 (Spring 2005): 41–48.

Shaw, Susan M. "Gracious Submission: Southern Baptist Fundamentalists and Women." *NWSA Journal* 20, no 1 (Spring 2008): 51–77.

Sider, R. D. "Structure and Design in the De resurrectione mortuorum of Tertullian." *Vigiliae Christianae* 23, (1969): 177–196.

Smith, Nicholas D. "Plato and Aristotle on the Nature of Women." *Journal of History of Philosophy"* 21, no. 4 (October 1983): 467–78.

Stauffer, Dana Jalbert. "Aristotle's Account of the Subjection of Women." *The Journal of Politics* 70, no. 4 (October 2008): 929–941.

Steenberg, M.C. "Impatience and Humanity's Sinful State in Tertullian of Carthage." *Vigiliae Christianae* 62, (2008): 107–132.

Steinmetz, David C. "Theological Reflections on the Reformation and the Status of Women." *Duke Divinity School Review* 41, (1976): 197–207.

Surburg, Raymond F. "The Place of Woman in the Old Testament." *Springfielder* 33, no. 4 (1970): 27–37.

Sutton, Agneta. "The Complementarity and Symbolism of the Two Sexes: Karl Barth, Hans Urs von Balthasar, and John Paul II." *New Blackfriars* 87, no. 10 (July 2006): 418–433.

Thompson, Becky. "Multiracial Feminism: Recasting the Chronology of Second Wave Feminism." *Feminist Studies* 28, no. 2 (Summer 2002): 336–360.

Thompson, John L. "Creata ad Imaginem Dei, Licet Secundo Gradu: Woman as the Image of God According to John Calvin." *Harvard Theological Review* 81, no. 2 (April 1988): 125–143.

_____. "Patriarchs, Polygamy, and Private Resistance: John Calvin and Other on Breaking God's Rules." *The Sixteenth Century Journal* 25, no. 1 (Spring 1994): 3–27.

Valantasis, Richard. "Body, Hierarchy, and Leadership in Chrysostom's On the Priesthood." *Greek Orthodox Theological Review* 30, no. 4: 455–471.

Weiler, Anton. G. Barker and J. Barker "Desiderius Erasmus of Rotterdam on Marriage and Divorce." *Dutch Review of History*, no. 84 (2004): 155.

Weisner, Merry E. "Beyond Women and the Family: Towards a Gender Analysis of the Reformation." *Sixteenth Century Journal* 18, no. 3 (Autumn 1987): 311–321.

_____. "Women, Gender, and Church History." *Church History* 71, no. 3 (September 2002): 600–620.

Welter, Barbara. "The Cult of True Womanhood, 1820–1860." *American Quarterly* 18, no. 2 (Summer, 1966): 151–174.

Williams, Daniel K. "Jerry Falwell's Sunbelt Politics: The Regional Origins of the Moral Majority." *Journal of Policy History* 22, (2010): 125–47.

Zamfir, Korinna. "The Quest for the 'Eternal Feminine.': An Essay on the Effective History of Gen1–3 with Respect to Women." *Annali Di Storia Dell-Essegessi* 24, no. 2 (2007): 501–522.

INDEX

Abel 10
Abelard, Peter 133
Abigail 33, 34, 35
Abimelech 15, 16
Abraham 10, 15, 16, 27, 28, 46, 57
Absalom 25, 26
Adam – Aquinas 135, 136;
 Augustine of Hippo 108–112;
 Calvin 190–192; Chrysostom
 87–89, 91; Clement of
 Alexandria 74, 76–78; Donne
 204–205; Edwards 226–227;
 Erasmus 176; Graham 278;
 Jerome 99; Lindsell 278;
 MacArthur 283; Luther
 180–183, 186, 187; Mather,
 Cotton 211; Milton 222–224;
 Philo 48–51; Tertullian 79–82
African Methodist
 Episcopal (AME) 304
Ahab 31, 32, 200
Ainsworth, Henry 206, 206
Alexander, Archibald 264
Allen, Sister Prudence 256
Allison, Emily 285
Ambroister 152

Ambrose of Milan 45, 150
American Baptist Churches USA
 (ABCUSA) 293, 299
American Lutheran
 Church (ALC) 295
African Methodist Episcopal
 Church Zion (AME) 304
Amnon 25
Ancrene Riwle 163
Angela of Toulouse 170
Anselm of Canterbury 158
Apocrypha xv, 11, 13
Apostolic Constitutions
 74, 121, 122
Aquinas, Thomas xvi, 42,
 130–136, 138–142, 156, 158,
 160, 171, 309
Aristotle xv, 37, 42–45, 51, 66, 131,
 134, 204, 309
Arius 98
Asherah 32
Assemblies of God 272,
 301, 302, 306
Assumption of Mary 157
Athena 69
Augustine of Canterbury 149

Augustine of Hippo xv, 39, 45, 73, 106–117, 129, 130, 132–134, 140, 142, 143, 150, 151, 164, 181, 190, 204, 222, 309
Augustus Caesar 60
Avignon Papacy 127
Avila, Teresa 160

Baal 32
Babylonian Captivity 127
Bancroft, Elizabeth 221
Barr, Beth Allison 286, 293
Barr, Jane 103
Barret, Donna L. 302
Bathsheba 23–25, 35, 98
Bead, Noel 177
Beecher, Lyman 234
Beguines 147–149, 171, 199
Bellis, Alice Ogden 12
Bendroth, Margaret Lamberts 266, 267, 269
Benedict, David 229
Bernard of Clairvaux 142, 145, 158, 160
Bird, Phyllis 2–4
Bishop, Bridget 219
Blaesilla 105
Blaugdone, Barbara 221
Bloom, Edward 246
Boaz 18, 21, 22, 29, 34
Boleyn, Anne (queen of England) 171, 200
Bolton, Robert 206
Bonaventure, Saint 133
Booth, Catherine 244
Boryczka, Jocelyn 210
Bracton, Henry 138
Brenner, Athalya 33
Bromyard, John 162

Bruno of Olmutz 148
Bude, Guillaume 179
Bulkley, Peter 217
Burk, Denny 290

Cain 10, 84
Calvin, John xvi, 171, 174, 190, 191–199, 20, 203, 207, 206, 227
Campbell, Alexander 236
Campbell-Read, Eileen 304
Canon Law xiv, xvi, 129, 137, 138, 150, 154, 180, 251, 252, 297
Carolingian Dynasty 149
Carter, Jimmy 280
Cathars 165
Catherine of Aragon (queen of England) 199, 200
Catherine of Siena 159–161, 171
Cato 168
Christians for Biblical Manhood and Womanhood (CBMW) xvi, 285, 289, 290
Charlemagne 165
Charles I 206, 220
Charles II 220
Christ 53, 55, 59–68, 70, 71, 74, 75, 81, 83–86, 90, 91, 94, 100, 104, 105, 113, 114, 115, 116, 118, 119, 121, 122, 139, 140, 142, 145, 151–153, 155, 156, 158–160, 162, 169, 176–178, 184, 187, 188, 191, 192, 196, 197, 201, 211, 212, 223, 224, 226, 227, 231, 233, 242, 245, 248, 255, 257, 259, 261, 263, 264–267, 277, 278, 281, 284, 289, 290, 291, 301, 305, 307, 308
Christian Methodist Episcopal (CPE) 304

Christians for Biblical Equality
  (CBE) xvi, 292, 305
Chrysostom, John xv, 73,
  86–96, 130, 164
Church of God – Cleveland
  (GOGC) 302
Cicero 94
Clare of Assisi 147
Clark, Elizabeth 86, 224
Clement of Alexandria xv,
  39, 45, 73–79
Codex Alexandrinus 11
Codex Sinaiticus 11
Codex Luris Canonici 150
Codex Vaticanus 11
Coffin, Judith 213
  Doctrine of Faith 258
Conrad of Marchtal 144
Cotton, John 214
Council of Epon 74, 124
Court of Ferrara 364
Council of Florence 140
Council of Loadicea 74, 152
Council of Lyons 148
Council of Macon 74, 124
Council of Nicaea 74, 120
Council of Paris 149
Council of Trent 97, 132
Council of Vienne 148
Cranmer, Thomas 200
Cromwell, Thomas 200
Cybele 61

Daly, Mary 252, 253, 262
Damian, Peter 145, 158
Damasus 97
David, King 15, 22, 24, 25, 29, 31,
  34, 35, 98, 203
DeBoer, Willis P. 197

Deborah 2, 33, 106, 197
Decretum 150, 151
Delilah x, xv, 20, 21, 203
Demosthenes 39
Denhollander, Rachael 292
Deuterocanon 10, 11
Deville, Tammy 270
Dexter, Samuel 211
Didascalia Apostolorum 74,
  118, 119, 121
Di Giovanni, Francesca 260
Dionysius 62, 64, 119
Dobson, James 282, 283
Dodds, E.R. 107
Dominican Order 146
Donatus 118
Donne, John 204
Durandus, William 150
Dwight, Timothy 234
Dyer, Mary 222
D'Angouleme, Marguerite 173

Eagle Forum 276
Eddy, Baker Mary 270
Edwards, Jonathan xvi,
  226–227, 229
Edwards, Morgan 228
Edward VI (king of
  England) 200, 203
Elah 33
Eleanor of Aquitaine (queen of
  England) 160
Elijah 32, 157
Elizabeth I (queen of England) 204
Elliot, Elisabeth 274–276
Elliot, Jim 274
Ellison, Emily Joy 291
Episcopal Church 293, 296, 297
Erasmus, Desiderius xvi, 174–179

Esau 27, 28
Esther 2, 33, 36, 106
Eternal Functional Subordination (EFS) 290, 291
Eucharist 119, 130, 141, 149, 155, 161, 255
Eve – Apocrypha 13; Aquinas 132, 134, 135; Augustine of Hippo 109, 110; Calvin 190–193; Chrysostom 86–92; Clement of Alexandria 74–75, 77–79; Edwards 226, 227; Erasmus 176; Graham 278; Jerome 99, 100, 104; Lindsell 278; MacArthur 283; Malleus Maleficarum 168, 169; Luther 180–183, 186, 187; Mather, Cotton 210, 213; Milton 222–224; Philo 48–51; Tertullian 79–84

Fall, The 2, 6, 7, 8, 12, 51, 70, 74, 76, 78, 81, 82, 88, 91, 99, 109, 111, 112, 122, 135, 140, 181, 183, 186, 223, 226, 191–193, 198, 205, 210, 212, 227, 256, 265, 284, 308
Falwell, Jerry 274, 280, 281
Farley, Margaret 133
Fell, Margaret 221
Fifth Ecumenical Council 157
Finney, Charles xvi, 232, 233, 235
Fiorenza, Elisabeth Schüssler 262, 263
Fletcher, Mary 225
Flowers, Elizabeth 288
Focus on the Family 282, 283
Fourth Lateran Council 128, 140

Fox, George 221
Fox, R.L. 85
Franciscan Order 146
Friedan, Betty 273, 277
Funderburk, A.R 269

Gabriel 84
Gataker, Thomas 204
Gelasius, Bishop of Rome's letter concerning women at the altar 74, 124
Gonzaga, Elisabetta 173
Gouge, William 204
Grace Bible Seminary 290
Graham, Billy 277, 278
Gratian 140, 150
Green, Ashbel 234
Green, TeResa 304
Greenham, Richard 202
Gregory of Nazianzus 97
Gregory of Tours 125
Grimke, Angelina 239, 240
Grimke, Sarah 239, 240
Grudem, Wayne 286, 290
Guidobaldo of Urbino 173

Hagar 15, 46
Hannibal 177
Hardesty, Nancy 293
Harris, Barbara 297
Harris, Katherine 218
Helena 98
Helvidius 105
Helwys, Thomas 221
Hempstall, Anne 221
Henry VIII (king of England) 171, 199
Herndon, E.W. 240

Hilda 143, 171
Hildegard of Bingen 160, 161, 171
Hill, Susan Lindley 214, 298
Hippolytus 117, 118, 164
Hodge, Charles 264
Hooten, Elizabeth 221
Hopkins, Ann 214
Hopkins, Edward 214
Horace 97
Hudson, Susanna 222
Hutchinson, Anne 216, 217, 222, 227
Hutchinson, Lucy 215

Immaculate Conception 156, 157, 189
Inquisition 149, 165–167, 170
Investiture Controversy 127, 145
Isaac 16, 26–28, 48
Isis 69

Jackson, Jesse 304
Jacob 27
Jatta, Barbara 260
James 59
Jehu 32, 33
Jephthah 14
Jerome xv, 73, 96–106, 114, 116, 143, 151
Jezebel x, 20, 31–33, 200, 227
Joanna 58
Joan of Arc 161
Job 1, 29, 203
John (Apostle) 104
John (The Baptist) 118, 121, 153
Johnson, Mary 245
Jonadab 25

Joram 32, 33
Joseph 59, 84 103, 105
Josephus 55
Jovian 99, 102
Judah 21, 28, 29
Julian of Norwich 160
Junia 71
Juvenal 97

Kempe, Margery 160, 161
Knox, John 196, 203, 204
Kramer, Heinrich 166–168

LaHaye, Beverly 276, 277, 279, 288
LaHaye, Tim 276, 279
Latimer, Hugh 200
Leah 46, 48
Lilith 4, 5
Lindley, Susan 214, 238, 240, 252, 280, 298, 304
Lindsell, Harold 278, 279
Lot 14, 26
Louder, John 219
Loveland, Anne C. 245
Lucilla 118
Luther, Martin xvi, 171, 174, 177, 180–190, 193, 196, 198, 199
Lutheran Church America (LCA) 295, 296
Lutheran Church Missouri Synod (LCMS) 195–296
Lycurgus 176

MacArthur, John 283–285
Macartney, Clarence 270
Machebeuf, Joseph 241
Magnus, Albertus 164
Mallet, Sarah 225

Marian Dogmas 158, 159
Marshall, Daniel 228
Marsha, Martha Stearns 228
Marshall, Molly 293
Martin, Susan 219
Mary Magdalene xi, 11, 58, 59, 143, 155
Mary mother of Jesus 2, 57, 59, 84, 104, 105, 106, 113, 114, 118, 138, 141–143, 155–159, 171, 188, 189, 206, 207, 227, 240, 244, 257, 276, 309
Mary of Bethany 155
Mary of Guise (queen of Scotland) 203, 204
Mary I (queen of England) 201
Massee, J.C. 270
Mather, Cotton xvi, 210–214, 217, 219, 222, 226, 227
Matthews, Marjorie Swank 295
May, Susan 221
McLoughlin, William 232
McPherson, Aimee Semple 303
Mendicant order 127, 146
Michael, Archangel 69
Michal 203
Miller, Richard 149
Miller, Samuel 264
Milton, John xvi, 9, 222–224, 226
Mishnah 55, 56
Mohler, Albert 290–292
Monica 106, 107, 116, 309
Montgomery, Helen Barrett 300
Moody, Dwight L. xvi, 232, 245–248, 267
Moon, Charlotte "Lottie" Digges 23, 238
Moore, Beth 285
Moore, Russell 290, 292
Moral Majority 274, 276, 280

More, Thomas 173
Morgan, Edmund 212
Morgan, Marabel 274
Moses 11, 19, 46, 57, 58, 104, 176
Mosley, Sara B 299

Nabal 34, 35
Naomi 210, 21, 34
Nathan 24
National Baptist Convention of America, Inc. 304
Northern Baptist Convention, USA (NBC) 299
Neoplatonism 130
Nettleton, Asahel 234
Noah 10, 23

Olympias 95, 96
Onan 18, 28
Origen 39, 45
Original Sin xv, 73, 87, 88, 106, 110–115, 129, 135, 152, 156–158, 186, 210, 227, 228
Orpah 34

Pachomius 142
Palmer, Phoebe 242–244
Pandora 11, 169
Pan Lutheran Council of 1969 295
Patricius 106
Patterson, Dorothy 288
Patterson, Paige 267, 288, 289, 292
Paul, (Apostle) xi, xv, 5, 23, 53, 59–71, 82, 83, 85, 87, 93, 95, 130, 142, 192, 197, 198, 107, 234, 240, 257, 307, 309
Paula 105, 106
Peach, Bernard 219
Perkins, William 205
Perpetua 85

Peter, Apostle 75, 259, 263, 276
Philadelphia Eleven 297
Phillip 76
Phillips, Euclid 270
Phillips, J.A. 169
Philo xv, 37, 44–51, 55, 56
Piper, John 286–287, 310
Plato xv, 37, 39–42, 44, 45, 51, 309
Poor Clares 147
Pope Alexander IV 165
Pope Benedict XV 252
Pope Benedict XVI 258, 259
Pope Boniface VIII 146, 148
Pope Eugenius III 160
Pope Francis I 259, 261, 305
Pope Gregory IV 146
Pope Gregory IX 150
Pope Gregory the Great 149, 155
Pope Gregory VII 145
Pope Gregory XI 160
Pope Honorius III 150
Pope Innocent III 155
Pope Innocent VIII 166
Pope John Paul II 255–259, 261
Pope John XXIII 253–255
Pope Leo XIII 241, 242
Pope Martin 157
Pope Paul VI 258
Pope Pius XI 252, 253
Pope Pius XII 157, 253
Pope Zachary 149
Porete, Marguerite 148, 161
Potiphar 46, 103
Powell, Adam Clayton Jr. 304
Presbyterian Church in the United States (PCUSA) 298, 299
Pseudepigrapha 10, 12, 13

Rachel 46, 48
Rebekah 16, 26, 27

Rice, John R. 269
Riley, William Bell 268
Rogers, Adrian 288
Rogers, Joyce 288
Ruether, Rosemary Radford 77, 262, 303
Ruth xv, 2, 18, 20–22, 32–34, 36

Sampson, Elizabeth 222
Samson 20, 21, 203
Sarah 2, 12, 15, 16, 33, 46, 48, 138
Saul 34, 164
SBC Ethics and Religious Liberty Commission (ERLC) 290
Schlafly, Phyllis 276
Scholz, Susanne 273
Sears, Jonathan F. 234
Second Lateran Council 145
Second Synod of Orleans 74, 124
Semple, Robert 228
Seneca 168
Seth 2, 10
Shaw, Susan 293
Shelah 28
Sicard of Cremona 150
Siricius, Bishop of Rome's Decree on Clerical Celibacy 74, 123
Sly, Dorothy 48, 51
Smiley, Sarah 245–247
Smith, Bailey 270
Smith, Henry 203
Smyth, John 220
Sankey, Ira 245
Snorton, Teresa 304
Socrates 39
Solomon, King 15, 22, 23, 24, 30
Solon 176
Southern Baptist Convention (SBC) xiv, 237, 238, 268, 271, 272, 289, 292, 293, 306, 309

Southern Baptist Theological
    Seminary (SBTS) 290
Soteriology 209, 233, 248, 272
Sprenger, Jacob 167, 169
St. Benedict, Rule of 144
St. Raymond of Pennaforf 150
Stanton, Elizabeth Cady 240, 247
Stokes, Claudia 233
Stone, Barton 236
Strachan, Owen 290, 291
Strange Woman in
    Proverbs 2, 30, 31
Straton, John Roach 267, 268
Sunday, Billy 266, 267
Synod of Carthage 74, 123
Synod of Gangra 120
Synod of Orange 74, 124
Synod of Nimes 74, 124

Tamar (daughter of David) 25
Tamar (wife of Er) xv, 15, 17, 23,
    26, 28, 29
Taylor, Nathaniel 234
Tertullian of Carthage xv, 73,
    79–85, 164, 204
Third Ecumenical Council 156
Thomas, Arabella 221
Theotokos 156, 189
Timothy 89, 71, 192
Titus 70
Tobias 12
Tobit 11, 12
Townley, Frances E. 299
Trible, Phyllis 25

Trier 166
Trinity 74, 79, 106, 108, 148

United Methodist Church
    (UMC) 294, 295
United Presbyterian Church
    of North America
    (UPCNA) 298, 299

Vatican II 254, 255, 260
Von Bora, Katie 183
Vulgate 11, 97, 174

Waldensians 165
Walters, Barbara 277
Ware, Bruce 290
Warnock, Raphael 304
Weinstein, Harvey 291
Weld, Thomas 216
Welter, Barbara 232
Wesley, John xvi, 225, 236
Wesley, Samuel 225
Wesley, Susanna 225
Whitefield, George 272
Willard, Frances 245, 247
Winthrop, John 214–215, 222
Woman of Folly (Proverbs) 30
Worthy Woman (Proverbs 31) 33

Young, Andrew 304

Zimri 32, 33
Zipporah 48
Zwingli, Ulrich 174